Future of Business and Finance

The Future of Business and Finance book series features professional works aimed at defining, describing and charting the future trends in these fields. The focus is mainly on strategic directions, technological advances, and challenges and solutions which will affect the way we do business tomorrow. We also encourage books which focus on the future of sustainability and governance. Mainly written by practitioners, consultants and academic thinkers, the books are intended to spark and inform further discussions and developments.

More information about this series at http://www.springer.com/series/16360

Hubert Tardieu • David Daly •
José Esteban-Lauzán •
John Hall • George Miller

Deliberately Digital

Rewriting Enterprise DNA for Enduring Success

Springer

Hubert Tardieu
Paris, France

José Esteban-Lauzán
Madrid, Spain

George Miller
West Wittering, West Sussex, UK

David Daly
Nottingham, Nottinghamshire, UK

John Hall
Warrington, Cheshire, UK

ISSN 2662-2467 ISSN 2662-2475 (electronic)
Future of Business and Finance
ISBN 978-3-030-37957-5 ISBN 978-3-030-37955-1 (eBook)
https://doi.org/10.1007/978-3-030-37955-1

Disclaimer: Throughout this book we use many industrial, societal, and personal examples to illustrate and emphasize the points we are seeking to make. The worlds of technology and business are incredibly fast moving, and whilst we have taken care to ensure that the facts we use are correct and relevant at the time of writing, we can make no guarantee that the specific situations we reference will not have changed by the time you are reading them. As far as possible, we have endeavored to make each chapter accessible as a standalone text, cross-referencing to other sections where necessary. This inevitably results in a few instances of key messages being repeated for the sake of maintaining appropriate context.

This Springer imprint is published by the registered company Springer Nature Switzerland AG
The registered company address is: Gewerbestrasse 11, 6330 Cham, Switzerland

Foreword

For the last 20 or so years, I have had the privilege of witnessing and participating in the development of the economics of the digital economy. My academic home, the Toulouse School of Economics, has been in the forefront of the development of the theory of platforms, in particular, through the work of my colleagues Bruno Jullien, Jean-Charles Rochet, and Jean Tirole in respect of two-sided markets.

It has also been my great pleasure to discuss and argue with many policy-makers in both public and private spheres about the application of these theories to the practical problems which they face. Among these discussions, those with Hubert Tardieu and his colleagues at Atos stand out in two respects. Firstly, Hubert and his collaborators are deeply involved in the day-to-day challenges faced not only by Atos, but also by its many clients. They search for practical, concrete, and applicable solutions. Secondly, they also understand more deeply than most that these solutions can only be useful if they rest on a rigorous, practical, and tested conceptual framework. We have had great discussions exploring the ways in which economic theory informs business practice and the ways in which business practice challenges economic theory.

Now, as "Deliberately Digital" makes clear the authors read and absorb not only economics, but also business strategy, sociology, and other relevant areas and scholarship. And, furthermore, they are great technologists. The result will be invaluable to many managers who must guide their organizations through our turbulent and exhilarating times. They will find a framework for organizing their thinking—I probably should have written frameworks: The authors make clear that one needs to combine different ways of thinking to make sense of the complexity of the problems that decision-makers face. They will find practical advice, informed by more than a century of collective experience(!), on how to put these frameworks to work for the benefit of their organizations and their customers.

I hope that "Deliberately Digital" is also read by public decision-makers, regulators, and my fellow academics. It provides a unique window on the concrete, real-world challenges created by digital transition and will help them understand how our regulatory frameworks, education policies, and public investment strategies can help firms, non-profits, and public administration meet these challenges (as well, of course, as ensuring that the technology is indeed put to use for the benefits of citizens). The seven detailed industry case studies at the end of the book will provide useful material to start along this path.

As all good books of this type, "Deliberately Digital" will be the focal point of many discussions. The managers who use it as a guide will want to share their experience, and I hope that the authors will create a forum[1] where they can do it. I am looking forward to taking part in those discussions.

October 2019

Jacques Cremer
Professor, Toulouse School of Economics
Toulouse, France

[1]https://deliberatelydigital.com is available as a central information point for a discussion forum relating to the topics raised in this book.

Acknowledgements

The authors would like to thank the following people for their invaluable support.

Professor Dr. Herbert Weber, for his encouragement to move beyond the early draft stage of this book.

Dr. Natalia Jiménez, for her specialist input relating to DNA science.

Dr. Charles Zaiontz, for his expert review of the statistical analysis examples.

Numerous colleagues and clients who have provided invaluable insights over many years.

Most of the work that the authors have done in relation to digital transformation has taken place during their tenure at Atos: the European digital champion, to which one of the case studies is devoted. Besides the case study and occasional citations of Atos-specific items (such as StratHacks or Journey), authors have made all necessary efforts to present a neutral and balanced account of transformation, based on their engagements with hundreds of clients and peers in other companies and institutions.

About This Book

Digital is changing almost everything in the world of business. However, most attempts at enterprise digital transformations fail—largely because of a lack of coherent strategy and the absence of an effective transformation plan. Deliberately Digital takes the lessons learned from the rise of the digital platform giants and explores how they can be adapted and effectively applied to established businesses, allowing them to compete within this new business paradigm.

Taking a holistic view of the business and technology landscape, this book describes the megatrends, evolution, and impact of digital technologies and related business models. It brings together what for many is a disjointed set of business transformation imperatives and creates a realistic guide for digital success.

Using the authors' decades of experience in supporting transformation and innovation, this book lays out a path to progressive iteration of business change and value realization, balancing the perspectives of revolutionary transformation and change-enabling optimization. All authors' royalties from the sale of this book are being donated to "ATD (All Together in Dignity) Fourth World", a movement of solidarity against poverty. This is an international non-governmental organization with no religious or political affiliation. https://www.atd-fourthworld.org.

Introduction to Deliberately Digital

Abstract

Digital Transformation is now a business imperative for every company. Those businesses that are currently lagging behind in the realization of the potential of digital technologies need to act in a way that intentionally delivers the kind of radical changes that will alter their very corporate DNA. Those businesses that are digital start-ups or leading adopters need to embrace continuous innovation and transformation if their models are going to bring lasting success. Whatever the starting point, a deliberate strategy for digital business will be the key to future and on-going business success.

Transformation—A Compelling Need

The advent and maturing of digital technologies have already had an immense impact across all sectors. In the consumer and media market, this is evidenced by the rise of the so-called digital giants (including Google, Apple, Facebook, Amazon, Alibaba, and Netflix). In manufacturing, through Industry 4.0[2] (initially crafted in Germany 8 years ago), we have seen the emergence of a significant new trend which started with the automation of production and has led to the launch of data-driven industrial smart services. In financial services, we see disruptions like open-banking platforms, Pay as You Use insurance, and cryptocurrencies. And now in 2019, at the time of writing this book, we are entering into the age of autonomous systems and artificial intelligence. But with all the incredible digital success stories, there also comes a host of examples of previously viable businesses that are struggling to both embrace and compete with the power and speed of digital. Indeed, there are questions now raised as to whether it is even possible for them to transform in ways and at a scale and pace that will fully re-establish their ability to compete.

[2]Industry 4.0 describes the trend toward automation and data exchange in manufacturing technologies and related processes.

Data—A Powerful Ally

At the heart of business success in the digital age is data. Data drives knowledge and insight; data informs and enables customer engagement; and (used appropriately) data is an intrinsic source of new value propositions and efficiency—bringing operational, tactical, and strategic advantage. We can distill these driving characteristics down to:

- Enabling "*Intimacy with customers*" through value-added, contextualized, differentiated, and trusted engagements. In this context, a customer is seen as any entity that is in receipt of products and services within a supply chain.
- Enabling "*Scale in operation*" through efficient, informed, responsive, and scalable processes. This dimension is concerned not only with scaling up but scaling out across networks of business opportunity.

The mission for businesses that want to reach digital leadership status is to achieve both these outcomes concurrently. For digital start-ups and new market entrants, that typically have digitally enabled customer intimacy as a given, the challenge is one of efficiently and effectively scaling their operations to drive market share and influence. For market incumbents who currently enjoy market share (albeit supported by legacy business models), the challenge is one of transforming their approach to customer intimacy to defend against new entrants and grow their market further (Fig. 1).

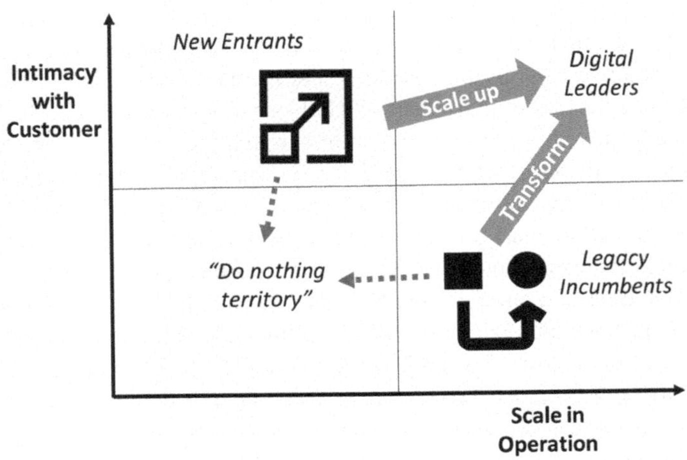

Fig. 1 Routes to digital leadership (authors' own figure)

The Path to Digital Leadership

The nature of the required transformation or scale-up is dependent both on the business's current operating models and the characteristics of the market in which they operate. The question prevails: Which will prove to be the winning course?

What is clear is that failure to appropriately and deliberately respond to the challenges and opportunities presented by the relentless evolution of digital technologies will lead to inevitable decline in business performance and relevance.

This book will explore the forces at work in the new "economy of data" paradigm and will show how businesses can successfully navigate the path toward digital leadership.

In Part I, we look at the imperative for digital transformation considering the factors that can enable and hinder both customer intimacy and operational scalability.

In Part II, we examine the target model for achieving digital leader status, paying particular attention to data-centric platform[3] models, a common operating model of many of today's digital giants.

In Part III, we consider the transformation journey options facing a business wishing to move from legacy incumbent to digital leader, whether this be via digital optimization or business model reinvention.

Old Paradoxes, New Thinking

For the past 30 years, we have seen Information Technology being applied in the transformation of business processes and capabilities; however, from the perspective of some, this has been tempered by the Solow paradox: "*You can see the computer age everywhere but in the productivity statistics*" (Solow 1987). As we enter the third decade of the twenty-first century, can and how will digital transformation address this paradox?

In the business world, we are seeing two major trends:

The first is the emergence of the *Economy of Data*. For two centuries, industries have tended to be fragmented into defined value chains, where every player is specialized in the production of goods or services which, when combined, bring an optimized production process. At every stage of the value chain, competition operates to enable cost reduction and profit maximization. Only recently have businesses realized that they were creating data which could be combined by the various players of an ecosystem to create mutually beneficial additional value.

[3]A *platform* is a business model that facilitates (data-driven) value creation and exchanges between interdependent groups of consumers and producers. Please refer to the Glossary at the end of this book for a more complete synthesis of platform variants.

Coase in his famous theorem[4] describes the economic efficiency of resource allocation in the presence of externalities (costs or benefits to a party who did not choose to incur them). The theorem states that if trade in an externality is possible, and there are sufficiently low transaction costs, bargaining will lead to the most efficient outcome regardless of the initial allocation of property.[5] In short, industrial data (often seen as an externality) can be traded within an ecosystem of partners to bring a value outcome which might otherwise be prevented by systematic competition.

In some part, the rapid growth of the economy of data has been achieved thanks to gaps in data privacy regulation: In Europe, regulations now require prior consent from data subjects, applying control over the usage of data after such consent has been given; in much of the rest of the world, the jury is still out as to whether privacy belongs to the past or if it is an essential constituent of national policy. This could well be a deciding factor in the viability and effectiveness of emerging digital business models.

The second trend, *Artificial Intelligence*, perhaps has a higher profile because it delivers mythical promises of data being processed in such a way that industrial processes (through machine learning and algorithms) can be automated without predefined reasoning devised by human beings, the dream being that of autonomous industrial productivity gains through the simple accumulation of data. However, this dream still seems a distant one, since first implementations have shown the necessity to rely heavily on human experts for labeling valid outcomes of the learning algorithms. We also have seen notable failures of AI applied to the Health sector, driving one of its pioneers to wonder whether industry was actually ready for AI. Could we be witnessing the next iteration of the Solow paradox?

In this book, we shall address three questions which we have repeatedly been asked by businesses facing the challenge of digital transformation:

1. Why do we need to undergo digital transformation?
2. What will it mean for my company?
3. How can I ensure a sustainable digital transformation?

We believe that the time has come to propose a set of principles and a methodology to help business leaders bring new thinking to the design of a sustainable digital transformation which anticipates the challenges they will have to face.

It is critically important to recognize that success in transformation is far from being a technology-only problem. Consider the following quote from "The Second Machine Age" (Brynjolfsson and McAfee 2016):

---

[4]https://www.investopedia.com/terms/c/coase-theorem.asp (accessed 26/10/2019).

[5]Economists call it a Pareto optimum which is a resource allocation where there is no alternative that would put the players in a better position.

Years later, when that hallowed General Purpose Technology electricity replaced the steam engine, engineers simply bought the largest electric motors they could find and stuck them where the steam engines used to be. Even when brand-new factories were built, they followed the same design. Perhaps unsurprisingly, records show that the electric motors did not lead to much of an improvement in performance. There might have been less smoke and a little less noise, but the new technology was not always reliable. Overall, productivity barely budged. Only after thirty years—long enough for the original managers to retire and be replaced by a new generation—did factory layouts change. The new factories looked much like those we see today: a single story spread out over an acre or more. Instead of a single massive engine, each piece of equipment had its own small electric motor. Instead of putting the machines needing the most power closest to the power source, the layout was based on a simple and powerful new principle: the natural workflow of materials.

The "new generation" which was a catalyst for transformational impact in the second industrial revolution is now happening in the context of the IT and digital revolution. Could the resulting cultural change be the means of finally delivering the full potential of digital?

References

Brynjolfsson, E., & McAfee, A. (2016). *The second machine age: Work, progress, and prosperity in a time of brilliant technologies*. New York: W. W. Norton & Company.

Solow, R. (1987). We'd better watch out (p 36). New York Times Book Review.

Contents

About the Authors

Hubert Tardieu is Advisor to the Atos CEO and Co-chairman of its Scientific Community created in 2009 and comprising Atos' 150 best scientists. The Scientific Community contributes to building the five-year vision for Atos and publishes its report every 2 years. He has been Member of the Executive Committee successively in charge of telecom, finance, and more recently consulting and systems integration. He is author of several books on information system design methods.

David Daly has worked within the technology industry since 1999 in a variety of roles ranging from software engineering and leading development teams, through to driving operational excellence and Agile and DevOps transformations.

He is a Fellow of the British Computer Society, a Chartered IT Professional, and a regular public speaker who has a passion for proving that alternative approaches can produce better results.

José Esteban-Lauzán has been working passionately in Innovation and R&D since 1997. He has directed large international research projects and driven transformation initiatives in the public and private sectors.

José engages with clients on transformation and thought leadership, supports innovators and intrapreneurs, mentors young talent, and likes to challenge the status quo.

José is heavily involved in technologies such as artificial intelligence and additive manufacturing, with a current focus in unpredictability and machine behavior.

John Hall is a Chartered Engineer who has over 30 years' experience of working in a variety of industries, but always with an IT and digital transformation focus. He has a passion for innovation and change leadership, with a very hands-on approach to exploring the potential of new technologies. He is a regular public speaker who enjoys inspiring others to think differently about digital disruption. Current areas of focus include blockchain, quantum computing, and ethical considerations for AI.

George Miller has spent his entire career as a product and services innovator, and for the last 20 years in business technology innovation working across all industry verticals and for clients that include a number of the world's leading firms. His current research interests include new business models, autonomics, artificial intelligence and mixed reality.

Part I
The Digital Imperative: The Need for Transformation

Introduction

Abstract What do we mean by "digital" and how has the historical advancement of technology led us to where we are today? Which business and societal trends must be understood? What are the key technologies that organisations must leverage now, and which ones should they be planning to harness in the future? We analyse why many digital transformations struggle to deliver the expected benefits and explain why we believe that a deliberate strategy for ongoing transformation, which requires that the very DNA of an organisation must be re-written, is necessary in order to achieve digital leader status.

In Part I, we will be focusing our attention on the imperative for digital transformation. In doing so, we will consider various forces at play from technology, society, and business trend perspectives and explain how these are interacting to drive seismic shifts in the way that value is both perceived and delivered.

We will contextualize why we have condensed the measures of digital success down to the two axes of "*Intimacy with Customer*" and "*Scale in Operation*" and discuss what is behind these somewhat nebulous terms. We will not be exploring how best to influence the progression along each axis (i.e., the objective of Part III); however, we will be signposting the opportunities and challenges to be faced (Fig. I.1).

It should become very clear that not only has the game changed in terms of the possibilities afforded by rapidly evolving digital technologies, but the rules of the game have changed as well, particularly in terms of customer expectations, perceptions of value, and perspectives on how and even if those possibilities should be adopted.

Digital can be a significant enabler of customer intimacy, but it can also be a huge constraining force if used inappropriately. Gaining and maintaining intimacy with customers is so much more than seeking to understand and influence their buying behaviors. It involves demonstrating deep insights into their market, building credibility, trust, and even shared-value partnerships. In business-to-

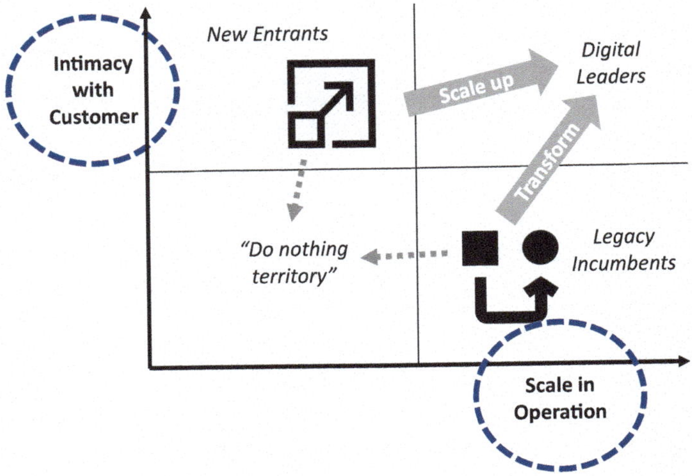

Fig. I.1 Driving forces behind digital leadership (authors' own figure)

business relationships, it might demand the creation of trusted ecosystems of data exchange that support integrated and orchestrated supply chains. Failure to get the balance right will risk businesses being left languishing in the zone of legacy, with ever-declining relevance in the markets in which they operate.

With regard to "*Scale in Operation*," once again digital technologies are key enablers, but the focus cannot solely be on ruthless efficiency and vertical integration[1] of supply chains, but also on understanding and leveraging the dynamics of multi-sided markets and value networks.[2] Scale in operation demands agility and flexibility in response to data-driven insights about market demands and trends.

[1]"A strategy whereby a company owns or controls its suppliers, distributors, or retail locations thereby controlling its value or supply chain" https://www.investopedia.com/terms/v/verticalintegration.asp (accessed 26/10/2019).

[2]Platform-driven enablers of incremental value creation through direct interactions and exchanges between two or more customer/supplier groups.

1 The Birth of Digital—A Brief History of Digital Technologies

1.1 What Is "Digital"?

What exactly is "digital" and how did it ever become "a thing"? The term digital has become the kind of complex, multilayered, hyped, and overused concept that often obfuscates more than it reveals. We tend to use it rather glibly and confidently, never quite stopping to reflect on its precise meaning because, well, everybody knows what we mean! As a result, we may think we have successfully communicated about it when, in fact, people's understanding of digital is far from binary and may be open to substantially different interpretations.

As a polysemic, multilayered term, it allows many definitions. The science- and tech-savvy may define it as the representation of information using binary digits (ones and zeros) or perhaps as all the technologies based on data that are represented in this way. Those who are more business-oriented may understand digital as a purpose, giving rise to business models that are (mostly) based on the virtual world, with an emphasis on intangible assets (such as digital data) to tap into new sources of value. Such people often use digital as shorthand for the strategy that will, hopefully, lead to the attainment of such a purpose. Marketing-oriented people might refer to digital as a new form of consumer perception and engagement based on digital technologies. Many people, across the whole spectrum of backgrounds, will define it as one of the biggest fads so far in the twenty-first century.

Based on the numerous engagements and collaborations that the authors have had with clients and partners, with the objective of trying to maintain a clear business focus and for the context of this book, we propose the following pragmatic definition:

> Digital is a mindset that seeks to leverage technology, data, and ways of working to establish new business and service models for the achievement of a higher purpose and value.

H. Tardieu et al., *Deliberately Digital*, Future of Business and Finance,
https://doi.org/10.1007/978-3-030-37955-1_1

1.2 The Transformation Imperative

The first successful digital businesses are known under a variety of nicknames such as "Digital Giants," FAANG (Facebook, Apple, Amazon, Netflix, and Google) or "the Digirati".[1] They are seen by some as the benchmark against which other businesses are measured in their digital efforts. They have grown at lightning speed into huge companies that have reached quasi-monopolistic status in their foundation markets and even in adjacent ones. And this is precisely why all businesses (including public sector organizations) feel the pressing need to digitally transform. If traditional companies and organizations do nothing to embrace the possibilities and tap into the new sources of value that digital technologies bring, they seem destined to disappear or wither into entities that hold only vestigial value.

1.3 The Timeline of Digital Technologies

Digital is the result of nearly a century of discoveries and developments which have recently started converging into vortices of significant possibility and radical change. But even the early phases of the digital revolution brought impressive economical, lifestyle, societal and business growth during the second half of the twentieth century driven by conceptual and implementation breakthroughs in key areas of information and communication technology (ICT). Information theory, microelectronics, and radio communication were the cornerstones for the exponential growth of information storage, computing, and telecommunication.

Personal perceptions of digital differ quite widely, partly because people have lived and experienced different parts of the history of digital technologies and their impact. Let's take a quick walk along the technology timeline to understand why those different perceptions have arisen.

In its infancy, in the 1940s, computing technology was essentially limited to military/defense applications and was embodied in a very few, almost prohibitively expensive machines that occupied entire rooms, weighed many tons, and had ridiculously poor storage and compute capabilities compared to today's standards. Beyond the real specialists, few people knew what digital meant, and most would still think of a person, not a machine, when hearing the term "computer."

By the 1960s, ICT had found its way into corporations, in the form of very expensive large cabinets (mainframes), which were manipulated by specialists and whose use was rationed (queued). By the 1980s, computers were becoming much smaller and more widespread across all kinds of organizations; personal computing was starting to emerge with PCs finding their ways into homes via practitioners, hobbyists, teenagers, and children. During those decades, mass media and

[1]A term that refers to the "digital literati": organizations or individuals that are well versed in digital matters (technologies, business models, etc.).

audiovisual information were distributed and exchanged via analog means on physical media: vinyl records, audio cassette tapes, and cassette-like videotapes, which were played on expensive and bulky reproduction machines. And, of course, we had paper-based books, magazines, and newspapers.

By the 1990s, computers were commonplace both at work (one per desk) and at home (with their use climbing up the age ladder toward parents). Analog media began the transition to digital media: CDs and DVDs which were much lighter, more reliable, and more capacious than their analog counterparts. The 1990s also saw the appearance and popularization of mobile phones and the Internet (the World Wide Web or Web). The latter enabled the interconnection of the many millions of computers that had until that time been islands of compute power. This in turn led to the mass creation and consumption of electronic content around the world (though mostly using just text and low-fi images). E-mail address lists were the social networks of the day. Phones were basically just phones: good only for talking through and perhaps listening to music, albeit on the move. The second half of the 1990s saw the birth of Google, Amazon (an online bookseller in its early days), early social networks such as Myspace, and online forums.

In the 2000s, the Web had reached a significant proportion[2] of the population, e-commerce became widespread, and peer-to-peer (P2P) protocols emerged to cope with bulky information exchanges at a time when broadband Internet access was nonexistent or a luxury. By the mid-2000s, next-generation social networks appeared (e.g., Facebook). Physical digital media (CDs, DVDs, mp3 players) started being virtualized through real-time streaming, and Netflix appeared and wiped Blockbuster out of the picture—Blockbuster eventually filed for “Chapter 11” bankruptcy protection in September 2010 (de la Merced 2010). Then, the arrival of the iPhone began an inexorable revolution of personal mobile computing, ushering in the era of the handheld personal computer (the reference to “phone” in the device’s name was mostly a tongue-in-cheek allusion to the past). Newspapers and magazines also began making their transition to the Web during this decade, most of them in a reactive rather than an intentionally transformative way: not exploiting the full potential of the Web but directly transposing their paper formats and mind-sets over to the electronic world.

This decade also saw the market adoption of fundamental technologies such as big data, after Google’s MapReduce paper (Dean and Ghemawat 2004); cloud (led by the bookseller Amazon); and geospatial (location), with Google Maps taking the world by storm. At this stage, computers, tablets, and smartphones (with intuitive user interfaces and purposeful applications) were making it easier for “seniors” and less technology-savvy consumers to enter the digital world.

Around a decade after the introduction of the iPhone, we can ask virtual assistants for directions, which we get immediately, accurately, and for free (in purely monetary terms, at least); we can find almost anything we want and purchase

[2] 1.8 billion Internet-connected people (>25% of global population) by December 2009 according to https://internetworldstats.com/ [accessed 26/10/2019].

it immediately, paying for it via a seamless process (if required); we interact virtually with family members, friends, or colleagues as much as (if not more than) we do physically; we can find training courses on almost any topic in three taps or swipes of our fingers.

However, the 2010s have also seen something of a rebalancing or even a tipping point where the utopian possibilities of digital technology developments are being tempered by the emergence of less positive consequences. The FAANG have consolidated into digital juggernauts that continue to exploit platform economy first-mover advantage, lack of industry regulation, and data protection illiteracy of the masses to acquire and maintain near-monopolistic positions. The popularization of digital technology, coupled with the inherent anonymity of the Internet, has led to unintended consequences such as cyber-bullying, cyber-stalking, fake news, and opinion echo chambers which, rather than helping people communicate and understand each other better, have isolated them into communities of like-minded people, radicalizing some areas of society into highly polarized and confrontational segments. Such negative aspects are under the spotlight at the very end of the 2010s because of their unexpected nature, and because the record speed of adoption of the underlying technology was largely driven by a somewhat positively biased view of their benefits.

The decade of the 2020s is probably going to see the introduction of powerful AI into our devices and apps, which when coupled with advances in networks, robotics, HMIs (Human–Machine Interfaces), and the devices themselves will once again transform the way we live and work in ways that are both expected and unexpected. Cyber-security will become even more important since, together with economics and finance, it will gain prominence as a proxy battlespace for physical wars. The world may become cashless, with digital payments made possible by all sorts of contactless and frictionless mechanisms. Cyber-physical systems will further blur the distinction between the physical and the virtual worlds.

1.4 Digital Has Eaten the World

Marc Andreessen famously wrote that "*software is eating the world*" (Andreessen 2011). This metaphor can be taken even further. Scientists define "human microbiota" as the set of all microorganisms that inhabit the human body. Each of us hosts a myriad of microorganisms in their skin, saliva, or intestines. It is common knowledge that many of them are fundamental for the correct functioning of our physiological processes (e.g., intestinal flora is key for the absorption of nutrients). However, very few of us realize that their number is such that in each of our bodies there are at least as many non-human cells as there are human cells, and some estimates put the ratio at a staggering 3:1!

All manifestations of digital technology (data, models, sensors, programs, etc.) can be viewed as the digital microbiota of the physical world. Digital entities will soon outnumber physical ones,[3] and they are increasingly more deeply ingrained into all things around us. Stop all hardware or software for just a few moments, and you would wreak havoc in most societies, with both foreseeable and unforeseeable consequences. We act as we do, we engage as we do, and the world runs as it does thanks to the pervasiveness of digital technologies. This trend is expected to continue such that, in a few years, the world (including human beings) will be an inseparable continuum of the physical and the virtual. Digital will cease to be a discernible thing because it will just be an integrated part of a new norm.

References

Andreessen, M. (2011). Why software is eating the world. *The Wall Street Journal*, 20/08/2011. Source https://www.wsj.com/articles/SB10001424053111903480904576512250915629460. Accessed October 26, 2019.

de la Merced, M. (2010). Blockbuster, hoping to reinvent itself, files for bankruptcy. *The New York Times*, 20/09/2010. Source https://www.nytimes.com/2010/09/24/business/24blockbuster.html. Accessed October 26, 2019.

Dean, J., & Ghemawat, S. (2004). MapReduce: Simplified data processing on large clusters. In *Sixth Symposium on Operating System Design and Implementation*. San Francisco, CA: OSDI'04, pp. 137–150. Source https://ai.google/research/pubs/pub62. Accessed October 26, 2019.

[3]As a bit of trivia, data created and copied annually is estimated to reach 44 zettabytes in 2020, about the same as the total number of grains of sand on the earth's beaches. Source: https://www.bmc.com/blogs/master-the-wave-of-data-for-competitive-advantage/ [accessed 26/10/2019].

Business Trends—The Changing Nature of Business Offerings and Ecosystems

2

2.1 History Repeats Itself

Since the dawn of humanity, goods and services have been traded, but it is only during the last four or five hundred years that the rise of capitalism brought a clear framework to the way that work, investment, and value were perceived, organized, and exchanged. A myriad of opportunities to create prosperity were pursued by business entrepreneurs, some of whom grew their enterprises to titanic proportions.

Historically, the early mega-corporations tended to be those associated with railroads, mining, and banking: They were the engines of wealth generation and the enablers of radically different ecosystems of trade. The rise of capitalism transformed communities, nations, and ultimately the world. But the journey of capitalism has not always been a positive one: There has always tended to be a divide between the "haves" and the "have nots". Workers, who were the fundamental source of value creation, were often exploited and did not always get a fair recognition for their efforts. The largest enterprise s tended to dominate the market, dictating trading terms and suppressing the smaller players. Regulation, societal reform, and consumer rights helped to redress at least some of the imbalances.

In today's digital world, it could be argued that not much has changed: The capitalist goals have, for the most part, stayed the same, it's just the methods of reaching those goals that are going through a physical to digital transformation.

The previous mission of the railroad industry to provide strategic communication and trade links has been taken up by the Internet that is now able to bring ubiquitous connectivity at the speed of light; as well as mining for raw materials, we are now mining data to search for new sources of insight and value; industry platforms are becoming the new banks for trusted exchange and monetization of data: Data has become a new currency.

H. Tardieu et al., *Deliberately Digital*, Future of Business and Finance,
https://doi.org/10.1007/978-3-030-37955-1_2

And still the mega-corporations tend to dominate, only they are very different from the industrial giants of the past. The exploitation of data rights is a new proxy for the historic exploitation of workers' rights and, as before, we are seeing a push back from consumers, society, and regulators.

It seems that a number of fundamental lessons can be learnt from history, but just how can they be appropriately applied to the new digital capitalism and business ecosystem that is emerging?

Much has already been written by others on the impact of topics like free market capitalism of economic models, production processes, supply chains, globalization, etc., so it is not the intent of this chapter to revisit those foundational principles in the context of business trends. Instead we will focus on what is changing as digital ways of working increasingly supersede the ways that traditional business is perceived and conducted. Setting aside for the moment considerations of the shifting dynamics in business leadership and employee engagement (these will be covered in later chapters), we will address four fundamental cornerstones of business operation and what trends we are observing. They are:

1. Business models and scope.
2. Digital value ecosystems.
3. Strategies for delivering and scaling business value monetization.
4. Hyper-connected supply chains.

2.2 A Big Picture View

Identifying business trends within the context of fast-moving and disruptive technology changes is no mean feat. There is always a risk of overgeneralizing or over-extrapolating; this is not our intention so, in an attempt to evidence the reality of trend perception, we have dedicated a significant proportion of this book to a number of industry-specific case studies. Nevertheless, we feel it is appropriate and helpful to take something of a general big picture view of the changing nature of business in the digital era since this helps establish a backdrop against which our transformation recommendations are made.

The largest and most influential businesses in today's world are digital, be that in relation to technology products, digitally enabled services or both. Several of them have grown from initial launch to market-dominating size and status in less than a decade. They tend to enjoy a premium in terms of market capitalization that at times belies their real operating profitability. Many have directly and indirectly influenced significant and disruptive change within society and business supply chains; some have even changed the way that business value is perceived. How they have achieved this and the implications for other businesses will be considered in due course.

If we look historically at the lifespan of businesses that head up the various stock market leader boards, we see that back in the 1950s market-leading companies had typically been around for an average of 60 years. Growth in size and reputation had been hard-won over decades, usually through strategic cycles of investment, creation of intellectual property, and the steady building of brand reputation and market share. Looking at the markets today (e.g., S&P 500), we see that the average age of leading companies has plummeted to less than 20 years. New enterprises that are growing at the speed of digital are pushing aside the legacy competition who are, as a result, suffering relegation down the market value league table or even total collapse (Fig. 2.1).

According to Harvard Business School (Bock et al. 2017), leading digital companies generate better gross margins, better earnings, and better net income than organizations in the bottom quarter of digital adopters: Leaders are typically generating gross margins of 55%, compared to 37% for digital laggards. Legacy businesses must find a way to respond to this challenge if they are to maintain relevance. A concerning truth is that there are a number of large, long-established organizations that believe that they cannot be digitally disrupted and that they are too big to fail. They therefore feel that there is no compelling need to transform, particularly if key stakeholders have a personal vested interest in playing it safe.

Despite the reticence in some organizations to undertake radical digital transformations, there are some notable examples of large legacy businesses that have been able to successfully reinvent themselves through a combination of organic transformation and/or smart acquisitions of digital start-ups which might ultimately have grown to become a competitive threat (such success stories include The Disney corporation, Walmart, and Hasbro).

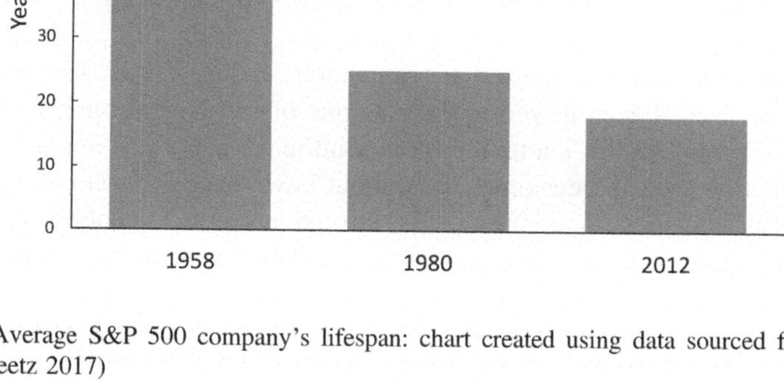

Fig. 2.1 Average S&P 500 company's lifespan: chart created using data sourced from Credit Suisse (Sheetz 2017)

2.3 Business Model and Scope

The meteoric rise of companies like Facebook (achieving a 2020 market value of $633 billion from its launch in 2004) might suggest that success in the digital era is easier for newcomers who are able to take a greenfield approach to implement innovative business models and capturing or creating a market share.

While we might marvel at the speed at which the Digital Giants have grown to a position of market leadership, we should also take sobering lessons from the speed with which today's heroes can become tomorrow's tainted firms. Just look at Facebook and Apple from the famous FAANG quintet. While still among the most valuable firms ever built, they have both been hurt by recent missteps:

> Facebook has suffered because they failed to keep pace with changing sentiment on privacy expectations; failed to safeguard customer data in a world increasing sensitized to this; and over-reached in terms of their ambition to realize value from customer data. And now there are serious questions being posed on whether Facebook Founder & CEO Mark Zuckerberg has the required credibility and skills to navigate the business successfully through these challenges.

> Apple has suffered because they have become hugely dependent for their growth on their incredibly successful iPhone product and on sales of this product into the Chinese market. As smart phones reached saturation globally, and as China's high growth economy faltered, Apple was forced to issue a revenue warning to investors. Tim Cook has yet to come under the kind of pressure to step down that we have seen for Mark Zuckerberg, but he is being questioned on the ability of Apple to sustain its performance; and analysts wonder whether and when Apple can come up with a new disruptive and scalable concept to get revenue growth back on track.

The digital honeymoon period can be short and market differentiation can soon disappear, especially where digital processes are relatively easily emulated by the competition, and consumer opinions and preferences are fickle. Copycat behavior is in principle much easier in the world of digital business: A market-leading concept, for example, in online banking, can soon become a "me too proposition" as the rest of the pack quickly follows. Take the example of connected personal home assistants: Amazon launched the Echo in 2015, and it is projected that revenue from Echo could reach $11 billion by 2020. One year later, Google released its almost identical Home device. Then in 2018, Apple released the HomePod. It seems unlikely that consumers will have all three devices in their homes, so which one will win out?

We would suggest that customer intimacy is a key driver for maintaining business relevance (hence its prominence as one of the axes in our path to digital leadership schema). In this context, customer intimacy is not just about connection to and affiliation with the customer, it is about how "sticky"[1] you can make your services. If as a business I am able to offer, through a single AI enabled, easy-to-use interface, everything from home shopping and delivery to music streaming, and

[1]In this context a "Sticky" service is one that encourages customers to remain with a given service provider either because it continues to deliver the best value for money or because the cost of moving to an alternative outweighs the benefits of doing so.

from VoIP (Voice over IP) calls to expert knowledge bases, why would my customers look elsewhere? Add to this a platform that allows other businesses to use my interface for offering their own services, then I gain further revenue opportunities and richer consumer behavioral insights while at the same time reinforcing the indispensability of my connection to the consumer.

What is your business doing to reinforce customer connection and intimacy?

A significant mark of sustainable digital business is that of continued and rapid strategic innovation. Strategic does not necessary imply significant, it is normally incremental but with a bigger long-term outcome in mind. As Geoffrey Moore commented "What makes modern business different? Simply put, speed plus disruption. Wave after wave of next generation technology, is continually transforming the landscape of business" (Moore 2015).

Transforming legacy businesses must recognize that undertaking a one-off digital transformation is not enough.

Enduring success demands achieving sustainable digital leadership status. For start-ups, this involves quickly achieving sufficient critical mass (independently or via strategic and collaborative partnerships) to support continuous evolution of their market value-added. And for transforming enterprises, it demands operating in such a way that established processes and principles do not act as an inertial constraint to the implementation and effectiveness of their desired digital model. Neither the transforming business nor the newcomer can rest on their laurels in terms of perceived value add: Continuous innovation is required to at least stay competitive in a world where loyalty is no longer helped by the challenge of switching to another service provider; value differentiation can be easily assessed and compared; and the shift to "everything as a service" removes the lock-in of CAPEX[2] depreciation. As we will see, digital transformation is not a one-time event, it demands a continuum of change. The nature of this change will in many ways be dictated by whether a business seeks to be a leader in innovation or an efficient emulator of others. The Digital Giants of today excel at this continuous evolution of their value propositions.

And yet there seem to be still further forces at work, since up to now the digital era is marked by both a strong "first-mover advantage" and a "winner takes it all" ethos. As a result, we are starting to see a trend toward increased polarization of the business landscape: Companies either grow into pseudo-monopolistic behemoths or evolve as small, nimble organizations, with a decline in the middle ground where many traditional businesses operate. Does your strategy contemplate transformation into one of those polar opposites? If not, does it address how to achieve and sustain a position in that shrinking middle ground? How easy is it for a digitally transforming business to become a digital leader, and on what battleground can they beat the "digital by design" competition?

[2]CAPEX stands for "Capital Expenditure" or "Capital Expense", which is the money spent on fixed assets (buildings, equipment, land, fleets, etc.). It contrasts with OPEX ("Operational Expenditure"), which reflects ongoing expenses (utility bills, external security services, external janitorial services, etc.).

How do established businesses respond? Resist or emulate? Trying to emulate can be a dangerous vanity, unless you are genuinely willing to invest to compete. In many cases, it is better to embrace digital capabilities by being a part of the digital supply chain and working out where your genuine value-add and differentiation lies.

2.4 Digital Value Ecosystems

A common feature of several of the largest and arguably most successful digital businesses is that they have been able to exploit the potential of data platforms. This concept is described in detail in the chapter on Platforms and Ecosystems. Platform businesses can be:

1. *Data-driven* with value being derived from the way that data (perhaps from industrial processes or end customer interactions) is gathered, refined, and monetized.
2. They can be *network-effect-driven*, with value multiplication being generated from the orchestration of the supply and demand side of digital marketplaces to the mutual benefit of all actors within an ecosystem.

The real power of the platform emerges when it is able to be both data-driven AND network-effect-driven.

It is our strong belief that platform models will become a dominant force over the next decade and will be a significant factor in successful digital transformations. Almost all businesses will need to decide how they will engage in some form of platform-based data ecosystem (whether this is as part of a collaborative supply chain or as a mechanism for direct customer engagement). Will they create their own platform; use that of a third party; or adopt a hybrid approach that selects a multi-platform strategy based on the nature of business interactions and the sensitivity of data being exchanged?

Clive Humby (the architect of supermarket Tesco's Clubcard) is widely credited as the first to coin the phrase "*Data is the new oil.*" He went on to comment "*It's valuable, but if unrefined it cannot really be used.*" The objective of a data platform is not only to provide a usable "well" of data but to provide the tools for its refinement and processing and for distributing the derived value. Implemented correctly data platforms will respect the security and privacy demands of all parties engaging in the associated ecosystem, while at the same time extending the reach and impact of business network engagements way beyond that achievable with traditional business models.

It should be noted that there is no simple formula for determining the most appropriate model. There are many factors (including regulatory, political, cultural, and business strategy) that will influence how successful a given platform model will be.

2.5 Delivering and Scaling Value Monetization

The world of digital has in many ways turned the perception of added business value on its head. In today's business-to-consumer (B2C) world, digital tools like online messaging, knowledge bases, collaboration environments and Wi-Fi network connections are all offered for free, and at availability and service levels that rival previously paid for models. Of course, such services are not really "free," operators still need to recoup the cost of things like servers and storage, but they do this through the direct and indirect monetization of the data that results from customer interactions: data from individuals who are, e.g., willing to share information about their buying trends and preferences, allowing suppliers to offer personalized and targeted offers.

Another major trend is in the shift to "servitization." This term has been coined to reflect the way that, in certain areas, products are increasingly sold as "services." Notable examples include:

- Cloud-based IT services that have no consumer CAPEX cost element but are charged for purely on a consumption basis, e.g., Amazon Web Services or Google Cloud Platform. This model has led to the relentless commoditization of IT infrastructure services for all but the most specialized of use cases.
- High-value CAPEX products that are now charged for on the basis of business outcomes. Instead of selling products, organizations sell services that are wrapped around the product, e.g., printer/photocopiers services are sold on the basis of page impressions, with paper and toner replenished as part of a managed service. Rolls-Royce was an early pioneer of this model when around 50 years ago they started selling aero-engine power availability (power by the hour) rather than selling ownership of the engine itself. Comprehensive telemetry[3] data from the engine in operation allows Rolls-Royce to determine and deliver optimized maintenance programs that maximize the availability and efficiency of its engines. Even though the process of manufacturing the engines may run at a loss, the lifetime maintenance revenues from outcome-based services enable a viable end-to-end business model.
- The gig economy[4]. While freelance working is far from being a new concept, digital platform businesses like Uber have taken the convenience and perceived value of such engagements to a new level. From food delivery (e.g., Just Eat and Deliveroo) to technical support (e.g., PeoplePerHour), the way that people resources are engaged is going through a transformation. Forward-thinking businesses are even exploring how gig economy principles might be applied to internal workforce management processes. While of course there are all manner of questions to be addressed regarding trust, local employment regulations,

[3]"The collection of measurements or other data at remote or inaccessible points and their automatic transmission to receiving equipment for monitoring https://ui.adsabs.harvard.edu/abs/1987STIN...8913455./abstract [accessed 26/10/2019].

[4]A labour market characterized by the prevalence of freelance work instead of permanent jobs.

fairness, and intellectual property, the attraction of only paying for suitably qualified individuals when you need them is particularly compelling in an era of rapidly evolving and scarce digital skills. Another interesting feature of this business model is that it is typically relatively asset-free: Uber uses the vehicles belonging to its registered drivers and Airbnb uses the real-estate belonging to its hosts. This asset-free model has been instrumental in removing some of the inertial forces that would otherwise restrain the market growth.

It should be noted that in a servitized world where service characteristics (outcomes) are well defined, similar offerings can usually be readily compared against one another. In the retail space, this has helped lead to the growth of comparison websites and a whole new realm of possibilities for multi-sided platforms. For example, online comparisons for vehicle insurance might quickly identify the best value for money deal for a given consumer, but in the process, it will also glean data about consumer needs and behaviors, which can then prove to be a rich source of marketing insights for supplier participants in the platform ecosystem. In a platform economy that, by its very nature, drives an increase in commoditization of services, identifying such additional sources of value and revenue is essential. The topic of servitization in the specific context of platform ecosystems is covered in detail in Part II in the chapter on Business Models.

2.6 Hyper-connected Supply Chains

Digital is a significant disruptor in supply chains for five key reasons:

- Data exchanges between supply chain partners allow a whole new paradigm of *collaboration, flexibility, and visibility.* This has a dual effect of enabling much closer interaction between parties (e.g., through near-real-time responses to up-stream or down-stream changes), but also the potential disaggregation of supply chain elements as switching of suppliers or logistics companies becomes much easier (both at a consumer level and a business-to-business interaction level).
- *Automation and AI* through digital technologies is one of the major influencers in transforming supply chains:

  – Automation and AI leads to the elimination of some supply chain elements (including a potential reversal of the historical trend for off-shoring and outsourcing). The nature of certain tasks that were traditionally off-shored (e.g., repetitive and predictable back-office processes or certain service desk functions) are now prime targets for automation using AI virtual agents or robotic process automation.

  – Analytics and AI will lead to new supply chain optimization insights. This area is covered in greater detail when we discuss the economy of the data lifecycle in the chapter on Business Models.

- *Provenance of supply*. There is an increasing trend among certain demographics to support sustainably and ethically sourced products and services. The insights available from digitally enabled supply chains are expected to become significant differentiators not only in market value perception, but also in regulatory compliance.
- *Customer intimacy*. Digital technologies enable a completely different level of customer intimacy than was previously possible (we dedicate the Customers chapter to this topic). But the bottom line is that those businesses who are able to gain control of the interface with the customer can then disintermediate and control the rest of the supply chain and drive incremental value from harvested customer engagement data. Businesses like Amazon or Comparethemarket.com have been highly successful at this. For many consumers, Amazon is the first go-to-place for finding products, reading reviews, getting recommendations, and making purchases, even though Amazon is actually a marketplace for an estimated 5 million sellers. Despite all the rich variety of companies selling their products through Amazon, it is Amazon that owns the direct customer relationship and, consequently, most of the related data-driven personal insights.
- *Digital enablement* of elements of the supply chain can become part of a business's differentiation and therefore brought into its core value proposition rather than outsourced, e.g., Amazon Prime warehousing and logistics.

References

Bock, R., Iansiti, M., & Lakhani, K. R. (2017). What the companies on the right side of the digital business divide have in common. *Harvard Business Review*. 31/01/2017. https://hbr.org/2017/01/what-the-companies-on-the-right-side-of-the-digital-business-divide-have-in-common. Accessed October 26, 2019.

Moore, G. A. (2015) *Zone to win*. Diversion Books.

Sheetz. (2017). https://www.cnbc.com/2017/08/24/technology-killing-off-corporations-average-lifespan-of-company-under-20-years.html. Accessed October 26, 2019.

3 Societal Trends—The Changing Influences on Business Strategy

The first quarter of the twenty-first century seems to be one of those times in history that is marked by a mood of "the change of an era." It seems to be a moment when the models, structures, and ideals that provided the backbone for the twentieth century (first turbulent and later affluent) are losing momentum and validity. However, the new models, structures, and ideals that will characterize the current century do not yet seem to have consolidated. In fact, there is continued (occasionally heated) debate on whether we have entered a period of Secular Stagnation[1] (as first proposed by Alvin Hansen in the late 1930s) or just a transitional phase of Schumpeterian Creative Destruction.[2] Even if the major Central Banks and other financial authorities speak of a "zero-growth" era for the coming years (the 2020s possibly), we think that these times will, in hindsight, be considered a period of creative destruction: a structural transition between two markedly different models of the world.

Let's explore Societal Trends: A multi-faceted family of trends that embody the perception of such times of change. Their outworking will drive behavior and allegiances at all levels and for all relevant business stakeholders: investors, entrepreneurs, workers, citizens, clients, partners, and users. Understanding these trends and their interplay is crucial when mapping the context (present and future) and defining the business strategy for digital transformation.

[1]A state of a market-based economy in which there is negligible or no growth for a very prolonged period of time.

[2]The "process of industrial mutation that incessantly revolutionizes the economic structure from within, continually destroying the old one, and creating a new one" (Schumpeter "Capitalism, Socialism and Democracy", Schumpeter 1942).

H. Tardieu et al., *Deliberately Digital*, Future of Business and Finance,
https://doi.org/10.1007/978-3-030-37955-1_3

3.1 Macroeconomic Trends

Looking at the wider picture with cyclic models, such as Nicolai Kondratiev's (Nefiodow and Nefiodow 2014) or Ray Dalio's (Dalio 2018), we seem to be at the end of a long debt cycle. Such phases are marked by huge amounts of debt at all levels: public (from national all the way down to the municipal level), private (both financial and non-financial companies), and household. Ultimately, debt means bringing to the present money that would otherwise only be made in the future. Since debt must normally be repaid with interest, a world overloaded with debt is a world in which a significant proportion of future income will be devoted to servicing that debt, and therefore, not available for consumption, investment or other use. It is very likely that the reader does not need such a simplified summary, but it serves as a powerful reminder of the business scenario for the next couple of decades.

The issue of debt is compounded by the so-called zero-era: near zero level interest rates, inflation, and growth. If current and anticipated future growth seems to be at best tepid, it may not be advisable to rely on huge consumption-based revenues or investment capacities. Unexpected spikes of inflation, coupled with salaries that are no longer indexed to CPI (Consumer Price Index), could further decrease the purchasing power of households, many of which already devote much of their income to servicing housing or education debt. An unexpected increase in interest rates, albeit not very large, could cause many businesses to be unable to service their current debt and as a result enter insolvency and bankruptcy. A meaningful digital transformation strategy must take these factors into account.

The last few decades have also seen a growing business dependence on exacerbated consumerism and programmed obsolescence, as well as near obsession with monetization. The monetization of everything reflects the phenomenon of commodification[3]: the way that certain aspects of life that were previously not considered to be the subject of an economic transaction begin to enter the economic and financial arena, e.g., services that enable a person to have someone else wait for them in a queue; the commercial exchange of human organs for transplant purposes; or the corporatization of education.

Commodification has led some to speak about the "death of capitalism," either in the classical Marxian fashion or in the sense of a rebirth: is capitalism being reimagined? This thinking is compounded by the fact that new digital businesses tend to have markedly different characteristics in terms of physical ownership of assets, reproducibility of processes, operational vs capital expenditure, etc. New economical concepts have been proposed such as "capitalism without capital" and "intangible economy" (Haskel and Westlake 2017), "global collaborative commons," and "zero marginal cost society" (Rifkin 2015). A digital strategy and transformation roadmap must take these reflections into account. Although apparently more philosophical or theoretical, they do hold practical value. Is it possible to

[3]The action or process of treating something as a mere commodity.

represent everything as a transaction? And, if it is, will stakeholders perceive the approach as something valuable and positive?

Currencies are also subject to experiments. Since the financial crisis of 2008, central banks of major currency areas (USA, EU, UK, Japan, and recently, but to a lesser extent, China) are playing the roles of friend and foe at the same time: They coordinate monetary policies in order to reach much needed equilibria in a complex hyper-connected world, yet they are also engaged in currency and trade wars between their respective geopolitical blocks. Some monetary areas (such as China, Russia, and Australia) seek direct agreements outside the traditional playing field of the former superpowers. Such "currency wrestling" may end up yielding winners and losers, or some form of union under a common basket of currencies.

Cryptocurrencies promise total independence from such traditional parties, with multi-issuer coins being freely used and transacted (pseudo) anonymously in a (usually) decentralized manner, although early experiments such as Bitcoin are yet to deliver against their promise. A currency must be very liquid, a unit of account, a medium of exchange/transaction, a means of value storage and a standard of deferred payment. Bitcoin in particular has failed to meet some of these critical criteria: Its value has been very volatile, it has been subject to a speculative bubble in 2018–2019 (with owners hoarding it), it is not a common and widely accepted currency for transacting, and it has not always been easy (or cheap) for its holders to convert it to a traditional fiat currency. In addition, totally unregulated major exchange houses have been hacked, with the result that the equivalents of millions of US dollars have been irreversibly stolen from their owners. In mid-2019, a consortium led by Facebook has proposed the cryptocurrency Libra,[4] triggering calls for caution and regulation from international monetary institutions.

Cryptocurrency controversies aside, some countries are experimenting with cashless environments, in which physical forms of currency are fully substituted by digital tokens, be it under a central bank-issued digital currency or under a decentralized cryptocurrency.

Is your business prepared to cope with the possible wild swings in currency exchanges that may result? Are you already experimenting with cashless environments (at an end-customer level or with employees)? Do cryptocurrencies feature in your strategic plan for digital transformation? If not, has it been a conscious decision or an unaddressed item?

3.2 Regulatory and Legal

Regulatory and legal measures tend to be implemented somewhat after the emergence of the principles, processes or events they are seeking to address. This is not necessarily a bad thing: societies need a "proof of the pudding" and some time to

[4] https://libra.org/ [accessed 26/10/2019].

reflect before deciding on what is permissible. However, when regulations and laws do appear, their impact on business can be significant.

In the current environment of major technological, business, and societal changes, the most notable sets of regulation seem to relate to privacy and data protection, the free market, and sustainability (in the wider sense of the word: i.e., economic, environmental, and societal). Ethical considerations are now on the rise, particularly with respect to the development and use of AI.

Regulation and law can be perceived as either a constraint or a catalyst for business. Some think that the very restrictive European regulations on privacy and data protection hinder the growth of Digital Giants in the EU for no good reason since, they argue, meaningful digital privacy does not really exist any longer. This line of thought applies to most forms of digital technology but especially to B2C digital platforms (*à la* Amazon or Google) and to AI (data being the fuel for AI). Kai-Fu Lee dismisses the future significance of Europe in AI, mostly on the grounds of the impact of regulatory constraints (Lee 2018). The very significant penalties contemplated by GDPR (Europe's data protection regulation) seem to back the claim, with fines that can be up to €20 million or 4% of the firm's worldwide annual revenue for the previous financial year, whichever is highest. However, a counterargument suggests that, spurred on by the same regulations, organizations and businesses may find new sources of value when providing goods and services that still comply with strict privacy and data protection laws. It is too early yet to judge the accuracy of each perspective. It is even too early to see if regulation may force some Digital Giants to abandon certain geographical areas and markets, or voluntarily split themselves up into a set of smaller legal entities.

If your company or organization operates in an area with strict privacy and data protection regulations, are you just complying? Are you sure that your compliance is not being achieved at the expense of substantial lost opportunities? In this regard, and aside from the purely financial view, you might even be perceived by clients and partners as a company that is too constrained; one that does not feel comfortable in the emerging digital world. If you are at the other end of the spectrum, taking considerable risks with regard to regulation or operating in a lax zone, you may want to consider public perception; the risk of a penalty (if any) may have been factored into your calculations, but what about the negative impact on people's perceptions and their potential viral spread?

There are sets of regulation that call for a "freer market," with the enhanced competition, lower entry barriers for players and wider, less friction-ridden access to consumers. One such example could be the European Payment Service Directive (PSD2), which requires banks to respond to the permissioned requests for exchange of certain basic financial information, to encourage (new) third parties to provide services in competition with traditional banks and financial institutions. Perhaps understandably, PSD2 was not very well received by the incumbent traditional institutions, which saw it as a threat to their market, with no possible upside. However, on further reflection, PSD2 might serve a powerful purpose for them: to push them into entering the new platform economy, a leap that intimidates most non-natively digital enterprises. Since PSD2 forces the opening and sharing of data for third parties to extract value from, why not benefit from others' data as well as from the ecosystem of new entrants? Bear in mind that most of the new entrants are financial start-ups (the so-called FinTechs) that could well become value-add partners and not competitors.

Have you included such reflections in your digital strategy? Would your business or activity be prepared for a substantial market-oriented regulatory change (designed to enhance competition)? Have you thought about how regulatory compliance could be an asset rather than a cost? What business opportunities or capabilities could come from apparently less favorable regulatory frameworks? In particular, do you have a strategy concerning digital platforms? Have you evaluated the pros and cons of building/owning your own platform, versus those of joining an existing one? Are you leveraging any digital platforms to increase your market share? Or even break into adjacent markets? Do you have a strategy for defending your business from the entrance of a digital giant into your space?

3.3 Environmental

The environment has been one of the, if not *the*, main targets of negative externalities during the twentieth and early twenty-first centuries. Besides moral and ethical considerations, numerous studies on wide-ranging environmental topics are leading scientists and experts to label the current era of Earth history as "Anthropocene": The era in which the influence of humans on nature is greater than the historically traditional influence of nature on humans (Subramanian 2019).

Fossil fuels, on which the human economy and civilization heavily depend, could have reached an inflection point. Climate change could begin to make very populated areas of the planet uninhabitable in the short or mid-term. International organizations such as the UN are urgently calling for concerted action within the next 10 years, after which a point of no return could be reached in certain aspects (extreme heat, droughts, and floods). We have conflicting trends of population concentration in mega-cities on the one hand, and issues with water and air quality on the other. In the last few years concerns are growing about plastic contamination in the oceans (and within animal and human bodies). Very recently we are seeing alarming reports about major losses of biomass, and specifically, the amounts of insects (Javis 2018) and plankton (Chu 2019) seem to have reduced in some areas by 50% or more. Such a huge change in numerical proportions is even more dramatic considering the fundamental role of insects and plankton in the trophic chain and in bio-ecosystems: Both are foundational components in the food pyramid, with insects also contributing to key processes such as decomposition and pollination.

Circular Economy principles promise to help reverse some of those trends. They represent a new formulation of economical processes that consciously break the linear "extract-use-discard" logic, which was fundamental to the mass consumption markets of the twentieth century. Instead, they favor closed loops that make much better (re)use of resources and assets. On the positive side, the very technologies that contributed to the old, damaging practices, may be employed to master the new Circular Economy, with notable additions such as renewable energy and additive manufacturing.

Has your digital strategy considered environmental aspects? Are they a constraint or nuisance, or are they a source of value (economical, financial, brand-related)? Are you hedging against possible climate-related events which are very likely in the coming years? Could your organization absorb insurance-related costs, either to damages suffered or damages caused? This is not an area that can be ignored or treated lightly as witnessed by the fact that US utility PG&E declared bankruptcy and saw its CEO ousted after being found responsible for the devastating October 2017 California wildfires (McLean 2019).

3.4 Security

Early in the second half of the twentieth century, humankind reached the potential for mutually assured destruction which, according to game theory, would prevent any one side from attacking the other, at least under rational considerations. A few decades later, after the fall of the USSR and the Iron Curtain, Francis Fukuyama famously posited "the end of history" (Fukuyama 1992), with Western liberal democracy becoming the universal and final form of human government, an end certainly at odds with history's notorious knack for cycles.

Far from witnessing such universalization of Western liberal democracy, the twenty-first century is seeing a form of democracy that is receding or weakening in its home turf. Large-scale armed conflicts persist, while at a smaller, more granular level they have increased (through terrorism and gang violence). Significantly, the very complexity and cost of physical world intervention, together with the power of new technologies, have caused the conflict to move to the virtual world. Wars of the twenty-first century will be, and arguably are already being, fought in the virtual world, with cyber-warfare and financial-economic operations taking the lead role, albeit perhaps not yet fully in the public eye.

We start to see hardware and software that originates from certain geopolitical areas being closely scrutinized or rejected by consumers in other areas, for fear of built-in malware, backdoors, or other hazardous features. This has been the case with Huawei, whose products where banned in the USA in 2019 (Spadafora 2019). In addition, data protection and privacy regulations have become a "silent weapon." B2C platforms that exploit individuals' data have different equivalents in different regions, for example, the US-originated Facebook, WhatsApp, Twitter or YouTube vs the Chinese WeChat, Tencent QQ, Sina Weibo, or Youku Toudou.

On the business side, intellectual and industrial property-related piracy, as well as direct cyber-attacks (some aided by social engineering) are on the rise. And there is near certainty in the fact that the real scale of the problem is much bigger than estimated, due to numerous unknown events. However, security (mostly cyber by now) continues to be perceived as a cost, not a core necessity of business. Do you regularly conduct cyber-security assessments, internal or external (with the aid of ethical hackers, for example)? Can you be certain of the number, extent, and damage of the attacks your organization has suffered? Is security one of the main drivers of your transformation strategy? Have you taken out insurance against cyber-security events? Are your products and services architected and produced with a security-by-design mindset? Are you sure your data and applications are more secure in your own premises than in a trusted third-party cloud? Does security and data privacy sit at the heart of your company values and processes? We consider these questions further in the chapter on Security.

3.5 People and Communities

People-related trends (individual or collective) are numerous, so we will focus on the ones most relevant for a business's digital transformation.

Demographic and generational shifts are crucial driving forces. Some countries' populations are rapidly aging, with a concerning inverted demographic pyramid (Japan, Italy, Germany), while others are experiencing notorious population booms (many African countries). As far as generations are concerned, we are starting to see the coexistence of up to five generations in the workplace, at least as far as technology-related culture is concerned. With the oldest cohort of so-called Gen-Y (millennials) approaching their 40s as we write these lines, generational shifts in terms of ethics, consumption patterns, household composition, and purchasing power are starting to have material impacts. The difficulties of some consumer staple brands, such as Kraft Heinz in the food sector (whose stock price fell 28% in a single session in early 2019 (Giammona 2019)), are mostly attributed to their lack of adaptation to such generational shifts. Regarding purchasing power, younger generations have less income than their predecessors did at the same age, they face much higher debt burdens (especially higher education loans) and struggle to enter the housing market which is again at an all-time high after the housing bubble burst in 2008. Businesses must include these factors in their strategy, both internally (talent attraction and loyalty) and externally.

These times of change display apparently contradictory trends or behaviors. On one hand, the world might have better educated populations, wider access to basic goods and services (although still very far from perfect) and a never-before-seen amount of easily available information. On the other hand, hoaxes abound, as does fake news, or trends that undo notable advances (anti-vaccination, flat-earthers, etc.). We seem to be "Amusing ourselves to death," as the Neil Postman book put it decades ago (Postman 1985), with notable public unawareness of the crucial problems faced by society. Social networks have favored the creation of echo chambers, where people are steered to only engage with others holding similar views. Social networks themselves are also riddled with fake news (including click-bait and behavior inductors) and are natural grounds for gambling-like interactions and escapism which deter meaningful action. People are becoming more and more polarized, precisely when the means exist for enhanced exchange and communication. Some people even feel uneasy about expressing their views, anticipating possible backlashes. Companies must navigate these uncertain waters, facing the conundrum of establishing brand values that are well perceived and clear, while avoiding the trap of polarizing topics.

After the 2008 financial crisis, there is a growing inequality in traditionally affluent societies, which have so far used the Welfare State as a mechanism to dampen social differences that might otherwise have damaged social and economic development. Tensions arise as the gap between the haves and have-nots widens, and the middle class is depleted. Discontent is capitalized by opportunistic populist figures and demagogues, which are becoming more preponderant, often fueling nationalistic, isolationist feelings, and policies.

Such inequality translates into polarization in the market, with the luxury segment growing profusely and the rest of the market drifting toward low-cost or good-enough products and services. The trend is driving major makers of luxury goods (including technological devices) to launch their own lines of second-hand or refurbished products under the same brand as new products (Gartenberg 2018). If your organization is in that shrinking mid-market, your strategy should take this into account as a potential lever for transformation.

The evolution of consumers into prosumers has not been as homogeneous as, perhaps naively, anticipated. Most consumers are prosumers only as unconscious producers of the data-trails that Digital Giants devour to perfect their algorithms. True prosumers, who consciously and purposefully produce high-quality information, are scarcer. Some of them have taken an intermediary role as so-called influencers, although the trend seems to be declining: True grassroots influencing in social media has frequently been overshadowed by astroturfing[5] or just plain poseurs.

Polarization may also become a trend in the labor market. AI and Automation are expected to replace human labor in many blue and white-collar activities, with less impact on the middle of the spectrum. At the ends of the spectrum, humans may still reign in highly skilled analytical jobs or in highly social and adaptive ones. On the positive side, crowdsourcing and crowdfunding, for personal or professional purposes, have matured. They are ready for businesses to exploit them wisely, for ideas, people, financing or other assets. Even more interestingly, some of them are morphing into digital platforms, such as P2P (peer-to-peer) insurance (Friendsurance, Lemonade). In addition to B2B (business-to-business) or B2C (business-to-consumer) digital platforms, P2P/C2C (citizen-to-citizen) platforms can provide interesting options for a business's digital strategy.

[5]The deceptive practice of presenting a marketing or public relations campaign in the guise of unsolicited grass roots comments from members of the public.

3.6 The Transformation Challenge

These Societal Trends are perhaps the hardest to master, due both to their sheer number and varied nature. In further sections we will explore some specific trends in more detail, looking more deeply at possible actionable proposals. However, there is no real substitute for an in-house exercise in context awareness and trend analysis that will serve as an input to your continuous reflections on digital strategy. While businesses and organizations used to focus on creating value for a few stockholders and major societal actors, now they are required to satisfy the expectations of a myriad of stakeholders (not just stockholders) that until recently were buried in the long tail of the user/client distribution.

References

Chu, J. (2019). *Phytoplankton decline coincides with warming temperatures over the last 150 years*. Phys.org, 07/05/2019 https://phys.org/news/2019-05-phytoplankton-decline-coincides-temperatures-years.html. Accessed October 26, 2019.

Dalio, R. (2018). *Principles for navigating big debt crises: The archetypal big debt cycle*. Bridgewater. Accessible online at https://www.principles.com/big-debt-crises/. Accessed October 26, 2019.

Data Protection in the EU. (2015). *European Commission*. Published online at https://ec.europa.eu/info/law/law-topic/data-protection/data-protection-eu_en. Accessed October 26, 2019.

Fukuyama. (1992). *The end of history and the last man*. Free Press.

Gartenberg C (2018) *Apple is selling refurbished iPhone 7 and 7 Plus phones now*. Theverge.com, 01/02/2018. https://www.theverge.com/circuitbreaker/2018/2/1/16960568/apple-selling-refurbished-iphone-7-plus-store. Accessed October 26, 2019.

Giammona, C. (2019). *Kraft Heinz faces existential crisis after $16 Billion rout*. Bloomberg, 22/02/2019. https://www.bloomberg.com/news/articles/2019-02-22/kraft-heinz-faces-existential-crisis-as-stock-tumbles-to-new-low. Accessed October 26, 2019.

Haskel, J., & Westlake, S. (2017). *Capitalism without Capital: The rise of the intangible economy*. Princeton University Press.

Javis, B. (2018). *The insect apocalypse is here: What does it mean for the rest of life on Earth?* New York Times, 27/11/2018 https://www.nytimes.com/2018/11/27/magazine/insect-apocalypse.html. Accessed October 26, 2019.

Lee, K. F. (2018). *AI superpowers China, silicon valley and the new world order*. Houghton Mifflin Harcourt.

McLean, R. (2019). *California utility PG&E replaces CEO amid bankruptcy worries*. CNN Business, 14/01/2019. https://edition.cnn.com/2019/01/13/business/pge-ceo-departure/index.html. Accessed October 26, 2019.

Nefiodow, L., & Nefiodow, S. (2014). *Kondratieff cycles*. Published online at https://www.kondratieff.net/kondratieffcycles. Accessed October 26, 2019.

Payment services (PSD 2) - Directive (EU) 2015/2366. (2015). *European Commission*. Published online at https://ec.europa.eu/info/law/payment-services-psd-2-directive-eu-2015-2366_en. Accessed October 26, 2019.

Postman, N. (1985). *Amusing ourselves to death: Public discourse in the age of show business*. Viking Penguin.

Rifkin, J. (2015). *The zero marginal cost society: The internet of things, the collaborative commons, and the eclipse of capitalism*. Palgrave Macmillan.

Schumpeter, J. A. (1942). *Capitalism, socialism and democracy*. Harper & Brothers.

Spadafora, A. (2019). *Trump order bans US firms from dealing with Huawei.* Techradar.com, 16/05/2019. https://www.techradar.com/news/trump-order-bans-us-firms-from-dealing-with-huawei. Accessed October 26, 2019.

Subramanian, M. (2019). Anthropocene now: Influential panel votes to recognize Earth's new epoch. *Nature*. https://doi.org/10.1038/d41586-019-01641-5 Accessible online at https://www.nature.com/articles/d41586-019-01641-5. Accessed October 26, 2019.

Technology Trends—Historical and Future Drivers of Change

4

There are several technologies and technological trends that are now reshaping the world (society and business alike) usually in unpredictable ways. The 2000s and early 2010s were characterized by a focus on a few culprits (Social, Mobile, Analytics, Cloud: collectively known as S.M.A.C.) and were marked by a techno-optimism[1] that just a few years later seems quite naive.

Since the second half of the 2010s, technologies, the interactions between them, and their applications seem to resist being straight jacketed into simple 4-letter acronyms. More importantly, techno-optimism has started to give way to a more balanced and nuanced view on technological adoption: one that puts values, ethics, and the social impact of technology on an equal footing with the initial promises.

It is also important to note that the pace of change seems to be continuing to accelerate. Therefore, even if we manage to succeed in providing a non-too-momentary account of the main technological trends, this chapter could be partially obsolete by the time you read these lines. Besides asking for your understanding, it is worth reflecting on how to incorporate such rapidly changing trends into digital business strategy.

4.1 Artificial Intelligence (AI)

Artificial intelligence (AI) represents the different approaches and multiple algorithms that aim to reproduce human intelligence in certain tasks (narrow or weak AI), or in general, multi-task domains (general or strong AI). The main approaches

[1]The often-misguided belief that new technologies (mostly digital) will rather easily solve big problems of humanity (such as war, totalitarianism or famine). It usually overestimates the power of technology and greatly underestimates the complexity of the problems it addresses.

H. Tardieu et al., *Deliberately Digital*, Future of Business and Finance,
https://doi.org/10.1007/978-3-030-37955-1_4

are symbolic AI (based on human-readable representations and logic), Bayesian networks (probabilistic graph-based[2] models), evolutionary algorithms (where potential solutions play the role of individuals in a population, subject to fitness functions) and Deep Learning (artificial neural networks with many layers, originally and vaguely inspired by biological nervous systems).

Symbolic AI was the predominant paradigm until the late 1980s. The recent boom of AI has been driven by Machine Learning (algorithms that learn from data instead of processing data according to explicit, given instructions) and especially deep learning. Deep learning has already reached or surpassed human performance in certain tasks such as image recognition and classification.

AI has been very hyped during the last few years, a situation which poses two challenges to businesses: firstly, to anticipate exaggerated results for the technology, which will fail to materialize; secondly, the risk of missing business use cases where the technology can bring real demonstrable value because such value is obscured by the clutter of hype. Both cases can, and do, misguide investments, and must be avoided. Examples of good uses of AI techniques include traffic prediction, facial recognition, nuanced sentiment analysis, automated classification of documents or information, automated surveillance, or fraud detection. Chatbots and speech/text recognition are other good examples of AI applications and will be addressed in the section on Human–Machine Interfaces and Natural Language Processing.

AI-based systems must wisely balance machine and human intelligence. In addition, there are significant efforts directed at making black box algorithms transparent (Explainable AI), avoiding bias in the training data and training processes (which may have negative and hard-to-detect consequences on performance), and at algorithm-specific security (avoiding or detecting the malicious injection of data which is aimed at derailing or hacking the algorithm's performance).

4.2 Internet of Things (IoT)

The Internet of Things is a discipline or meta-technology focused on the connection of objects, sensors, actuators, software, and computing hardware in networks or meshes. Its ultimate purpose is to interconnect all relevant objects in order to enable the intelligent and remote management of virtually anything.

This enables the automatic or semi-automatic remote management of many aspects of everyday life at home or at work, including meeting rooms, parking spaces, stadiums, houses, cars, and industrial equipment. There are already many positive use cases, but the full power of IoT is yet to come. To fully realize it, several challenges need to be solved including: the cost of deploying and

[2]A structure composed of objects (called "nodes") which may be related to one another by links. Graph s are studied by "graph theory" and are widely used in communications, semantics, computational biology, and many other fields.

maintaining the connected objects; the risk of objects or data being attacked or vandalized; and high communication latency due to substantial data transfer, limited power duration, or autonomy.

4.3 Blockchain

Blockchain has become famous as the technology that supports the Bitcoin cryptocurrency, but the underlying technology potentially offers much more than that. Blockchains, and distributed ledger technologies[3] (DLTs) in general, enable trust in otherwise trustless environments, doing so in a decentralized way without the need for intermediaries or trusted third parties.

They act as ledgers for transactions, enabling their traceability. They can be applied to such things as the commerce of valuable goods and luxury items and the issuance of education certificates or real-estate deeds. They can also be used as the basis for smart contracts that auto-validate when a transaction meets certain conditions, automatically triggering further processes. In addition, they can support the tokenization of analog or physical entities, allowing them to be subject to digital treatment and monetization.

The Bitcoin Blockchain (a so-called public chain) has limitations in certain aspects, such as scalability (it doesn't always perform well as the number of transactions increases), speed (it is not quick enough for certain use cases, such as toll payments), or energy efficiency (large amounts of energy are consumed in the mining process required for consensus proofs). For these reasons, alternative protocols and consensus mechanisms are being explored. Some of the previously mentioned limitations pertain only to public Blockchains and DLT's, and they are being solved or circumvented through private Blockchains. This approach has opened a rather heated debate on whether a private Blockchain really is a Blockchain at all, since it usually reintroduces controversial aspects like centralization, third-party trust guarantors, and permissioning. Operational models relating to DLT s are in their early stages, so a significant amount of exploration is to be expected until some concrete models prove their value and are widely adopted for specific business situations.

4.4 Cloud and Virtualization

Cloud technologies are the visible commoditization of computing. Big and expensive computers hosted by and dedicated to specific enterprises are substituted by cheaper and much more numerous computers clustered in gigantic remote data centers, which offer computing "as a service." Despite its name, the "public" Cloud

[3] A digital system for consistently and immutably recording transactions in multiple locations in a shared and synchronous manner.

is in fact in private hands (Amazon, Microsoft, Google, etc.); the term "private" is reserved for the data centers under the control of the companies and organizations using them (even if data center hosting and control may be outsourced). Hybrid cloud refers to the automated and efficient orchestration of both types.

Cloud computing comes in different flavors: Infrastructure as a Service (IaaS), Platform as a Service[4] (PaaS), and Software as a Service (SaaS). Under IaaS, the user accesses remote infrastructure resources as needed but has to configure them and manage the full application stacks that run on them; an example is Amazon Web Services (AWS EC2). Under PaaS, the infrastructure services are provided as part of a platform and are largely transparent to the user, who focuses on developing and deploying applications; an example is Google App Engine. Under SaaS, the user accesses the application, without any development, deployment, or maintenance concerns: Everything is transparent except the functionality; examples are Dropbox and Salesforce.

Many digital organizations are "Cloud native," meaning that their systems and applications were designed and developed on, and for, the Cloud. Most traditional organizations have a complicated mix of legacy and new systems and applications: Some of these will never leave the corporate data center, some will be migrated to the Cloud, others may have already been migrated or are Cloud native. Managing a mixed legacy and new technology environment can be a significant challenge for "IT" and for the business divisions. This tends to be because legacy solutions are generally business critical, costly and not very flexible; this can make such environments unsupportive of the demands for speed, flexibility, and experimentation that digital business strategies generally require.

4.5 Hyper-commoditized Computing (Serverless and Beyond)

Public cloud started by offering compute and storage as a service, but this has evolved to offer virtualized computers and many other services (task scheduling, security monitoring, etc.). The latest wave is serverless computing, where most operations (i.e., infrastructure-related) activities are hidden. The ultimate goal is to automate all operations (a trend dubbed No-Ops), enabling a developer to send only code to the cloud platform, which will then handle all the necessary remaining steps to run the code. Coupled with the ever-decreasing cost of compute and storage, this could have a dramatic cost-saving impact on the delivery of computing environments, savings which could be reinvested elsewhere.

[4]"Platform" in this context should not be confused with the much broader business-model-driven concept of Industry Platforms.

4.6 Edge and Swarm Computing (The Shift to the Edge)

As public clouds accumulate huge computing capacities in centralized clusters (let's call it "the center of the cloud") other connected objects are rapidly growing in number, memory and processing power (smartphones, tablets, objects, sensors, etc.). This trend is shifting the center of gravity of compute power and data processing away from large central data centers and toward the "edge of the cloud." We are now seeing this model extend further and further into distributed computing at the edge (hence the name Edge Computing), where individual objects possess local intelligence, avoiding unnecessary movement of data, from the edge to the center and back, something which is very inefficient in terms of time and energy.

In addition to such hyper-connectivity and distributed computing, Swarm Computing can also bring intelligence in the way that edge objects combine their efforts to accomplish common objectives, autonomously adapting their performance to changes in themselves or their environment. For example, wind turbines in a wind farm could monitor their individual and collective performance: If several of them malfunctioned, the rest would modify their operating regime to ensure their total output remained as close as possible to their operational objective.

4.7 Additive Manufacturing

Additive Manufacturing is popularly known as 3D printing: the process of manufacturing things by successively depositing layers of materials in a defined manner. The cheapest and most popular 3D printers use plastic materials (polymers), but it is feasible to print with other materials including certain metals, ceramics, and concretes. The name Additive Manufacturing stems from the fact that the object is manufactured by continuously adding material, unlike in most traditional processes where raw material is removed to achieve the desired form. In Additive Manufacturing, an object is formed by print heads following a series of digital instructions that contain the material deposition path and the associated feed parameters (temperature and speed). This technology is seen as revolutionary since it permits the use of much less raw material (50–80% less), it enables the realization of designs that were hard or impossible to manufacture before, and it can drastically reduce the need for transport and storage: Parts do not always have to be centrally manufactured and then distributed; they can be simply printed at, or close to, the place of use.

4.8 Augmented Reality and Virtual Reality (AR and VR)

Augmented Reality (AR) superimposes digital objects, perceptual artifacts or information layers onto an observer's view of the real world, in order to enrich (augment) the experience of the viewer. For example, captions can be overlaid onto a human's view of the world to provide information about points of interest or show pictures of the inside of a building that is being viewed from the outside. The technology was first used for gaming and education, but it has moved into other areas such as marketing, tourism, and industry (e.g., to aid a field worker during a repair or maintenance operation). In contrast, virtual reality (VR) creates a scenario which is entirely virtual (even though it may represent real objects and situations) in which the person is fully immersed in the virtual experience. VR has found uses in entertainment and training, but it does not seem to have lived up to its promises. Even though the cost of the technology has decreased significantly, a "killer application" is yet to appear. Also, some users feel discomfort ("VR sickness") due to the dissonance between the virtual reality perceived by the eyes and the actual reality perceived by other senses.

4.9 Human–Machine Interfaces (HMI) and Natural Language Processing (NLP)

Human–Machine Interfaces are devices that enable humans to interact with computers, ideally in a very natural way. The most widespread examples are keyboards, mice, joysticks, and touchscreens. More advanced HMIs involve gesture, touch (haptic), or language interfaces. These tend to be more natural for a human since they enable interactions that are much closer to those used in regular human to human interactions. However, advanced forms of HMI are yet to experience mass adoption due to a combination of factors, such as comfort, user experience, cost or lack of integration/interoperability with existing software and hardware.

Natural Language Processing (NLP) is a field that uses different techniques and approaches (rule-based, statistical, AI) to process natural human language. It addresses all different aspects of human language (syntax, semantics, discourse) as well as its uses (language understanding, language generation, translation, summarization, etc.). It generally also includes speech recognition.

With a shift of compute power to the edge of the cloud, many of the objects around us could exploit HMI and NLP to unleash a revolutionary way for humans to engage with machines. We already see the first steps in some conversational assistants (Cortana, Siri, Alexa and others), but the future could involve direct communication with smart objects without the need for virtual intermediaries. Following the serverless and No-Ops trends presented above, conversational coding could be the most natural way to program and send code (or just goals or requirements) to the cloud. In the long term, the ultimate objective would be "ambient intelligence" or "the invisible computer": in other words, being surrounded by a ubiquitous computing continuum, accessible through natural language.

4.10 Digital Twins and Internet of Twins

Digital Twin s are digital replicas of physical objects or systems, endowed with data analytics and simulation capabilities, so that they can virtually reproduce or simulate the performance of their physical counterparts under diverse conditions. The twins can simulate individual performance steps or entire processes. Their capability can be valuable at all stages of a physical entity's lifecycle: in the design phase, to test the performance and characteristics of alternative designs; in the testing phase, to submit virtual models to all kinds of tests (lowering the cost or accelerating the generation of results from physical testing); in the production phase, by feeding data obtained from the physical object or system into its twin and carrying out predictive and prescriptive analytics; and in the operational phase to help optimize performance and feedback design improvements.

Digital Twins are being developed in different fields, such as health care or industry. In the former, a human heart can be modeled as a combination of three virtual systems: mechanical, electromagnetic, and fluid dynamic. The Digital Twin can be "personalized" to match the heart of a specific person and used for example to design a customized stent. In the case of industry, Digital Twins are being developed for various machines and systems, such as wind turbines, to optimize their design and performance, or to study and predict malfunctions.

The Internet of Twins would be the natural extension of the Internet of Things, where for every object or system, different twins could exist and interact with each other.

4.11 Quantum Computing

Quantum Computing is an emerging technology, but one with game-changing potential. It takes advantage of the properties of matter at sub-atomic scale to perform computations on quantum bits, or qubits. Whereas a classical bit can only hold a value of 0 or 1, a qubit can take those values or any intermediate combination (coherent superposition) of both. This can enable the execution of certain algorithms thousands or millions of times faster than with classical computers.

Which algorithms might benefit from Quantum Computing (not all of them can) is still a research question. Shor's algorithm, which enables the factorization of a number into its prime number components, is certainly one of them. Since this algorithm is one of the primary bases for data encryption, as soon as a sufficiently powerful quantum computer appears, most current encryption keys will be decipherable by brute force, rendering many existing cyber-security measures useless, including some Blockchains! That is why, in parallel to the research and development relating to quantum computers, there is significant work devoted to the development of Quantum-Safe Cryptography.

Today, Quantum Computing is still in its infancy. Among other limitations, current quantum computers do not have many qubits (a long way from thousands or millions) and quantum decoherence[5] is not well controlled, causing interactions of the quantum computer with its environment to ruin computations. Quantum simulators are classical computers that can simulate the performance of a quantum computer. They are a useful and affordable means to introduce Quantum Computing into business today. They are starting to be used in physics, chemistry, pharmaceutical and financial services: These are currently the fields where the use of quantum computers is considered to be the most promising.

4.12 Nanotechnology

Nanotechnology refers to the manipulation and engineering of matter at a molecular or atomic level and can have many different applications: from the extension of device physics, to the direct control of matter at atomic scale, or the development of new materials.

At the nanoscale, materials can sometimes exhibit properties that are markedly different from those at the macroscale: opaque materials can turn transparent, inert ones can become catalysts, etc. The same applies to atomic level structures such as nanopillars, nanorods, or nanotubes.

They could be applied in electronics (micro-electromechanical systems or MEMS), biomedicine (tissue engineering, targeted drug delivery), aerospace (smart regenerative materials) and many other fields. There are, however, concerns to be elucidated, such as the potential toxicity and environmental impact of nanotechnology, as well as the associated security implications.

4.13 Genomics and Health Care

Genomics is the field of science that focuses on the genome, i.e., the complete set of DNA for a living organism. Genome editing is a technique that permits the insertion, deletion, modification, or replacement of bits of an organism's DNA in a targeted way. Since DNA is the "code of life", genomics and genome editing hold the potential to positively hack the code of life, for example enhancing organisms or eradicating diseases. Of course, such benefits must be carefully balanced against the inherent risks and ethical considerations that such techniques present. However, it is a rapidly evolving field, and we can expect notable breakthroughs, together with associated ethical and societal debates, in the next couple of decades.

[5]A quantum physical property, necessary for the functioning of quantum computers, but which can be destroyed by interactions with the environment.

Health care could undergo a revolution if advances in genomics are coupled with the real-time predictive and prescriptive analysis of many other sources of relevant data (besides genetic data): proteomics, metabolomics, lifestyle, medication history, electronic healthcare records (EHR), wearable sports and health monitors, etc. Under this new paradigm, health care would be a continuous affair, including the preventive phase where no pathology exists. Furthermore, it would be truly personalized (unlike today's coarse protocols) and participative.

4.14 Timelines from a Strategic Perspective

These technologies have a historical and a future development path. Due to their different levels of maturity, pace of evolution, etc., you may choose to incorporate them into your operations at different points in the timeline—Table 4.1 summarizes our recommendation. Since they are generic recommendations, some of the individual points may not apply (fully, yet or ever) to your specific line of activity:

Table 4.1 Strategic timeline for technology experimentation

	Maturing in 2015–2019 You should be doing this:	Maturing in 2020–2024 Pilot this now:	Maturing in 2025–2029 Watch and experiment with this now:
Artificial intelligence	Proven cases, including RPA, predictive analytics, computer vision	Advanced cases: prescriptive analytics, enterprise AI	Artificial Intelligence: "futuristic" cases
Internet of Things	Proven and financially sound cases	Low power and latency, mid-high volume of devices	High/very-high volume of devices & massive roll-outs; internet of twins
Cloud	Cloud strategy; public and hybrid solutions	Serverless: evolution from cloud or leapfrog beyond cloud and DevOps towards NoOps	Serverless: NoOps and further commoditization (new architectural practices, FinDev)
Additive manufacturing	At least for prototyping or spare parts	Focus on industrializing the process	Full integration of the technology after its industrialization
Augmented reality	Implement use cases in marketing, sales, education, field services …	Full business processes, truly immersive remote collaboration	Move towards multiple realities, their coexistence, sharing and navigation
HMI and NLP	Voice commands, language understanding and generation	Haptics, gestures, advanced language processing	Move towards disappearing interfaces and devices

(continued)

Table 4.1 (continued)

	Maturing in 2015–2019 You should be doing this:	Maturing in 2020–2024 Pilot this now:	Maturing in 2025–2029 Watch and experiment with this now:
Digital twin	At least simple simulations, connected to lifecycle management	Elaborate, multimodal simulations connected to business and IT systems	Digital twins as BAU and internet of twins business scenarios
Blockchain	Ideating and piloting processes, identity and tokenization	Sound business models and processes	Seamless integration in digital platform(s) & IT landscape
Edge and Swarm	Early experimentation	Edge computing: bring intelligence and connectivity to objects at the edge of the cloud	Swarm computing: self-organizing intelligence of objects at the edge of the cloud
Quantum computing		Start experimenting with it using simulators to understand its potential	Advanced experimentation and initial solutions (as accelerator)
Genomics and healthcare		P4 medicine, impact on your people and business	Advanced P4 medicine, impact of -omics on your people and business
Nanotechnology			Identify scenarios of use

Table compiled by authors

Keep in mind that your strategy and transformation actions must contemplate not only the isolated impacts and consequences of each of these technologies (and others you may add yourself), but also their possible combinations and interactions.

5 Digital Frustration—Why Do Organizations Struggle to Transform Successfully and Sustainably?

5.1 Why Is Digital Transformation so Hard?

If the potential of digital is demonstrably so significant, why do so many businesses struggle with reaping the benefits? In fact, is there any real lasting hope for traditional businesses seeking to transform their models into ones that can compete effectively with digital leaders?

Digital leaders share several common traits that have been widely publicized: They are data- and analytics-driven, based on platform models (see chapter on Platforms and Ecosystems) and tend to be quite independent of physical assets and supports. However, they also share other traits that have not been so popularized, at least until recently: the real Digital Giants have grown in relatively regulation-free environments; they often directly or indirectly use physical assets whose cost is borne by others; they focus on one-to-many, business-to-consumer (B2C) models and markets (with extremely high fragmentation and low bargaining power); and their quick growth has given them considerable investment ammunition, which has only kept growing.

Traditional organizations, those facing the transformation imperative, start their journey practically from the opposite position: most are regulated (some heavily so); they can be somewhat burdened with physical infrastructure and assets; many have tight business margins (and few have the investment power of the digital natives); and many of them focus on B2B models with radically different approaches to trust, engagement, and bargaining power.

Moreover, again unlike Digital Giants, given their generally long histories, traditional organizations are often deeply embedded within the socio-economic fabric. The consequence of this is that they are subject to closer scrutiny and are expected and required to conform to higher societal standards. Imagine the consequences of a traditional bank or telco profiting from private data (à la Facebook) based on flaky End User License Agreements? We believe that a successful digital transformation will be measured by its societal adoption, no matter how well defined its "hard" business KPIs might be.

H. Tardieu et al., *Deliberately Digital*, Future of Business and Finance,
https://doi.org/10.1007/978-3-030-37955-1_5

All things considered, digital transformation is a huge, David-and-Goliath type of challenge that traditional organizations face. It is one which they may proactively embrace or wait to be forced to embark on, but it cannot be avoided. It's no wonder that (notwithstanding hype and fad) digital transformation is often considered hard, sometimes explicitly resisted, and usually subject to very personal perceptions. But what are the bases of such perceptions and how valid are they?

As we look at the main challenges faced by transforming businesses, it is worth remembering that pursuing a digital strategy is no surefire guarantee of success, whether you are pursuing a transformation strategy, or a digital native strategy. There are many external factors that seem to be in a constant state of flux, and which may heavily influence the outcomes of what, at one point, seemed to be the most compelling of digital propositions:

- A breakthrough technology could render established digital models vulnerable or obsolete. For example, Quantum Computing could break current cryptographic security mechanisms, threatening digital banking, online trading, IP protection, etc.
- Legislation driven by public opinion could block certain digital business models, e.g., gig economy employment models impacted by new employee rights legislation.
- Societal values could constrain the adoption of certain technologies or lead to a rejection of established ones, e.g., concerns over personal data exploitation blocking the willingness of smart energy meter users to share their consumption data.

Businesses must be fully aware of such external complication factors; however, the fact remains that more than 80% of digital transformations fail primarily because of internal cultural factors that can largely be summed up as an "unwillingness to change".

5.2 The Challenge of Culture Change

Digital transformation is not only about technology, it is just as much about people, processes, and culture, and a failure to deal with these points holistically is a recipe for failure. Changing long-established cultural norms is a huge task, and concurrent operation of dual cultures, as waves of transformation are executed, can be divisive and obstructive.

True transformation must go to the very heart of an organization and for the most part needs to be led from the top-down (to give the right to break the shackles of long-established processes and governance), but not all organizations are prepared to do so. There are a number of reasons for this which are explored below. Digital newcomers are for the most part not subject to such constraints. They can start from a clean sheet and therefore have distinct advantages in terms of flexibility and agility, and they have the freedom to explore and experiment.

Let us now consider some of the key behaviors that we have observed within enterprises that lead to sub-optimal or failed digital transformations.

5.3 Digital Mavericks

Nature abhors a vacuum and where digital transformation is not explicitly driven from the top, then it is often the case that some groups or individuals will seek to fill the gaps because they believe it is the right thing to do. This can yield some positive results, but it can also take the focus away from needing to follow more of a corporate-led transformation.

The nature of digital allows bottom-up innovation as enabling technologies are often accessible and relatively cheap. Cloud-based services allow individuals to easily spin up environments and build/host applications that are largely outside of the visibility of corporate IT services. In many organizations, we have seen a significant rise in so-called shadow IT, where business users take their own initiative and embark on covert or even overt breakaway IT initiatives. The likely outcome of shadow IT initiatives is that they are rarely well integrated with core IT systems and therefore suffer from inefficiency of independence; they may expose the business to security or data privacy risks; they tend to add cost rather than remove cost (as they sit alongside and are incremental to legacy systems); and they ultimately lead to frustration from users who perceive corporate IT falling further and further behind in terms of delivering against business needs. Nevertheless, such initiatives can be a positive catalyst for change and an incubator for innovation. If corporate IT departments can work more effectively and collaboratively with such shadow initiatives, then transformation can become more potent. Failure to realize such collaboration will relegate the corporate IT function to the "department of no".

But maverick behavior can only go so far and tends to hit roadblocks when it comes up against traditional established processes. Examples of areas of conflict could include: The risk profiles of loosely defined agile programs are not acceptable within the rules of traditional approval models; potential fin-tech start-up suppliers fail Dun & Bradstreet checks and so are blocked by corporate procurement; digital SMEs don't want to work with large corporates because of untenable payment terms.

Transforming businesses need to find a way to successfully harness the energy and creativity of digital mavericks in their organization, using them to intentionally drive digital initiatives that are a coherent part of a wider transformation strategy. One successful approach we have seen is to work bottom-up, leveraging pockets of expertise and enthusiasm, and then build out scalability from local successes.

5.4 Digital Varnish

The pressure (both internal and external) to deliver short-term, demonstrable results from digital transformations can be significant. This often leads to somewhat parochial and limited scope activities that deliver "skin deep" results. They give an illusion of something different and new but, in reality, the underlying core business processes are still reliant on legacy, old-world processes, and technology; we call this "digital varnish". When the new digital functions work well and as predicted, everything can seem good, but significant problems and frustrations can arise when circumstances demand more complete end-to-end process digitalization. A good example might be that of online purchasing of rail tickets: everything works seamlessly when a customer purchases a new standard ticket, but if ticket amendments have to be dealt with manually (involving physically printed tickets being sent by recorded delivery to the purchaser's home address), the whole digital experience breaks down. Processes are only as good as their weakest link: truly transformative models demand end-to-end (digital) customer experience centricity.

It's not just about end customer engagement transformation. If you want to move your employee experience to one of virtual/home working, then you must have good collaboration tools, knowledge platforms, and networks. Failure to provide the right tools that allow people to do their job will lead to inefficiency and employee frustration, to say nothing of the impact this has on client facing activities. New ways of working demand different policies, different leadership, and different management styles: Too often we see businesses pushing employee flexibility and well-being initiatives while at the same time continuing to impose constraining, legacy management processes. Be prepared to let go of some of the controls that may well have been seen historically as "sacred cows".

Another form of applying digital varnish comes from overpromising on the expectations of digital. Failure to realize the promised benefits will inevitably lead to disappointment. There is a clear need to give a compelling vision for transformation; and equally to avoid the hype and make sure that there is commitment to deliver against the expectations raised. This does not necessarily imply that you need to have all the answers up front, but that there is senior sponsorship for addressing challenges as they emerge.

5.5 Having a Dog and Barking Yourself

For many, the path to digitalization is unknown and seen as fraught with risk; there is (perhaps inevitably) a degree of skepticism and caution over fully embracing new ways of working and letting go of the old ones.

We have observed many examples where businesses have outsourced the provision of certain parts of their operations to a digitally capable third party, yet they still retain a full-size internal governance team that, for example, dictates the architecture of the solution. Often the internal governance team has little experience in the new technologies that the outsourcer is deploying, and they apply old-world thinking to overlay what are perceived to be the necessary controls to comply with familiar, tried, and tested processes. An example might be that of using waterfall project management[1] approaches for overseeing agile development programs. Almost inevitably this leads to sub-optimal outcomes at best.

In other examples, businesses may deploy robotic process automation to some of their back-office processes but then fail to redeploy the employees who previously executed those processes. This results in an under-realization of the expected business benefits, and even a conflict in the way processes are operated as employees seek to maintain control.

If specific digital transformation initiatives do not deliver the anticipated cost benefits or change, they will tend to be viewed as failures. This can taint the ways that wider transformation programs are perceived.

Hanging on to historical assets relating to what you know or what you have can be a real constraint to realizing the benefits of digital, whether these assets be tangible or intangible. An extreme example would relate to migration to the cloud from business-owned data centers. Moving workloads to public cloud environments will only fully deliver the anticipated cost savings once the costs of legacy data centers (physical assets and operational costs) can be eliminated. This is a challenge when the cost drivers associated with owning physical assets tend to be quite binary (i.e. you cannot eliminate them until all usage has been stopped).

It is interesting to reflect on the fact that some of the most disruptive digital platform businesses have exploited (at least initially) other people's assets rather than trying to optimize the cost of their own (e.g. Uber, Airbnb, Netflix).

5.6 A Little Knowledge Is a Dangerous Thing

It is relatively easy in the current Internet age to become an "expert" on emerging digital technologies. MOOCs (Massively Open Online Courses) and Internet-based accreditation programs abound. Many transforming businesses look to their employees to engage in self-learning in order to make themselves ready for the new world of digital. However, applying theory to real-world applications demands more than a YouTube video. Unforeseen challenges like integration with legacy systems, dealing with regulation challenges (e.g., data privacy, security accreditation) can cause apparently simple digital initiatives to fail, sometimes in risky ways, leading the established IT department to say, "I told you so" and clamp down on the application of unsolicited digital activity.

[1]A model for project management in which activities are broken down into sequential phases, each depending on the completion and deliverables of the previous one.

5.7 Technology Waves

We saw earlier in this part of the book that the evolution of technology over the last few decades has been incredible, almost beyond what could have been reasonably predicted. And this rate of change only seems to be accelerating. This creates a significant challenge for businesses looking to establish a digital investment strategy. How can payback be ensured when chosen technologies may well be obsolete before the end of deployment programs? When should the next groundbreaking idea be embraced and investments in other areas written off? These dilemmas can often lead to paralysis in decision making, where it is thought that making no decision is better than making the wrong decision. Indeed, at one level, cost avoidance might be seen by some as a viable strategy, but this can only ever be a short-term plan.

Many companies will adopt a "follow-the-leader" attitude: When digital solutions are seen to work for others, they are deemed as a safe territory for investment. However, this will mean being permanently behind the leaders, who will inevitably have moved onto the next wave of innovative approaches by the time copycat investments start to bear fruit. True digital leaders will be relentless in their drive to maximize the differentiation and benefits that evolving technology can offer.

Businesses need to learn to work through overlapping waves of transformation where incremental changes deliver tangible benefits, learning how to "skate where the puck will be." If you're a laggard now, you should consider how you can wisely skip some steps and aim at an anticipated future state, or you'll always be a laggard. If you're very late at adopting DevOps, aim to adopt serverless models. Anticipation of these emerging trends demands situational awareness, a sense of how technologies are evolving, where are the leaders investing, and how might emerging thinking ultimately converge.

5.8 A Compelling Need

For all the above reasons and more, we believe that now is the right time for businesses to take the digital transformation challenge seriously. Past practices are mostly unsustainable, and conventional growth and business models are quickly losing relevance. This book is aimed at helping the emerging generation of businesses practitioners and leaders to successfully achieve enduring digital transformations.

6 Rewriting Enterprise DNA—Achieving Fundamental and Intentional Transformation

We can think of business organizations as living organisms composed of cells (individuals), capable of forming organs and tissues (physical and virtual teams), performing physiological functions (internal and business processes), and connecting through complex and intricate biological pathways (collaboration and interdependencies between the teams).

In a similar way to living organisms being defined and regulated by the genetic instructions contained within their DNA, the elements of complex business machinery are coded by what can be referred to as the "corporate culture" or "enterprise DNA" of organizations. The organization's DNA can be thought of as the "cultural macromolecule" that holds the code for all traits of the enterprise: the kind of talent it tends to attract, its approach to risk taking, the kind of growth that it is keen to promote, or its inclination toward hierarchical interactions. All are coded in and directed by the DNA of the company.

Continuing the analogy with the molecules of life, digital transformation processes can be considered to be the equivalent of genome editing: a technique involving the manipulation of the DNA sequence of a cell. By means of targeted insertions, deletions, replacements, or modifications, the DNA code is intentionally altered to achieve beneficial purposes. The latest mechanism to perform genome editing is called CRISPR[1]-Cas9, it uses key molecules to target specific parts of generic code and modify the associated DNA at precise locations. The enzyme molecules used in this process are sometimes referred to as "programmable DNA scissors."

[1]Clustered Regularly Interspaced Short Palindromic Repeats.

H. Tardieu et al., *Deliberately Digital*, Future of Business and Finance,
https://doi.org/10.1007/978-3-030-37955-1_6

The impact of genome editing has proven to be very positive in domains such as biomedicine and agriculture, where it is used to research different diseases that affect humans, increase crop yields, and control plant diseases.

We draw a comparison between corporate digital transformation and genome editing because we consider that the purpose of the former should be to consciously alter, in a precise way, the DNA of an organization. The intended goal would include such things as favoring the development of an enhanced strategy, guaranteeing solid business cycles, creating new business models, shortening the time to market, and enhancing its adaptation capabilities to changing conditions.

Bearing in mind the changing business trends we have described previously, attaining the position of digital leadership requires that enterprises will need to master two major digital business breakthroughs:

- *Servitization*, which is a modification to customer/supplier value chains within a given "pipeline" supply chain (see chapter on Business Models and Glossary). Continuing with our genetic themed analogy, this would be like a modification driven by external factors (epigenetic[2] modification) that transforms the behaviors of an organization without fundamentally altering its underlying DNA.
- *Multisided markets*, where either the dominant player of an ecosystem or an industrial platform player are driving the rewriting of the genome of participant organizations by inserting their own genome at the junction between the two sides of the market. This alters the organization's behavior from a pipeline model into a platform business model, as well as changing the DNA of the wider market being served (Fig. 6.1). The type of data exchanged between the sides of the market could be seen as the "digital DNA scissors" that result in the underlying business algorithms of the platform.

The genome editing methodology has three main steps: design, edit, and analyze; the same stages are applicable to digital transformation in business. *Design* helps to find where to define the two or many sides of the market (through which the data exchanges will take place), *Edit* defines the algorithms to apply to this data, and *Analyze* assesses the potential additional business opportunities or undesirable effects arising from such editing.

Having presented the compelling need for corporate digital transformation, and having drawn some parallels with biological genome editing, the following parts of this book deal with the execution of enterprise digital transformation. We pay

[2]The study of the way in which genes can alter their "expression" due to external temporal influences.

Fig. 6.1 Rewriting Enterprise DNA through Digital Transformation. Naomi Hall created the image, which is used with her permission

special attention to the pre-digital and digital DNA characteristics and the required approaches to achieve fundamental and intentional change (enterprise DNA editing). We also consider the challenges and solutions that non-digitally native organizations are facing.

Part II
The Digital Business: Designing the Transformation

Introduction

Abstract In Part II of this book, we seek to help you identify the specific ways in which your own organisation will need to transform. We start by examining how strategy and business models must change to take advantage of digital and, in particular, how the opportunities presented by platforms and ecosystems must be embraced. Then we look at how digital businesses must engage with their customers, demonstrate leadership, structure themselves internally, inspire their staff and innovate relentlessly. We also consider how evolving security challenges must be faced. Each chapter in Part II concludes with a set of practical recommendations which will assist you in designing a tailored digital transformation for your business.

In Part I, we have considered the imperatives behind the need for digital transformation. We are now going to spend time looking at the target model for aspiring digital leaders (Fig. II.1). It is clear that there is no "one-size-fits-all" answer to this target, although there are some very evident similarities between the models used by those businesses that have been successful in growing to digital giant status.

The common features we observe are an ability to excel at establishing, maintaining, and leveraging customer intimacy, and to do so at scale. While not exclusively the case, many of the exemplars have harnessed the power of highly scalable data platforms to create multi-sided markets and establish extended value ecosystems. It is for this reason that we will devote a significant proportion of our Part II thinking to the principles of the data platform business model.

Not only do data platforms allow data-driven insights into market demands, operational performance and consumer satisfaction but, implemented correctly, they facilitate direct and frictionless interaction with customers (whether they be end consumers or other businesses). It is this ownership of direct customer relationships that is so instrumental in driving successful digital business. If you own customer digital interaction, you can differentiate your products and services according to direct buy-side signals; you can shape the market through targeted incentives; and

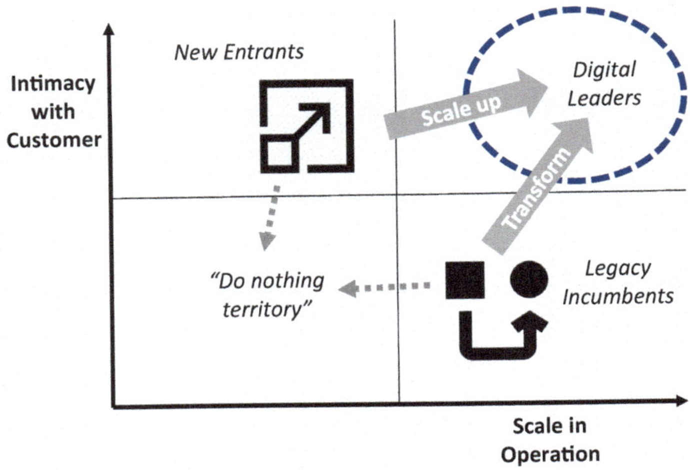

Fig. II.1 Driving forces behind digital leadership—attaining leader status (authors' own figure)

you can build a direct and engaging rapport with customers using innovative digital channels. Of course, it is possible to get such interactions wrong—and customers will respond accordingly, sometimes in ways that have further reaching consequences than losing a single piece of business—social media can be a powerful tool in delivering negative feedback on a product or service that can easily deter many others from buying.

Perhaps just as significant is the fact that businesses that fail to hold direct client relationships put themselves in danger of suffering the relentless pressure of increasing commoditization as they become relegated to being just a link in what might be a highly dynamic and even fickle supply chain. This is of course why product businesses are increasingly looking to exploit the potential of digital by moving up the value chain through the servitization of their products, delivering valued outcomes to their customers.

The ability to build such customer intimacy at scale is a mark of the digital giants. In many cases, they have scaled to almost monopolistic status, owning the customer interface and shaping the market. For example, Amazon and Alibaba are seen by many consumers as the go-to-places for almost any retail purchase. As a result, they can understand individuals' buying behaviors and maximize revenues through knowing how to develop consumer perceptions of value and service. What's more, if they own those insights, it is much harder for the competition to glean and exploit them.

Similar thinking can be applied in the context of business-to-business relationships, where the stakes are potentially higher, and the revolution in business model thinking even further reaching.

Strategy—The Two Routes for Achieving Enduring Digital Success

7

7.1 Digital Strategy Must Be the New Strategy

"Business strategy" is one of those terms whose meaning is often taken for granted but which may elicit very different notions in people's minds. Business management literature will quickly inform us that the final goal of business strategy is to accomplish specific business objectives. But with regard to what "business strategy" actually is, we can find many more varied definitions. The most common include the following words and phrases:

- Dynamic definitions: a course of actions, set of decisions or competitive moves, a combination of proactive actions and reactions, etc.
- Plan/map definitions: A master plan, high-level plan, working plan, management's game plan, long-term plan of action, long-range roadmap, etc.
- Vague definitions: the choices that business makes about how to achieve their objectives; the means by which it (the company) sets out to achieve its desired ends (business objectives); etc.
- Pragmatic definitions: what needs to be done; a summary of how a business plans to achieve its goals; etc.

There are elements of truth in all these terms: A business strategy should be long term, define what the business should look like within a given timeframe, define the context and direction of the business, as well as describe a roadmap of actions and likely choices to arrive at the desired endpoint.

However, in the course of professional practice, we have found substantial evidence of major challenges, such as the absence of a strategy, the lack of adherence to the strategy, a confusion between strategy and tactics, or a confusion between strategy and storytelling. A notable challenge must be added: the specific definition of "digital strategy" and, more importantly, its consideration as a subset of overall business strategy.

H. Tardieu et al., *Deliberately Digital*, Future of Business and Finance,
https://doi.org/10.1007/978-3-030-37955-1_7

Just as we think that terms like "digital world" and "digital business" will soon simply become "world" and "business" (as digital elements are seamlessly integrated, and the population becomes increasingly "digitally native"[1]), we contend that "digital strategy" will soon be seen as just "strategy" or "business strategy." It is in an enterprise's interests to affect that change of mindset right now. Make your "digital strategy" your strategy, incorporating whatever elements of the original strategy make sense. If you make your digital strategy a mere subset of your existing strategy, you will likely be looking at the future with old perspectives, missing many possible sources of value.

In the following sections, we will examine some key challenges associated with strategy in the context of digital transformation. We will also provide recommendations and questions for self-evaluation.

7.2 Some Key Challenges of (Digital) Strategy

Before covering strategy in the context of digital transformation, let's review some of the key associated challenges. If these are found to exist in an organization, they must be addressed and solved first. If not, they must be kept in mind in order to perform sanity checks during strategy definition and rollout.

The absence of strategy. It is not uncommon to find companies that do not have a strategy, either because they do not have an explicitly stated one, or because they do not have one at all. Having an explicit, communicated, and accepted strategy is crucial for a business at any moment, and especially in moments of deep change and transformation.

Lack of adherence to the strategy. The strategy does exist, but it is deemed by some members of the organization to be "theoretical": as if it needs to be there in case someone asks but it is not really meant to be implemented. Perhaps it was created by internal or external consultants, who stayed at a safe distance from the coalface of business, and as a result is not found actionable. Or maybe it's a perfectly good strategy, but the management team is not committed to implementing it, under the perception that it straightjackets decisions and actions or spawns needless debate.

Lack of communication of the strategy. The strategy exists, be it good or bad, but it is not communicated appropriately to all levels of the organization. Of course, parts of it will be very sensitive and confidential, not for all employees' eyes. But the essentials of the strategy can and must be layered and formulated in a way that they can be communicated to all levels of the organization, to create a common sense of purpose and direction. This is especially true in the context of digital transformation.

[1]A term used to describe someone born or raised during the age of digital technology and therefore instinctively familiar with its capabilities and uses.

When strategy means tactics. Since the strategy defines what an organization wants to be and how to get there, it must be anchored in the long term. However, the term "strategy" is often used to describe shorter-term, tactical moves. No matter how brilliant such moves might be, and even if they are perfectly implemented, they will only enhance or optimize the organization; they will not take it to a different, more evolved stage. We will say a bit more about the obsession with the short term below.

Strategy or storytelling? Some strategies are cut-and-paste, patchwork pieces of storytelling. They portray past success cases as lighthouses and past failures as cautionary tales, distilling the whole lot into generic goals and courses of action from which little value can be extracted. Storytelling is good, especially for articulating a vision, since humans are very sensitive to narrative for communication, memorization, and learning purposes, but storytelling should not be seen as a substitute for a properly crafted strategy.

The "trickle-down dilution". This is a significant and potentially very damaging challenge in digital transformation efforts. Let's suppose that an organization has a great (digital) vision and strategy, and it sets out to communicate and execute it. As the message and expectations cascade down, the multi-layered nature of strategy (corporate level, business level, functional level, etc.) leads to discordance: The further the strategy trickles down in the organization, the more concrete, fine-grained, and pragmatic it becomes. As a result, the required actions are perceived as more and more disruptive and distant from the operational status quo by the very people responsible for executing them. For example, the data center staff involved in public or hybrid cloud implementation; the central functions (HR, Finance, IT, etc.) involved in business process automation; the middle managers involved in Enterprise Decision Management, etc.

The obsession with the short term. Short-termism is one of the signs of our time. We see it at play in many democracies, where long-term endeavors such as large-scale civil construction or environmental management are impeded or abated by much shorter electoral cycles. Short-termism is equally damaging to the digital transformation of businesses. As mentioned above, a good strategy is anchored in the long term. Its execution and re-evaluation require navigation between different timescales and abstraction levels. As we will see in the next section, an obsession with the short term in the form of so-called quick wins can delay or impede truly transformational objectives which are implicitly deemed as mere "slow wins."

Lack of situational awareness. It is always important to be aware of the context and situation when setting ambitious objectives and roadmaps to accomplish them. This is true for short-term change initiatives and for periods of stability, and it is crucial for longer-term initiatives and for periods of marked change, which are key features of digital transformation. However, most strategies suffer from a lack of situational awareness and are built with a static rather than a dynamic mindset. One technique we have found rather useful is "mapping," as proposed and extended by Wardley (2015, 2017). Wardley maps are a visual and context-specific representation of lines of business—Fig. 7.1 gives an example map for a specific financial services context. A Wardley map is anchored around the client, with the vertical

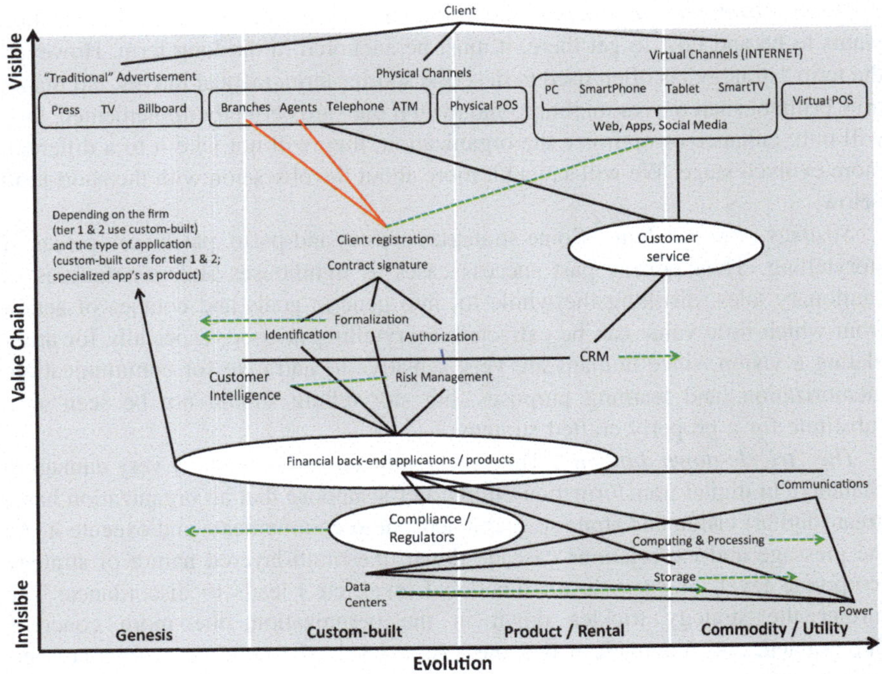

Fig. 7.1 Example of a Wardley map for a financial services business. Based on a map created by one of the authors in 2014 during an internal Atos session on Wardley maps

axis of the map representing how visible each element of the value chain is to the client: The lower the element is, the less visible it is to the user. The map also represents evolution, with the horizontal axis representing the different stages of maturity of the elements in the value chain, from genesis to commodity/utility status. The map can be enriched with additional features like arrows that depict the evolutionary trend of a component (is it moving toward custom-built or toward utility?), vertical bars (akin to walls) that depict inertia against change, or colored lines that depict past and future value chains. Mapping helps achieve situational awareness and sparks crucial strategic debates in the organization. Once the organization's value chain is pictured against the landscape and the forces that shape it, key insights appear.

7.3 The Case for a Bi-modal Strategy

While we insist on the importance of strategy-led digital transformation, we are witnessing a disproportionate focus among commentators and analysts on digital strategies that deliver quick-win results at the risk of rushing toward a non-sustainable digital ambition. Such an approach can ultimately result in destroying value rather than creating it. We are seeking to establish enduring principles for transformation, that may still include some quick-win initiatives, but will be primarily focused on altering the very DNA of a business. It is important to stress that there is no "black-and-white position": Winning approaches will tend to be strongly bi-modal in nature. In Part III, we share insights on how to maintain an effective balance between quick wins and longer-term initiatives, thereby avoiding bias toward either of the extreme positions.

At the heart of any digital strategy is the question: "How can I exploit 'digital' to create differentiated and sustainable value propositions in my chosen market(s)?". Research would suggest that only around a quarter of executives are confident in the belief that their business has really understood the full potential that digital strategies can offer.

In our experience, businesses seeking to transform tend to focus on digital marketing and customer engagement, but there is a significant risk of such strategies becoming "digital varnish" (referred to in Part I). Creating digital engagement channels (mobile, online, social media, etc.) is important, but not enough to re-imagine your value propositions and ensure that you can compete with the truly disruptive players.

A digital transformation strategy can be approached from two very different perspectives.

- *Optimization and transformation of existing business processes* with little or no change to the core business model.
- *Fundamental transformation of the business model* to deliver new services and products in new and disruptive ways. This might be affected through the establishing of a separate digital division.

It is important to understand that for most businesses, these do not represent an either/or choice. The expected outcomes of both approaches are generally complementary and interdependent (e.g., making a single leap from a legacy model to a fully digital model would be economically and culturally unsustainable in most cases). Undertaking a first wave of digital optimization may be a critical enabler (from a cost and skills perspective) of more radical transformation. There are, however, some situations where phased transformations will present untenable risks and so dual, separate strategies will need to be pursued.

Let's summarize each of the approaches in turn to establish their context. The specifics of how to affect their related transformations will be addressed in Part III.

7.4 Optimization and Transformation of Existing Business Processes

Although meaningful transformation strategies must avoid the trap of quick-win bias, optimizing and transforming business processes should normally be the first strategy to be implemented. They are the easiest to justify, the most measurable, and the least risky. They may also be the means of releasing operational costs for reinvestment into the wider transformation program. It should also be remembered however that, to stay ahead of the pack, optimization cannot be viewed as a one-shot initiative: Continual optimization is the required new norm.

Focus should be on delivering improvements through:

- *Increasing asset utilization and performance.* This should include assessing whether to use own assets or those of others (e.g., move to cloud, platform sharing).
- *Increasing employee productivity.* Reducing or eliminating the friction of legacy ways of working can be one of the most significant drivers of culture change and operational flexibility.
- *Delivering cost reductions by process automation.* Not only can process automation deliver cost savings, but it can also improve quality, reduce risk, and release people capacity for other transformation activities. Be careful, however, not just to automate existing processes "as is." First remove or streamline legacy processes wherever possible. Consider carefully the sequence in which to automate processes (i.e., avoid complex processes with complex interdependencies as the first movers).
- *Identifying new revenue opportunities and sources of data-driven value.* This calls for different thinking about the insights and value that you can glean from the existing data that you have; how you can meaningfully (and legitimately) exploit data from other sources; and how you can create monetized services. Thinking about how you might servitize your business model can be a significant enabler in this process.
- *Improving customer experience and engagement.* This is looked at in depth in the chapter on Customers, but a critical point to note is the importance of direct customer feedback. Consider customer journeys in the context of the digital world, look at true end-to-end engagement models and think (where relevant) about your customers' customers.

The real challenge of digital business optimization is that the "digital art of the possible" is often so extensive that it is impossible to pursue its full potential. It is therefore necessary to select a portfolio of the most attractive and beneficial projects, ranking them using the models we describe in Part III based on return on investment, timescale, and certainty.

One approach that we have found particularly helpful and productive is that of the "StratHack": a conflation of the words Strategy and Hackathon.[2] StratHacks can take various forms, but the approach we would recommend involves highly focused, cocreation workshops targeted at reimagining transformation problems through the lens of digital possibilities and persona journeys. They bring together creative inputs from across an organization and often include trusted partners who can bring fresh thinking and thought-provoking inputs from other companies and industries. They can be very effective at prioritizing transformation initiatives and ensuring maximum stakeholder buy-in (since stakeholders are part of the solution!).

Each transformation theme, workstream, or activity may have its own particular metrics. However, it is important that they are combined in a way that clearly identifies their collective consistency and contribution to the overall business improvement objectives (as measured according to the five categories described above).

7.5 Fundamental Transformation of the Business Model

It is much harder to define "what good looks like" when referring to new business models. By their very nature, they will be innovative and different, they will open up new sources of value that consumers may not even have realized they needed or wanted ("*A lot of times, people don't know what they want until you show it to them.*"—Steve Jobs, Apple).

Here is an attempt to capture some of the most desirable characteristics of digital business models and the manner in which they are conceived and executed:

- *They are engaging.* It is easy for customers to buy products and services in the first instance, but engagement does not stop after the initial purchase: there is ongoing and growing intimacy of engagement in terms of additional value-add and personalization.
- *They are scalable.* They are able to leverage network-driven effects to grow rapidly without customers experiencing your growing pains.
- *They jealously guard the direct relationship with customers*, allowing ongoing innovation to be targeted at proven market demands in a much more effective manner.
- *They seek to employ servitization* as a means of encouraging the continuity of business engagement, and of securing access to customer usage data relating to the operational performance of services.
- *They encourage seamless integration of supply chains*, but at the same time disintermediate certain elements to maintain flexibility and agility in response to changing demands.

[2]A time-limited event in which people with different skills in software development (designers, architects, programmers, etc.) get together to create a functioning prototype or product in response to a set of business needs or a similar challenge.

- *They are not afraid to challenge conventional market boundaries* (e.g., Amazon moving from online bookseller to cloud provider and then to media company and IoT service platform).
- *They are obsessive about the use of data*, both to drive optimization into business processes (predictively and prescriptively) and also to create new customer value propositions.

It is this last point that is perhaps the most important foundational characteristic of business model transformation. Digital businesses must have a *Strategy for Data*.

In our definition of "Digital" (see Glossary and chapter on The Birth of Digital), we included a clear component of data centricity. A digital strategy cannot be complete without a clear and deliberate view of how data will not only be used to enable business operations but how it will serve as a fundamental source of business value creation.

In many ways, data is a new natural resource but, unlike other resources, one that is growing in abundance rather than being progressively depleted. For centuries, we have learned how to organize our society around the exchange of scarce resources according to agreed rules and value principles. The provision of data-centric or data-enabled services is now giving rise to a whole new set of economic business models, most of which behave quite differently from traditional models.

7.6 Recommendations

- *Assess your organization's strategy ruthlessly.* If you do not have a strategy, it is obsolete, or it is internally thought of as a theoretical exercise (to keep the Board, the analysts or the market happy), then you should embark on a serious digital strategy definition exercise. If you have a traditional strategy and a (nascent or actual) digital strategy, you should work toward having a single strategy which is Deliberately Digital.
- *Avoid easy recipes:* Do what Google did, avoid doing what Blockbuster did, be the Uber of your market sector. Looking around at representative success and failure cases can be a great source of inspiration, but do not fall into the trap of simply copycatting others' strategies. Also, avoid storytelling past success and failure cases in a backward-looking mash-up wrapped up as future strategy. Storytelling will play a fundamental role in the way that leaders engage employees in their strategy (as we will comment in the chapter on Leadership).
- *Anchor your strategy in the long term.* Do not draft a set of tactical moves for the *status quo ante* (the state of affairs that existed so far). Avoid falling into the trap of just chasing quick wins: If they don't detract from the bigger picture transformation, go for them; however, avoid them if they are going to turn into the kind of battle victories that makes you lose the war. This can so easily happen by delaying or diverting resources from essential actions, for example.

- *Adhere to your strategy.* Transforming an organization's DNA, corporate culture, and business model is not a quick and rosy affair. The journey will be long and often bumpy, so stepping back into the comfort zone will be a recurring temptation. Do not be lured. Stick to the strategy, re-evaluating it continuously in quantitative terms (digital KPIs) and qualitative terms (situational awareness).
- *Do a mapping exercise (perhaps using Wardley maps, as mentioned before).* Picture the components of your existing and future business value chains against their stages of evolution. See where current technology and business trends are taking each component. Imagine what will come next as components are commoditized. Assess possible inertial forces as well as disruptive moves and evaluate their impact on your organization in financial and people terms.
- *Address disruption.* Looking at the trends mentioned previously (in the chapters on Business Trends, Societal Trends and Technology Trends), how could your business be disrupted? And how could it disrupt its own sector or other sectors? Are you a retailer with too much dependence on e-commerce giants, who could leverage their ability to scale and copycat you out of existence? Are you a logistics company making a substantial part of its revenue from industrial parts, which could be manufactured on site (with minimal storage and transport) using 3D printing technology? Does your business use labor that does not perform significant added-value tasks, and which could easily be automated out?
- *Keep the innovator's dilemma in mind.* Incumbents may fail by seemingly doing the right thing every single step of the way. By focusing on clients' needs as expressed by the clients themselves, incumbents may miss game-changing disruptions that those same clients will buy from unexpected competitors later! Clayton Christensen (Christensen 1997) describes how Seagate (leading manufacturer of 5.25 in. drives) missed the 3.5 in. drive disruption and Bucyrus-Erie (leading manufacturer of cable excavators) missed the hydraulic excavator disruption. Both companies produced early prototypes of the novel products but shelved them due to marketing decisions. It is frequent that incumbents fail at embarking on new products or services because their initial sales will be much lower than the established portfolio, at least until the former booms and the latter tanks. This calls for businesses to keep the faith in well-considered digital strategies and not revert to type at the first hint of failure.
- *Address leapfrogging.* In times of radical change, assets can become liabilities. For example, a huge network of physical offices used to be an asset to a bank, but the need for such real estate has been drastically downsized in digital times. Explore where this is true for your organization and identify liabilities in both your own organization and your competitors. In particular, can your organization leapfrog others? Can you skip some of their maturity steps, often dictated by their history and assets, and find a shortcut ahead, instead of mimicking their roadmap?
- *Leverage your analog assets.* If your organization is not digital by birth but is an incumbent, think of the assets that give you a real or potential competitive advantage and fully leverage them in your strategy. These might include your brand, your network of clients and partners (and the trust they have in you), the data that you have (even if siloed) or that you can easily tap into with moderate

effort, or your physical assets that are not redundant in the digital economy. Note that some digital banks are now recognizing the value of strategically sited physical branches in helping to reinforce certain aspects of customer intimacy and trust.

- *Design and implement a bi-modal strategy.* Some key reminders:

  - Beware quick wins that create non-sustainable situations and destroy value.
  - Avoid a shallow transformation mindset (focused only on marketing and customer engagement) which leads to the kind of "digital varnish" that preserves rather than disrupts the status quo. Later, in Part III, we will describe a transformation model that encourages a range of initiatives that span areas such as strategy, customers, leadership, and organization structure.
  - Combine wisely and purposefully the two approaches to transformation: optimization of existing business processes and fundamental transformations of the underlying business model(s). Do it in a way that ensures each approach complements and reinforces the other.
  - Achieve the optimization of existing business processes by working on the five categories: asset utilization and performance, employee productivity, cost reduction by process automation, new revenue opportunities and sources of data-driven value, and customer experience and engagement.
  - Start working on the fundamental transformation of your business model(s) by exploiting the results of your mapping exercise. Also, make sure you have a strategy for data on which this effort is founded.
  - Consider using StratHacks to prioritize transformation initiatives and ensure maximum stakeholder buy-in.

- *Storytelling at the right time.* Once your new strategy is well defined, use storytelling to create the best narratives to communicate it to the whole organization. Use communication (two-way, not unidirectional) and change management to avoid the "trickle-down dilution" we mentioned earlier. The more that people understand what is going on, for which purpose, how their role fits in, and the benefits that await, the more internal resistance to change and damaging inertial forces will be neutralized.

In the next chapters, we will cover the main dimensions of transformation design, which must be properly addressed and covered in the strategy. These are business models, platforms and ecosystems, customers, leadership, organizational structure, people, and innovation. We will start by looking at data-driven digital business models, servitization, and the role of platforms.

References

Christensen, C. (1997). *The innovator's dilemma: When new technologies cause great firms to fail.* Cambridge: Harvard Business Review Press.

Wardley, S. (2015). *Situation normal, everything must change.* Simon Wardley Keynote at OSCON 2015 (21-24/07/2015, Portland, OR, USA). O'Reilly Accessible at https://www.youtube.com/watch?v=Ty6pOVEc3bA. Accessed October 26, 2019.

Wardley, S. (2017). *Wardley maps.* Online book published between 2016 and 2017. Accessible at https://medium.com/wardleymaps/on-being-lost-2ef5f05eb1ec. Accessed October 26, 2019.

Business Models—Servitization and Platforms as the DNA Scissors for Transformation

8

In this section, we shall explore the basics of *Digital Business:* a paradigm in value creation that bases its foundations not on goods and services, but instead upon *data*. Data is a very general term that describes a piece of information formatted in a particular way. In its broadest sense, it can be represented through media ranging from the earliest cave paintings and Sumerian writings through to music and video. For our purposes, we will use the term data to mean the representation of information using digital technologies (essentially bits and bytes). It must be recognized that the shift of emphasis from representations of information (and value) that are physical, to those that are digital, brings with it a whole new dimension of challenges and opportunities for business leaders, economists, and regulators to wrestle with. This is why digital business models are generally fundamentally different from traditional ones.

In the context of business value, data is different. It is not discrete and in principle can be easily copied and distributed; on its own, it may have zero intrinsic value but combined with other data assets, it can bring highly valuable insights; its ownership can be uncertain; and its value can be highly transient. Dealing with data as an incremental business asset demands a reinvention of business models at both a micro- and a macro-level.

Data becomes useful (and valuable) when it can be associated with decisions or actions which themselves hold economic value. However, it is usually the case that raw data (e.g., sensor data, online purchase transaction data, and system logs) needs to be checked, analyzed, and processed according to the downstream events it is to influence or inform. Only then can the appropriate value be extracted (and monetized). To further complicate matters, it may well be the case that the business entity that gathers the raw data is not the same as that which is able to refine and therefore impart value to the data.

When data is exchanged between different parties, there are new business model perspectives that need to be considered: From an ownership perspective, the usage of data needs to be treated differently from its generation, even though the generator

H. Tardieu et al., *Deliberately Digital*, Future of Business and Finance,
https://doi.org/10.1007/978-3-030-37955-1_8

of the data can hold onto it for use in other services; the data generator might also require the data user (buyer) to declare its usage intentions.

Simple data business models can take two basic forms:

- *Business-to-Consumer (B2C):* where consumers consent to share their data with a business in exchange for a free or subsidized service (or product) from that business. The service is typically a transaction which is directly associated with the data being shared. There is likely to be an implicit agreement with the consumers that their data may be further used in relation to adjacent services, so long as those services are delivered by business partners that fall within the scope of the original consent.
- *Business-to-Business (B2B)*: where two different companies decide to share data between each other instead of sourcing it separately from the market. If companies have to buy data from the market, they may be exposed to variable and possibly unpredictable transaction costs, but if they share their data (with specific agreements as to ownership rights), they can enjoy a mutually beneficial zero-cost transaction.

In both cases, the willingness and ability to share data generates *network effects* (sometimes called externalities); a network effect is the impact that an additional user of a good or service has on the value of that product to others. When a positive network effect is present, the value of a product or service increases in some relationship to the number of consumers. For example, we can have a positive network effect when the number of users of a telephone network increases, since the potential scope of interconnections increases accordingly.

A negative network effect can occur when an increase in users leads to a perceived decrease in the value of a product or service. For example, as the number of vehicles using a given road network increases, there will tend to be an increase in traffic congestion. Network effects are rarely monotonic[1]; they can have tipping points that invert their impact. In the road network example, to begin with having more cars is beneficial, as it encourages investment in additional services like petrol stations or breakdown services, but a limit is reached when all these perceived benefits are negated by grid-lock traffic jams.

8.1 The Service Economy

At the same time that data is establishing its own economic importance, we see an increase in the relative importance of services associated with product offerings. Products today tend to have a higher service component than ever before; this evolution is sometimes referred to as the "*servitization*" of products. The previous

[1]Mathematically, a monotonic function is one whose values either never increase or never decrease.

dichotomy between products and services is now being replaced by a continuum that spans both, with a growing emphasis on services that are designed around a desired outcome. For example:

- Instead of buying a car, consumers might buy a mobility service.
- Instead of buying a physical train asset, a rail operator might buy passenger kilometers through a fully managed service provided by a train vendor.

In both cases (B2C or B2B), the commercial models are built on consumption-based charges for the use of an underlying asset or service.

The servitization model ultimately leads to contracts that are based on devolved risk outcomes where not only the quantity of a measured service, but also its delivery quality is used to calculate its market price.

This somewhat linear type of service model is referred to as the "*pipeline model*" since it describes a clear economic flow between buyers and sellers. Historically, it has proven to be a very useful model, but it is one that shows its limitations when describing the impact of network effects (a capability which is becoming increasingly important when data is an integral part of more complex economic transactions).

To better model network effects, economists have introduced the concept of *"two-sidedness"* where two types of agent exist in a market. The utility of a given agent depends on the number of agents on the other side of the market. For example, in the card payment market, we can distinguish two sides: the consumers and the merchants; any consumer will see the utility of their card increase whenever an additional merchant is able to accept it. Conversely, a merchant will see an increase in the utility of accepting a type of card every time a new consumer chooses to adopt it.

Platforms and Ecosystems are two of the most innovative parts of digital transformation because they bring a new type of business model which disrupts the traditional pipeline model. There are some noticeable and key differences between the way they operate in Business-to-Consumer and Business-to-Business interactions.

8.2 Platforms and Ecosystems in the Business-to-Consumer World

This model has been the foundation of the incredible success of the Digital Giants and was initially analyzed and documented by economists under the name *"two-sided markets."*

The seminal work in this field was published by Jean Charles Rochet and Jean Tirole in 2003 (Rochet and Tirole 2003), with Jean Tirole receiving the 2014 Nobel Prize in Economic Sciences for his work.

Initially, the authors concentrated on an explanation of what it is that allows a market with network externalities to be successful in domains like software, media, payment systems, and the Internet.

To quote them:

> Platforms devote much attention to their business model, that is, how they court each side while making money overall. This paper builds a model of platform competition with *two-sided markets. It unveils the determinants of price allocation and end-user surplus for different governance structures (profit-maximizing platforms and not-for-profit joint undertakings)*

Jean Tirole's work applies primarily to the Business-to-Consumer world, explaining how it is possible to be successful as a platform operator by "courting" the two sides of the market. For example, in the context of payment cards mentioned previously:

- What value propositions should be offered to a potential cardholder to convince him/her to sign up for card (ease of use, lower risk, loyalty benefits, etc.)?
- What advantages can the merchant get (customer data-derived marketing insights, increased loyalty, etc.)?

The platform operator should build an engagement proposition for each side, for example:

- For the customer, an annual price to get the card, with a possible additional fee per transaction.
- For the merchant, an annual price to install the point-of-sale terminal and a subsequent fee for each transaction.

Carrying the costs for network, platform, and marketing acquisition, the platform operator needs to design a strategy to ramp up engagement and quickly reach the critical size for each side of the market.

In the two-sided market, the platform launch will usually require significant operator investments, but if successful the platform operator will be in a strong position, bringing efficiency and even a tendency toward market monopolization.

This is why the ongoing work of Jean Tirole and the Toulouse School of Economics (TSE) has been concentrating on the regulation of two-sided markets, a challenge which is far from being sorted out when considering the dominant position not only of the Digital Giants but also of other platform businesses such as Booking.com (hotel reservations) or Uber (transportation networks).

The pioneering work of Jean Tirole considers the platform as a "black box" that exhibits behavior which is capable of being modeled. We will use the concept of the *economy of data lifecycle* to help explain the internal functioning of the platform.

This model was first proposed by Atos in 2014 (Lidbetter et al. 2014) and has proven to be very useful, even in the context of recent developments relating to GDPR and artificial intelligence.

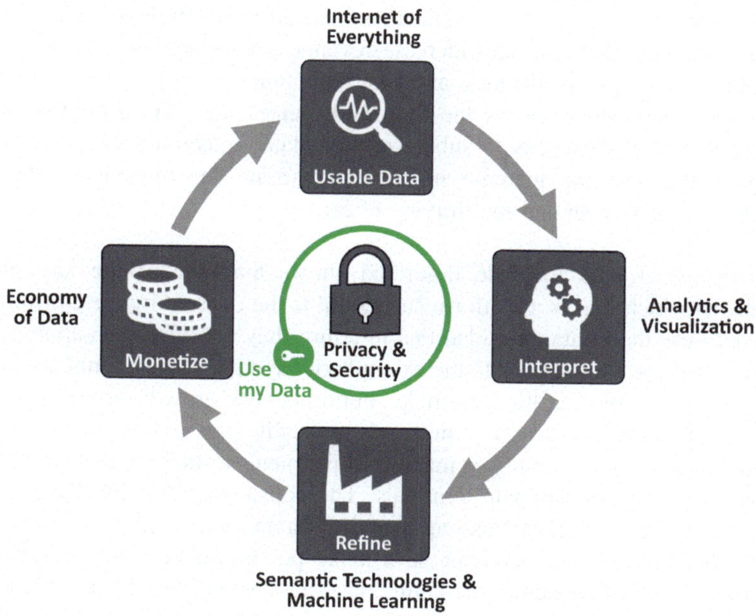

Fig. 8.1 Economy of data lifecycle for B2C. Based on original concept from Atos (Figure modified with permission of Atos, based on Fig. 6 on page 16 of Journey 2018 (Lidbetter et al. 2014)

The schema in Fig. 8.1 gives an overall view of the data life cycle for B2C exchanges.

It needs to be read starting from the top-left position:

1. The Internet of Things allows the collection of raw data from all manner of connected consumer-related sources (online transactions data, social media, even connected product data).
2. Respecting *Privacy and Security* is a necessary prerequisite for allowing raw data to be transformed into *usable data*. A useful model for establishing trust in this area is the "*green button*" (an American concept used in the energy sector for consumers to provide explicit consent for selected third parties to use their related personal data). In a similar way, in May 2018, GDPR defined regulations relating to data usage consent and, in a limited way, to its control. Furthermore, the *International Data Spaces Association* has recently further refined both the specification of data usage control and the management of privacy policies for its data exchange architecture.
3. Usable data is interpreted through analytics and visualization to help consumers take appropriate decisions, often within the context of specific applications or services.

4. Businesses can use analytics, semantics, and artificial intelligence to generate further insights that can help increase revenues, margins, and consumer satisfaction through personalization and cost reduction.
5. The final step which closes the loop and creates the B2C economy of data lifecycle is for businesses to subsidize their data collection/management costs through the resulting increase in revenue/margin. The objective is being to establish a self-generated multiplying effect.

The economy of data lifecycle described shows that one of the key internal mechanisms which makes a platform successful is the consent by the consumer for suppliers to use their data, provided that in return they are offered an appropriately subsidized service. Going back to the example of payment card systems, we can see how the economy of data lifecycle helps build network growth through participation in a platform ecosystem: consumers typically pay a few euros per year (sometimes zero) for the ability to make card payments to many merchants who, in turn, pay for their point-of-sale terminals. The consumer normally doesn't pay a premium to make card payments (compared to paying with cash), except for their annual subscription. The merchant pays a fee per transaction but benefits from access to a wealth of consumer marketing data that comes from the use of cards. In addition, merchants might offer loyalty programs that enable the gathering of additional data about their customers, who in return receive discounts on future purchases.

In this instance, the platform operator is carrying the risk of offering payment services to consumers that spend very little and to merchants who have other competitor card vendors offering similar services.

Further examples in the B2C world include:

- Trivago offering hotel reservation services to consumers that pay no subscriptions, and hotel owners that pay registration and transaction fees to the platform operator.
- Lyft offering transportation to consumers that pay no subscriptions and drivers that pay registration fees and receive a travel fare (minus the commission charged by Lyft).

The main challenge for platform business partners is to gain access to the market data collected by the platform. In the two previous examples (Trivago and Lyft), the platform operator insists on leading the customer engagement process and therefore business partners have little or no explicit rights of access to the market data, potentially leaving all the benefits in the hands of the platform operator.

Historically, platform operators may have sought to increase their revenues by using consumer data beyond the scope of the consent given, including reselling of consumer data to business partners that were not an explicit part of the consumer agreement. With the introduction of GDPR in May 2018, the whole economy of B2C platforms has been challenged. As a consequence, an intimate understanding of the data lifecycle and its implications has become essential to avoid the huge potential penalties that might be incurred by platform operators if they breach the regulations (up to 4% of their annual turnover).

8.3 Platforms and Ecosystems in the Business-to-Business World

As we have done for the B2C world, let us now present the economy of data lifecycle in the B2B world.

It can be summarized with the schema shown in Fig. 8.2, first published by Atos in 2016 (Esteban et al. 2016).

We can see general similarities with the B2C data lifecycle but also some significant differences.

The schema should be read starting from the top left with the whole value cycle being primed and fed by a range of raw data sources. These could include events collected by sensors in the real world or human interactions expressed through commands or decisions made in companies belonging to the ecosystem and relevant to its purpose. Continuing clockwise round the lifecycle diagram:

1. Internet of Things and human–machine interfaces deliver raw data (production data, usage data, etc.) which are collected separately (partner by partner) in the ecosystem.
2. The privacy and security components of the platform ensure that all data sovereignty[2] and permissions aspects are respected before transforming raw data into usable and shareable data.
3. The orchestrated ecosystem platform builds a common data lake[3] and applies analytics and machine learning after the data collected by the various partners of the ecosystem has been interpreted, according to a *data reference architecture* agreed by all the partners.
4. Each partner can then use the refined industrial data according to their market understanding and their own processes to prepare appropriate decisions in order to increase their efficiency, improve the flexibility of their processes, and reduce their time to market (through shorter and more insightful innovation cycles).
5. Beyond the appropriate use of common industrial data which has been collected as part of the ecosystem (within agreed data usage control), each partner will also use their own machine learning to further refine data and merge shared ecosystem data with their own proprietary data.

[2]The International Data Spaces Association defines **Data Sovereignty** as: **"The capability of a natural person or corporate entity for exclusive self-determination with regard to its economic data goods."**

[3]A large-scale repository for data is generally designed to store all the raw data of an organization (thus avoiding departmental data siloes) for later exploitation. Unlike data warehouses, data lakes use flat, non-hierarchical architectures.

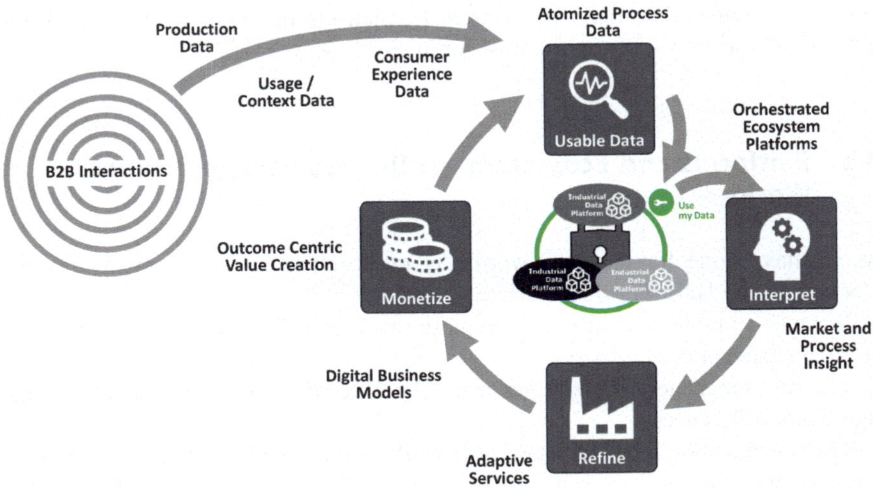

Fig. 8.2 Economy of data lifecycle, extended to the B2B platform context. Based on original concept from Atos (Figure modified with permission of Atos. Based on Fig. 4 on page 14 of (Esteban et al. 2016)

6. All these analytics and machine learning processes are the basis for the adaptive services that support digital business models and create outcome centric value.

In summary, B2B multi-sided platforms take advantage of a large variety of data collected by partners of an ecosystem, while still respecting each other's data sovereignty and intellectual property. Industrial data is interpreted according to a common and agreed data reference architecture, with every partner deriving their own benefits through creating or enhancing services which will improve their business.

The benefits for each partner of the ecosystem are obvious, but what are the benefits and the challenges of the *Platform Operator?* We will discuss this in the following chapter on Platforms and Ecosystems.

8.4 Recommendations

- *Identify what data you currently have access to*. Consider what data you already collect or have access to. Which person or business produces this data and whose data sovereignty needs to be respected in its use? What benefits could you imagine being realized from this data?
- *Understand what data (that you do not already have access to) your business could benefit from.* Is this data already being collected by someone else (a partner,

supplier, or client perhaps)? How is this data different to the data you already do have access to? Could there be benefits in exchanging this data?

- *Consider how your current products could be (further) servitized.* What different charging models can you imagine which more closely bind your revenues to the value created for your customers? To what extent would you need to digitalize your existing products to achieve this? Could this digitalization create additional value (particularly from the data that could be collected)?
- *Determine whether there is a way in which you or your clients could benefit from participation in platforms.* Would these platforms be single-sided or multi-sided? Would these platforms be B2C or B2B? What critical mass of participation would be needed and what barriers can you foresee to achieving this? How could these barriers be overcome? Where do you see the role of your company in the platform: participant or operator?
- *For platforms that may be of potential interest, consider how they would relate to the Economy of Data Lifecycle.* What specific security concerns can you imagine? Where will raw data be sourced from? How could the data be interpreted and refined? What strategies could you legitimately use to monetize the data collected?

References

Esteban, et al. (2016). *Journey 2020: Digital shockwaves in business*. Atos. Accessible at https://atos.net/content/mini-sites/journey-2020/index.html. Accessed October 26, 2019.

Lidbetter, et al. (2014). *Journey 2018: The third digital revolution—agility and fragility*. Atos. Accessible at https://atos.net/wp-content/uploads/2016/06/atos-ascent-journey-2018-whitepaper.pdf. Accessed October 26, 2019.

Rochet, J. -C., Tirole, J. (2003). Platform competition in two-sided markets. *Journal of the European Economic Association*, 1(4), June 2003. Accessible at https://onlinelibrary.wiley.com/doi/10.1162/154247603322493212. Accessed October 26, 2019.

9 Platforms and Ecosystems—Supporting a Company's Digital Strategy

9.1 The Role of Platforms

We refer to the digital service which facilitates the match-making between the two sides of a market as a multi-sided platform. On their own, users on either side of the platform do not have the ability to force an increase in the number of agents on the other. Instead, it is the platform operator that will build or facilitate propositions that are attractive to both sides. This is done with a clear expectation that when agents commit to engaging on one side of the platform, they will see a corresponding increase on the other side.

It is important to realize that there is no obvious continuum between a sophisticated pipeline business model that only recognizes one side in the market, and a platform business model that relies on network effects between two sides of a market to build a critical mass (although data platforms can and do support pipeline models).

In the B2C market (which is the most mature in this context), platform operators have tended to stimulate growth in platform usage by offering incentives to participants on one or both sides of the platform. This is continued until the number of consumers makes the platform attractive enough for agents on the business side to engage on normal terms (and vice versa). The multi-sided platform operator acts as a catalyst bringing viability to a market which would otherwise be unable to take off.

In the B2B market, the mechanism of the platform plays out slightly differently: The platform operator usually commits to the companies participating in a common ecosystem that instead of having to incur the cost of buying, selling, and exchanging industry data, they will be offered zero-cost bi-directional data transactions through the platform. This will be in exchange for the platform operator gaining the rights to using the data that has been shared. The platform operator acts as if it and the companies participating in the ecosystem are all integrated parts of the same company, even though they maintain their own management independence (Fig. 9.1).

H. Tardieu et al., *Deliberately Digital*, Future of Business and Finance,
https://doi.org/10.1007/978-3-030-37955-1_9

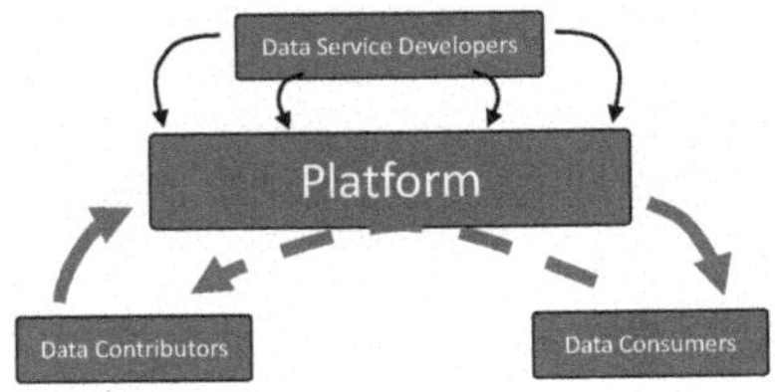

Fig. 9.1 Platforms in the B2B market. Authors' own figure

Let's look at some examples of platforms in practice.

The platform operator "HERE" (the former cartography division of Nokia) has recently provided the opportunity for stakeholders to share data collected from each of their "connected cars" irrespective of their brands (Audi, BMW, Daimler, etc.). This offers an unprecedented capability to gather valuable road-related data that might help, for example, accelerate the advent of autonomous vehicles. In this example (at least initially), there is only one type of agent (car manufacturers) and therefore one side of the market.

HERE anticipates the future additional value that can be brought by making "refined data" available to other market participants (e.g., public sector for management of road quality and congestion, insurance companies for insights into driving styles and related risks, and logistics operators for optimization of journey times). The intent is that this platform then becomes the foundation for a multi-sided market.

As we mentioned earlier, platforms in the Business-to-Business world can be either *one-sided* (as in the example of HERE where all participants are potentially bringing and using the same type of data) or *multi-sided* (including *two-sided*) where the participants in the ecosystem are bringing different types of data (see example of Skywise below, where Airbus brings production data and EasyJet brings operational and customer feedback data).

The case of one-sided platforms is already well documented and doesn't need further development. We shall instead concentrate on multi-sided platforms (which are sometimes referred to as *Industrial Data Platforms*) where several industry partners, involved in a given market for delivering products and services, decide to form an ecosystem to exchange industry data via a contractual relationship.

The value of such an ecosystem can be summarized as "Benefitting from vertical integration in the management of industrial data while each partner of the ecosystem maintains its management autonomy and guarantees its data sovereignty."

Establishing such integration is one of the aims behind Industry 4.0. Through applying Industry 4.0 technology and processes, companies aim to increase their flexibility, reduce their time to market, and improve their efficiency. However, few companies have full access to all the supply chain production data, operations data, and customer feedback required to deliver the necessary end-to-end perspectives. B2B platforms can bring significant value in enabling multi-sided markets that help address some of these hurdles. Nevertheless, there often remains the issue of data ownership and intellectual property protection.

GDPR is a first attempt to regulate data sovereignty for natural persons, but it suffers severe limitations in the case of mixed data which is generated by natural persons but is then used for industrial purposes (e.g., data generated by autonomous vehicles, smart energy meters, or health monitoring services).

In terms of data protection, GDPR is not limited to access control but includes usage control which needs to be handled through specific policies that dictate how data is handled after access has been granted.

In contrast to B2C platforms where the platform operator is “courting” the two different sides, in B2B platforms all partners of the ecosystem want to be treated equally and therefore will probably want to participate in:

- Data sovereignty policy definition
- Data reference architecture definition

The platform operator is therefore expected to manage the industrial data platform with total respect for the agreed policies without favoring any of the partners, and to do so at a reasonable cost.

Two possible options can be considered for platform operation:

1. A joint venture between the members of the ecosystem.
2. An outsourcing company with a well-defined contract (scope, commercials and term).

It is highly unlikely that members of an ecosystem will tolerate one of them stepping forward to act as the platform operator.

However, one example of just such a breakthrough in collaborative data value exchange is that of Skywise (a platform for the airline industry, operated by Airbus).. In the Skywise data ecosystem, Airbus is the owner of production data, while its airplane customers (e.g., Air France, Lufthansa, and EasyJet) generate operational and customer feedback data. The Skywise platform enables ecosystem members to share their industrial data through a zero-cost transaction capability, as if they were a single operating entity, while at the same time allowing them to maintain their management independence. From a platform user perspective, the incentive to engage is the provision of access to data that could allow them to engineer better products and services and to realize faster innovation cycles (Fig. 9.2).

Today, the Skywise platform has already been adopted by Airbus and EasyJet, and it is expected that other airline companies will join them. It should be noted that EasyJet is perhaps in a favored position since it only uses Airbus planes and therefore only has to consider participation in one platform ecosystem. Operators such as Lufthansa or Air France have a more challenging data sharing issue: As they operate both Airbus and Boeing airplanes, they would need to participate in membership of two different platforms (Skywise and its equivalent with Boeing).

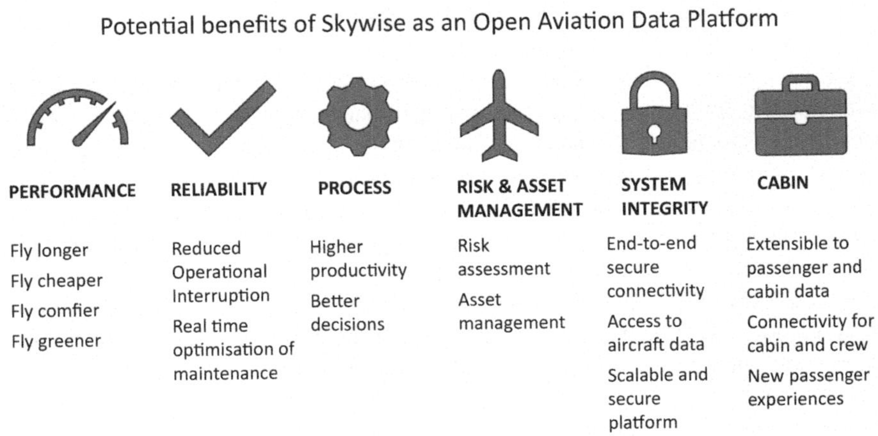

Fig. 9.2 Potential benefits of an open aviation data platform—adapted from Skywise scheme. *Source* Coninx (2017)

Already competing (but somewhat parochial) platforms are emerging from the likes of Pratt & Whitney (Engine Wise), GE (FlightPulse), and Rolls-Royce (R2 datalabs). It remains to be seen how these platform models will play out: Will vendors jealously guard their data, constraining themselves to more of a pipeline model, or will "neutral" platform operators emerge, creating the means for trusted exchange of data that will then drive value adding network effects?

Whatever the challenges to be overcome, it is clear that because of the rapidly emerging economy of data, the service industry needs to consider a business model strategy that allows it to undergo a non-linear metamorphosis from a pipeline model to a platform model.

9.2 The Consequences of Platform Introduction

Once a platform reaches its critical size (economic viability), it will naturally tend to attract more participants. As network effects catalyze further growth, there can be a tendency toward market monopolization. Even if new, better platforms emerge, competition inertia may come into play as platform users face data and operational migration challenges: Sometimes it is just too much effort to switch. This is particularly relevant where there are complex contractual, intellectual property and data sovereignty considerations to manage.

In order to avoid manipulation and distortion of the market, we expect to see industry bodies, regulators, and company procurement departments encouraging or even enforcing competition between similar platforms (exactly as we have seen with Open Banking regulations and the PSD2 initiative).

Switching between platforms is not the only challenge to be faced in complex data ecosystems. It will increasingly become the case, especially in complex and diverse supply chains, that data from a given party needs to be distributed and even duplicated across multiple platforms: so-called *multi-homing*.

An example of multi-homing in the B2C market might be that of retail loyalty cards. Different supermarkets or petrol stations, for example, might offer their own loyalty schemes allowing customers to accrue "points" that can then be redeemed via a partner ecosystem. A given consumer might hold several different and disconnected loyalty cards, each of which have their own defined redemption options. Platforms like Nectar or Avios have created "independent" loyalty markets, where loyalty card points accrued through the purchase of a given product or service from one partner can be converted to value from another (apparently disconnected) one within its partner network (all the while accruing useful data about consumer spend behavior).

In B2B markets, large industrial companies will tend to have multi-source purchasing policies (e.g., Air France will buy from both Airbus and Boeing). As a default position, each product vendor will tend to propose its own platform for documenting and storing its design, build, operate, and maintain data. This gives product users a challenge when trying to optimize the global coordination of its operations, because the support data they require is distributed across multiple platforms. Such disaggregation can happen at multiple levels throughout a supply chain and is particularly problematic when each platform operator seeks to have a monopoly relationship with its buyers, with a view to strongly influencing the pricing of services. Which platforms do supply chain participants engage with and how do they get a holistic view across their service providers when operational data is distributed across the supply chain landscape?

The multi-homing challenge can potentially be solved by "independent" service providers that are able to offer the same service irrespective of the underlying platform. However, for all kinds of reasons, this is not a trivial task, particularly with regard to the protection of intellectual property, honoring contractual and commercial constraints, and the respecting of legal data protection obligations.

Multi-homing can also be addressed within an ecosystem of industrial partners who have decided to share their respective industrial data using agreed common representations. This is done in such a way that any partner of the ecosystem can use industry platform data regardless of which company collected it. Excellent progress is being made in respect of standardized data taxonomies and structures through initiatives like the International Data Spaces Association which has created a reference architecture for sharing industrial data. Nevertheless, there remains the problem of who owns and operates the platform itself. This calls for enforceable trust and robust collaboration agreements.

9.3 The Specific Case of Platforms Mixing Industrial Data and Personal Data

With the introduction of GDPR, an unexpected situation has occurred for mixed data which relates to data that is collected in an industrial context, but which is seen by consumers as their personal data.

Examples of such data are:

- Smart energy meter platforms which have been installed to reduce the cost of collecting energy consumption data, but which also have a key role to play in managing the energy network and dealing with the challenges of an increasing share of intermittent renewable energy generation.
- Connected car platforms which have been installed to offer services to car users, but which have become essential contributors to car manufacturers for supporting vehicle maintenance. This will become even more relevant in the era of autonomous vehicles.
- Electronic health records (EHR) which are a key enabler of precision medicine and the control of healthcare spending.

In all of these cases, the raw data collected can rightly be seen as personal, and therefore, GDPR is applicable. However, consumers may not realize the potential benefits of their data for energy management, autonomous cars, or health progress, and therefore, by default, don't permit access to their data. Individual preferences (and ill-informed assumptions) may, as a result, become an obstacle to realizing the full potential benefits of otherwise transformative digital solutions. This situation will not only be detrimental to the use of analytics to help offer better services, but it could also preclude data collection for machine learning. This might result in the unanticipated consequence of introducing bias into AI systems that have to rely on being trained predominantly with unregulated data or data that only reflects the particular demographics that are willing to share their data.

Three options can be considered:

- The regulator can exhaustively describe the cases where consent will not be required, thus avoiding ambiguity and risk on the part of the platform operator.
- Consumers can themselves decide which usage scenarios they will accept for their data, with a guarantee from the platform operator that their data sovereignty will be respected. Consent may be encouraged through the offering of consumer incentives.
- Shared data can be anonymized to the extent that data privacy laws are not breached while, at the same time, not all of the data value is eroded.

It is essential to implement data sovereignty principles as an extension to GDPR in such a way that data privacy is not limited to data access but fully includes data usage control, otherwise there is a risk that individual perceived risks can prevent the realization of benefits from industry data platforms.

9.4 Strategy Challenges and Demands for Platform-Based Ecosystems

Digital platforms are still a relatively recent phenomenon, but they have proved to be an extraordinarily efficient mechanism for the generation of profitable growth. Platform-based firms can generate the same revenue as a non-platform-based organization but achieve it much more quickly, using a fraction of the employees, and with substantially greater margins.

However, it is by no means the case that platforms are a straightforward route to wealth creation. The platforms we see today are the survivors; for every success, many others failed along the way. In the last part of this chapter, we'll share some leadership lessons on what it takes to create, scale, and evolve a platform successfully.

Take a business systems perspective. As they mature, platform-based ecosystems involve multiple parties and operate beyond traditional business boundaries. The relationships between participating parties are both fluid and dynamic. What binds these participants together is the ability to access large numbers of customers cheaply and easily, to enable their offerings using pre-existing platform tools and data, and to benefit from network effects which create positive feedback loops.

Know what it takes to win. Platform orchestrators need to achieve scale quickly, or else risk being overwhelmed by the competition. This requires them to invest substantially in the early years and to potentially accept substantial losses as they build their position.

80% of successful ecosystems achieved 50% market share within their first five years and then went on to reach an average market share of 80% within seven years. This contrasts with those that didn't take off: they reached only 8% share within five years, and 13% at their peak. In the first few years, ecosystems which ultimately proved successful had on average negative profit margin of −60%. (source: BCG Henderson Institute).

Platform concept. Digital leaders need to think carefully about why their ecosystem partners will be interested in working with them in a new way, and they need to consider which side of the market they wish to address first. Most often, the side chosen is that of the customer, which is why we see so many high-profile attempts by platforms to aggregate as many customers as possible.

"Chicken & Egg" problem. At the outset, there is a key challenge all platforms have in common, which is how to make network effects work when you have so little to offer. Some ways to address this include:

- Make a substantial and credible up-front investment commitment. Microsoft did this at the beginning of their X-Box gaming business, with a $500 million commitment to promote the new platform and attract game developers.
- Find others with a commitment to collaborate through your platform. Google did this when they launched their Android operating system for mobile phone, aligning in advance with mobile manufacturers.
- Initially take the role of product producer as well as that of platform operator, like Apple did with the manufacture of their iPhone.
- Offering free initial platform membership, with charges only being applied at the point when value is realized (e.g., sales revenue is generated).

Platform scope. Platforms will encourage network effect growth when they enable multi-sided markets. Established leaders typically add more sides to their platforms over time as they become more and more useful, for instance, through growth in customers, content, and services.

It turns out that the likelihood of success is increased for the platform operator if it avoids taking on too many market sides at the same time; the issue here being that the required effort overwhelms them, and when the platform is still immature, it can lead to confusion for participants. Even a one-sided market approach can initially prove highly effective; for instance, Amazon took this approach in the beginning when they only sold books on their platform, and they did so directly to consumers.

Keep evolving. Ecosystems are dependent on maintaining platform momentum to retain the engagement of participants. BCG's Henderson Institute research found that winning platforms increased their scope twice as fast as others, implementing on average one major move every three years. Effective ways to evolve platform scope include:

- Attract more types of ecosystem participant.
- Increase the range of products and services accessible through the platform.
- Broaden out the platform offer into entirely new market areas.

Technology evolution. The pace of evolution in technology can present serious problems for platforms. For instance, Facebook was originally built for a world of PCs, and then suddenly consumer behavior changed radically with the rapid evolution of smartphones. For a while, a big question for Facebook was whether they could make the social network compelling on mobile devices for advertisers. This was a serious challenge for the firm, and they responded with major mobile platform acquisitions in the form of Instagram and WhatsApp.

Competing standards. It is common for platform orchestrators to find they are competing to establish their standards as the prevailing model, against others trying to do the same with different and incompatible standards. For instance, many years ago, Sony's Betamax video tape format had most of the then fast-developing market for home video, until the arrival of a competing VHS standard. VHS had a couple of critical advantages which helped it win out. Firstly, it offered a significant performance advantage over Betamax: Its tapes could run an entire two-hour movie, whereas Betamax's tapes could only run for sixty minutes, so requiring a change part way through. Secondly, VHS quickly attracted a wide range of manufacturers. Sony tried to bring in other manufacturers for Betamax too, notably JVC, but moved too slowly.

Ecosystem relationships. Platform orchestrators can struggle to balance competing interests between their own organization and those of complementary firms operating on their platform. One of the key decisions for a digital leader will be the degree to which the platform they orchestrate should be "open" or "closed." The more open the platform, the more control they will cede to other participants.

9.5 Recommendations

- *Consider how you will incentivize participation in B2C platforms.* In what ways can you incentivize consumers to participate in relevant B2C platforms? How can you ensure that you create a strong connection with the consumer when creating or participating in a B2C platform ecosystem?
- *Identify potential benefits of vertical integration in the end-to-end supply chain.* What benefits could participants in your existing supply chains (both up and down-stream) gain from sharing data? What constraints or challenges would arise from such data sharing?
- *Determine approaches to implementing such data sharing.* Which organization is best placed to build a platform to enable this data sharing: your company, another company in the existing supply chain or, more likely, a joint venture or independent trusted third-party provider? What legal agreements will be needed between participants in such a platform?
- *If you are seeking to create a platform, define a clear strategy for achieving scale.* How will you encourage sufficient platform users (be they people or businesses) to generate a large enough network effect to make the platform viable? How will you eliminate or minimize any negative network effects as usage of your platform increases? How will you ensure that, at a technical level, your proposed platform can scale smoothly to support future volumes?

Reference

Coninx. (2017). https://www.aviation24.be/manufacturers/airbus/airbus-launches-new-open-aviation-data-platform-skywise/. Accessed October 26, 2019.

10 Customers—How Great Digital Businesses Truly Put Customers at the Heart

"Customer-first" is treated as an essential part of many businesses' value statements. Despite this, we continue to observe that there is a massive gap between those organizations which authentically practice "customer-first" and those that are just paying lip-service to it.

The belief systems of those that get it right typically go along these lines: "In putting the customer first… we will develop a rich understanding of their changing context… that helps us to anticipate their changing requirements… so developing more valuable products and services… which differentiate us from others… accelerated and enabled by our strong 'innovation value web' of partners… further strengthening our position of trust… building customer loyalty… increasing our share of wallet… gaining active customer advocacy… reducing our cost to serve… mitigating our business risk… enabling us to accelerate our investments in business quality and innovation… attracting and retaining the very best people in our industry… assuring our continuing profitable growth… and through this attracting long-term shareholders who understand the inherent value of the business."

You will notice that this customer-first belief system has strong, positively reinforcing feedback loops embedded within it. These feedback loops can enable firms to create powerful momentum which can drive out the competition. As competitors begin to feel the pressure, it is not untypical for their own "customer-first" ambition to be undermined by another belief system, one that is focused on protecting revenue, cash and profits (i.e., short-term business value at the expense of customer value).

If we solely put financial performance first, there is a risk of creating a negatively reinforcing feedback loop: "We will earn the future right inside our business to re-invest in our customers… in the meantime we will take short-term measures to cut our costs, even if customer service might be negatively impacted… we will protect our cash flow, even if this means that our partners are not paid on time… we will insist that our customers pay for services we have delivered, even if they are dissatisfied… and we will defer investment in product and service innovation, even if powerful business cases are evident… the fact that customers no longer advocate

H. Tardieu et al., *Deliberately Digital*, Future of Business and Finance,
https://doi.org/10.1007/978-3-030-37955-1_10

our business is regrettable, so we will drive our delivery people harder to win back trust… the fact that our offerings are less differentiated is disappointing, so we will drive our sales people harder to make up for this… the fact that our existing customers don't wish to buy more from us at this time is concerning, so we will focus our efforts on winning new customers even if this is typically a more expensive and risky option… and the fact that we are struggling to attract and retain the best talent is unfortunate… so we will exploit the option of hiring less demanding, cheaper people more compliant with our current needs… this will all add up to delivering the short-term expectations of our demanding shareholders, who will otherwise dump the stock."

The unfortunate reality for those which follow such a path is that the market will not be slow in detecting a lack of sustainable long-term strategy; as a result, businesses that fixate on a financial-first belief system can enter into a downward spiral from which they might never recover.

10.1 The Importance of Customer-Centricity

For many organizations, customer engagement and experience are where digital transformation begins. These are certainly essential considerations because the ability to attract and retain a customer is a primary requirement for any business. However, the concept of true customer-centricity is not synonymous with customer engagement and experience; it goes much deeper in seeking to genuinely put the customer at the heart of how a business operates.

There are three key dimensions of customer-centricity:

1. *Customer-Centric Culture* (how firms build customer empathy, insight, and understanding throughout their organizations). While marketing and sales teams have naturally focused intensely on understanding customers, this has not always been so true for all other areas of business. When markets moved slowly, perhaps this mattered less than it does now, but in today's digital world of accelerating change, it is increasingly essential for businesses to have a deep and shared understanding of their customers across their whole organization. And more than this, for everyone in the business to understand the business's customer strategy and use this to drive their day to day actions and behaviors.
2. *Customer-Centric Operations* (how businesses function for customers in a coherent manner, including front and back-office processes). It is no longer enough for only front-office operations to be aligned with customers; back-office operations also need to be aligned, and so must the business's entire executive leadership team (we cover this in more detail within the chapters on Leadership and Organization Structure). Such alignment is essential because customers now expect businesses to interact with them in a coherent manner. Where customers (whether B2B or B2C) sense incongruence, they are very quick to point this out and have become used to doing so on social media in a manner that can sometimes be designed to create maximum embarrassment.

3. *Customer-Centric Commerce* (how businesses optimize value for customers and for themselves). It is this holistic approach to digital that separates the best from the rest. Businesses now have the potential to source much more detailed data on customers, helping them to improve their understanding as to how to meet their needs in the most mutual value creating way. They also have more useful data that they can share with customers to help enable closer customer/supplier collaboration, and ensure this value is realized in practice.

These three elements need to work together to ensure businesses put the customer at the heart of the way they think, act, and operate. By starting from the perspective of their customers and working back into their own business processes, brand owners within organizations can avoid adopting technology for its own sake. Instead, they can support the never-ending journey toward "knowing their customer," "reaching their customer," and "innovating effectively against customer needs." What's more, they will do so in a way that maximizes customer value while at the same time creating optimum value for the business.

10.2 The Digital Enablers of Customer-Centricity

Until relatively recently, most marketing strategies were grounded in what are essentially linear processes based on variants of the AIDA model (Awareness, Interest, Decision, Action). The principle behind this was that customer growth should be regarded as a sequence of events (or customer journeys) in the shape of a funnel, with the marketing and sales organization in control of this process through a sequence of "push" activities.

Over the past ten years or so, organizations have found that customer journeys are better represented by a more interactive set of feedback loops with multi-way interactions. These reflect deeper interconnectedness with the customer and the wider ecosystem around them. The most successful businesses understand that the effective realization of compelling customer journeys means that they need to orientate their entire organization toward serving their customers. It no longer works to treat sales and marketing as a "front end" which can be viewed as independent from other parts of the operation (such as distribution, service delivery, manufacturing, and supply chain).

Why has this change taken place? And how can businesses deliver compelling customer journeys in practice?

The key driver of change has been the continuing, rapid evolution of digital technologies, and the inventive application of these technologies in entirely new ways of interaction. This applies externally with customers and internally across organizational boundaries and leads to more coherent business responses to customer needs.

Customers and organizations are interacting differently today *because they can*, and both are finding they derive great benefits from doing so. Those firms that lag behind in this respect, risk coming across to their customers as both out of date and increasingly irrelevant.

We believe there are three critical enablers to creating a customer-centric business. It is helpful to summarize these before exploring how evolving technologies have introduced a new "art of the possible" in each area:

- *Knowing your customer:* All businesses ultimately live or die by their ability to understand what it is that their customers value (even if these customers are effectively intermediaries to the end customer); to anticipate how this may be changing; and to respond with products and services which delight them, in a more compelling manner than the competition.
- *Reaching your customer:* Every business has always sought efficient and effective ways to reach their customers, and through this communicate their value, sell their products and services, and provide after sales support as the customer requires.
- *Innovating against customer needs:* The raw nature of competition has always demanded that businesses continue to evolve their offerings to keep ahead of the pack. This capability is especially powerful in today's digital world given the pace at which competition can create a "fast follower" response (or indeed leapfrog concepts with something significantly better).

10.3 Knowing Your Customer

It is now possible to "know" the changing tastes and preferences of every single customer you have, even when there are millions of them distributed around the world; to "walk in their shoes" through their own unique life experiences; to "live" alongside them in their homes every day; to "observe" customers as they shop; to "see" how they are consuming your product or service; and to "understand" how their needs may be evolving. All this comes from the ability to capture, assimilate, and explore vast volumes of data created through myriad customer interactions, for example via mobile devices, and through the rapidly growing number of embedded IoT devices which track and monitor consumer behavior and even product usage.

The sheer power of these technologies is such that it has attracted strong and growing regulatory interest. The current direction we are going in is to put the customer in control of their data, to ensure businesses only retain the data that the customer has permissioned them to hold, and to transparently delete data when the customer wishes. Any business that fails to retain their customers' trust in this regard is highly likely to find itself at a massive competitive disadvantage.

Let's consider some of the technology developments that have transformed the way that businesses can know their customers (Table 10.1):

Table 10.1 Evolution of "know your customer" enabling technologies Table compiled by Authors

Time period	Knowing your customer capability evolution
1970–1999	Brands get more connected to customers (viewing laboratories/large-scale telephone interviews)
2000–2004	Rise of online surveys; emergence of rich contextual customer insight based on online behavior (what people search for; what they spend time looking at)
2005–2009	Brands learn to assimilate and process vast volumes of customer data (big table databases/Hadoop[a]). Marketers create inferred customer insights from the amalgamation of disparate databases and use cheap, scalable compute power to look for patterns in this data. There is a rise of mass real-time feedback via smart mobile devices
2010–2014	Data "runs riot;" custom APIs enable brands to see marketing data in real time across all channels in one place, implement omni-channel optimization and track what happens online and offline, with a direct connection to paid ads
2015–2019	Awakening of the need to safeguard customer data and to put customers back in control of their data. Recognition that brand owners must work hard to earn and retain customer trust; complete rework of customer data practices
Futures 2020–2025	Automated, intelligent insight into every customer individually. This insight becomes available to brands all the time, in real time. Brands begin to anticipate customer needs (before the customer even realizes this need themselves); brands are able to understand "customer lifetime value" in a dynamic sense and respond accordingly

[a]Popular name of the Apache Hadoop software library: "a framework that allows for the distributed processing of large data sets across clusters of computers using simple programming models" https://hadoop.apache.org/. Accessed October 26, 2019

10.4 Reaching Your Customer

Reaching customers in a highly connected digital world is (in theory) easy and cheap, and there are multiple channels available for doing so. What's more, it is also easy and cheap for all your customers to interact with each other about the brands they use, and potentially easy and cheap for them to interact with your business should you enable that.

The critical challenge for businesses arising from this is how to ensure that the channels now available to them are used together seamlessly. This demands the creation of "a single customer view" across all touch points. It requires the ability to visualize this single view within the context of the entire customer journey and ensure that this view is available in near real time to all those interacting with customers (whether this is done using people or automated robotic processes). Get this right and you can deliver a coherent approach to "next best action," informed by detailed insight (derived increasingly from AI and machine learning).

Once again, let's consider the evolution of technologies that have contributed to transformation in the way that you can reach your customers (Table 10.2).

Table 10.2 Evolution of "Reach your customer" enabling technologies (Table compiled by authors)

Time period	Customer reach capability evolution
1970–1999	Rise of globalization/global brands (affordable access to target audiences globally); rapid growth in targeted direct mail (affordable targeting of consumers in their own homes); emergence of one-to-one marketing (use of geodemographics[a] to conduct rudimentary profiling)
2000–2004	Marketing communication goes "digital," initially with "brochure-ware;" viral marketing; emergence of on-going brand interaction online; "permission marketing" (Godin 1999); customer ability to influence others begins to scale exponentially This period also saw the launch and rise of platform marketplaces. eBay, Amazon marketplace, price comparison sites all created unprecedented customer connection possibilities even for the smallest of trading companies
2005–2009	Communication and distribution channels proliferate (YouTube, Facebook, Twitter, Snapchat, Instagram, etc.); omni-channel management becomes a critical challenge; emergence of marketing automation and SPAM (digital equivalent of junk mail); e-commerce begins to take off; and customers begin to "take control" of brands (brands become "ideas that people live by")
2010–2014	Google and Facebook come to dominate digital marketing; social marketing grows to huge scale (YouTube, Facebook, Snapchat, Instagram, Twitter); rise of social influencers (over $1billion now spent annually on social media influencers (Mediakix 2019); rise of myriad peer-to-peer networks; companies can respond to customer feedback and make real changes faster than ever before; customers become active and powerful brand ambassadors and advocates with extensive reach; emergence of "context" as a challenge in the digital media world; online celebrity brand endorsement model takes off on YouTube; and emergence of immersive marketing, for example using "gamification"
2015–2019	"Social" goes mobile (mobile comes first: 90% of Twitter video views and 60% of YouTube views are now originating from users on mobile device); social Media Stories become key part of brand marketing (Instagram "Stories;" YouTube "Reels"); video on demand becomes a key marketing tool (YouTube viewers watch a billion hours of video each day; Facebook users consume over 8 billion videos every day; 82% of Twitter's audience views video content on the platform) Rise of artificial intelligence, and evolution of chatbots (60% of Millennials now say they have used chatbots—2018 number; 80% say they are interested in using them—2018 number (Arnold 2018)) Programmatic media buying works hand-in-hand with AI and real-time bidding to automate media buying
Futures 2020–2025	Brand communication experiences evolve to become individual and contextual; emergence of "Zero Shopping" (predictive and prescriptive engagement)

[a]The study of populations and their characteristics, according to geographical bases

As you consider transforming the way you reach your customers, look particularly at what happened in the early 2000s when platform businesses began to take the market by storm. We have already described the potential of platform business models and their associated ecosystems and would recommend that even if you are not proposing to establish your own platform, you should look for existing ones that you can leverage: Today, the most celebrated and valuable businesses on earth are (in some way) platform operators. Platforms can be massively powerful for their business users because they provide access to large numbers of customers and their associated data; they include many valuable pre-built tools and resources which can help refine and improve the experience your business provides; and they are typically created on scalable cloud-based architectures which enable user businesses to grow in a virtually unbounded way.

For example, Facebook is now used by over 60 million small businesses as a growth platform. These enterprise s benefit through a combination of potent qualities: Facebook has attracted a global usership of over 2.2 billion people, so its advertising services can give firms extraordinary reach; equally the rich, data-driven user insights Facebook can create enable firms to target their preferred audiences in a highly forensic manner. Once you begin to engage your audience, Facebook has many additional tools to support you, such as: App Install which enables customers to install your own businesses mobile app directly from your Facebook page; Web site links which enable you to direct your customers to a given page on your Web site; Facebook App Engagement Ads which help you to encourage customers who have downloaded your app to go to a specific area within it (such as a travel page); and Facebook lead generation which helps you provide your target customers with very simple digital forms that they will be more likely to fill in.

10.5 Innovating Against Customer Needs

The very nature of how new products and services are developed has changed fundamentally and now reflects the agile development methodologies we see for software. Firms used to launch products and services only once they were finished. Now, the more successful innovators are much more likely to adopt an iterative "test-learn-test" approach, with "beta" versions launched initially on a small scale, followed by rapid innovation cycles as new offers are evolved. An interesting retail example is that of fast fashion, with Zara clothing collections able to go from design to being in-store within a period of only 4 weeks (Wharton 2016).

As firms progress through their innovation cycles, we see them doing so in an increasingly collaborative manner with many others beyond the walls of their business. Third parties engaging in this process include customers, suppliers, partners, universities, opinion shapers and formers, and other expert communities. This collaboration occurs throughout the innovation lifecycle, including insight creation, ideation, development, testing, feedback, and launch (Table 10.3).

Table 10.3 Evolution of customer-centric innovation enabling technologies Table compiled by authors

Timing	Innovation capability evolution
1970–1999	Emergence of techniques to shadow consumers; artificial physical shopping environments; accompanied shopping; shadowing consumers in their homes as they use a product
2000–2004	Development of discrete camera technology enables in-home behavioral analysis
2005–2009	Firms able to collaborate with customers much more easily, affordably, and on a bigger scale than ever before. Cocreation, personalization, and mass customization become possible, enabled by accompanied changes in business operations
2010–2014	Brands learn to innovate at "digital" pace
2015–2019	Additive manufacturing/3D printing enables more localized and responsive product innovation
Futures 2020–2025	Unique/bespoke "through life"/end-to-end experiences offered to each customer; offerings evolve into deeply intermeshed products and services that extend into each aspect of the customer journey

Table 10.2 shows a summary timeline for the way that approaches to innovation have evolved over the last 50 years.

10.6 A Specific Focus on Artificial Intelligence as an Enabler of Customer-Centricity

Underpinning many of the digital enablers of customer-centricity is some kind of data analytics, artificial intelligence or process automation. Such technologies are transforming the way that brands interact with their customers, creating new possibilities to design and enrich customer-centric experiences. Businesses can use AI to learn about customer tastes and preferences (for example, using image processing, emotion recognition, and sentiment analysis); to engage in conversation (using chatbots enabled by Natural Language Processing, often referred to as NLP); to provide personalized, and increasingly customized, products and services (using preference analysis based on their search history); and to predict customer behavior (using algorithms that recognize traits associated with certain behavioral patterns). The potential to exploit such competitive advantage cannot be ignored.

There is a growing trend for customer interaction through AI-enabled voice channels. According to Alpine.AI online voice searches had reached 1 billion per month by January 2018, and according to PwC research, 50% of all online searches will be voice-based by 2020 (Nikku 2015). It turns out that voice interaction with digital services has evolved the point where customers simply find it easier, and increasingly more relevant, as messaging becomes more tailored.

Businesses too can benefit from using AI-enabled voice: Chatbots were initially used by firms keen to reduce their cost to serve, but they have now evolved to enable significant value creation through the additional customer data they generate.

One example of a firm making good use of this technology is Sephora: Customers are invited to take an interactive quiz based on their use of cosmetics; once this data has been collected, Sephora use their chatbot to make personalized tips and recommendations; finally, Sephora's chatbot directs users to their Web site to make their purchases. Sephora also has a bot with a Virtual Artist feature, allowing customers to upload a selfie and create their own customized look.

Chatbot technology is evolving rapidly: Google made a breakthrough in 2018 with a chatbot capable of holding natural conversations with a human at the other end of a phone call to perform everyday tasks (Google 2018), such as booking an appointment for a haircut or booking a table at a restaurant for dinner. What caused a significant media stir was that the chatbot made these calls "undetected": As far as the human they engaged was concerned, they were dealing with another human being. A few remarkable features of these calls included: The voice intonation was very human-like, with entirely natural modulation; and the way of speaking was also very human, including "ums" and "errs." But perhaps the most impressive thing was the ability of the chatbot to handle conversations elegantly when they didn't go quite as expected.

Chatbots are now being embedded into customer journeys to support seamless engagement across multiple touch points, including messaging apps such as WhatsApp, Facebook Messenger, and WeChat; and in-home digital assistants such as Alexa and Google Home.

A key challenge for firms now is to make effective use of all the new data that chatbots are generating.

10.7 Creating a Customer-Centric Operating Model

To become authentically customer centric, firms need to ensure their operating model puts the customer at the heart. This demands effective collaboration, co-ordination, and alignment across the whole business. Achieving this requires having an Executive Committee member responsible for customer-centricity and end-to-end customer experience.

Key requirements for success include:

- Customer-centric governance to drive the right behaviors.
- Strategy built from the basis of creating the best customer value, supported by the most compelling customer experience.
- Shared customer insights, with clarity throughout the business regarding the customer value proposition.

- Channels working seamlessly together for customers, with shared real-time intelligence, and the ability to serve customers based on their preferred means of interaction.
- Product and service design aligned with an evolving view of changing customer needs.
- Support functions such as Finance, HR, Procurement, and Marketing-driven to ensure that the firm's front and back-office processes work in a streamlined manner.

The increasing rate of change in customer expectations means that many organizations now realize that they must listen to customers. And increasingly we see them acting boldly to make good use of the insights they obtain:

- *Listen with purpose*: Design Thinking is proving a powerful means to create innovative new concepts. For readers less familiar with Design Thinking, this can be an excellent way to map customer journeys, understand customer needs and wants, identify the "pains" and "gains" associated with these, and define new concepts for further development and evaluation.
- *Build minimum viable products/services*: Firms in many industries now operate innovation centers, and are opening these up to partners, as well as actively inviting tech start-ups to work alongside them. And we see an increasing use of "open innovation hackathons focused on strategic market opportunities which enable them to crowdsource ideas and early-stage concepts.
- *Engage a partner ecosystem*: Most large organizations have deep relationships with their technology vendors, who are understandably eager to support their innovation efforts with funding, skilled experts, and access to other assets. Beyond this, and especially in certain markets such as banking and insurance, we see firms going a step further and creating an ecosystem of smaller start-up technology players. These start-ups are used to help them access more disruptive technologies, and to explore their value potential early.

Nevertheless, there is a significant challenge that remains. At executive management level, many firms tell us that they struggle to deploy successful new concepts at scale through aligning efforts across their enterprise. There seem to be too many things getting in the way: project delivery teams already overburdened and too busy to engage; budgets stretched to breaking point with existing workloads; difficulties in adapting current processes and working methods to accommodate a new concept; complexities in aligning key stakeholders across the business (especially challenging for businesses with more federated organizations); concerns over assessing, and possibly adapting, the innovation to take account of regulatory and compliance concerns; and change fatigue among employees reluctant to re-train so they can take advantage of the innovation. The chapter on People gives a hint as to how to break this vicious circle.

It turns out that a great *employee* experience is critical to a compelling *customer* experience. A 2017 research study by Temkin Group (Temkin and Lucas 2017) showed that those firms with a customer experience significantly better than their competitors, typically had employees who were 60% more engaged. Improved employee engagement is a powerful differentiator because it points to a degree of passion and commitment on behalf of employees that goes beyond them just treating their work as a job to be done.

Achieving higher levels of employee engagement demands a concerted effort, including: ensuring the firm has a purpose that employees can feel passionate about; listening to employee needs and wants; designing a great employee experience to make their lives easier and more productive; supporting and encouraging employees to interact and collaborate with each other across teams and divisions; and enabling lifelong learning for personal development and skills enhancement.

If you have frustrated or disgruntled employees, this will inevitably show through in their engagements with customers. Remember, your most impactful salespeople are not necessarily in your sales team!

10.8 Recommendations

- *Implement best-in-class solutions for knowing your customers,* reaching your customers, and innovating against their needs. Using the timelines we present in this chapter, check which of the evolutions in 2015–2019 you are already using. Check that you are already evaluating those that we have identified for 2020 and beyond.
- *Ensure that the customer voice has senior representation within your company.* You should have at least one member of the Executive Committee who has defined responsibility for ensuring that the organization pays constant attention to customer needs.
- *Build a business culture that puts the customer-first* in a truly authentic manner.
- *Design and evolve your customer journey* in a manner that is inclusive and participatory: work with your customers to inspire future products and services for your business.
- *Work with your customers and partners* to improve the products and services you offer. Collaborate closely with your customers and partners to understand their needs and to find new, innovative ways of addressing them.
- *Use data to better understand your customers.* Use the data you collect about your customers, together with artificial intelligence and machine learning, to provide better products and services that are more attuned to your customers' needs.
- *Use technology to elevate the customer experience.* Make wise use of chatbots, social media and other related technologies to improve the quality of service that your customers receive.

- *Create a truly customer-centric operating model* that enables deployment of new concepts at scale through aligning efforts across your enterprise, and beyond into the wider ecosystem.
- *Introduce the Agile way of working* to drive your customer-centric evolution at the required speed and quality.
- *Enable your employees* to support your customers more effectively by ensuring that the employee experience you provide gives them the tools they need to be effective.

References

Arnold, A. (2018). *How chatbots feed into millennials' need for instant gratification*. Forbes. January 27, 2018 https://www.forbes.com/sites/andrewarnold/2018/01/27/how-chatbots-feed-into-millennials-need-for-instant-gratification/. Accessed October 26, 2019.

Godin, S. (1999). *Permission marketing: Turning strangers into friends and friends into customers*. Simon & Schuster.

Google. (2018). Google duplex: A.I. assistant calls local businesses to make appointments. https://www.youtube.com/watch?v=D5VN56jQMWM. Accessed October 26, 2019.

Mediakix. (2019). *Instagram influencer marketing is a 1.7 billion dollar industry*. Mediakix.com, March 07, 2019 https://mediakix.com/blog/instagram-influencer-marketing-industry-size-how-big/ Accessed October 26, 2019.

Nikku, A. (2015). *Voice is the transformational new frontier in financial services: How can you get up to speed?* PwC https://www.pwc.co.uk/industries/financial-services/insights/digital-voice-assistants-how-to-get-up-to-speed.html. Accessed October 26, 2019.

Temkin, B., Lucas, A. (2017). *Employee engagement benchmark study*. Temkin group and qualtrics XM Institute. It can be ordered online at https://www.qualtrics.com/xm-institute/employee-engagement-benchmark-study-2017/. Accessed October 26, 2019.

Wharton. (2016). *Zara's 'fast fashion' business model*. Knowledge Wharton High School, February 18, 2016 http://kwhs.wharton.upenn.edu/2016/02/zaras-fast-fashion-business-model/. Accessed October 26, 2019.

Leadership—What Is Required of Leaders and Leadership to Achieve Digital Success?

11

11.1 The Changing Context for Leadership

As we have seen in Part I, the rate of change in business, society, and technology is increasing. Business leaders (and especially CEOs) tell us that a consequence of this acceleration is that they now have opportunities to create or destroy value faster than any of their predecessors.

So, what lessons can be learned as to how digital leaders need to operate if they are to help their organizations to thrive? We have found that there are certain "eternal" leadership qualities that have become even more relevant in this new context. We have also found that becoming a successful digital organization can pose new challenges for leaders (see Fig. 11.1). How can they successfully evangelize new digital strategies and business models? What is their role in new flatter, less hierarchical organization structures? And what new demands does the changing composition of an organization's workforce place on them?

11.2 Eternal Leadership Qualities that Are Even More Relevant for Digital Organizations

Given all the hype about digital, one might expect that some revolutionary, amazing new qualities are required of digital leaders, in stark contrast to the somewhat outdated qualities of their non-digital forbears. The truth is more complex and nuanced.

Leadership qualities such as integrity, authenticity, empathy, humility, situational awareness, flair, and fortitude are just as important today as they have ever been. For leaders to attract followers, they need to show consistency between their values and their actions, and they need to retain a positive, resilient outlook that encourages others to do things they might otherwise have thought to be impossible.

H. Tardieu et al., *Deliberately Digital*, Future of Business and Finance,
https://doi.org/10.1007/978-3-030-37955-1_11

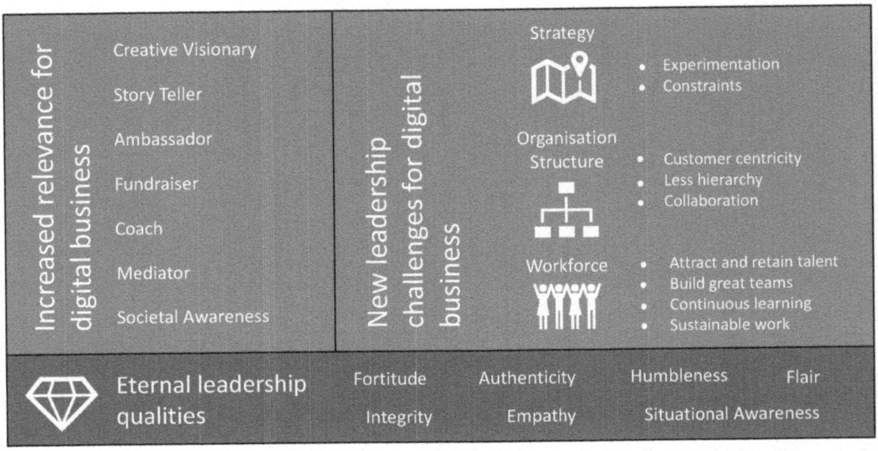

Fig. 11.1 Evolving nature of leadership qualities. Authors' own figure

Henry Ford of Ford Motor Company showed these qualities, once saying "*One of the greatest discoveries a man makes, one of his greatest surprises, is to find he can do what he was afraid he couldn't do.*" One example of Ford's applied leadership qualities was when he established the first moving assembly line in 1913. This quickly proved to be a breakthrough in manufacturing efficiency, enabling Ford to produce a complete Model-T chassis in just 93 min, as compared with the 728 min required by the previous approach of static production lines.

11.3 Additional Qualities Required of Digital Leaders

Digital business leaders require a combination of some very particular additional leadership qualities built on these "eternal" ones, which we'll now describe with examples.

Digital leaders not only need to be creative visionaries, they must be able to embrace continual disruption and intuitively respond to it. They must also be able to see beyond what others can see, with the ability to create the practical and continually anticipatory steps that make their vision a reality. This is critical because the best digital firms are in some way revolutionary: They seek to reshape the world and do things differently. To achieve this, they must paint a picture for their people which is beyond anything that currently exists. They must appropriately and authentically use storytelling to bring what they are trying to do to life for all those they engage, making it feel real to the wider executive group, to employees, and to other critical stakeholders.

For example, Steve Jobs is credited with the greatest corporate turn-around when he returned to Apple in 1997. In his return speech he described his vision of providing "relevant, compelling solutions that customers can only get from Apple," with Apple providing the breakthrough platform, systems integration and marketing power, and third-party developers bringing creative insight, market knowledge, and entrepreneurial energy.

A strong vision is just the starting point. Effective digital leaders need to turn their vision into something much more tangible, giving their people a clear sense of how to achieve their vision through a well-defined mission statement, and then backing this up with strong guidance on the products and services they will create and further develop. Apple makes both of these connections powerfully. Their mission is to bring the best user experience to customers through their innovative software and services. This mission is translated into compelling and unique solutions that combine beautiful design with smart technology selection, tightly focused on technologies that are in the ascendance.

As they develop and evolve their offerings, a particular complicating factor for digital leaders is that their work is forever in "beta," in the sense that their products and services are never "complete;" they are always undergoing continuous improvements arising from endless learning and experimentation. This requires a different leadership mindset and approach. Facebook's Mark Zuckerberg understands this very well, and from the very beginning of his firm, he embedded a "learn by making" culture, with team members engaged in regular hackathons, and being asked to present working prototypes rather than ideas expressed on PowerPoint slides.

Iterative development in this way can work very well until there is a sudden step-change in customer behavior which demands more radical action. Accelerating waves of technology and their associated disruption makes this happen with increasing frequency. As a consequence (and far more than their forebears), digital leaders must become adept at the art of the "pivot." One example is from 2013 in the way that Facebook confronted the rapid growth in adoption of smart mobile devices. It was soon clear to Facebook that the context for social media consumption on a mobile device was very different to that on a personal computer, and not just because the screen was smaller. When accessing mobile devices customers are often busy, moving around, multi-tasking, and looking for much more immediate interactions. Facebook's pivot required transforming their social media experience to reflect this reality, with many industry commentators questioning at the time whether this was even possible. To help Facebook's people meet this demanding challenge, Mark Zuckerberg introduced a mobile design think-tank which developed a set of mobile-experience best practices. He also placed a mobile design expert into every product team, so ensuring that this thinking was rapidly disseminated.

Having great products is one thing, having people buy them is another. Even as their teams create exceptional new products and services, digital leaders need to generate customer interest and excitement in their brand and in their latest offers. And they must do this against what can sometimes feel like a deafening roar of competitive noise. Steve Jobs was the arch-exponent of excitement creation as the star of Apple's annual presentations. Steve's shows always made a huge stir, not least with his iconic "one more thing" addresses toward the end of each performance (the moment in Apple's annual product launches when he would introduce their biggest innovation). Even after Steve's death, these presentations continue in a similar way and still generate a huge volume of free media coverage and online attention for Apple.

In addition to becoming skilled at inspiring customers, partners, developers, and distributors, digital leaders also need to become adept at engaging the financial community. Two key challenges they face are: Firstly, they are more likely than their forebears to find themselves pitching for funding for a radically new idea; secondly, they are more likely to find themselves reassuring investors about the achievability of expected high-growth projections. Like it or not, established firms, and especially those which are publicly listed companies, are accountable to their shareholders, usually at least once a quarter. For some digital leaders, it seems to come as a surprise that the standards to which they are held accountable are exactly the same as for other leaders, no matter what their individual brilliance, or the unique value they have created. A well-reported example is provided by Tesla's Elon Musk. Elon found himself frustrated on an analyst call in May 2018, and he ended up insulting analysts and refusing to answer their questions, causing an immediate share price fall. He subsequently apologized, but along with other unorthodox behavior, this undermined his standing.

As digital leaders secure the required funding for their ideas, they need to ensure they can maintain momentum behind their business's growth. Key to this is the creation of a strong culture aligned to their vision that enables a widening group of people to get on board, and the ability to adapt this culture over time to accommodate their changing business reality. Getting culture right has proved challenging for many digital leaders. For instance, Amazon has been described as "the greatest place I hate to work" (Whitney 2015) by former executive John Rossman, author of The Amazon Way. Interviews with current and former employees in different parts of the business describe a culture with very high demands, unmanageable pressure, and employee distress. There is a constant battle to reconcile these aspects with the thrill of matching the organization's ambition through value creation.

Google has also faced cultural challenges. From the very beginning, Google built an open culture based on free-thinking people who "don't do evil," which they found to be highly attractive to many brilliant and independent-minded people, who have undoubtedly been key to its extraordinary success. However, the sheer growth rate of the firm has led to rapid on-boarding of large numbers of new employees. The open, free-thinking culture which proved so compelling in the earlier years is now causing problems with some highly publicized cases of sensitive matters such as diversity and inclusiveness, involving employees getting into heated internal and increasingly external debates.

It should be noted that in some respects employee pressure of this kind can be helpful. Digital organizations need to reflect the populations they serve in order to ensure the right degree of insight and empathy into their customers' changing needs and to enable the required creativity in how these needs are addressed. However, addressing the issue of diversity is a new challenge for leaders, and it demands real sensitivity to cultural and social cues. A difficulty within Google right now, which we think arises from its cultural roots, appears to be an expectation from some employees that they should be able to say pretty much whatever they like to each other, which is creating a febrile atmosphere that management is struggling to address.

Google's culture has also placed constraints on its business growth. For instance, its "do no evil" roots prevented the business from operating in areas requiring censorship of content, most importantly China; and the way Google has celebrated those who created cool products, far more than it has celebrated those who could write contracts with large organizations, has arguably left the public cloud wide open to early exploitation by Amazon and Microsoft. Google is now seeking to change this, but it is having to play catch up.

The cultural challenges faced by the largest digital leaders and others are not unique. Leaders have always had to be attuned to the societal context in which they exist. However, as we have seen in earlier chapters, new digital business models raise new ethical, political and regulatory questions. Digital leadership requires keeping your company ahead of changing public opinions, political changes and new (or anticipated) regulation and legislation. When digital businesses are young and small, they tend to be cut a certain amount of slack. However, for larger firms this tends not to be the case, and this is especially true for the largest digital firms today. The key issue here is that there are now a number of digital firms which have become both richer and more powerful than many governments, and the platforms they support impact our daily lives in such deep ways that any irregularities can no longer be ignored. A number of incidents have arisen in recent years which serve to underscore this new reality, whether through data loss, fake news, trolling, inappropriate content, non-payment of taxes, anti-competitive practices, or any number of other legitimate concerns. Today's digital leaders need to anticipate and proactively address societal and regulatory compliance concerns, whether they relate to formal or informal expected standards.

11.4 The Impact of Digital Maturity on Leadership

A company's level of digital maturity has a significant influence on what the priorities of leaders should be. Firms are spread out across a digital maturity spectrum, with less mature ones not always wishing to admit it, or perhaps not fully realizing where they truly stand. Take stock of the reality for your company as you shape your leadership approach.

At the most basic level, you can be sure that most firms are now committed to the concept of digital business. According to a study recently undertaken by MIT with Deloitte, 85% respondents agree that "being a digital business is important for the success of my company." However, this research also revealed that firms are distributed across a bell curve of digital maturity, and they can usefully be segmented into those that are "Early-Stage" (where digital is mainly talk), "Developing" (where digital initiatives are taking place, but are disjointed), and "Maturing" (where the firm is becoming digital to the core).

The contrast in attitude and behavior between those firms which are Maturing vs those which are Early-Stage is stark. For instance, another MIT/Deloitte research finding was that 76% of respondents from Maturing firms agree they are "much more likely to use technology to conduct business in a fundamentally different way." This compares to only 36% of respondents from early-stage firms.

This supports our own experience which has shown that leadership approach must be informed by an organization's digital maturity. In a firm that is less digitally mature, far greater emphasis will need to be focused internally on how to create the right digital mindset and culture to deliver against external expectations (including those from customers, partners, investors, and the market). We think of leaders in these firms as needing to drive internal change in response to an "external pull."

In companies that have a high level of digital maturity, the leadership focus is on explaining the vision to stakeholders outside of the organization (customers, partners, investors), while also selling the value of what the company is doing. We think of leaders in these firms as needing to drive external change in response to an "internal push."

In between (where most companies actually exist) is what we call the "equilibrium zone." The danger of this zone is that there is no strong drive for change, either from within the organization or outside of it. For organizations in this zone, leaders have to play the role of disruptor: deliberately upsetting the balance in order to achieve progress (Fig. 11.2).

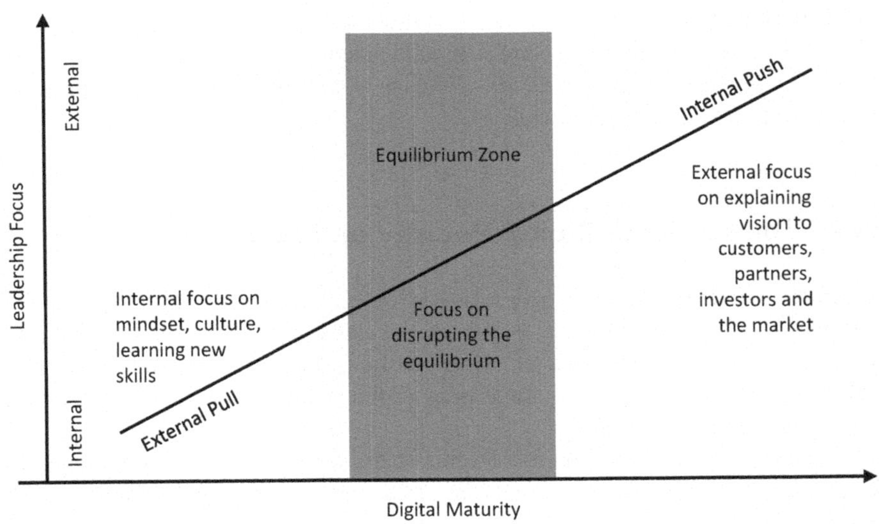

Fig. 11.2 Impact of an organization's digital maturity on the focus of leadership. Authors' own figure

11.5 Leading the Digital Strategy

As digital leaders seek to break new ground, they must embrace a test, learn, test approach, not just for the development of their products and services, but also for their strategy and business models, and even for digital transformation itself (something that we explore more in Part III and, in particular, in the chapter on Planning an Iterative Transformation). These experiments are usually undertaken in parallel, and for larger firms, this is now done on a significant scale. For instance: Facebook's Mark Zuckerberg has estimated that there are 10,000 versions of Facebook's social media site running at any given point (Clifford 2017). This is how they drive the continuous incremental improvements they believe to be necessary to keep their business as the pre-eminent global social media platform in the world.

Making the required level of experimentation possible demands that digital leaders need to first inspire, and then enable diverse teams to come together organically from across their organization and beyond. These teams need freedom to work in an agile manner, with delegated authority and empowerment (these topics are covered in more detail in the chapter on Organization Structure). Ensuring effective evaluation and learning necessitates an approach that is data-driven and results oriented. When executed effectively, this will result in rapidly growing data volumes and a need to analyze this data using effective digital tools and techniques. In order to avoid unnecessary delays and possible missteps, digital leaders must ensure their people have the required permissioned access to trusted data and that this is used to underpin decision-making.

As touched on previously, in less digitally mature businesses the level of insight into the strategic implications of new and emerging digital technologies and business models can be relatively weak. Digital leaders need to create the foundation for future success by improving insight and understanding in their organizations. This should start with the executive leadership because this group will need to sign-off on future digital strategies, plans, and resources (as described by the transformation model that we explain in Part III). In so doing, digital leaders need to encourage their peers to think beyond the traditional context of their business as they shape their vision and strategy. This is a critical moment for them because, even when these are well conceived, there will inevitably be a series of gaps and uncertainties which can only be navigated through subsequent experimentation and learning. Such gaps and uncertainties are the nature of digital business, but it is not necessarily in the nature of digitally immature firms to accept these and move forward; instead, their temptation will be to demand further reports until all outstanding questions have been addressed and, even if they can be persuaded to act, there is a strong likelihood that they will under-invest.

Less digitally mature organizations can find themselves in a dilemma. On the one hand, they are often facing challenges with a stressed legacy business model, which can lead them into a cycle of cost cutting; on the other hand, they are trying to catch up from behind in building their new business models, which can lead them to under-invest. An adept digital leader will need to learn how to work within these constraints to move the organization forward.

11.6 Leading in New Organizational Structures

In the next chapter about Organization Structure, we will see that the way people are organized into teams, and how cross-team collaboration is enabled, will often need to change to meet the demands of digital. These new structures, in turn, require new approaches to leadership.

As we have seen in the last chapter, customer-centricity is of vital importance for digital success. This means that leaders at all levels must relentlessly focus on their customers. Many, even most, businesses would claim this to be the case already, but with digital leaders, the obsession with customers leads them to behave in some very particular ways. They don't just listen to customers through qualitative focus groups or quantitative field studies, and they don't just observe customers through assisted shopping or in-home immersion studies. Digital leaders put themselves in the customers' shoes, and work to imagine entirely new services and experiences that could be transformational to customer well-being. As they do this, they experiment directly with their customers, gathering data on each and every one. This data is used to refine their thinking and to relentlessly iterate their products and service concepts.

With the flattening of organization structures, digital leaders must let go of top-down leadership models. Often, they will need to support the creation of diverse, cross-functional teams, bringing together a set of complementary mindsets, experience, and skills. Digital leaders need to promote a sharing culture in which knowledge, people, and other resources are used in a flexible way to support key projects as necessary. This support for cross-team collaboration is not only internal: We have found it helpful to work in partnership with others as part of a collaborative ecosystem including partners, customers, and even competitors. This is all part of creating an abundance mindset (as further discussed in the chapter on Innovation).

Working with competitors can be helpful for a couple of reasons: Sometimes, the work you are doing demands the establishing of industry-wide standards to be successful; sometimes there is a need for you to collaborate to increase customer acceptability for an entirely new service.

Working with partners is great because they can give you access to all kinds of resources that you would otherwise need to provide yourself. For example: access to required skills and talents you might otherwise lack; access to complementary innovation services and environments; access to pre-built platforms and capabilities; and even access to critically important customers.

Working with customers is essential to keep you on track. In the end, it is the customer who will be paying (in some way) for the new product or service you create. Working alongside them can help you stay in tune with what they truly value within your idea, ensuring that the new offerings you create maximize customer benefits while minimizing unnecessary investments.

11.7 Leading a Digital Workforce

As we will explain in the chapter on People, the nature of work is changing, as is the make-up and expectation of many organizations' workforces. Leadership styles have to adjust to these changes in order to attract and retain the best digital talent, set employees up for success, promote lifelong learning, and prevent burnout.

Because digital talent is scarce and hotly competed for, attracting and retaining it is important. Access to talent is one of the most critical success factors for an effective digital organization, and the qualities that attract this talent are not necessarily the traditional things such as a good wage, job security, and longer-term prospects. The best digital talent wants to work with the best digital leaders, and to do so on meaningful projects: projects that enable them to stretch their skills, do great work, and create outstanding outcomes. For this to happen, they know they need to be in a firm that understands digital, works in digital ways, and provides the right environment to increase the likelihood of success. Digital leaders need to create the right conditions for this talent, whether for people working directly for the company, or for others brought in as consultants, contractors or even via the gig economy.

Digital leaders need to ensure that teams contain the right mix of skills provided by a diverse set of contributors. This includes ensuring the right blend of technology expertise combined with specific industry knowledge. It also demands the finding of new ways to source and engage that talent in a scalable manner, whether from inside or outside the organization. Of course, attracting talent is only part of the picture: just as important is retaining it. The scarcity of digital talent means that digital leaders must always watch out for talent flight. This is especially true for early-stage firms. Digital leaders need to do all they can to ensure their talented people continue to have motivating, rewarding work; work that helps make the most of their skills; work that stretches and inspires them to reach for new possibilities; and work that ultimately makes them proud because they have in some way improved people's lives.

In our experience, the best digital leaders make time available for teams to be disruptive and creative, and they take the trouble to ensure they have a suitable working environment which supports creative activities. It is interesting to note some recent research undertaken by Harvard Business School into work environments (Camerota 2018): Their work suggests that the open-plan offices now favored by most businesses can cause distraction and discomfort for employees; these environments can also reduce their creative thought processes. Reasons include distraction by colleagues and by the endless noises from the growing array of workplace digital devices. Harvard's researchers propose complementing open-plan areas with more compartmentalized workspaces, including offices for quiet time and reflection. We have personally found that it is valuable to have a variety of spaces available for teams to use in a flexible manner, so they can select whatever space and resources they need at a given time.

Digital leaders also appreciate the truth in the expression "necessity is the mother of invention." Sometimes, having constrained resources can be a good thing, forcing a more iterative and collaborative approach, requiring teams to think about the minimum needed to solve a problem or prove a concept, rather than trying to come up with the "perfect" solution. At the same time, digital leaders also need to recognize when it is necessary to pivot from initial proof of value toward creating a scalable, robust product that can drive accelerated value creation for their firm (which will often require significant up-front investment).

The rate of change in our increasingly digital world demands continuous learning. Microsoft's CEO Satya Nadella observed the importance of this rather succinctly when he said he wanted his firm to move from a culture of "know-it-alls," to a culture of "learn-it-alls." The important point for leaders is to be role-models for lifelong learning and to find ways to nurture this in other people, ultimately enabling every employee to take responsibility for their own learning.

Leadership plays a vital role in attracting and retaining talent, enabling people and teams to be successful, and promoting continuous learning. In addition, they must ensure that the new demands of digital do not make work unsustainable and result in burnout. One of the great scourges of our time is the always-on, $24 \times 7 \times 365$ culture of availability and responsiveness. This relentless transactional focus is now a major long-term mental and physical health risk, and it also causes depleted energy levels and creativity. Digital leaders need to set an example for their teams, creating a more balanced collaboration and communication culture, one that enables employees to rest and recharge, while also leaving their minds free to wander in search of fresh ideas.

11.8 Recommendations

- *Develop and nurture the eternal leadership qualities that are even more relevant today for digital success.* Do leaders in your organization demonstrate consistency in their values and actions? Are they visionary? Can they communicate their vision and inspire people through effective storytelling? Are they the leading advocates of the company's products and services? Are they able to coach and support people, and act as mediators to bring people together? Do your leaders grasp the changing nature of society, business, and technology, and do they know how they may need to adjust their leadership style as a result?
- *Understand your firm's level of digital maturity.* What implications does your company's level of digital maturity raise for leadership? Do leaders need to evangelize digital internally to influence people's mindsets and advance the company culture? Or do they need to be more focused on people outside of the organization, explaining to them how digital transformation will benefit them and what part they will play in its success? Do your leaders need to act as the disrupting influence?

- *Ensure that leaders in your organization are equipped to formulate and articulate digital strategies.* Are leaders used to working in experimental test-learn-test cycles, not only for changes to products and services, but also for developing new business models? Do leaders understand and can they articulate how digital approaches can drive strategic advantage?
- *Anticipate how leadership will be impacted by changes to your organization's structure.* Do your leaders understand their role in a flatter organization structure where there is greater autonomy for staff, and more cross-team collaboration? Are they able to lead not just internal staff by using their positional power, but also people across the organization (and outside of it) by taking a collaborative and consensual approach?
- *Understand what demands will be placed on your leaders by the changing make-up of your workforce and changes to the nature of work itself.* Do your current leaders make it easier to recruit and retain the best digital talent? If not, what needs to change? Do your leaders lead by example when it comes to embracing continuous learning and reducing burnout and other negative work-related health impacts?
- *Evaluate how you recruit and develop leaders within your organization.* As we have seen, the nature of leadership required for a digital organization is significantly different to that in traditional enterprises. How do you evaluate candidates for leadership positions and is this aligned with the needs of digital? Do your leadership development programs sufficiently address the leadership styles and skills necessary for a digital organization?

References

Camerota, C. (2018). *The unintended effects of open office space*. Harvard Business School, 09/07/2018 https://www.hbs.edu/news/articles/Pages/bernstein-open-offices.aspx. Accessed 26 October 2019.

Clifford, C. (2017). How Mark Zuckerberg keeps Facebook's 18,000+ employees innovating: 'Is this going to destroy the company? If not, let them test it.' Cnbc.com, 05/06/2017.

Whitney, L. (2015). Amazon is not a 'soulless, dystopian workplace.' CEO says. Cnet.com, 17/08/2015 https://www.cnet.com/news/amazon-ceo-says-company-is-not-a-soulless-dystopian-workplace/. Accessed 26 October 2019.

Organization Structure—Allocating Roles and Responsibilities to Support Business Strategy

12

12.1 What Do We Mean by "Organization Structure"?

All organizations have a structure. When an organization is small this may be quite simple: for example, a business owner with two or three members of staff with specific responsibilities (such as a salesperson, a support engineer, and a software developer). In such cases, the company typically consists of one single team, with a single mission and purpose. Larger organizations will have more complex structures consisting of multiple teams. Each team might have its own mission and purpose, which should contribute to (but not necessarily be the same as) the business's overall mission and purpose.

The way that people are organized into teams, and the way that roles and responsibilities are distributed between teams and individuals, significantly influences the way that an organization performs. There are different approaches, each of which has their own advantages and disadvantages. For example, a structure that is optimized for efficiency will generally be so at the expense of speed and agility in execution. In this chapter, we explain how to balance these trade-offs in order to support the strategy, business models, and customer focus that we have described in the previous chapters. We will also consider how the structure can enable (or stifle) the required levels of innovation (as described in the next chapter).

12.2 Organizing to Meet the Demands of Digital

In Part I, we have seen how the rate of change and disruption is increasing and have considered the pressure that this places on businesses. Specifically, it means that businesses must be able to respond to change quickly. Agility and pace are required at three different levels:

H. Tardieu et al., *Deliberately Digital*, Future of Business and Finance,
https://doi.org/10.1007/978-3-030-37955-1_12

1. *Strategy*: being willing and able to pivot the overall purpose and mission of an organization in the light of new circumstances.
2. *Business models*: being willing and able to radically and quickly change business models as required.
3. *Execution*: being able to quickly deliver new solutions, both in response to changing or newly discovered customer needs, as well as to optimize internal operations.

12.3 The Digital Executive Committee

Let's start by understanding the impact of these requirements on the roles and responsibilities at the top of a company: its Executive Committee.

Table 12.1 describes the traditional remit of each role and some of the new challenges and requirements that are specific to digital businesses. To these traditional roles are being added the roles of the Chief Digital Officer and Chief Ethics Officer, which we will later consider more specifically.

12.4 The Increasing Link Between the CTO and CIO

The traditional distinction between CTO and CIO is that the CTO is focused externally on the products and services delivered to clients, whereas the CIO is focused internally on the technology needed to support internal operations.

But in digital businesses, this line has become blurred. For example, can Amazon's logistics solutions (including smart-lockers and online streaming of video) really be classed as internal IT, when they are so critical to the overall customer experience that Amazon delivers? In practice, we are often seeing that to create an overall end-to-end customer experience, no meaningful distinction can be made between internal and external IT.

Also, it has been normal for internal IT to focus on cost reduction and stability ("keeping the lights on" for less). Conversely, externally facing solutions are focused more on innovation and a faster pace of change in order to create and maintain differentiation from competitors. But digital businesses need to be able to innovate their internal systems at the same pace as externally facing solutions.

12.5 The Promise and Trap of the CDO

The role of Chief Digital Officer (CDO) is a relatively new invention and has been used by various firms to mean any one of the following:

Table 12.1 Impact of digital on the roles and responsibilities of the Executive Committee (table compiled by authors)

Role	Traditional responsibilities	Requirements for digital
Chief Executive Officer (CEO)	Overall responsibility for achieving the objectives of the organization	An ability to drive change at pace, particularly in strategy and business models
Chief Financial Officer (CFO)	Overall responsibility for all financial matters including accounting, financial reporting, and budgeting	Although most organizations will have regulatory requirements for frequency of reporting (usually annual or bi-annual), digital business demands that budgeting and feedback on financial performance occur in short cycles in order to respond rapidly to change and to gain feedback quickly New business models can also necessitate new ways to evaluate the potential value of investments
Chief Operating Officer (COO)	Overall responsibility for delivery execution and optimization	Recognize and use opportunities to leverage technology to improve delivery and optimize costs. See beyond a pure cost-cutting mentality and consider value creation and customer experience
Chief Technology Officer (CTO)	Responsibility for the technology strategy for the products and services delivered to customers	Drive the overall capability of the organization to leverage technology to achieve greater business success
Chief Information Officer (CIO)	Responsibility for internal IT and technology strategy	
Chief Market Officer (CMO)	Responsibility for all marketing and advertising activities	Act as the "voice of the customer" at the most senior level within the organization and ensure that everyone in the organization is relentlessly customer focused

- An evangelist for digital, promoting new technologies, practices, ways of working, and business models.
- The leader of a digital transformation project or program.
- The head of a team/department, building some or all of the digital solutions (typically new user interfaces for web/mobile).
- Someone with overall responsibility for making the organization "more digital."

To further complicate matters, many organizations are not clear on whether they see the CDO role as transitory (i.e., only necessary for a time-limited period until some benefit is realized) or as a permanent member of the organization's leadership team.

What should be clear from our description of the other roles, is that a CDO cannot be successful in any of these missions, without the support, buy-in, and commitment of the rest of the Executive Committee. For example, a CDO cannot successfully evangelize new ways of working, if the COO insists that everyone follows a specific process. Similarly, if their only remit is to build a thin digital veneer over existing products/services, then the benefits will be limited (Hall 2018; Daly 2017).

We believe that this is one of the reasons that we have seen the following anti-pattern occurring: A CDO is appointed, the CDO fails to deliver the hoped-for benefits, the CDO is blamed for the lack of benefits emerging and is removed from their position. In many of these cases, the CDO had neither the mandate nor the influence to successfully deliver the expected change. Often what was needed, rather than the addition of a CDO, was a change in (or a change in the approach used by) the CFO, COO, CTO, CIO, CMO, or even the CEO.

In summary, our advice regarding the appointment (or not) of a CDO is:

- Be clear about what you expect them to achieve.
- Consider whether they will have the mandate, influence, and budget required to deliver against expectations.
- Consider whether this scope really belongs to one or more of the other members of the Executive Committee.
- Potentially, rather than appoint a CDO, appoint a more specific role reporting into one of the Executive Committee members (e.g., VP Digital Transformation, VP Digital Solutions).

12.6 The Growing Emphasis on Ethics

The Chief Ethics Officer is another relatively new innovation, which recognizes the increasing importance of ethics within businesses. As we have seen in Part I, changing trends in society mean that there are not only more regulatory and legal requirements for businesses to operate in an ethical manner, but customers and staff are also now attracted to (or repelled from) companies based on their ethical credentials. In short, the ethical standing of an organization is no longer just a legal hygiene-factor or a nice-to-have, it has become a key factor driving company competitiveness.

12.7 Structuring Teams

Essentially there are two approaches to structuring teams within an organization (although they can be combined to create numerous different hybrids, as we will discuss later). Either you organize people based on what they do (a *functional* structure based on the skills people have and the activities they perform), or you organize them based on what they deliver (a *cross-functional* model based on the products they build or the services they provide).

12.8 Functional Organization

With a functional organization, teams will consist of people who share certain expertise and skills and perform similar activities. For example, in a car factory this would equate to having separate teams for engine, sheet metal, welding, and painting. For a software as a service company, it would equate to having separate teams for analysis, coding, testing, and support.

In a functional organization, delivering something of value to a customer (whether that be a specific car model or a new software feature) requires a complex interaction between each team of specialists. To achieve this, it is usually necessary to run a project or program of work, with some people (a project manager or project team) dedicated to coordinating the activities of each of the separate teams.

The main benefit of the functional model is efficiency from economies of scale, which are achieved via four main levers:

1. *Resource sharing*: By sharing resources (whether people or machines) between projects, a high degree of resource utilization can be achieved. For example, if there is not much testing to be performed on one project, then testers can work on another project instead.
2. *Knowledge sharing*: As people are organized by their specialisms, it is easier to enable knowledge sharing between them which, in turn, enables people to further develop their specialist skills.
3. *Standardization*: For example, it is easier to standardize on one method for welding car bodies, if all welding is performed by one team.
4. *Incentivization*: For people working in a functional area, it is usually easy to set personal targets (e.g., number of cars painted, number of test cases written) to drive performance for each team.

However, a functional organization usually achieves this efficiency at the expense of increased lead times (time taken from an initial customer demand to their need being met) and responsiveness (adaptability to change). The same four levers that drive efficiency can end up creating longer lead times and hindering responsiveness.

As resources are shared, the project team with the responsibility to deliver the overall solution will have to negotiate with each separate team over resources. In practice, there are usually many projects like this running in parallel in a large organization. Even with perfect planning, resources will sometimes have to be diverted without prior notice to address high priority unplanned work unrelated to the project they are assigned to. Furthermore, if a project is dependent on one department that happens to be especially busy at one point in time, then the project may be delayed: not because of the time taken to do the specific work for that project, but because of the length of time that the project must wait for resources to become available.

A team of specialists who share knowledge and standardize their practices may do so in a way that optimizes the performance of their team at the expense of the value delivered to customers. For example, they may see a benefit to using one tool (e.g., a saving on license costs), whereas individual projects could be delivered faster, more cheaply and more reliably, by using a range of specialized tooling.

Because the organizational hierarchy is not aligned with the delivery of value to the customer, there can be a gap between what the customer wants, and how people in each team are incentivized (explicitly or implicitly). For example, a helpdesk team may be more focused on optimizing its function (e.g., number of calls per agent per day), than on ensuring that the overall customer experience is positive.

12.9 Cross-Functional Organization

Whereas a functional organization is constructed based on people's skills, expertise, and the activities they perform, a cross-functional approach organizes people around the value that is delivered to the customer.

To expand on our previous examples, in a car factory this would mean a production line per model of car (first pioneered by Toyota and now universally accepted as the most effective approach for manufacturing).[1] For a software as a service company, it would equate to having separate teams for each product.

In order to build a cross-functional organization, you first need to understand what your organization does to bring value to the end customer (its value chain). Fundamentally, any business will use some raw materials, perform some value-adding activities and, in doing so, meet a customer need. While it is perhaps relatively easy to understand the value chain in, for example, a traditional manufacturing environment, for more digitally based enterprises it is not always so obvious. The raw materials can be data, the value adding activities can be created through analytics and AI, and the customer needs can be met digitally rather than physically (and may range from pure entertainment to life-saving insights). Furthermore, in multi-sided platform-based business models, customers may

[1]Note that even in the case of the recent innovation of "adaptive manufacturing lines", they are still organised around the creation of a product, rather than a function.

themselves also be the suppliers of raw materials. Nonetheless, understanding the key value chains inside your business is a pre-requisite to creating a cross-functional organization.

In a pure cross-functional organization, everyone needed to deliver a particular value chain will be part of the same team. By way of example, for a software company that builds three products, this would look as shown in Fig. 12.1.

As you can see, each team has every function present that it needs to deliver value to its customer(s). Note that, by itself, this model cannot be considered cross-functional, unless each team has the autonomy to decide how their respective activities should be executed. If every software developer in an organization has to follow a specific common process or use a particular technology, or if the HR processes are mandated to be the same for each team, then they are not truly cross-functional.

This is also only a cross-functional model if the value delivered to the customers is created by building the software. An alternative model for some businesses is to deliver value not through the sale of the core product, but rather through the customization, maintenance, and implementation of the product for specific clients. In this case, a cross-functional organization might look more like that shown in Fig. 12.2.

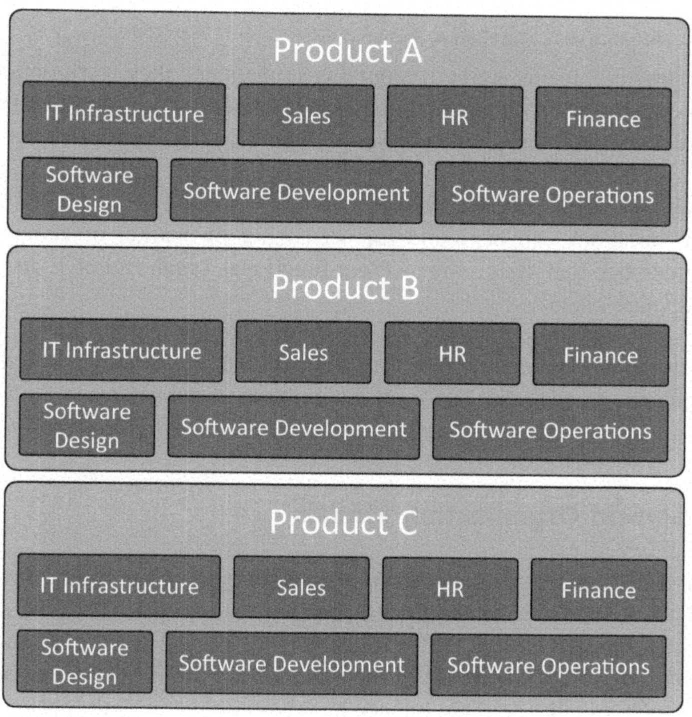

Fig. 12.1 Examples of cross-functional organization around products. Authors' own figure

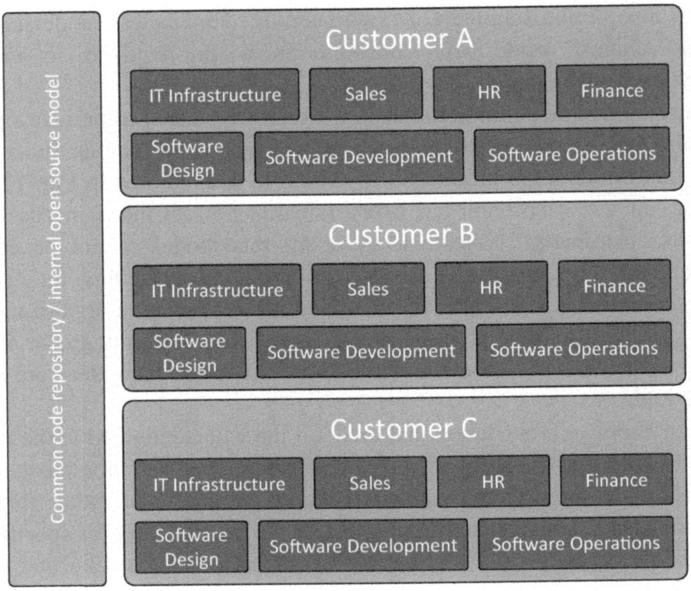

Fig. 12.2 Example of cross-functional organization around clients. Authors' own figure

In this structure, teams are built around customers and they work on a common product code base (using an internal open-source model). Often there will still need to be a small team to manage the product, but note that the customer teams are not dependent on the product team to deliver: They have full autonomy, control, and the capability to deliver for their client.

Similar variations can be found for organizing by market or geography, but always remember that it is only a cross-functional organization if its structure mirrors its value chains.

The benefits and disadvantages of cross-functional models are mirror images of those for the functional counterpart. Cross-functional organizations will tend to be more responsive to customer needs, at the expense of efficiency.

12.10 Hybrid Organization Models

In the cross-functional structures shown previously, you will probably have noticed that not all of the functions will necessarily be a key component of the value chain. For example, in a company building software products, it may be that the HR and Finance departments are not a critical part of the value chain. Similarly, it may be that the internal IT infrastructure does not impact the delivery of value to the customer. If this is the case, then a hybrid model makes sense, where people performing these functions

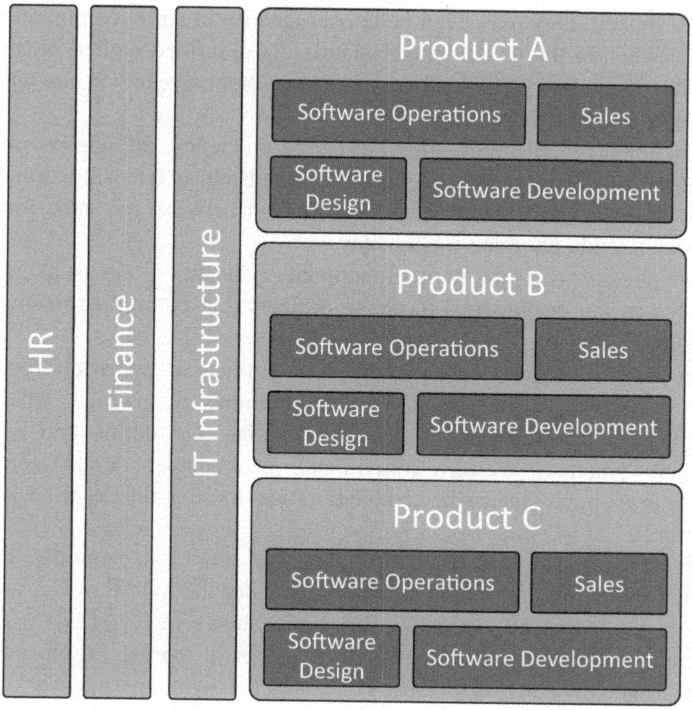

Fig. 12.3 Example of a hybrid organization. Authors' own figure

are structured into one team to gain the efficiency benefits of a functional organization, while cross-functional teams retain their independence for activities that primarily drive value for the customer (as illustrated in Fig. 12.3).

Note that these choices are very context dependent: If one of the product teams needs to recruit in a very different way (due to their location or the technologies that they use), and without this, they cannot deliver their products successfully to their customers, then organizing HR functionally may not make sense. A good way to help you decide if a function is a critical part of the value chain is to ask yourself whether a delay in any activity it performs could negatively impact the customer. If it won't, then it is unlikely to be a key part of the value chain.

12.11 Hierarchy and Cross-Team Collaboration

Whether you choose a functional, cross-functional or hybrid structure, as soon as you create teams you will, to some extent, create siloes: People will be more comfortable collaborating with people who are in the same organizational unit as themselves. Indeed, they may even be encouraged to do so by commercial models and targets (whether this is deliberate or not). As described earlier, creating these silos can have some benefit in the form of greater responsiveness to customer needs, or efficiency through economies of scale.

In a functional organization, silos can create efficiency, although sometimes to the detriment of responsiveness to customer needs. In a cross-functional organization, the reverse is true, as the lack of alignment between the same functions in different teams tends to create inefficiency.

We have already seen that, with a functional organization, the usual approach to deliver value to the customer is to create projects that coordinate resources from multiple teams.

With a cross-functional organization, the equivalent approach for crossing functional boundaries is the creation of communities of practice, which enable people with similar functions to share knowledge and define and agree with common good practices. We have found that a great enabler for such communities of practice is to have standardized collaboration tooling that is used across the organization.

The division of an organization into teams (or silos) will naturally lead to the creation of a hierarchy. For example, an org chart for the hybrid model we showed in Fig. 12.3 might typically look like the one as shown in Fig. 12.4.

This hierarchy gives a clue as to one of the main barriers to cross-team collaboration. Managers (such as the heads of product shown here) may seek to control access to the staff reporting into them. An example of a consequence of this is that a request from the Head of Sales for product A to the Head of Software Design for product B will have to go via the Head of Product A, the CEO and the Head of Product B (in an extremely hierarchical organization) or, at the very least, via the Head of Product B (in a less hierarchical one). This barrier can be psychologically quite significant and can easily be enough to prevent people from even trying to collaborate across teams. This, in turn, can lead to reduced initiative taking, reduced value being delivered to customers and large inefficiencies through duplication across functions in different silos.

We see that successful digital businesses seek to minimize this hierarchy effect in two ways: firstly, by keeping the levels of hierarchy to a minimum (i.e., larger teams with fewer layers); secondly, by implementing self-organization.

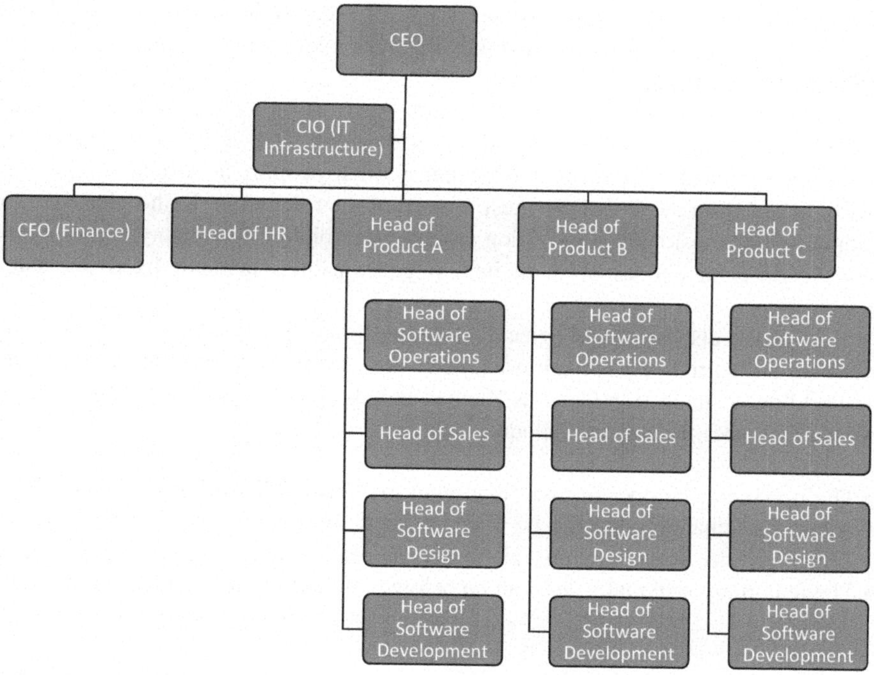

Fig. 12.4 Example of an organization hierarchy derived from a hybrid organization structure. Authors' own figure

12.12 Self-organizing Teams

Self-organizing principles can be applied both at the team level and/or at the organization level.

At the team level, the principle of self-organization is applied by allowing members of a team to self-select the tasks they work on. In order for this to be effective, there are four pre-requisites. Everyone on the team must:

1. Share a common vision and purpose.
2. Have a common view of what work needs to be done.
3. Mutually agree constraints that govern what tasks they can select (e.g., skills accreditation).
4. Have a clear view of what everyone else on the team is working on.

Only by sharing a common vision and purpose for what the team is trying to achieve can the members of the team reliably decide what they should work on in order to best achieve that goal. Our experience suggests that when employees have a high level of personal engagement with the team's mission, they will make good decisions about how they can best contribute. Conversely, we have also found that no amount of micro-management or detailed task allocation can compensate for a team that is disengaged.

A common view is needed of what work needs to be done. In a team context, this is usually referred to as a "backlog." It does not have to be fully prioritized; however, sufficient prioritization is needed so that people can select the tasks to work on based on those that are most in need of their attention. Rather than have a simple one-dimensional prioritization scheme from high to low, many teams prefer to have different classes of work item (e.g., expedite, standard, fixed due-date, non-urgent).

It is usually also helpful to agree a set of constraints that govern what people will work on. Sometimes this is manifested in a team charter, in "definitions of done," or in workflow visualization (such as Kanban boards). Such constraints help to guide people's choices. Examples include:

- The maximum number of tasks that team members will work on in parallel.
- A software change will only be released after it has been code reviewed.
- A high priority work item must always be chosen before a low priority work item.
- The maximum size that a task can be before it should be sub-divided into smaller tasks.

These constraints, when agreed and crystalized by the team, also give the team a rich set of levers to adapt and improve how they work together.

Finally, members of the team also need to have clarity about what other people are working on, in order to make good decisions about where they should focus their attention.

In practice, we have found that teams will adapt their ways of working when given these kinds of insights. For example, in one case, software deployment was a bottleneck and developers were quite willing to take on deployment activities when they could see that this was what was constraining delivery lead times. In another case, developers, an architect, and a test manager all picked up testing tasks to address a testing bottleneck, enabling the whole team to stay on track. We have also seen cases where team members volunteered to learn new technologies because they could see how it would alleviate a bottleneck.

Self-organization can also work at the macro level. In recent times, organizations like Lunar Logic, Haier, and Buffer have experimented with completely eliminating management hierarchy (sometimes called "extreme self-organization"). Lunar Logic (a software development company) reported that their "*financial results sky-rocketed*" (Daly and Brodzinski 2016) when they adopted this approach, something that they largely attributed to the increase in employee motivation that resulted from the increased autonomy.

Chinese appliance manufacturer Haier removed middle management and reorganized its 80,000 workers into 2000 self-managed teams (known as zi zhu jing ying ti or ZZJYTs). One example of this autonomy in action is their approach to launching new products and services (The Economist 2013):

> If ambitious employees spot an opportunity, they are free to propose an idea for a new product or service. A vote, which can include not just employees but suppliers and customers, decides which project goes ahead. The winner also becomes the project's leader. They form their team by recruiting from across the company; employees are free to join or leave ZZJYTs.

Since introducing this level of autonomy Haier has been judged the eighth most innovative firm worldwide. It has also seen a fourfold increase in revenue over 10 years and a sixfold increase in profits.

Buffer, who provide social media management tools, also achieved strong results, but have subsequently re-assessed their approach, concluding that "*The key realization was that people by nature have a unique place within Buffer that isn't created equal.*" (Widrich 2015)

It is recognized that if you remove a formal management hierarchy, then inevitably something else will fill the vacuum left behind (Compagne 2014):

> Without a formal structure, informal alliances will form, and soon enough you'll have replaced the formal structure with an implicit, hidden one that's much harder to change

Thus, organizations considering this radical approach must carefully define how the new approach will work. Example approaches include Holacracy (Holacracy 2015) and those described in Valve's employee handbook (Valve 2012).

Our view is that in most large organizations, at least in the interim, people will actually continue to be organized into teams and therefore there will be a corresponding hierarchical structure. However, as discussed previously, this structure should be designed to optimize for the delivery of value to the customer, it should be as flat as possible and, even then, it must be expected that people will collaborate frequently and openly with people from other teams. As Elon Musk put it: "*Anyone at Tesla can and should email/talk to anyone else according to what they think is the fastest way to solve a problem for the benefit of the whole company.*" (Bariso 2017)

Effective self-organization depends on a style of leadership that enables it. As described in the Leadership chapter, leaders must be able to articulate the core purpose of the company and their vision for the future so that all employees understand how they can best support these goals. When self-organization is successfully implemented, then we have seen that companies can achieve widespread and valuable collaboration across the firm to share ideas and information. It is also a factor that can make an organization more attractive to its employees as it gives them more opportunities to work across a number of topics and disciplines.

12.13 Recommendations

- *Review the roles and responsibilities of members of the Executive Committee.* Is everyone on the Executive Committee aware of how the demands of digital will impact their role? How are you addressing the increasingly intertwined objectives of the CTO and CIO? Have you made a conscious choice whether or not to appoint a CDO and, if you have appointed a CDO, have you clearly defined their remit ensuring they will have the support and resources to be successful?

- *Review your business value chain(s).* How does your organization deliver value to clients and how do you expect this to evolve in the future (taking into account our advice in the chapters on Strategy, Business Models and Platforms and Ecosystems)?
- *Understand your current organization structure.* Is it currently a functional (based on the tasks people perform and the skills they have), cross-functional (organized around your business' value chains), or hybrid model?
- *Identify how you might evolve your organization structure to better balance efficiency vs. responsiveness to customer needs.* Are there certain functions that are not a core part of your value chain(s) that could benefit from economies of scale? Are there current known pain-points in terms of long lead times and a lack of adaptability to changing market and customer requirements which might be addressed by implementing a more cross-functional structure?
- *Identify and bridge silos.* Which silos can you identify in your organization that in some way are limiting your business success? What mechanisms could you implement to increase the ease with which people can collaborate across these silos?
- *Implement self-organization at the team and macro level.* Are teams within your business enabling self-organization via the four pre-requisites we describe in this chapter? If some of these pre-requisites are missing, are they causing problems (e.g., people working on the wrong things) and, if so, how could you address them? Do you already apply self-organization principles? If not, how could you move toward a self-organizing model with a flatter structure and with greater autonomy for people to choose how they can best contribute to your company's purpose?

References

Bariso, J. (2017). This email from Elon Musk to Tesla employees describes what great communication looks like. Inc.com, 30/08/2017. https://www.inc.com/justin-bariso/this-email-from-elon-musk-to-tesla-employees-descr.html. Accessed 26 October 2019.

Compagne, O. (2014). Holacracy versus hierarchy versus flat orgs: actually, Holacracy is highly structured. Holacracy.org, 19/03/2014. https://blog.holacracy.org/holacracy-vs-hierarchy-vs-flat-orgs-d1545d5dffa7. Accessed 26 October 2019.

Daly, D. (2017). *Cargo cult digital transformation*. Atos, 03/11/2017. https://atos.net/en/blog/cargo-cult-digital-transformation. Accessed 26 October 2019.

Daly, D., & Brodzinski, P. (2016). *Giving a Damn*. devopschat.net, chat scheduled for 1st September 2016 @ 8 pm UK time. Accessible at http://devopschat.net/2016/08/02/1st-september-2016-giving-damn/. Accessed 26 October 2019.

Hall, J. (2018). Digital varnish—why we have only started to scratch the surface of the digital revolution. Atos, 05/11/2018. https://atos.net/en/blog/digital-varnish-started-scratch-surface-digital-revolution. Accessed 26 October 2019.

Holacracy. (2015). *Holacracy constitution version* 4.1. Holacracy.org, June 2015. https://www.holacracy.org/constitution. Accessed 26 October 2019.

The Economist. (2013). Haier and higher: The radical boss of Haier wants to transform the world's biggest appliance-maker into a nimble internet-age firm. The Economist, 11/10/2013. https://www.economist.com/news/business/21587792-radical-boss-haier-wants-transform-worlds-biggest-appliance-maker-nimble. Accessed 26 October 2019.

Valve. (2012). *Handbook for new employees*. Valve, March 2012. http://www.valvesoftware.com/company/Valve_Handbook_LowRes.pdf. Accessed 26 October 2019.

Widrich, L. (2015). What we got wrong about self-management: embracing natural hierarchy at work. Buffer. Originally written Aug 5, 2015. Last updated Aug 23, 2017. https://open.buffer.com/self-management-hierarchy/. Accessed 26 October 2019.

13 People—How Does a Digital Business Create and Engage with the Workforce of the Future?

The fact that a chapter on people appears relatively late on in Part II of this book, should by no means be taken as a measure of the importance that we place on the topic. Employees at all levels of an organization can be the biggest allies or the biggest blockers of transformation. Securing the buy-in and support of your staff at all stages of a transformation program is a critical success factor (as we describe in Part III).

In the digital world, the nature of work is experiencing a relentless revolution. An almost inevitable feature of most digital transformations will be some kind of automation, whether this is relatively formulaic robotic process automation or more sophisticated AI-enabled functions (e.g., virtual agents and recommendation engines). It is fascinating to see how such capabilities are maturing and consider the potential that is materializing, but it must be remembered that, when implemented, these capabilities will replace human jobs: Jobs that have previously helped to give individuals a feeling of worth.

Throughout history, industrial and technology revolutions have brought with them the fear that automation will lead to mass unemployment, but up 'til now that fear has not materialized. Instead, newer, higher-value roles have been created, bringing a growth rather than a decline in opportunity. Nevertheless, the transformation challenge is one of ensuring that individuals are able to be effectively reskilled for those new roles so that such opportunities can be exploited. This demands a deliberate program of sustained employee engagement to provide the tools and time to retrain. It also demands a clear leadership vision as to which skills are the ones that will be required in the future. As we saw in Part I, in a world where waves of technology development are landing at seemingly ever shorter intervals, anticipating and planning for future skills requirements is no easy task.

Ensuring a workforce of positive contributors demands having employees who are informed, equipped and enabled to do what is expected of them, and who feel motivated to carry out their daily tasks. Yet, particularly in times of business

H. Tardieu et al., *Deliberately Digital*, Future of Business and Finance,
https://doi.org/10.1007/978-3-030-37955-1_13

change, workforces can often find themselves ill-informed as to what is happening at a strategic level; ill-equipped to deal with new ways of working; and de-motivated because change and uncertainty are rarely seen as entirely positive.

So how can an enterprise successfully manage the transformation of its people?

13.1 Be Transparent

Firstly, two thought-provoking quotes:

> *A lack of transparency results in distrust and a deep sense of insecurity* – Dalai Lama.

> *Honesty and transparency make you vulnerable. Be honest and transparent anyway* – Mother Theresa

Transparency and truth are potent weapons in building trust, and they should be used habitually. Change usually brings fear about job losses, concerns over acquiring new skills, and uncertainty over aligning with different work cultures. Keeping people in the dark as to what is happening will only fuel the rumor mill and the negative "water cooler" chats, accelerating the inevitability of disengagement and even obstructive behavior. Targeted and timely communication will help counteract these negatives, but only if it is meaningful, understandable and actionable; it is easy to see through the corporate spin, inconsistent behavior, and condescending messaging.

We have observed transformations that were hailed by management as resounding successes. However, at a grassroots level the employees were totally unhappy, spending a significant part of their working day complaining about how they were being treated and trying to work out what on earth was going on. In these instances, there was a complete disconnect and lack of two-way communication, collaboration, and consultation between the different layers of the organization: Changes were imposed on people with no meaningful consultation and individuals were left to fend for themselves and draw their own conclusions as to what the future held.

On the other hand, being transparent nurtures meaningful feedback that will allow necessary adjustments to strategy that may otherwise be missed; it will make people feel like they are part of the solution and not just a part of the problem; it will help minimize the inefficient wheel-spinning that so often occurs when people do not know what they should be doing.

There may be occasions where transparency will reveal management vulnerabilities, but that is nothing to be ashamed of if positive leadership can be demonstrated in addressing those vulnerabilities. There will inevitably be certain strategic insights that cannot be freely cascaded throughout an organization, but be honest about things you cannot share and for which you don't necessarily have all the answers.

Transparency engenders trust, and trust engenders engagement. PwC in its 19th Annual Global CEO survey (Snowden et al. 2016) reported that employees who felt their leaders treated them with respect (i.e., trusted them) were 63% more satisfied with their jobs, 55% more engaged, 58% more focused, and 110% more likely to stay with their organization. Unfortunately, and conversely, a lack of trust in management is often identified in workplace surveys as a significant problem. Furthermore, most people leave their jobs because of their bosses and not because of the job itself. 93% of employees would be more likely to stay with their job if their bosses would show more empathy (Businessolver 2019).

13.2 Be Engaging

Research from the Hay Group has shown that businesses with highly engaged employees enjoy up to 30% better performance than those with low levels of engagement. The message is clear: If you want a high performing organization, make sure your employees are engaged with what you are trying to achieve. However, according to a 2018 Gallup State of the Global Workplace report (Harter 2018), only 15% of employees are engaged, 67% are disengaged, and 18% are actively disengaged, and that is across all businesses, not just those undergoing transformation. You should see your transformation program as an ideal opportunity to raise levels of engagement, by considering how you might:

- Put employees more in control of their destiny.
- Give employees the means to explore new opportunities and acquire new skills. Afford them the right to experiment and fail, but do so in a way that the impact of failure is minimized, and valuable lessons are learned. Note: this often works against established governance processes, so it calls for management as well as individual employees to be brave.
- Encourage regular two-way communications using a variety of channels. In particular, encourage open communication and collaboration across the boundaries of traditional organizational silos.
- Take the opportunity to find out what capabilities you really have in your organization (skills that may otherwise be hidden away).
- Identify new leaders and champions who will evangelize the future vision and strategy (such people may come from the most unexpected places). Make sure that your team of evangelists is appropriately diverse.

We have seen examples of good engagement where employees were encouraged to identify themselves as willing candidates for reskilling. This was done without prejudice, to avoid the fear that “sticking your hand up” would put you at the top of the redundancy list if things didn’t work out. The HR teams supported volunteers in identifying where they might best fit in the new skills framework, and employees were then provided suitable training courses to ensure they were properly equipped.

What's more they were then assigned mentors who were responsible for identifying opportunities for their new-found skills to be used and further developed. Needless to say, such initiatives are ideal ways for individuals to take responsibility for discovering their future talent fit.

Research has shown that companies that embrace employee freedom and control, typically achieve "engaged" levels for around 70% of their employees. This is exactly the kind of culture that transforming organizations need to establish.

In his book "*Drive: The surprising truth about what motivates us*" (Pink 2010), Daniel H. Pink highlights the need for intrinsic motivation when undertaking complex knowledge work. The three sources of intrinsic motivation are:

- Autonomy: having control over how you work and what you work on.
- Mastery: having the opportunity to learn and develop yourself.
- Purpose: finding meaning in your work that goes beyond monetary reward.

What we have learned from working with transforming organizations is that where there is a clear vision of where that organization is seeking to go, and where its employees are empowered to be actively involved in that journey, the workforce will typically be much more engaged. As a direct consequence, they will demonstrate the required levels of flexibility as their roles' transition to a new target state. Conversely, where there is a lack of clear vision and communication about change, there will tend to be resistance to that change, be it passive or active. We have seen situations where very significant investments in automation of business functions have failed, simply because the employees did not feel part of the solution and therefore resisted engaging in the necessary implementation process.

13.3 Embrace the Changing Nature of Work

From a skill and organization context, the starting point for transforming businesses is usually one that exhibits:

- Incumbent skill sets that are at risk of obsolescence.
- Rapidly growing demand for new scarce skills that are constantly evolving.
- Individuals holding established management positions who often have an incomplete appreciation of the potential of digitalization and the risks of failing to embrace it (such individuals will also tend to have little vested interest in wanting to change).
- Organizational and HR management models that are no longer fit for purpose.
- Managers and leaders who may have historically acted as trainers, coaches and mentors for "the way things are done round here," now themselves being coached and reverse-mentored by the new generation of "digital natives."

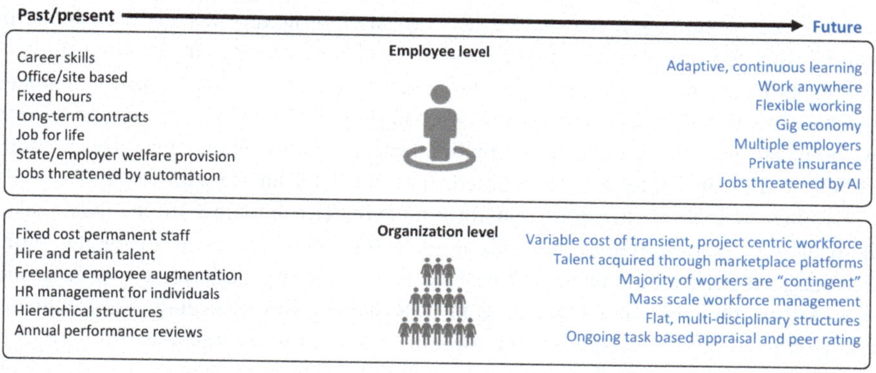

Fig. 13.1 Changing nature of work in the digital age. Authors' own figure

Change is inevitable whether or not it is welcomed and intentionally orchestrated.

There are several dimensions to people change both at the employee level and an organization level. The anticipated operational and behavioral shifts from the past/present to the future are summarized in Fig. 13.1. In the majority of cases, they represent significant changes to the people strategies currently pursued by most organizations, and hence, this part of your transformation demands significant focus, it cannot be dealt with as an afterthought.

There was an age when people took a job after leaving school or further education and then tended to stay in the same or similar job (hopefully with some career promotion steps) until they retired. This is demonstrated to some extent by the recent US statistic that gives the average tenure of workers in the 55–64 age bracket to be 10.1 years, more than three times the 2.8 year average for workers aged 25–34.

We would suggest that there are two main drivers behind this trend:

1. Younger workers aren't motivated by the same factors as previous generations. The goal of securing a job for life is superseded by that of achieving a good work-life balance and a sense of purpose beyond financial success. Only 12% of employees actually leave their job because they want more money (Source: CareerBuilder.com).
2. A growing need to regularly reskill. The half-life of skills[1] is dropping rapidly and is now widely reported to be only 5 years (in some technology areas it is even less). The mantra of "Learn at school, do at work" is no longer relevant. Regular reskilling is essential, and if this is not made possible within a given employment context, then what choice have people got but to change jobs?

[1]The period over which around half of a defined skill set is rendered obsolete by other advances.

Historically, having a reasonable level of staff turnover was no bad thing: it could bring new capabilities, fresh insights, and new energy. In an environment where skills are relatively portable and widely available, such turnover is manageable, but the skill demand profile is changing. Future skills requirements are evolving all the time leading to a situation where new skills are typically in short supply, and even if they can be sourced, they may not have much longevity.

Businesses that are digitally transforming have two choices: Either they make themselves so attractive to the job market that they have no problems with recruiting on-demand the latest and best skills, or they engage in an active program of reskilling their existing workforce in accordance with emerging requirements. We would suggest that the second option is the most sustainable one for the majority of organizations. However, while there are definite advantages in pursuing an active reskilling program, this must be seen as one which is properly aligned with the emerging business strategy and which will therefore lead to positive future opportunities. There must be buy-in from all parts of the organization, in the full recognition that there will inevitably be challenges with the internal restructuring of teams.

If people are not able to quickly and meaningfully apply their new-found skills, they will tend to lose what they have learned, or find themselves taking their new, highly marketable skills elsewhere. We have observed situations where individuals have been reskilled in key areas such as cloud computing or data science (sometimes under their own initiative), but their line managers would not release them from their legacy roles to a new area of the business. Needless to say, such an approach normally leads to two gaps needing to be filled: one in the new skill area and one in the legacy area! Unfortunately, we have seen this become a significant constraint to reskilling, with the short-sighted view being that of "As a manager, why should I invest in training programs, when I am personally unlikely to see any benefit, and will probably see pain?".

This calls for talent management programs that are driven from the very top of the organization where role flexibility and mobility are seen as the expected norm and even positively incentivized (see later comments in the chapter on KPIs). Such programs should look to clearly define and prioritize desired digital skills; assess people's backgrounds and create learning paths toward the target digital skills; assess people's willingness to retrain (you will find that some people are not willing to retrain); create a good mix of internal and third-party trainers; and define clear attainable goals and rewards (money, compensation, new positions, etc.). It may seem an obvious statement, but it must be recognized that many digital skills are quite technology-intensive and require both a solid level of core technology skills and a willingness on the part of the retrainee to engage. Retraining takes time (people don't become digital savvy after a one- or two-week course), so don't always expect immediate returns and be prepared to further invest in nurturing the skills acquired. Digital theory is not enough on its own, and there is a need to learn how to apply it to specific market demands and regulatory environments.

Disappointingly, retraining cost and time are often considered as an overhead (not an investment) by many organizations: it is one of the first discretionary spend items to be stopped when there is pressure to meet profitability budgets.

13.4 The Target Skills

One effect of the continually changing skills requirement is that it is virtually impossible to fully predict the roles that will be required in the medium to long term. The skills that will be required in 1–15 years may not be visible or understood today. This has significant implications not only for businesses, but also for the education system: What skills should schools, colleges, and universities be teaching in order to prepare its students for the future world of work? Who could have imagined, just 10 years ago, the need for roles like drone pilot, hologram designer, telemedicine doctor, or AI engineer? Or who would have predicted that long-established careers like administrators and accountants will soon drop off the list of in-demand skills?

Recognizing the fact that a number of repetitive, administrative roles are already, or will soon be, automated, we see a progressive shift in the skill sets demanded from new job applicants. Instead of searching for candidates with specific technical skills (which may quickly become obsolete), recruiters are looking for individuals who demonstrate what some would consider softer skills. The most in-demand individuals will be those who possess the skills that technology cannot easily replicate, and also those who are able to learn and adapt in a world of constant change.

Among the most essential future skill groupings, we see the following:

- Creativity, critical thinking, and complex problem solving.
- Wisdom, judgement, and cultural sensitivity.
- Leadership and communication.
- Adaptability, learning, and willingness to change.
- An ability to deal with information.
- A propensity to acquire and use specialist technical skills.

These are the kinds of skills that are hard to learn and hard to automate. They are the skills that will innovate the business models and technologies of the future and drive the next waves of change. They are the skills that will allow individuals to continually reinvent themselves and remain relevant in the future.

Don't assume that just because a skill appears to be connected to a digital technology, that it will maintain its relevance, even in the medium term. Some technologies are developing so rapidly that they are overtaken and become obsolete even before there is a chance to fully exploit them. Be prepared to continually evolve your employee's skills, and don't be afraid to change tack early, even though it may involve writing off some of your training investments. Keep in mind that skills which are capable of being automated or virtualized, probably will be (and sooner rather than later). Anticipate and prepare for long-term future skill iterations as well as currently emerging demands.

13.5 A Digital Strategy for People

A target model for people strategy is perhaps the most difficult to define in a transformation context. The problem is that we are all different. Many of those differences are to be encouraged in terms of positive benefits that properly managed diversity brings, but they also bring challenges with respect to how they can be effectively and efficiently managed as a coherent team, particularly in times of significant change. It is therefore not just the changing nature of skills that need to be considered, but changes in the way that those skills are engaged and applied.

With ubiquitous network connectivity and remote collaboration tools, work is less and less constrained by previously accepted physical boundaries:

- Homeworking is the expected norm, at least one day a week, for a whole range of roles that were previously office based.
- Desk spaces that were once considered to be personally assigned are now hot desks.
- Experts connect via video links through smart glasses worn by field engineers, guiding their remote colleagues to perform tasks that are above their inherent skillset.
- Chatbots and service desk agents perform call handovers with seamless precision.
- Defined shift times are replaced with flexible working arrangements.
- Corporate-issue IT equipment is now superseded by employees' own laptops, tablet s, and smartphones (so-called Bring Your Own Device or BYOD).
- Some individuals may find they spend their entire working day talking into their computers, meeting with dozens of people, but never engaging face to face.

New digitally enabled working styles may bring efficiency, and reduction in real-estate and travel costs, but this does not come without its problems. For example, homeworkers can often feel isolated and disconnected from the beating heart of the organization, creativity, and innovation are stifled, and personal development can become a promise that never materializes. In extreme cases, we have encountered individuals who have never met their line managers or immediate working team in person!

This is an untenable situation for businesses looking to transform their workforce into an engaged and motivated team. In a similar way that we observed in the chapter on Customers where leading businesses put their customers at the heart from an outward-looking perspective, here we also recognize that they should ensure that they put their employees at the heart from an inward-looking one.

Remember that engaged employees are significantly more productive than disengaged ones, so such approaches should not be seen as a cost burden, but as a guaranteed return on investment.

13.6 Equipping Your Team

A successful digital transformation, demands employees that are digitally equipped to do their work. Failure to have access to the right digital tools, applications or data will render most future digital roles impotent.

To help understand the people related forces that are at play (particularly for employees), it is useful to draw parallels with how individual consumer engagement with technology has evolved in the B2C space. It is largely these consumer experiences that are shaping employee expectations of IT in the workplace.

Positive digital consumer experiences and hence a perspective of "what good looks like" can perhaps be summarized as:

- *Ubiquity*: "so long as I have power and wi-fi, I expect to be able access whatever digital services I need."
- *Intuitive*: "I want to use digital applications that require little or no specialized training; it should be obvious what I have to do."
- *Autonomy*: "I am master of my own destiny in terms of choice of application and how I use it."
- *Robust*: "I expect IT to just work. If one bit fails, I will simply go and look somewhere else for a solution."
- *Easy*: "I expect digital processes to help me be more efficient. I do not expect them to be a painful chore."

Unfortunately, these expectations have traditionally been things that are difficult for corporate IT departments to live up to. This might be for a number of reasons:

- Corporate standards encourage a one-size-fits-all approach.
- Security and privacy considerations are often cited as a reason for blocking access to useful third-party applications.
- IT applications are often implemented to support the operation of established business processes, rather than to seek ways to adopt best practice in process digitalization.
- Internal governance, financial approvals, and general process latency often mean that corporate IT departments simply cannot operate with the flexibility and agility of external consumer services.

All this typically means that there is a significant disappointment gap between the corporate employee experience of IT and the private consumer experience of IT.

To make things worse, rather than embracing the expectations and skills of new employees, traditional businesses will tend to indoctrinate new employees in established ways of working. We have seen many examples of younger generation new starters who are well practiced in all manner of digital collaboration tools but who are expected to use corporate email solutions which are a complete anathema to them. Corporate IT functions are often seen as "the department of no!", a stance which often encourages individuals to go off and do their own thing through some kind of "shadow IT" initiative.

It is interesting to observe that many enterprises are choosing to delegate the problem of IT experience to employees themselves, by allowing them to bring their own technology (e.g., smartphones, tablets, and laptops). A set of company portal apps might be provided by corporate IT for accessing things like collaboration and admin tools, but beyond that the employee assumes full responsibility for ensuring their devices work. Of course, such models bring with them all kinds of challenges like data security and the rights of the employee to expect to be provided with appropriate tools to do the job. But could we be heading to the point where core IT equipment is such an integral part of everyday life, where bringing your own devices is seen as no different than bringing your own clothes?

Transforming businesses will need to decide just how far this freedom of choice extends. We have seen some businesses give employees choice over whether, for example, they use Gmail or Outlook as their corporate email interface; others allow different teams to select their own Agile development management tools. This kind of freedom of choice may seem to fly in the face of all conventional wisdom relating to corporate organization control, but for traditional businesses, the uncomfortable truth seems to be that employees that are given higher levels of individual and team autonomy are far more engaged and consequently far more productive and loyal.

13.7 Generational Shifts

In setting a strategy for people, it is important to recognize that we are facing significant generational swings in terms of the workforce population. By 2025, it is estimated that in the USA more than 55% of the workforce will represent Millennials and Generation Z (Fig. 13.2). These demographics exhibit quite different attitudes to life and work than many of their predecessors. They are natural networkers; have a propensity to share and co-innovate; they are more technologically fluent and more capable of multi-tasking; they love a challenge and are less risk averse.

Traditional management styles are not particularly well suited to get the best out of such individuals, so business cultures and ways of working will need to change in order to attract and retain Generation Z workers in particular.

New, transformed cultures need to consider things like:

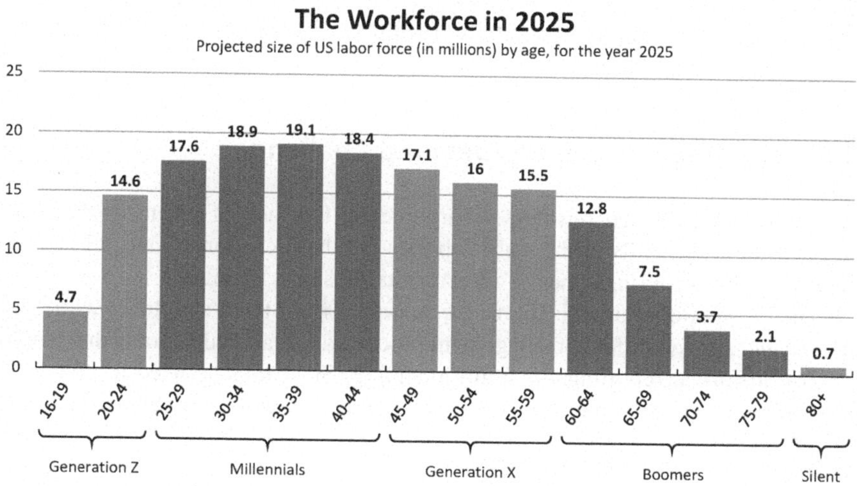

Fig. 13.2 Workforce in 2025—predicted size of US labor force by age. Based on chart from SelectHub (2019); *Data Source* Department of Labor

- *Workforce management*. How do you make this more agile and productive? Can you allow individuals to choose the tasks and assignments that they work on? (Please refer to self-organization within the chapter on Organization Structure).
- *Pay structures and appraisals*. How can they properly reflect the "digital worth"[2] of individuals, particularly in environments where having salaries linked to length of service rather than relevant skill sets makes no sense. There are some notable examples of digital businesses that use peer rating of employees to determine what each of them is worth to the organization.
- *Should people be paid by output rather than input*? Would this mean an end to the often-meaningless measure of time-sheet recording (just because I can show that I have been working for 37 h, does not mean I have been proportionately productive). There are perhaps some lessons to take from digital disruptors like Uber: Their "Gig economy" model allows workers to choose the way they work and they succeed or fail on the basis of the outcomes that they deliver. This gig principle of choosing when you work and how you work might also be applied to permanent employment roles and, in some ways, is reflected in the growing number of instances of business offering "unlimited holidays": employees have the ultimate choice of when and how they work.
- Does the organization structure reflect traditional management roles, or does it recognize the importance of leaders, who usually function at their best when not constrained by the overhead of governance and administration?

[2]The total sum of the value of the digital assets and competences of an individual or organization.

- *How can flexible ways of working be used to help balance supply and demand fluctuations*? This can be particularly helpful during times of transformation.

13.8 The Ongoing Supply/Demand Challenge

Even in well-established business environments, the task of ensuring the availability of the right skills at the right capacity can be a challenge, and this is very much exacerbated during times of fundamental business change.

In many traditional organizations, we see quite rigid team structures with cumbersome and slow workforce management processes and analytical tools that tend to focus on historical reporting for future planning. Such models need to change in almost all of their aspects, but we see four main areas of focus (as shown in Fig. 13.3):

(1) Recruitment and retraining strategy

   – The focus needs to be on building predictive models that intelligently anticipate resource requirements based on a variety of data feeds that go beyond traditional HR metrics. They should include, for example, sales plans, market trends, and customer strategies.

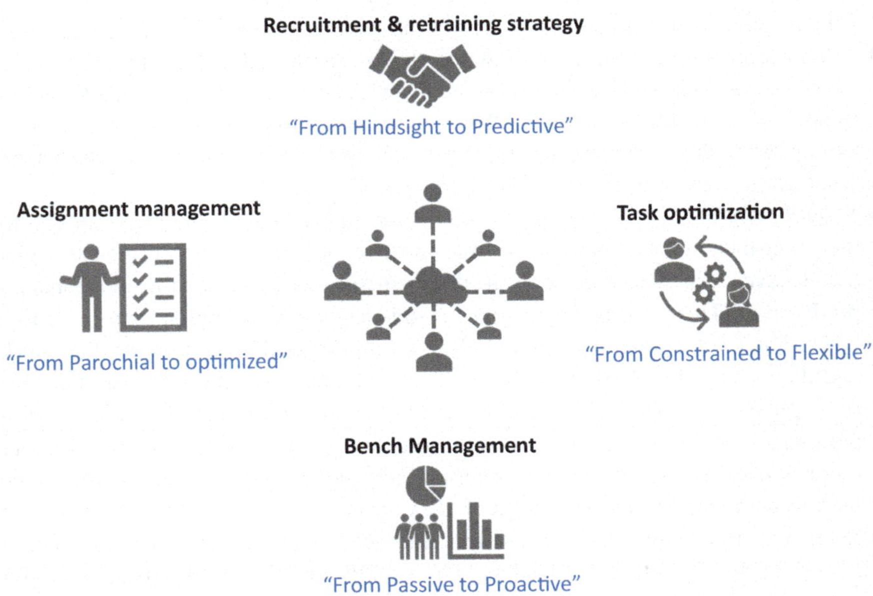

Fig. 13.3 Workforce management transformation. Authors' own figure

- There should be a clear policy for retraining and upskilling in advance of medium to long-term demand materializing.
- Be bold in building future capabilities, even though resources may not be immediately fully productive; leaving this until the last minute will be too late.

(2) Assignment management

- Ensure that you are aware of latent skillsets within your teams. Implement mechanisms for allowing people to work beyond the scope of their assigned skill boundaries. Seek to nurture "expert generalists" who are able to exhibit much greater role flexibility than "parochial specialists." Allow individuals to manage their own profiles within a common skills database.
- Use digital tools to augment employee capabilities and turn "smart hands" into experts. For example, a utilities field engineer with video or augmented reality communication links to a remote subject expert can be guided through maintenance tasks that would otherwise demand costly follow-up site visits.
- Create (virtual) multi-functional teams to avoid wasteful handovers between siloed divisions. (Please refer to chapter on Organization Structure).
- Use analytics and simulation tools to optimize assignments through, for example, minimizing travel time, or avoiding two specialist resources where one generalist would do.

(3) Bench management

- Recognize that especially during times of transformation, resources may not be fully utilized. Maximize these opportunities to encourage reskilling, job shadowing, and supporting internal transformation activities.
- Make sure that organization policies, targets, and incentives do not constrain the ability to make flexible use of bench resources.

(4) Task optimization

- Where possible, focus more on task allocation than assignments (i.e., shift from input-based to outcome-centric models).
- Allow individuals a degree of autonomy in terms of task selection. A gig economy-type model could be of help here, where work opportunities are presented, through a platform, as potential tasks for people holding the required skillset.

– Align individual incentives and measures so as to encourage employees to proactively maximize their contribution to business outcomes.

There is not likely to be a one-size-fits-all solution to the above approaches, but it is important to have a commonality of taxonomy across various tools and data sources that you might use (i.e., there is little value in having a sales forecast model that has skills demands described in a different way to the assignment management system). Keeping things simple and engaging for employees is a key to successfully transforming workforce management.

13.9 The Rise of the Gig Economy

90% of net new jobs in last 5 years were "off-balance sheet" (World Economic Forum 2018). An increasing proportion of the workforce is now made up of contingent workers or so-called gig workers.

The contingent model is a useful one, particularly in transformation programs when managing skill demand can be especially problematic. Just as cloud computing has allowed easy scale up and down of compute and data storage capacity, so contingent workers can be used to fill gaps in your people-based operational capability. However, you should consider the following:

- Use the gig model of defining output measured tasks rather than open-ended time and material engagements.
- Build an ecosystem of trusted gig workers that you can on-board to new tasks as efficiently as possible. You might achieve this through workforce management partners.
- Do not view contingent workers as an excuse to avoid reskilling your permanent employees.
- Be strategic in the skills that you deem as transient and ones which you view as core (or differentiating) for your business. Avoid satisfying core skill demand through contingent workers.
- Manage contingent worker demand as an integral part of an overall talent management program to ensure that, wherever possible, you are able to use internal resources first.

The gig economy is viewed by many with great skepticism. Concerns over employee rights, zero-hour contracts and lack of access to normal employment benefits are all seen as reasons for not embracing the model. However, just as we anticipate a steady shift to servitized (as a service) business models, so we expect human resources to be increasingly employed, measured, and rewarded on the basis of defined tasks and outcomes.

You will have hopefully gleaned from reading this chapter that the transformation of your people is probably the most complex part of an aspiring digital leader's journey. There is no "one-size-fits-all" answer and perfect solution. But, people (their values, attitudes, visions, etc.) are largely what defines the DNA of an enterprise. In many ways, if you can drive the necessary changes throughout your workforce, the rest will follow. When reskilling (in both soft and technical skills), seek an optimal balance that considers several dimensions: cost, opportunity, time, and societal impact. As a leader, be prepared to lead by example in learning and championing new technologies and working models, acting as both a mentor and a mentee.

13.10 Recommendations

- *Identify how you can make your organization more transparent.* What could you do to enable everyone in the company to have a clearer view of why and how decisions are being made, what the impact will be for them, and how they relate to your business purpose?
- *Assess the impact of the changing nature of work.* How will the changing nature of work impact your business and its staff? What do you need to do now to fully take advantage of this or mitigate against is (as appropriate)? Consider this, both at the employee level and at the organizational level.
- *Equip your people with the mindset, tools, and skills to do their job effectively.* Are you already aware of which people or parts of your organization do not have the requisite mindset, tools or skills to perform well in their role? How are roles in your organization expected to change to meet the demands of digital and how can you ensure that people will receive training and support for this? Think about not only whether people have the tools needed to do their job, but also are these tools the "right tools" and are they able to get the most out of them?
- *Understand the generational make-up of your workforce.* Assess the current generational make-up of your workforce and consider how you expect that to evolve, especially considering the future strategy of your company. What can you deduce from this about the current and future expectations that your employees are likely to have? What will need to change in the way you attract, manage, incentivize, and reward your employees?
- *Identify your current pain-points in terms of people and skills, considering how they are likely to change in the future.* What mechanisms could you implement now, and in the future, to better ensure that you have the right people available at the right time? Could you apply gig economy principles (either internally or externally)? What barriers do you see to having less rigid team structures and a more flexible workforce? How could you overcome them?

- *Take a balanced approach to creating your future workforce.* Reskill intentionally where appropriate; partner where necessary; engage university students to inject a fresh "learning" generation; and build a trusted network of contingent workers as a catalyst for flexibility and responsiveness to changing demand.

References

Businessolver. (2019). *2019 State of workplace empathy*. Businessolver. https://www.businessolver.com/resources/state-of-workplace-empathy#gref. Accessed October 26, 2019.

Harter, J. (2018). *Dismal employee engagement is a sign of global mismanagement*. Gallup blog. https://www.gallup.com/workplace/231668/dismal-employee-engagement-sign-global-mismanagement.aspx. Accessed October 26, 2019.

Pink, D. H. (2010). *Drive: The surprising truth about what motivates us*. Canongate books Ltd.

Selecthub. (2019). https://selecthub.com/hris/workforce-management/workforce-management-software-market/. Accessed October 26, 2019.

Snowden, S., et al. (2016). *Redefining business success in a changing world CEO survey*. PwC. https://www.pwc.com/gx/en/ceo-survey/2016/landing-page/pwc-19th-annual-global-ceo-survey.pdf. Accessed October 26, 2019.

Innovation—Recipes for Staying Ahead of the Competition in a Digital World

14

14.1 Innovation in the Context of Digital Transformation

Innovation originates from the Latin term "*innovāre*" which quite literally means "to change something by introducing a novelty." Innovation is not invention, where something new is created, and it is not an improvement, where something already being done is done better. Innovation is the introduction of an invented novelty into an existing good, service, or process with the objective of making it better but also different.

The use of innovation as a business term is in certain decline, after having been notoriously hyped in the first 15 years of this century. However, there is evidence that "*organizations that are consistently successful at managing innovation out-perform their peers in terms of growth, financial performance, and employment, and that the broader social benefits of innovation are even greater*" (Tidd and Bessant 2018). Therefore, innovation continues to be the key source of renewal for organizations. The declining popularity of the term only means that other, more fashionable terms are being used instead, sometimes ambiguously (e.g., change, transformation, etc.).

What have radically changed in the last 20 years are both the purpose and the context of innovation. In the last quarter of the twentieth century and early years of the twenty-first, there was a certain climate of complacency: geopolitical stability; a booming economy (even if punctuated by occasional crises); a markedly slower pace of change (in technology and consumption patterns among others); economic and financial models that were both consolidated and well-functioning; a certain appetite for risk; and so on. The business context was stressful, of course, but not plagued with disruptions. Businesses mostly feared a relatively slow death at the hands of their competitors, not sudden disruption coming from beyond their visible radar screen.

As we described in Part I, organizations now operate in the confluence of the post-crisis scenario and the acute need to undergo digital transformation. The challenge is significant: mastering the necessary transformation requires investing more

H. Tardieu et al., *Deliberately Digital*, Future of Business and Finance,
https://doi.org/10.1007/978-3-030-37955-1_14

and investing differently than in times of more stability. However, the post-crisis scenario is marked by much tougher economic, financial, and business conditions: low inflation, zero interest rates, excessive levels of public and private debt, and quite acute risk aversion in business, among others. Organizations need to innovate more and better, at precisely the time when risk aversion and cost contention plague decision making.

14.2 The Conundrums of Innovation

Individually and collectively, humans tend to display resistance to change. This trait has a healthy side to it, likely a product of the natural selection process that has brought us this far as a species: novelties need to prove their worth, in terms of greater benefits and equal or fewer side-effects than existing things.

Overcoming resistance to change is probably the key challenge of innovation. This is especially true in business, where objectives are ambitious, deadlines tight, and competition hard. If we add the context of digital transformation, executives now find themselves in front of more than one conundrum when it comes to leveraging innovation for the sake of business transformation. Let's examine a few:

Openness. Open Innovation seems more difficult to manage. It is potentially costlier, or at least the costs seem to be less clear and contained. It requires more careful and attentive management of intellectual Property. On the other hand, traditional (closed) innovation seems less promising for certain goals, since it is poorer in terms of skills, it is less diverse, it leverages less "brainpower," and it is more contaminated by internal fears, beliefs, and biases.

Investment effort. A significant number of investments are considered non-core, superfluous, or "a waste", at least when viewed with the excessive short-term perspectives now prevalent. On the other hand, not investing is a sure way to achieve nothing and may generate very negative perceptions in the market (customers, analysts, investors, etc.). To complicate things further, positive disruptions tend to be born out of investments that are initially considered non-core or simply strange.

Degree of ambition. Ambitious innovation (such as Google's "moonshot s"[1]) can be (or can be perceived as) too costly, too risky, too disruptive for "business-as-usual" corporate structures and processes. On the other hand, if innovation is not ambitious enough, why do it at all? After all, digital transformation and disruption require that extra dose of ambition, compared to more traditional innovation.

Time. Blinded by excessive concern with the short term, organizations place too much emphasis on "quick wins," and innovation is no exception. However, short innovation investments usually render only small, incremental results. What is worse, if the innovation becomes disruptive and is realized quickly, it may hurt the

[1]"Moonshot thinking" refers to choosing a huge problem that requires disruptive, non-conventional approaches to be successfully solved.

organization! In contrast, longer innovation investments tend to hold the promise of deeper, more disruptive results, at the expense of higher and/or more sustained investments, longer payback, etc.

Client-centricity. Client-agnostic innovations are perceived as narcissistic and less (or not at all) aligned with actual client needs, and they are therefore more difficult to introduce successfully in the market. However, client-centric innovation is not exempt from risks. For example, it may lead to the innovator's dilemma (please refer to chapter on Strategy) or, as the probably apocryphal Internet meme puts in Henry Ford's mouth, "if I had asked people what they wanted, they would have said faster horses" (Vlaskovits 2011).

As conundrums tend to induce immobility, it is better to address them and take action, even at the risk of failing, than to freeze in indecision. After all, failure can be skillfully managed into being fast, bounded, and conducive to learning.

14.3 Methodologies and Other Innovation Traps

Organizations can be confused by the abundance of design and innovation methodologies and by the claims made about their effectiveness. Approaches like Agile, Design Thinking, global innovation management technology, lean start-up, lean enterprise, open innovation, stage-gate process, human-centered design, crowdsourcing, Double Diamond, and Deep Dive, all have their advantages and disadvantages, their advocates and detractors. However, methodologies are just tools, a means to an end. Efforts should be focused on making sure that progress is achieved in accordance with the strategy (at corporate, digital, and innovation levels), and on avoiding common traps, some of which we list below.

The Theology of Methodology

The first trap organizations encounter is precisely that of engaging in wasteful, non-productive discussions (often dogmatic arguments) about which methodology to follow. Thus, the effort goes into debating how things should be done instead of actually doing them. Avoid these sterile debates in your organization. Assess the main characteristics of methodologies against your objectives, strategy and culture, and get the ball rolling.

Short-Cutting Methodology

Make sure you understand which facets of a given methodology are optional or adaptable to your organization, and which are non-negotiable. For example, some methodologies require the exclusion of certain levels of management from brainstorming processes, committing to invest in at least one grassroots project (decided bottom-up by employees), or allowing ad hoc teams to spend a substantial part of their time (more than 15%) on an innovation project. Adhering to non-negotiable facets will bear results but may entail some growing pains or risk taking. Neglecting such facets will likely lead to achieving the same kind of results you would get without the methodology, and/or a decrease in team morale.

The Killing Process

While methodologies are beneficial for focusing and channeling efforts by avoiding anarchic or haphazard approaches, they can be double-edged swords. Many innovation methodologies include expansive phases and convergent phases. In the former, barriers are eliminated to maximize freedom, creativity, abundance of ideas, and out-of-the-box thinking. In the latter, constraints are added to filter ideas into a more manageable number, favoring convergence and condensation. Unfortunately, it is very common that convergent phases eliminate all outliers, which include (apparently) stupid and unfeasible ideas together with truly disruptive and game-changing ones. Make sure you keep an eye on this and introduce measures to rescue potential diamonds from the innovation dustbin.

The Blame Game

One of the main inhibitors of innovation is a negative corporate reaction to certain initiatives and perhaps even teams. It is not very rational behavior, but it is quite common in organizations. Risk aversion and cost contention create a climate of nervousness, which may result in a backlash against investments that do not succeed (either at all or soon enough). The backlash may be directed at the topic or at a team, and usually translates into negative labeling: "*X* is a useless technology," "let's never spend a penny on *Y* again." This kind of behavior is very harmful: it makes learning impossible, it constrains growth possibilities by forbidding topics at a generic level, and it inhibits people's innovation attitude. The blame game is more frequent in organizations with an old-fashioned culture, or those where innovation is more of a patchy succession of one-off projects than a well-structured, well-governed, and well-managed strategic affair.

The Self-defeating Team

The innovation team can inadvertently inhibit their very goal and purpose. With the wrong governance and structure, the innovation team quickly turns into a box in the org chart. Consequently, "innovation" becomes whatever is done in that box, excluding and being disconnected from whatever is done in other parts of the organization. Make sure you have the right kind of structure and governance. Favor small innovation teams that have the mandate to inspire and facilitate, so that innovation can happen potentially everywhere in the organization.

Innovation as an Exotic Function

Innovation must exist as a core corporate function, like Finance or Marketing. It must not be secondary or isolated. Perhaps more than other functions, Innovation must run in perfect sync with top management, other corporate functions and business divisions: innovation must happen everywhere and its effects should be potentially disruptive (positively so, but disruptive nevertheless) for all parts of the organization. However, in some organizations, Innovation is a secondary function and/or does not run in perfect sync with others. When this happens, it is perceived as an exotic add-on and its results are neglected or resisted by the organization. Remember that "*organizations have habits and they'll stick to their habits even at the risk of their own survival*" (Anderson B, communication). Ensure you gain co-ownership and buy-in of all stakeholders in your innovation activities.

The Difficulty of Managing Innovation

Innovation is the kind of activity that mixes hard and soft aspects quite uniquely. It combines skills in mathematics, science, engineering, administration, and management, with skills in negotiation, communication, influencing, and persuasion. Its effects (primary and secondary, positive and negative) are often not fully predictable, since the activity takes place in fast-moving and uncharted territories. Practitioners may fall into the trap of favoring the soft side excessively, which may lead to results that are not not-fully working or are somewhat shallow. Conversely, it may be the hard side that is excessively favored, possibly leading to results that are misaligned with business, solutions that are looking for problems, or outcomes that suffer a lack of buy-in. One of the key difficulties of innovation management, that of justifying its return on investment (ROI), is covered later in this chapter.

Beware of Innovation fads

There are potentially many fads in innovation, so we will focus on a few of them that are especially relevant for digital transformation programs. Firstly, we must clarify that they are fads, not hoaxes or "snake oil." They may work totally or partially, and you may find them to be essential building blocks in your transformation effort. However, they are the subject of intense crowd enthusiasm while their goodness and benefits have not been properly researched and proven, at least not yet. Therefore, they could be adopted based on expectations that may prove unfounded once appropriate research is conducted. As the Latin adage goes, *caveat emptor*[2]: be cautious when adopting them, in case their benefits are not exactly as portrayed, or there are hidden costs to factor into the decision process.

Crowdsourcing

Crowdsourcing is a model in which certain activities are sourced to a large group of experts or users, mostly external to the organization. It received a lot of attention in the 2000s, when a number of successful experiences were reported. The model was considered key for enabling organizations to tap into the wisdom of the crowds: a vast and valuable resource outside the corporate perimeter.

In the case of innovation, crowdsourcing has been used for ideation activities and innovation contests. It can be interesting for certain activities, but its shortcomings (often downplayed) must be factored in. Among others, organizations tend to underestimate the necessary (and often substantial) management effort and tooling required to set clear goals and processes, ensure fluent communications, assess progress, manage potentially abundant and disparate feedback, and manage low-quality contributions. A significant portion of management effort can be outsourced through the use of available applications and platforms, but then costs, service level agreements, confidentiality, and other critical points must be evaluated.

Organizations must also address issues such as: the risk of bias in the skillset of the crowd; the lack of ascendancy over the crowd and how to react if the initiative deviates from the plan; the careful definition and implementation of reward or compensation mechanisms; and the balance between openness and confidentiality, as well as managing and communicating intellectual property aspects. For the latter, crowdsourcing can be adequately dimensioned and sourced among people within an organization and trusted third parties (such as partners, providers, or customers).

[2]Let the buyer beware.

Intrapreneurship

Intrapreneurship promises to unleash the entrepreneurial spirit and skills of employees in mid- and large-sized organizations. While being employees, intrapreneurs can propose novel, potentially disruptive ideas, and obtain resources (time, money, skills, and providers) to lead them to fruition. If successful, this paradigm unites the best of two worlds: the risk-taking attitude, extreme passion and out-of-the-box thinking of entrepreneurs, and the loyalty, confidentiality and business alignment of in-house affairs.

The reality of intrapreneurship, however, is far from rosy. The realities of the in-house environment usually outweigh the promises of freedom of movement within an organization. In particular, truly disruptive ideas are often killed during the pre-launch decision process or are subject to excessive scrutiny if they survive it. Intrapreneurs may find themselves between a rock and hard place, as their project competes for attention and dedication with day-to-day tasks, often creating friction with their line managers. If the idea pursued is truly disruptive, organizations (especially large ones) will react quite strongly against it. Also, the expected freedom of movement will not materialize as the processes and bureaucracy of the organization are imposed on the intrapreneur and its internal start-up.

Andrew Corbett has summarized the situation well: "*...no single individual, no matter how brilliant, can take a game-changing innovation all the way from idea to reality. Innovation has to be a company-wide endeavor, supported from top to bottom by systems, structures, and a company culture that nurtures transformative ideas and products. Companies need to institutionalize innovation rather than expect it to simply flow forth from intrapreneurs operating within existing structures.*" (Corbett 2018)

Open Innovation

Open innovation has been defined as "*a distributed innovation process based on purposively managed knowledge flows across organizational boundaries, using pecuniary and non-pecuniary mechanisms in line with the organization's business model*" (Chesbrough and Bogers 2014). By engaging relevant and trusted stakeholders in a well-organized innovation ecosystem, it promises a richer and more fluent path to innovation. Some of the shortcomings of crowdsourcing also apply to this model: management complexity, ownership and management of Intellectual Property, compensation and/or joint commercialization, etc.

After researching the realities of open innovation, Tidd and Bessant conclude that "*The proponents of open innovation tend to offer universal, and often universally positive, prescriptions whereas research suggests that the specific mechanisms and outcomes of open innovation models are very sensitive to context and contingency. This is not surprising because the open or closed nature of innovation is historically contingent and does not entail a simple shift from closed to open as often suggested in the literature.*" They add that "*the empirical evidence on the utility of open innovation is limited, and practical prescriptions overly general*" (Tidd and Bessant, op. cit.)

Business Model Innovation

Innovating the business models of the organization is one of the main objectives of digital transformation, so any elements of fad in business model innovation must be exposed for explicit investigation and debate.

Teece states that "*the 'business model' defines the way the company creates and delivers value to customers, and then captures a portion of this value to make profit and grow*" (Teece 2010). Therefore, business model innovation goes far beyond the definition of new products and services (which can take place in non-transformational, business-as-usual portfolio management) and focuses on new ways of creating value and novel revenue models.

In the previously cited article, Tidd and Bessant conclude that "*...perhaps too much of the current BMI* [business model innovation] *research adopts a narrow goal on how best to capture value, often downstream in the process, and typically in a business environment. Consequently, there have been a proliferation of typologies and case studies, but fewer significant insights into how innovation can create and capture value in different contexts. In contrast, innovation research and practice might benefit from a deeper focus on the capabilities and mechanisms which create value, in a broader range of commercial and social contexts*" (Tidd and Bessant, op. cit.)

In previous chapters, we have addressed digital business models, with an emphasis on servitization and platforms. The key take-away of this section is to realize that current and future research is likely to uncover new value creation and delivery models, perhaps outside the business environment, which can be adapted or serve as inspiration for additional transformation initiatives.

14.4 The Elusive Return on Innovation Investment (ROII)

We have mentioned the topic of ROII in the section on "Methodologies and other innovation traps," and we examine it here in more detail.

As with any type of investment, the return on innovation investment is a key indicator of critical importance during the decision-making process. With (ideally) abundant innovation ideas and always-limited investment budgets, the ROII is critical for go/no-go decisions, and for prioritizing pre-approved investments. The difficulty lies in the elusive nature of the ROII. Unlike its non-innovation counterparts, the ROII is often difficult to arrive at and validate because it needs to be based on necessarily uncertain factors: the maturity timelines of a number of technologies, yet-unknown interactions among novel technologies, uncertain adoption curves and timescales, societal and individual adoption or rejection models, etc.

Some argue that the very concept of ROII makes no sense. In general, it is based on so many wild estimations that its validity is nearly null, and this is truer the more disruptive the investment is. Kromer proposes discarding the ROII and understanding innovation as a financial option. Thus, innovation is like health insurance for a company, it has value if you make use of it, and it has value even if you do not exercise it. Investing in innovation is investing in the option to launch a new business, even if it might fail or we decide against it in the long run, the option still has value (Kromer 2015)! After all, not investing in innovation is equivalent to embracing decay and accelerating the path to obsolescence, maximizing the chances that some other organization will disrupt you.

Enjalbert and Vandi argue that there is no such thing as Innovation ROI, stating that "...*in our digital world, innovation covers too various types of endeavors to be tracked by a single definition of success. From improving your current products and services to exploring new markets, to digitalizing internal tools and processes, there is not one single way of measuring the ROI of innovation.*" (Enjalbert and Vandi 2018). Their claim is based on the sheer diversity of initiatives that may be conducted under the umbrella label of "innovation". However, they go on to propose the creation and management of an Innovation Portfolio with properly defined KPIs to deal with the diversity and complexity of innovation projects.

Even if these claims are quite correct, most analysts, consultants, and relevant stakeholders continue publishing methods of ROII calculation (Grajewski 2013; Kolk and Eagar 2014) and books on gauging the value of innovation (Phillips and Phillips 2018), mostly because CEOs and Boards keep requesting them. In spite of it, ROII calculation creators tend to explicitly highlight the special difficulties of the endeavor.

Interestingly, Accenture have reported a decrease of ROII in 2014–2018, in spite of increased innovation spending, which they attribute to non-core, ad hoc innovation efforts, and to an innovation mindset more focused on technologies than on business challenges and opportunities (Ross 2019).

We suggest maintaining a healthy dose of skepticism on ROII figures, given the imponderables often involved in their estimation. It is not unusual to see corporate ping-pong exercises where ROII calculations bounce back and forth between innovation teams and Finance teams, often in search of a figure that will satisfy executives, no matter how unrealistic. Such exercises clutter approval decisions and the posterior monitoring of investments.

14.5 Innovation for Digital Business

Digital Business requires a different style of innovation for several reasons:

- The pace of technology development drives all market sectors to reduce their time to market for offering new features.
- Servitization inherently requires frequent novelties to keep the service attractive, particularly when competitor service comparisons are relatively easy.
- The adoption of Agile development and DevOps as the necessary approach to deliver new applications drives the installation of new features at every sprint, putting them into operation on a daily or weekly basis. This acceleration of development pace gives the overall feeling of always being in beta mode, while quality still needs to be there to avoid customer drop out.

None of these are comfortable bedfellows with the task of managing and maintaining legacy environments and business models, where typically the prevailing attitude is one of minimum disruption and risk. Delivering digital levels of innovation is likely to be seen as too difficult a task for traditional IT departments. In any case, innovation ideas are increasingly driven by the business and not IT. Therefore, two options can be considered:

1. Delegate the digital service developments to external teams, generally start-ups, which will bring new ideas for business models and implement processes to deliver the new services.
2. Create new internal teams with a responsibility for digital innovation.

The first option requires a strong internal ability to control the task performed by the start-ups to avoid the risk of becoming entirely dependent on an external player. Although it has merit for encouraging "out-of-the-box" innovations, our previous considerations on open innovation and crowdsourcing apply.

The second option raises the problem of coexistence with the organization's IT department and the alignment with existing legacy applications used internally and by customers. Addressing this problem is the primary objective of digital transformation through optimization of existing business processes. If the digital transformation is properly designed and planned, it should normally be handled by an augmented IT Department.

14.5.1 The Need for a Few Long-Term Digital Investments

The acceleration of pace in new service deliveries is necessary but not sufficient to reap the benefits of digital transformation. Longer-term strategies are also needed which might demand sustained investment commitment to reap longer term, albeit potentially significant, benefits. Two key opportunities for long-term investment to support business model innovation can be summarized as:

- Identification of *Industry data platform* opportunities. Platforms will be the enabler for unlocking all manner of data-centric insights and hence service innovation opportunities.
- Creation of *API* connected ecosystems, both internal (to guarantee service reuse) and external (to facilitate open interfacing to other services or objects). Allowing trusted partners to bring their innovative service enhancements into your solution set should bring significant value add. Some of the driving force behind regulations like PSD2 was precisely to encourage innovation and competition through enforcing the move to API connected markets.

Building APIs is a more technical investment which is essential to reap the benefit of digital transformation. Service-oriented architectures (SOAs) rely heavily upon the reuse of generic services. Companies such as Amazon have built their entire platform architectures upon a very limited number of APIs which have tended to be invariant over time while the generic services that use them have improved year after year. Internal APIs require very strict discipline by software developers to use published APIs to access generic services, rather than creating similar bespoke services. In addition, open APIs help to organize the interface with the external world to facilitate interoperability of services and interfaces.

14.5.2 Build a "Customer-First" Innovation Ecosystem

In the Leadership chapter, we talk about the accelerating rate of change experienced by executives in today's more volatile and uncertain world. Navigating this uncertainty demands that firms get closer to customers and at the same time bring themselves (together with customers) into a strong partner ecosystem, one that offers immediate access to complementary IP, skills, and capabilities.

Such ecosystems have strong implications:

- Say "goodbye" to the "office fortress" and create a coworking area within your work environment, but outside the corporate "firewall." This enables partners and other third parties to work alongside your employees on a more day-to-day basis without compromising confidential information assets.
- "Mindset of abundance": one of the wondrous things you find when you visit Silicon Valley is the enthusiasm everyone has for "making the cake bigger" as opposed to debating how to "share the cake." This abundance mindset works best when market opportunities are new and high-growth.

One of our team recalls being in San Jose in 2007 at a time when Cloud Computing was becoming a big thing. They were frankly amazed to see the heads of cloud from IBM, HP, and others sharing the challenges they saw and comparing notes on ways to address them. When asked about this they said simply: "*There are 4 billion people on Earth today with access to our technology platforms; we are after the next 3 billion!*" And from a cloud perspective, the common interest for all parties was to build client appetite to adopt cloud, and so bring forward the market opportunity.

As you might expect, this "mindset of abundance" works less well as markets mature and competition intensifies. For instance, we are now seeing a pivot by Apple to "grow our own share of the cake" as smart phone sales flatline globally.

However, looking at the relative newness and high potential of the technology enabled business transformation opportunities available in all sectors of the economy today, we suggest that the "mindset of abundance" is the best one to adopt. The key is to get in early and accelerate learning, and to recognize that the only way to build credible solutions at the right pace is to partner actively.

14.5.3 The Human Organization to Deliver Innovation in the Digital Age

There is no silver bullet to getting organized to deliver innovation.

The approach typically used by digital native organizations (particularly in their formative years) is allowing their people to spend one day a week in developing new concepts which will, when ready, become proofs of concept or proofs of value. They follow a strict evaluation process through which ad hoc teams are created to develop innovative projects which are reviewed at regular milestones. They are discontinued if they do not deliver or are scaled up and out into business offerings when successful.

The approach is similar to that of intrapreneurship, which we described earlier, and is not exempt of limitations. We mentioned a few that appear in traditional companies, but even employees of Digital Giants report the growing weight of politics and "popularity contests" within their organizations.

14.6 Recommendations

- *Innovate despite cost consciousness and a potentially challenging financial context*. In addition, you will need to balance incremental and disruptive innovation, with more emphasis on the latter than in previous decades.
- *Ensure that the innovation function is core in the organization*, and in perfect sync with other corporate functions. Favor a streamlined team that works jointly with innovators in all areas of the organization.
- *Avoid pushing excessively for short-term results*, be it deliverables or return. Some critical investments with disruptive potential will take time and may have a slow start in terms of sales or efficiency. Have a clear exit strategy for floppers, but also one for valuable yet slowly maturing projects. Data platforms and API-connected ecosystems are typical cases of long-term investments.
- *Balance wisely the opposites of each innovation conundrum:* openness and closeness, client-centricity and client-agnosticism, etc. Client-centricity is essential, but a healthy dose of agnosticism and occasional stubbornness may help you avoid the innovator's dilemma.
- *Avoid the traps we have listed in the section "Methodologies and other innovation traps"*: giving more importance to the methodology than to the goals, tailoring methodologies to fit the worst traits of your organizational culture, killing game-changers together with silly ideas (they'll both appear as outliers in many processes and tools), avoid the blame game when failure happens and learn from it, avoid too large and/or disconnected innovation teams, and remember that innovation comprises a challenging mix of soft and hard skills, and achieving the right balance is crucial.
- *Crowdsourcing, intrapreneurship, open innovation, and business model innovation are key paradigms that you need to leverage*. However, keep in mind that

they have significant fad elements and do not buy them simply at face value. Do some investigation to separate actual gains from hype and to identify their inherent challenges before you put them in practice.

- *Maintain a healthy dose of skepticism on ROII figures*, given the imponderables often involved in their estimation. Otherwise, approval decisions and the future monitoring of investments will be cluttered. Innovation is a fuzzy affair compared to established business processes or investments. Therefore, ROII is subject to a much higher degree of uncertainty and should be viewed very differently from regular ROI.

References

Anderson, B (Communication). Brad Anderson, Former CEO of best buy, as reported by Rita McGrath. https://www.youtube.com/watch?v=22C3qWM1VPk. Accessed October 26, 2019.

Chesbrough, H., & Bogers, M. (2014). Explicating open innovation: Clarifying an emerging paradigm for understanding innovation. Oxford University Press.

Corbett, A. (2018). The myth of the intrapreneur. *Harvard Business Review*, 26/06/2018. https://hbr.org/2018/06/the-myth-of-the-intrapreneur. Accessed October 26, 2019.

Enjalbert, N., & Vandi. C. (2018). There is no such thing as Innovation ROI. NUMA, 28/03/2018. https://medium.com/numa/there-is-no-such-thing-as-innovation-roi-daff48654235. Accessed October 26, 2019.

Grajewski, B. (2013). *Analyze the ROI of your innovation idea, step by step*. Forbes, 27/12/2013 https://www.forbes.com/sites/theyec/2013/12/27/analyze-the-roi-of-your-innovation-idea-step-by-step/#1f4784204c76. Accessed October 26, 2019.

Kolk, M., & Eagar, R. (2014). How to manage your return on investment in innovation—Reaping the most from innovation investments. PRISM/1/2014. Arthur D. Little. https://www.adlittle.com/sites/default/files/prism/ROI.PDF. Accessed October 26, 2019.

Kromer, T. (2015). The ROI of Innovation—What is it? https://grasshopperherder.com/the-roi-of-innovation/. Accessed October 26, 2019.

Phillips, J. J., & Phillips, P. P. (2018). *The value of innovation: Knowing, proving, and showing the value of innovation and creativity*. Wiley

Ross, A. (2019). Innovation spend is increasing, but ROI is decreasing, says Accenture, 30/01/2019. https://www.information-age.com/roi-is-decreasing-says-accenture-123478678/. Accessed October 26, 2019.

Teece D. J. (2010). Business models, business strategy and innovation. *Long Range Planning, International Journal of Strategic Management*, Elsevier.

Tidd, J., & Bessant, J. (2018). Innovation management challenges: From fads to fundamentals. *International Journal of Innovation Management*, *22*(05), 1840007. https://doi.org/10.1142/S1363919618400078. Accessed October 26, 2019.

Vlaskovits, P. (2011). Henry Ford, innovation, and that "Faster Horse" quote. *Harvard Business Review*, 29/08/2011. https://hbr.org/2011/08/henry-ford-never-said-the-fast. Accessed October 26, 2019.

15 Security—Business Constraint Versus Enabler of Trust

15.1 Security: The Perfect Excuse to Remain in the Past

One of the (few) fundamental topics that all society and business stakeholders agree upon is the importance of security in all its manifestations: physical security, information and data security, identity and privacy, safety, etc. In the context of digital transformation, it is often the case that security transcends the category of concern to become an excuse, the perfect ally of negative inertia that seeks to avoid change and maintain the organization in the comfortable-though-deadly present. Particularly, Executive Committees and Boards wield the "security wildcard" to avoid the organization's transition from a pipeline model to a platform model, arguably perceived as the most difficult transformation step since it challenges decades of culture and process optimization. "How are we supposed to open our confidential business data and share it in a platform with an ecosystem of players?" "How would we ensure control of the data and Intellectual Property?" "Wouldn't we increase our attack surface irresponsibly?" Resolving these apparent dilemmas requires paying attention to two basic aspects: lack of awareness about the current state of affairs and lack of awareness of technology-based solutions.

The first basic aspect is that businesses display a worrying lack of awareness about the current state of security in their own organizations. Furthermore, even when aware, organizations tend to hide security issues that are not publicly evident. As a consequence of the former, and of other short-term pressures (cost, priorities, time-to-market, etc.), businesses often do not take appropriate security measures. This diagnosis is not only a perception of the authors, but widely reported in the business literature, as the following examples show:

- "*The study…reveals that 50% of global companies do not currently take measures to protect themselves—and their clients—from cyber risks.*" (Paragon 2018)
- "*But there is also another type of cyberattack, the kind that we are less likely to read or hear about. These are the attacks that target proprietary corporate*

H. Tardieu et al., *Deliberately Digital*, Future of Business and Finance,
https://doi.org/10.1007/978-3-030-37955-1_15

information, seeking to find out what is 'beneath the covers' of an organization" (Moreno 2017)
- "*Only 36% stated that they've provided cybersecurity training to their employees. And more than half of the businesses (59%) don't have a cyber incident action plan*" (Cisomag 2019)
- "*Half of management teams polled in 12 countries, including the UK, are unaware of business process compromise (BPC) attacks*" (Ashford 2018)
- "*…only 16% of the board of directors have a clear understanding of the impact of loss or interruption associated with cyber threats while the rest are still unaware of the fact that a single attack can make or break a business. The highlight of the research is that almost 96% of the companies have a cybersecurity strategy in place, while only 12% of them have actually tested their plan. The rest of them still aren't sure what their in-house measures could yield when the success parameter is taken into account.*" (Goud 2018).

The objective of our highlighting such a state of affairs in security is not one of finger-pointing. If most organizations find themselves in such situations, there must be powerful, complex reasons for it. The crucial point is this: if the actual state of affairs is so distant from good practice, there are very significant competitive advantages to be gained by leveraging transformation to get up-to-date in security matters. Each defensive, change-opposing question at Executive Committee or Board level can be neutralized with arguments and figures, turning them into opportunities to be materialized via digital transformation.

The second basic aspect is that digital technologies and digital transformation programs offer the means (tools, solutions, approaches, and processes) to put security at the required maturity level. Not many years ago there was widespread concern about the security of public Clouds; nowadays, the top providers of public Cloud are considered more secure than the majority of organizations' data centers and IT systems. A serious inspection of digital security is likely to show your organization that a similar situation is taking place in the case of in-house, pipeline-model processes and solutions versus platform-model ones.

15.2 Why Is Digital Security so Important?

Protecting the integrity of your business may seem like an obvious responsibility, but the fact of the matter is that many enterprises don't take security and the threat of cyber-crime as seriously as they should. No matter how good the rest of a business's digital strategy and operations might be, poor security can lead to outcomes that are hugely damaging and costly.

Security risks and cyber-crime can take a variety of forms: from malware to phishing, and denial of service to zero-day exploits, with the motivations of the perpetrators usually being related to one or more of the following:

- Theft or extortion of money
- Theft of intellectual property/sensitive data
- Desire to discredit the parties under attack
- Just to prove that a system can be breached.

It is interesting to observe the way that motivations for trying to break digital security have evolved over time. Perhaps the first high-profile example of code breaking was that of cracking the Enigma code in World War Two: a feat that was said to have saved many thousands of lives and considerably shortened the war. In the 1960s, the earliest computer hackers were motivated by seeing "who was the best" at breaking into or altering software code; in the early days there did not seem to be much malicious intent behind the hacks.

Then in the 1970s, hacking turned to thoughts of getting personal gain from breaking the system. The first major hack came against the telephone network when someone worked out how to make free calls.

In the 1980s, we saw an explosive increase in the number of personal computers and a move to connect to the newly created Internet. Groups of hackers going by names like "Legion of Doom" and "Masters of Deception" tried to outperform each other in breaking into supposedly secure systems.

Since then, the reasons behind people writing viruses and malware or orchestrating DDOS attacks have evolved further. Individuals and groups continued to "test the system" and prove their prowess in coding (sometimes this was done with a sense of pseudo morality as they targeted enterprises that were deemed to be acting unjustly), but it wasn't long before money began to play a defining role. New threats involving identity theft, social engineering, and ransomware emerged. The rise of (pseudo) anonymous cryptocurrencies made it possible to carry out crimes that used malware to block access to computer systems until a "ransom" is paid. While such attacks began by targeting individuals, they quickly moved into the enterprise space. In 2018, the WannaCry cyber-attack was reported to cost the UK National Health Service a total of £92 million.

The change in motivation and impact of cyber-attacks was driven by a recognition that:

- Individuals and corporates were becoming almost totally dependent on their digital systems.
- Personal data had intrinsic value, particularly where it included payment card details or could be used for identity theft.

Customer information databases became prime targets for hackers. Governing bodies sought to drive responsible business behavior through the implementation of regulations such as the European General Data Protection Regulation, but even the threat of massive non-compliance fines (in addition to the reputational damage caused by high-profile breaches) did not always have the desired effect. Notable examples of the impact of data privacy breaches under GDPR include:

- British Airways being handed a proposed £183 million fine for breach of customer data. If upheld, this would amount to 1.5% of their global annual turnover.
- In July 2019, Marriott hotels received notice of an intended fine of £99 million for failing to protect personal data of 339 million guest records.
- In June 2019, EE were fined £100,000 for sending over 2.5 million direct marketing messages without customer consent.
- In November 2018, Uber were fined £385,000 for failing to protect customers' personal information during a cyber-attack.

The really sobering thought is that the "bad guys" are not only on the outside trying to get in. A disgruntled employee with the right access and know-how can do as much damage as the most sophisticated of external threats.

Even worse than these "fast jobs," are "slow jobs": attacks that are progressively prepared and carried out over weeks or months, either to be triggered as a fast job at a certain later date or to be undetected before, during and after the attack: data is not a physical item that you will miss because it's missing, it can be replicated outside of your perimeter and still look perfectly safe in your IT systems.

It should be clear from the above examples, that in an increasing data centric economy, the data that gives rise to new routes to value must be protected as seriously as the traditional currencies that we hope it will generate. This ethos must be an inextricable part of any digital transformation strategy and target model.

Referring back to our "Routes to Digital Leadership" schema, first shown in Fig. 1, we saw that growing and maintaining intimacy with customers is an essential factor in reaching digital leadership status. If trust with individuals or the wider market is lost, such intimacy and hence leadership position cannot be sustained.

15.3 How the Security Challenge Is Evolving

In the digitally transforming world, the problem of IT security is very different from that which many organizations are used to dealing with. There are a number of reasons for this, including:

- The potential attack surface[1] is growing. A conventional security strategy would be to minimize an enterprise's potential attack surface. With the move to cloud and edge, and ever-increasing system interconnectivity, the total attack surface is hard to define, never mind protect. The attack surface is now introducing risks beyond those of revenue and reputational damage to matters of life and death, as critical national infrastructure and healthcare solutions are increasingly connected and digitally enabled.

[1]The attack surface represents the different points where unauthorized users can try to breach system security.

- Attack vectors[2] are becoming more varied and sophisticated. It must be remembered that the same exciting and innovative technologies that are available to create all kinds of new digitally enabled products and services, are also available to people who would use them for malicious intent. What's more, such people are not constrained by regulations or morals in the way we would expect law abiding enterprises to be.
- Increase in compute power. Brute force attacks can now be readily applied to things like guessing passwords or personal identification numbers, thereby allowing unauthorized access to systems through the same route as authorized users. Brute force techniques can also be used to attempt to decrypt encrypted datasets. This threat is of growing concern with the anticipated advent of quantum computers that are predicted to be able to perform, at exponentially faster speeds, the very mathematical computations that cryptography is built upon.
- The size of the prize is increasing. With so much inherent value being tied up in data, and with digital payment channels (including debit and credit cards) gaining an ever-dominant share of commercial transactions, the "rewards" for data related criminal activity are significant and growing daily.

We have already referred to the fact that the somewhat intangible nature of data has advantages in the scalability and pace of its use, but it also has distinct disadvantages in terms of maintaining its integrity and exclusivity. Data can be readily copied (stolen) and altered in a way that potentially renders it useless. Loss of valuable digital Intellectual Property can negate competitive advantage at a stroke (e.g., copying of digital designs, 3D print files or media files can spoil countless hours of creative effort and even be used to hold individuals and businesses to ransom). In 2014, Sony Pictures were hacked by a group calling itself the "Guardians of Peace": as well as stealing and subsequently leaking information about Sony Pictures' executives' salaries, employees' families, and unreleased films, the hackers also deployed malware in an attempt to further damage Sony's IT infrastructure. They then went on to demand the withdrawal of the planned release of a comedy film about a plot to assassinate the North Koran leader Kim Jong-Un. It is still unclear who was behind the hack and the full extent of the damage that was caused.

As our information technology increasingly moves toward the "edge," it is harder to differentiate between the "inside" and the "outside." Traditional perimeter-based security no longer affords the necessary protection, and with botnets[3] able to crawl Web sites and systems looking for any vulnerabilities, reactive responses to breaches are mostly ineffective. The nature of automated attacks and the speed at which they can propagate to exploit identified vulnerabilities mean that for

[2]Attack vectors are the means by which a hacker gains access to IT equipment in order to deliver a payload or malicious outcome.

[3]A botnet is a number of Internet-connected devices running malicious code, that are used to perform distributed denial-of-service attacks, steal data, send spam, and allow access to target devices.

responses to be effective they not only need to use automated response techniques but also need to shift their emphasis to predictive and proactive security operations.

The "inside" and "outside" differentiation also blurs on the human side. There are "outside jobs," attacks coming from parties external to the organization, and "inside jobs," but some of the most devastating attacks are a clever mixture of high-tech-enabled outside activity with social engineering to persuade insiders to inadvertently collaborate in the attack. This highlights the importance of adherence to security policies, which we mention later in this chapter.

15.4 The Need for a Proportionate Response

All the previous points may lead you to conclude that the risks associated with exploiting digital technologies may outweigh the positive benefits they offer. But, in general, there are perfectly viable mitigations that can be put in place so long as you are aware of the potential threats and deal with them in a proportionate manner. A measured response will avoid the dual trap of either overestimating or underestimating the security risks being faced. The simple fact is that IT security must be seen as an essential hygiene factor for all businesses and approached in a way that does not unnecessarily constrain your business. In fact, quite the opposite: as discussed, it should be seen as a positive means of market differentiation. Any business wishing to attain and maintain digital leader status must have a strong security mindset. This must embrace "security by design" and not as an afterthought.

There are many practical and pragmatic guides for cyber-security. One helpful example is "*The 10 Steps to Cyber-Security*" (NCSC 2018) that is published by the National Cyber Security Centre of Great Britain. This particular document focuses heavily on user awareness, policies, monitoring, and control. It urges that cyber-risk is seen as a priority for boards and that proportionate risk management is flowed down through the business. A significant element of cyber-risk comes from people's ignorance or carelessness. For example, clicking on suspect e-mail attachments, sharing USB drives with third parties, weak passwords, obsolete but undeleted user accounts, or loss of laptops.

A lot of relatively simple measures can be taken to mitigate these kinds of risks. Things, like password policies, encrypted hard drives and USB drives, limited user privileges, and automated security patching regimes, will be highly effective not only in reducing external threats but also in reducing the knock-on impact of disproportionate responses to given threats. For example, some organizations place a total ban on the use of removable media devices like USB drives for fear that sensitive data will be lost, and however, such measures can be quite restrictive when trying to perform perfectly legitimate data transfers. Using strong encryption on reputable makes of USB drives, although never 100% infallible, should offer an acceptable level of security. The simpler and more seamless you are able to make security measures to work with, the less the tendency for legitimate users to try to circumvent them, for example, electing to use personal e-mail accounts to transmit data that is otherwise unnecessarily blocked in corporate e-mails systems.

Vulnerabilities in passwords can be overcome by enforcing minimum complexity policies and by using 2-factor authentication (typically requiring "something I have" and "something I know"). But you should also try to find ways of removing the human risk: it never ceases to amaze us that we still see people with their passwords written on sticky notes! New innovative security techniques make use of combinations of physiological (e.g., facial recognition and finger prints) and behavioral measures (e.g., typing rhythm) to prove an individual's identity.

It is interesting to note that many corporate security breaches occur as a result of failure to adhere to policies and procedures (e.g., falling behind on security patching regimes; unencrypted data transmission; failure to respond to security alerts in a timely manner; ignorance about security risks resulting in individuals behaving in a naïve manner and, for example, falling victim to phishing scams). Scam e-mails or service desk calls may seem crude and obvious to most, but they only have to work with one individual out of thousands for a breach to occur. Reducing the level of dependency on human interaction for maintaining security standards is a very important consideration.

Analytics and Automation are significant allies in the fight against cyber-attacks. Real-time analytics and Deep Learning algorithms can now be used to monitor security logs, network activity and system user behavior to identify unusual and suspect behavior to proactively neutralize the risk before it fully materializes.

While, for many, the cloud is seen as a risk, there are significant benefits of moving your data and applications to it. Cloud providers are likely to be able to invest in far more security and backup measures than individual companies. But you still have to use them: In early 2019, over 108 million records of bets made at Web sites belonging to an online casino group were found to have been stored on an Elasticsearch server that hadn't been secured with a password. At about the same time, a Facebook-integrated app called "At the Pool" exposed over 22,000 users' passwords through a backup in an Amazon S3 bucket that stored the passwords as plain text.

When considering using the cloud, don't be constrained by adopting a "highest common denominator" approach to data security. We have observed many companies who didn't understand their own data well enough to determine how sensitive it was. Everything was therefore deemed to require the highest (and therefore costliest) level of security.

Digital businesses need to understand that the full value of data insights is usually only realized when they are appropriately shared with others within a complementary ecosystem. Don't constrain the realization of this value by being paranoid about sharing data. This is especially important when looking to exploit platform business models.

The security mindset needs to extend beyond the normal, logical threats. For example, particularly, if you are a high-profile organization, you need to accept that there are some actors who will do whatever they can just to make a point. In the case of the Olympic Games, IT service providers have to defend against hundreds of millions of security events in order to maintain a resilient and safe experience for viewers around the world. Those wishing to cause disruption would seem to have little to gain but the disruption itself and the potential to claim bragging rights in cyber superiority, but the cost of defending against such mentality is considerable.

15.5 Recommendations

- *Leverage, perceive, and communicate digital transformation as an opportunity to reach best-in-class status in security* as opposed to wielding security as an excuse to entrench on pre-digital ways. The latter is based on a very dangerous false sense of security originating from a lack of awareness of the actual state of security in the traditional pipeline model.
- *Treat security as a necessary hygiene factor. It* is a means to an end and not an end in itself, so be proportionate in the measure you employ. Nurture a security mindset within your business and make it as easy as possible for people to comply with policies.
- *Use analytics, automation and cloud where possible and appropriate*. This will help reduce human factor risks. Be proactive in using analytics and AI to pattern match and find unusual behaviors. Respond automatically to identified threats: things happen too fast to have extended debates about what action to take.
- *Prevent rather than respond*. Actively monitor for vulnerabilities (system, policy, and behavioral) and address them proactively.
- *Do not be held back by security paranoia*. Especially when implementing platform business models, if you are not willing to appropriately share data, then you will not get anywhere.
- *Perimeter security alone is not good enough*. Consider what you need to change as you look to exploit edge and IoT capabilities.
- *Security problems will almost inevitable occur at some time*, so have policies and procedures to deal with them as effectively as possible.

References

Ashford, W. (2018). *Half of business leaders unaware of BPC cyber attacks*. Computerweekly.com, 07/12/2018. https://www.computerweekly.com/news/252454061/Half-of-business-leaders-unaware-of-BPC-cyber-attacks. Accessed October 26, 2019.

Cisomag. (2019). *UK mid-market businesses lose £30 billion to cyber-attacks*. Cisomag.com, 19/07/2019. https://www.cisomag.com/uk-mid-market-businesses-lose-30-billion-to-cyber-attacks/. Accessed October 26, 2019.

Goud, N. (2018). *Boards of directors of most UK companies are unaware of Cyber Attack repercussions*. https://www.cybersecurity-insiders.com/board-of-directors-of-most-uk-companies-is-unaware-of-cyber-attack-repercussions/. Accessed October 26, 2019.

Moreno, K. (2017). *The Cyberattacks we don't hear about but should*. Forbes, 14/02/2017. https://www.forbes.com/sites/forbesinsights/2017/02/14/the-cyberattacks-we-dont-hear-about-but-should/#34285ed33a2f. Accessed October 26, 2019.

NCSC. (2018). *10 steps to cyber security*. National Cyber Security Centre, UK, 17/11/2018. https://www.ncsc.gov.uk/collection/10-steps-to-cyber-security. Accessed October 26, 2019.

Paragon. (2018). *Half of companies around the world unaware of cyber threats*. Paragon Relocation. https://paragonrelocation.com/half-of-companies-around-the-world-unaware-of-cyber-threats/. Accessed October 26, 2019.

Part III
The Digital Transformation: Executing the Transformation

Introduction

Abstract In Part III of this book, we explain how to organise and execute an ongoing digital transformation. We describe and explain our recommended transformation model and governance. We address how to identify and analyse your company's current state and its opportunities to improve; how to prioritise workstreams to maximise the value of the transformation (taking into account return on investment, timescale and risk); and how to deliver workstreams iteratively (whilst balancing long-term strategy against short-term agility). We also explain how to define meaningful KPIs, not only for the successful management of the transformation itself, but also to support your transformed business.

In Part I, we have seen why there is an urgent need for many organizations to transform themselves in response to the rapidly evolving changes in business, society, and technology. In Part II, we have provided recommendations for how organizations must function in order to fully leverage the opportunities created by digital, ranging from strategy through to customer engagement and innovation at scale. Now, in Part III, we will see how a company can make the journey to transform from where they are today toward a state where they successfully and continually harness the promise of digital (Fig. III.1).

First, we will look at how the transformation can be initiated and planned. Then, we will look at how the progress of the transformation can be measured and how KPIs used to measure and manage a business may need to be adjusted. Finally, we will look in more detail at how the transformation can be implemented and sustained.

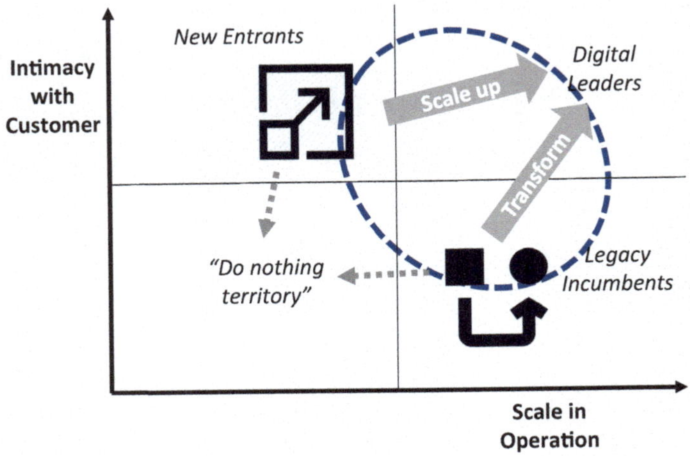

Fig. III.1 Different but interdependent routes to digital leadership (authors' own figure)

It is obvious that not all businesses can achieve digital giant status, but becoming a digital leader within a defined market is within the gift of many enterprises if they are willing to take on the challenge of Deliberately Digital transformations.

Starting the Transformation—Establishing the Right Foundations 16

In Part I, you have seen the key societal, business, and technology trends that are impacting organizations' ability to achieve customer intimacy and scale in operation, and which make up the *transformation context* for your business. They are the external forces and drivers that simultaneously create a need to transform and also enable the transformation.

Based on the concepts and recommendations presented in Part II, you will no doubt already have formed some ideas about the ways in which your company may need to scale up and transform in order to achieve digital leader status.

One important part of initiating the transformation is to refine these ideas (in collaboration with a wide range of stakeholders) and then group them into *transformation workstreams.* We have found it helpful to think of transformation workstreams in the context of eight groupings of *transformation themes* as shown in Fig. 16.1. Note that while we have not explicitly included security within this diagram, we have previously stated that this should be an all-pervasive consideration that needs to be included within all transformation workstreams.

Exactly which workstreams are identified as relevant will vary from company to company. However, we would typically expect to see a spread of workstreams, with one or more in each of the transformation themes. Balancing the workstreams across the transformation themes and prioritizing and selecting specific workstreams to progress is one of the key inputs the Executive Committee must make to the digital transformation. This is covered in more detail in the chapter on Planning an Iterative Transformation.

You will see that we have also further grouped the transformation themes into two categories:

- *Foundational*: these are the workstreams that will be likely to fundamentally change your business. They could transform your business strategy and/or business models and will typically require you to leverage business platforms or ecosystems in some way. Perhaps most importantly, these workstreams may create a new or revitalized sense of purpose for your organization. They may require

H. Tardieu et al., *Deliberately Digital*, Future of Business and Finance,
https://doi.org/10.1007/978-3-030-37955-1_16

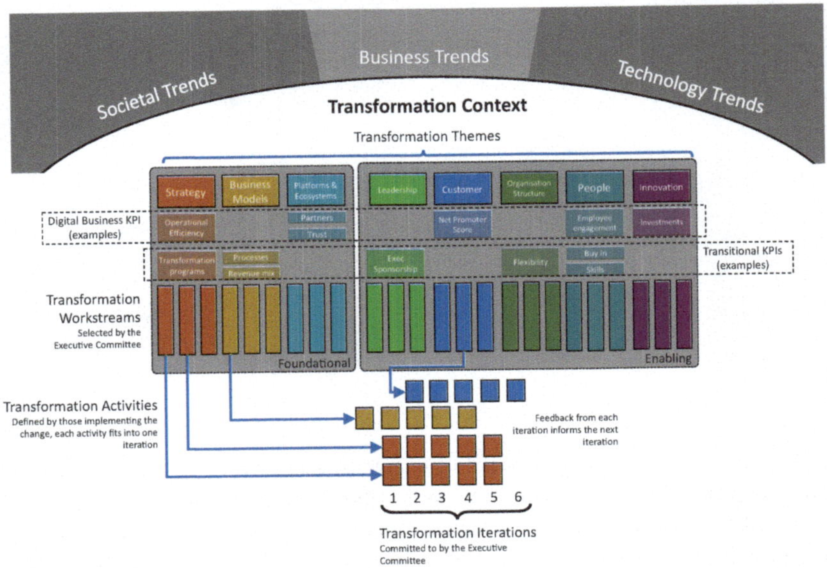

Fig. 16.1 A model developed by the authors for how to achieve enduring digital transformation. Authors' own figure

leaders to develop and articulate a vision that helps people across the organization understand what else needs to be transformed in order to support this vision, and why it matters.

- *Enabling*: these are the workstreams that will tend to optimize your business operations. They may drive efficiency and scale, but they will not (by themselves) impact the fundamental nature of your business.

In general, *foundational* workstreams will have a bigger impact on customer intimacy but may also positively impact your ability to drive scale in operations. Conversely, *enabling* workstreams will tend to have a bigger impact on your ability to successfully scale your operations, but may also result in increased customer intimacy.

The reason this distinction between foundational and enabling workstreams is necessary is that often you will need to agree upon and start progressing the foundational workstreams as a priority. Not doing this can easily lead to you focusing your transformation efforts on optimizing the wrong things. Far better to create the right foundations in your strategy, business models, platforms and ecosystems, and then optimize, than to waste effort on optimization that will never bring you to a position of Digital Leadership. These foundational workstreams are so critical that we discuss their formulation in more detail in the following chapter.

There is one important exception to be aware of: sometimes optimizing current operations can be a necessary step to creating the budget and capacity to implement the foundational workstreams. This topic is covered in more detail in the chapter on Planning an Iterative Transformation.

You will also notice that we identify two categories of KPIs:

- *Digital business KPIs*: These will be the new "business as usual" KPIs for your enterprise. Traditional methods of measuring and managing performance do not always make sense in a digitally transformed business, and therefore, the KPIs you use will need to be transformed accordingly.
- *Transitional KPIs*: These are KPIs that are introduced to track the progress of transformation workstreams. They may be adapted over time, but they are unlikely to be required permanently.

We discuss both categories of KPIs (and the overlaps and interplay between them) in the chapter on Measuring the Transformation.

Workstreams are further subdivided into *Transformation Activities*, each of which can be delivered within a single *Transformation Iteration*. How this is done is described in more detail in the chapter on Enduring Digital Transformation.

Figure 16.2 gives an overall view of the transformation process. In the following chapters, we will explain each step in more detail, and we will describe how feedback is built-in to ensure that the transformation is both adaptable and sustainable, while successfully balancing a short-term need for results with a long-term vision.

But first, let's understand why this approach combines top-down and bottom-up methods for understanding your organization's current state to secure buy-in from across the organization—a key pre-requisite for success.

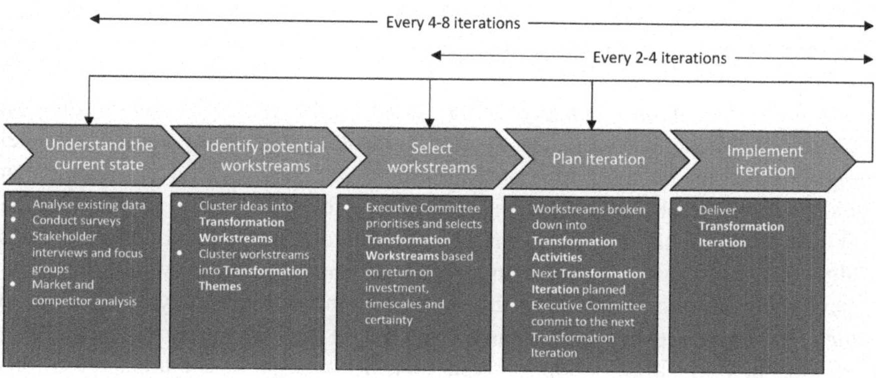

Fig. 16.2 Overview of the transformation process. Authors' own figure

16.1 Buy-in as a Critical Enabler of Transformation

The most common cause for the failure of a change program is "*employee resistance to change,*" with "*management behavior not supporting change*" coming a close second (McKinsey 2008). In other words, if people do not buy-in to the change, it is unlikely to succeed.

It also turns out that getting people's buy-in for a transformation and, if necessary, achieving a shift in organization culture, is often the part of transformation that requires the most work [with some estimating that it constitutes up to 70% of the effort involved (Syntec 2016)].

These two facts should not be surprising. There is no point rolling out new tools if nobody uses them. There is no point implementing new ways of working if people do not adopt them (or only pay lip-service to them). For change to achieve results, the people in the organization have to be fully engaged with it, support it, and make it happen.

A commonly held view is that "people don't like change." And yet this statement is clearly not true. If people do not like change, then why would they ever go on holiday? Why would they ever apply for a new job? Why would they have children, or watch a new movie, or move to a new house? If change is so universally dreaded by all people, why would they behave in a way that, in fact, clearly demonstrates that (at least under certain circumstances) they embrace and welcome change?

The reason is that when people believe that a change will be beneficial (for themselves and/or for some higher purpose), they will pursue that change with vigor and determination, even if there is a significant personal cost to achieving it.

However, if people see no benefit to a change, then why would they invest any effort in it at all? And if they anticipate that the change may, in fact, be detrimental, or even if there is just a risk of the change being detrimental, then naturally, they will invest their time and energy to try and stop or slow down the change.

This is illustrated nicely by the words of Stephen Bungay when he said that "*organizational sociology starts with the empirically verifiable assumption that most organizational behavior is rational given the position of each individual within the organization*" (Bungay 2011). Based on this principle, and building on the work of Michel Crozier, The Boston Consulting Group developed a model suggesting that the behavior of people (or groups of people) within an organization could be explained by understanding their goals, resources and constraints (BCG 2000). If you find that individuals are not supportive of the transformation, there is a high likelihood that the people involved are behaving rationally, and that they believe that resisting or blocking the transformation is the best way for them to achieve *their* goals (using *their* resources and within *their* constraints). The thinking from Boston Consulting Group suggests that, if you wish to see a change in this behavior, then you should seek to change their goals, resources, and/or constraints.

We see that firms who achieve digital leader status understand in particular the importance of aligning the goals and sense of purpose of individuals within the organization, with the goals and purpose of the organization itself. By way of example, consider that new recruits at Zappos are, after their 4-week initial training program, offered $2000 to leave: "*Zappos wants to learn if there's a bad fit between what makes the organization tick and what makes individual employees tick, and it's willing to pay to learn sooner rather than later.*" (Taylor 2008)

Digital leaders also understand that this sense of alignment is very much a two-way street: for the people of the organization to support the organization in achieving its purpose, the organization must itself enable people within it to fulfil their own sense of purpose. Indeed, it should enable its people to help each other toward achieving their goals.

We cannot emphasize enough the importance of such alignment. Jim and Michele McCarthy, who in the 1980s led hundreds of software engineers at Microsoft to build cutting edge products, have since dedicated two decades to researching and understanding organizational dynamics. One of their conclusions has been:

> People often see a shortage of resources where no such shortage really exists. Problems are then misdiagnosed as being caused by too little time or too few people, or both, and wrong strategies are subsequently employed. In a properly aligned team, most talent and time shortages are resolved by uncovering the untapped talent of the people already in place. (McCarthy and McCarthy 2002)

So, beware: if you are receiving feedback that people do not have the time or money or other needed resource for the transformation, more often than not it will actually be the case that the goals of the transformation are not sufficiently aligned with the goals of the organization's people. Which underlines again why securing buy-in is so important.

16.2 What Is Buy-in?

Let's now clarify what it means to have buy-in to the required changes needed to deliver a digital transformation. We believe the three components of buy-in are:

- Consensus across the organization about what needs to change and that there will be a benefit from the change (at least in the long term).
- Commitment from people to make the change happen.
- Accountability of people to make the change happen.

Let us now clarify what we mean by these three terms. Consensus does not mean that everyone agrees. Rather, it means that:

- Everyone understands what is proposed.
- A significant majority agree with what is proposed.
- The remainder agree to support (not block) what is being proposed.

It is also important to be clear about what is meant by a commitment in this context. Specifically, those who commit to a change must:

- Commit to providing the needed resources (time, money, emotional energy, etc.).
- Commit to completing certain actions and steps that may be required.
- Commit not only to performing tasks/actions, but to doing their best to achieve the overall goals of the change.

In literal terms, accountability means having to explain (give an account of) your actions and the results they have (or have not) achieved. Later in this chapter, when we describe transformation governance, and also in other chapters, where we talk about KPIs and measuring benefits, you will see how people and teams can be held accountable for the delivery of a digital transformation. When it comes to accountability, however, there may seem to be a dichotomy between holding people accountable for making change happen and having a "no-blame" culture that values learning from mistakes much more than it seeks to punish individuals for making them. However, we actually find that having a high-accountability culture and a no-blame culture are symbiotically linked (and they both create the capability for an organization to learn from experience).

If, when something doesn't go as planned, a person says that it was "because of X" where X was outside of their control, they are effectively saying that the idea was doomed from the outset and there was nothing they could have done to make it a success. For real learning to take place, such statements must start with "It didn't go as planned because I…". Only when accountability has been accepted and responsibility taken for how events unfolded, can meaningful learning take place. However, having such true accountability (and the learning that flows from it) is impossible if people fear that any mistakes will be punished. As one of our colleagues once said, "people aren't afraid of blame, they are afraid of the consequences that come with blame." A successful digital transformation is built on people making commitments, and those people being held accountable for delivering on those commitments. But the goal of that accountability is to learn as quickly as possible what works and what doesn't, not to chastise or punish anyone.

Let's bring together these three components of consensus, commitment, and accountability by way of a simple analogy: climbing a mountain. Firstly, any team would need consensus about their desire to climb a mountain. They would have to understand what it is that they seek to get out of it (both personally and as a group)? Is it personal satisfaction? Friendship? The desire to complete a difficult challenge? Is it to raise money for a worthwhile cause? This purpose will inform other decisions on which consensuses will need to be reached as planning progresses, for example, which peak to climb and which route to take. People on the team will, at some point, need to commit toward the goal, declaring themselves "in" or "out." This doesn't mean that everyone will have to climb to the summit: there will be many parts to play in a successful ascent. But everyone needs to be committed to the team achieving the goal: by putting in the necessary resources (time, effort, and financial), completing the needed intermediate actions (including physical training and the learning of relevant skills), and making best efforts to enable the team to be successful in its mission. Finally, everyone will need to feel accountable for the team reaching the summit. One way of achieving this is to create external accountability: perhaps by collecting sponsorship for a charitable cause, or through some other form of public commitment. However, members of the team will also need to create internal accountability between each other: challenging everyone to demonstrate that they are delivering against the commitments they have made.

16.3 Whose Buy-in Is Required?

As we have seen in the chapter about Organization Structure, a digital transformation can only be successful with the full support of the Executive Committee. Indeed, the digital transformation may require changes to the roles and responsibilities of those serving on the Executive Committee. They typically have significant positional power (people reporting to them, control of budgets, etc.) as well as indirect influence over many parts of the organization. This makes their buy-in critical to the success of the transformation.

However, it is a mistake to think that it is only the senior leaders whose buy-in needs to be secured. Taking this view could result in a purely top-down approach to transformation, where everyone else's role is relegated to simply following orders. As we have seen throughout Part II (and, in particular, in the chapters on Leadership, Organization Structure, People and Innovation), this is the antithesis of the organizational culture required for a successful digital business.

One final point to make regarding buy-in is that, in practice, not everyone will be ready, willing or able to support the transformation. In some cases, this means it will be appropriate for them to leave the organization. If this is the case for anything more than a small minority, then you should consider whether the transformation being proposed is the right one, and instead seek to secure more buy-in from a wider range of stakeholders. However, achieving buy-in from 100% of the people in an organization (no matter what level they are at), is unlikely to be a realistic goal. Therefore, the fact that some in the organization will not be ready to participate in the transformation is something that must be expected and planned for.

16.4 How to Secure Buy-in

Fundamentally, to support a change, people need three things. Firstly, they need to believe that the change will result in a future that is in some way better than it would be if the change is not made. Secondly, they need to believe that it is feasible to implement the change (even if this belief is based on trust rather than evidence). Thirdly, they need to believe that the cost (emotional, financial, etc.) of making the change will be worth it for the anticipated benefit. To summarize: they must believe in the goal, they must believe in the plan, and they must believe that the results will be worthwhile. These beliefs are far more likely to be engendered within people when they have directly shaped both the goal and the plan or been meaningfully involved in doing so.

This is why it is important to engage with people from across the organization at the outset to understand how the organization currently functions, to determine what the goal(s) for the future should be, and to build a plan for achieving the transition. In the following sections we will describe approaches to understanding the current state of your organization that will also start to naturally create buy-in for the transformation. It will help you learn what your company currently does well and where there are opportunities to improve. In addition, we will explain a transformation governance structure that aims to ensure that buy-in can be created and sustained across the organization and at all levels.

16.5 Statistical Analysis

Many organizations already have access to substantial datasets covering financial (and market) performance, customer satisfaction and employee engagement. In large organizations, it is usually possible to segment the results (e.g., by geography, market, or organizational unit) and look for trends. You can, for example, see if higher customer satisfaction correlates with higher profitability. If it doesn't, you can ask yourself why? If it does, you can try to understand what is leading to high customer satisfaction in the segments that are scoring well (and what is leading to low scores for those that aren't). All of this analysis will be useful as a starting point for discussion as you begin to engage stakeholders from across the organization with the definition of future goals.

For those readers that are interested in how to use statistical analysis to identify trends, we have included some hints and tips in the Appendix. This contains information about commonly available tools and simple but effective visualization techniques. Following the approaches outlined can yield powerful insights that will be of immense value to your transformation program.

16.6 Survey Design

Once you have looked at existing data sources, you may wish to complement these with one or more surveys which you will conduct to help you understand what needs to change in more specific detail.

Such surveys can be a rich source of data. We recommend carefully considering the following points when designing your survey:

- Be clear about what you are trying to find out. What is the main question you are trying to answer? What secondary questions are you trying to answer?
- Try and avoid disguising two questions inside one. For example, if you ask, "To what extent do you feel our internal tools are reliable and easy to use?" you will not know from the results whether a low score indicates low reliability, poor usability, or both.
- If most or all of the questions can be answered on the same scale (e.g., strongly agree, agree, neither agree nor disagree, disagree, and strongly disagree), this is usually easier for the respondent than if each question has a unique set of responses. These types of scales are collectively known as "Likert" scales.
- Many people feel strongly about whether or not to include a middle (or neutral) option in the list of possible responses. The problem with providing no neutral option is that it forces anyone who has a genuinely neutral view to "pick a side." If you then make statements based on the results like "80% agreed or strongly agreed," this can be open to challenge because some of those people may not have agreed (but did not disagree either). Providing a neutral option will lead to less polarized results. However, a potential downside of providing a middle option is that it can sometimes be seen as the "easy answer" which people choose simply to complete the survey quickly, rather than because it reflects their true viewpoint.
- It is good practice to include a "Don't know" or "Not applicable" for any questions where these could be legitimate responses. For example, a question like "Do you feel passionate about your work?" is a question which you could reasonably expect everyone in the organization to be able to answer. However, a question like "Do you enjoy working from home?" should have a "Not applicable" option for those who do not work from home. And a question like "Are you paid a market competitive salary?" should have a "Don't know" option for those who are unaware of how their salary compares to what competitors are offering their staff.
- You will almost certainly wish to capture some demographic information about respondents such as number of years of service, role, and business unit. You may even wish to extend these questions to how positive they feel about the company. Some of the reasons for collecting this information are explained later.
- Keeping the number of questions as low as possible (but not at the expense of combining more than one question into one, or making the answer choices more complex) is a major factor in improving response rate. Aiming to make the survey take no longer than 10 minutes to complete is a good target.
- Test the survey. One of the best practices we have found is to sit with someone while they take the survey. Every time they ask you a question about how to respond, this signals that the survey design could be further improved.

It is often useful to include in your survey freeform text fields where people can suggest what they would like to see improved. While it can be somewhat harder to analyze this type of data, it can prove to be a rich source of potential improvements. One point to note is that it is possible to restate almost any problem as a solution and vice versa. For example, "we don't automate enough" can become "we should automate more." Because of this, our advice is that, in the early stages of collecting ideas and proposals, you should not worry too much about this, but rather allow people to express themselves in whatever way they prefer.

One final point regarding survey design, which is often missed, is that you must consider how completing the survey is likely to make respondents feel. Remember that one of the goals of understanding the current state inside your organization is to secure people's buy-in. Will completing the survey inspire and enthuse people about the possibilities that may be opened up by the transformation to come? Or might it make them feel negative or defensive about what lies ahead?

16.7 Who to Survey

Once you have designed the survey, you will need to determine which group of respondents you will target. One factor to consider is how many people you will need to survey in order for the results to be representative. In other words, if you have an organization of 10,000 people, how many people (and what mix of people) do you need to survey to have confidence that the results represent the whole company? Fortunately, there are many calculators available which will tell you the sample size (number of people who complete the survey) needed for a given population size, confidence level, and margin of error.[1] In our example, the population size would be 10,000 (total number of employees). Confidence level is the probability that the results from the people surveyed will represent the total population (the industry standard is 95%). Margin of error is the amount by which the scores would be different if the entire group (of 10,000 employees) was surveyed rather than just the subset of the population (the sample): 5% is an industry standard value for this. Confidence level and margin of error are interrelated: a confidence level of 95% and a margin of error of 5% are together saying that if you ran the survey 100 times, on 95 of those occasions the results would vary by 5% or less from the results obtained by surveying the entire population. As you can see from Table 16.1, in our example, we would need a sample size of 370 people to achieve this.

All of the above assumes that the sample is not unusually biased. If our example is a multinational organization with offices in 80 countries, but the 370 respondents are all based in the UK, then it is unlikely that the results will be representative of the company as a whole. Similarly, if those 370 are selected from the top 10% of earners it would not be reasonable to assume the results represent the total population of the organization's employees. This is one reason for collecting demographic information as described earlier: to ensure that the mix of people responding to the survey is representative of the make-up of the whole population.

[1]There are many survey size calculators available for free online, for example: https://www.surveymonkey.com/mp/sample-size-calculator/.

Table 16.1 Sample size needed for a given population size and confidence level

		Population size						
		100	200	500	1000	2000	5000	10,000
Confidence level	95%	80	132	218	278	323	357	370
	90%	74	115	176	213	238	256	262
	80%	63	91	124	141	152	159	162

Assuming 5% margin of error. Table compiled by authors using the Survey Monkey sample size calculator. https://www.surveymonkey.com/mp/sample-size-calculator/ (accessed 26/10/2019)

Of course, it is also sometimes valid to target a specific population (depending on the question you are trying to answer). If what you want to know is: "what do managers think about x," then it makes complete sense to target one category of staff. Note that as the population size decreases, the percentage of people that you need to survey will increase. If you have a population size of just 200 top managers, then you will need to survey 132 of them (as shown in Table 16.1), for a confidence level of 95% and margin of error of 5%. This is also something to keep in mind when you compare responses between different demographics, as the sample size for each demographic may become too small to meaningfully represent them.

As survey response rates rarely achieve 100%, you will have to send your survey out to more people than your target sample size. Actual response rates will depend significantly on how incentivized or motivated people are to respond. Response rates of higher than 50% can be achieved when there is a significant push (for example reminders, management cascades, prizes, etc.). Without concerted efforts, a response rate of around 10–20% is more realistic.

Response rates will be higher if you can commit to sharing the results with survey participants and to taking some action based on the survey results. In fact, we would say these are very reasonable expectations from respondents: why should they spend their time answering your questions if they won't gain any new insights and if nothing will change as a result? Remember that one of the key goals (and possibly the main goal) should not just be to gather information, but to engage people with the transformation. By making a commitment that the results of people's feedback will be shared transparently and that concrete actions will be taken as a result, you will engender greater buy-in for the digital transformation (provided, of course, that these commitments are also followed through).

The actual response rate you achieve can also give you some useful insights into how people feel about the subject of your survey. Low response rates can suggest that people do not consider the subject important or that they do not believe anything will change as a result. You may also see the response rate vary between different types of people (another reason to collect demographic information), again giving you some insight into how passionate or ambivalent these groups are regarding the topic of your questionnaire.

16.8 Stakeholder Interviews and Focus Groups

Although analyzing existing data sources and conducting surveys are both very useful, we strongly recommend that you do not limit yourself to these types of analysis alone. We have found that focus groups and stakeholder interviews with employees, partners, and customers can be extremely effective. Not only do they act as a sense check for other data sources, but they also illicit stories that can be very powerful in helping others to understand the need for change. We would recommend interviewing at least all of the senior leadership in the organization (N-1 and N-2 from the CEO). Then complement this with targeted interviews to ensure you have coverage of recent joiners, technical specialists, middle managers, and most geographies. We recommend using a standard structure for these interviews (e.g., a list of prompts) which are focused on the goals of the transformation and potentially seek to validate some of the conclusions reached through data analysis and surveys. However, successful interviewing of stakeholders requires that they are at ease and comfortable when answering questions. Therefore, it is important not to stick too rigidly to a script. If the interviewee is comfortable for the discussion to be recorded, this can make things much easier as it enables note taking (that might otherwise interrupt the flow of the interview) to be completed later. We suggest that, wherever possible, such interviews are conducted face to face, although we have seen that they can be managed via phone, especially where the interviewer and interviewee already know each other. A written commentary describing the main points arising from the interview should be written up for each interview. Note that this approach of a standard structure and write-up is particularly important when the interviews are to be conducted by a number of different people. In such cases, it is useful for the interviewers to have regular feedback sessions together so that the outcomes of early interviews can inform future interviews.

The value of a focus group versus a one-to-one interview comes from the interactions between participants. Sometimes, it is possible to get great energy in the room with people quickly bouncing ideas off each other and building on each other's thinking. We have found that this is very difficult to achieve via a conference call, even when the participants know each other. Instead, a face-to-face environment setup to enable creative thinking (comfortable furniture, plenty of whiteboard space, etc.) is greatly preferred. Because the value in a focus group comes from the cross-fertilization of ideas, it is useful to bring together people from different backgrounds. In this situation, some kind of icebreaker exercise should be considered essential to start things off but try to make it an "icebreaker with purpose" rather than something that is perceived as meaninglessly bland or banal. Then, to address the questions you wish to explore around digital transformation, we have found that it is best to use an element of fun and games to do this, rather than a traditional round-table discussion. Try to make the expression of opinions as interactive and collaborative as possible—we have found the use of voting with colored stickers or placing bets on a range of options using poker chips can be highly engaging and thought provoking.

Consider whether the proposed make-up of the group might make people less willing to share their honest views. A classic example would be that if you invite several people and their boss, it is unlikely that many (or any) of the participants would be willing to publicly go against the opinion of their manager!

It is very important that people who participate in interviews or stakeholder workshops know in advance how the information will be used (in fact, this can be a major factor in how fully they will engage). Our recommendation is that you apply the Chatham House Rule: information disclosed during a meeting may be reported by those present, but the source of that information may not be explicitly or implicitly identified. If any information collected during an interview or focus group is to be shared with attribution, clearance should be obtained from that individual first.

16.9 Competitor and Market Analysis

Of course, understanding the current state should not only look at the internal workings of your company. In addition, you need to discover what your competitors are doing and planning to do, and what is happening more broadly in the markets you serve. For this, we have found that it can be useful to work with external analysts/consultants who can advise you on these topics. However, we must add a cautionary note: as Tom Peters once said, the danger of competitive benchmarking is that "*we pick the current industry leader and then we launch a five-year program, the goal of which is to be as good as whoever was best five years ago, five years from now.*"

16.10 Setting up Transformation Governance

In the last few sections, we have looked at how statistical analysis, surveys, stakeholder interviews, focus groups, and competitor and market analysis can be used to understand the current state of your organization and also, more crucially, secure buy-in for the digital transformation. Let's now look at what transformation governance should be put in place to sustain this buy-in and to turn the insights gained into tangible transformation activities.

In Fig. 16.3 we show the key components of the transformation governance that should be put in place from the outset.

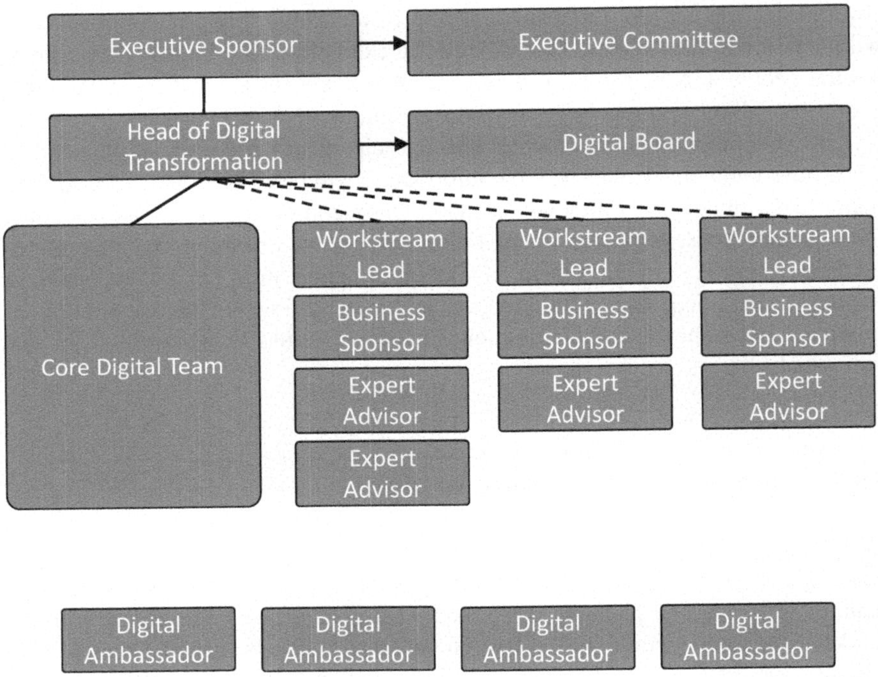

Fig. 16.3 Key components of a digital transformation governance structure. Authors' own figure

Here is a brief summary of how each component of this governance structure fits with the transformation model that we outlined earlier:

The *Executive Committee* prioritizes and selects workstreams which will form the basis for planning downstream transformation iterations. This ensures that the strategic direction of the transformation is set and supported from the very top of the organization.

The main link between the Executive Committee and the digital transformation program itself is the *executive sponsor*. The executive sponsor should be a full member of the Executive Committee. They may be especially focused on the digital transformation (e.g., a CDO), or they may have responsibility for a wider portfolio. They could even be the CEO. However, crucially, they must have sufficient time and enthusiasm to dedicate to the transformation in order to successfully manage it via the *Head of Digital Transformation* and the *Digital Board*. The Digital Board is chaired by the executive sponsor and has responsibility for selecting which activities will be in each iteration. In addition, it monitors the execution of each iteration. The Digital Board should be comprised of senior managers from different parts of the business, as well as experts in relevant fields. The Head of Digital Transformation has overall responsibility for delivering the transformation. In terms of line management, they will usually report directly to the executive sponsor and will report progress updates to, and seek guidance from, the Digital Board.

The Head of Digital Transformation will also have reporting into them the *Core Digital Team*, which will manage the overall coordination of the digital transformation.

Workstream Leads are responsible for identifying activities to be included in their workstream and for managing their implementation. They have a "dotted line" report into the Head of Digital Transformation. Each workstream will also have a *Business Sponsor* allocated to it. Their role is to champion their respective workstreams within the organization, provide advice on business related matters, and also be a first point of escalation for the Workstream Lead. We would expect them to be quite senior (usually at least N-1 from the Executive Committee). In addition, each workstream will have one or more *Expert Advisors*. They are not dedicated to a single workstream and they are not line-managed by the Workstream Leads. Their role is to provide expert guidance on topics that are relevant for the workstream (e.g., on business models or specific technologies). The team members who are considered to be relevant Expert Advisors within a workstream may change as the workstream evolves.

The *Digital Ambassadors* are a network of people from across the organization who will support the activities of the digital transformation and enable information exchange and collaboration across different parts of the business. Workstream Leads, the Core Digital Team and the Head of Digital Transformation will tap into this network, as required, to deliver the digital transformation.

16.11 Communication

As we reach the end of this chapter, you may have noticed that we have not specifically discussed the creation of a "communication plan" or similar for the digital transformation. This is quite deliberate: we believe that the best kind of communication is that which takes place through the collaborative process of designing and implementing the transformation itself. While occasional broadcast communications or management cascades may be appropriate, communication should primarily result from the actions required to make the transformation happen. Genuinely seeking people's feedback about what needs to change, enabling senior leaders to steer the direction of the transformation in a meaningful way, and training people in new tools, technologies and ways of working, are all better ways of communicating that your organization is undergoing a transformation than a newsletter or an all-staff conference call (although these do have their place when used appropriately).

Individual transformation activities are likely to involve the identification of their stakeholders (including anyone who will be impacted by the change) and will require decisions as to how to engage these people in order to achieve the objective(s) of that transformation activity. However, this, combined with our recommendations for transformation governance structures, securing of buy-in, and enabling people to contribute to the design of the transformation, should constitute almost all of the communication effort that is required.

References

BCG. (2000). *A framework for analyzing organizational behavior. Strategic workforce engagement: Designing the behavior of organizations for competitive advantage.* Boston Consulting Group. Accessible at: https://www.bcg.com/documents/file14006.pdf (Exhibit 2). Accessed October 26, 2019.

Bungay, S. (2011). *The art of action.* Nicholas Brealey.

McCarthy, J., McCarthy, M. (2002). *Software for your head.* Addison-Wesley Professional.

McKinsey. (2008). *McKinsey quarterly transformation executive summary.*

Syntec. (2016). *Report of the Syntec DevOps Camp-Paris*, February 2016.

Taylor, B. (2008). Why Zappos pays new employees to quit–and you should too. *Harvard Business Review.* 18/05/2008. https://hbr.org/2008/05/why-zappos-pays-new-employees. Accessed October 26, 2019.

Foundational Transformation Themes—Putting in Place Servitization and Platform Ecosystems

17

In the previous chapter, we described how to get started with your digital transformation by understanding the current state of your organization. We also identified that there are three key foundational transformation themes: strategy; business models; and platforms and ecosystems. These require special attention early on in any digital transformation: the decisions you make regarding them will have a significant impact on the content of the other transformation themes, and on the success of the overall digital transformation. In this chapter, we look in more detail at how each of these foundational transformation themes should be approached.

17.1 Strategy

As we have seen in the chapters about Strategy and Leadership it is important to ask yourself how your strategy will:

- Align with the fulfillment of your organization's core purpose.
- Exploit digital to create differentiated and sustainable value propositions.
- Fundamentally transform your business model(s).
- Optimize and transform existing business processes.

In most cases, you will not have a complete answer to these questions to begin with. Therefore, a priority component of your digital transformation will need to be workstreams that are tasked with clarifying them. The approaches adopted could range from conducting market research, and engaging with clients and partners, through to conducting small-scale, safe-to-fail strategy experiments.

H. Tardieu et al., *Deliberately Digital*, Future of Business and Finance,
https://doi.org/10.1007/978-3-030-37955-1_17

17.2 Business Models

When considering the changes that you need to make to your business model(s), there are two main approaches you should consider:

1. The *servitization* of products and/or services.
2. Leveraging *business platform ecosystems*.

Let's now discuss the specifics of each approach in turn.

17.3 Servitization

The servitization of products/services generally follows a pipeline model to transform the relationship between the seller and the buyer, reflecting an increasing service focus within product delivery. There are three key steps in servitization.

Firstly, the existing products must be fully or partially digitalized. While in principle servitization can be implemented with non-digital products, in practical terms some degree of digitalization is normally needed. Digitalization reduces the marginal cost of supply and increases immediacy for the consumer, both of which makes a servitization business model more viable and compelling. Implemented well, this digitalization will also increase customer intimacy, resulting in better, longer-term relationships between the supplier of the service and the client. In some cases, the product or service will remain almost entirely physical (as would be the case, for example, if switching to a power-per-hour charging model for airplane engines). However, even in these cases, some level of digitalization is still needed in order to enable the metered charging model. In addition, digitalization can enable service enhancement through data-driven insights. By way of example: although, in principle, the Spotify music streaming service could have been implemented by sending people CDs through the post, the reality is that such a non-digitized implementation would have failed because the cost of supply would be too great (not to mention the lack of immediacy for the user). Furthermore, shipping CDs through the post would not enable a metered charging model (i.e., pay per month of access to music) nor would it enable the service to be enhanced through sophisticated data-driven insights (e.g., recommendations based on actual listening habits).

Secondly, metered charging models should be implemented. An example would be "pay as you drive" for a car, rather than a fixed one-off cost for purchasing a car plus additional (and often unpredictable) maintenance and running costs.

Finally, move toward outcome-based contracts. Products achieve a higher level of servitization the more the charging model is aligned to the creation of value for the customer. So, for example, in the case of a car, paying per kilometer driven or per journey completed achieves a higher degree of servitization than paying per hour of travel or per month of having access to the car.

Servitization requires a shift in revenue recognition models as consumption/outcome revenues (typically OPEX based) replace the selling of products on a one-off basis (typically CAPEX based). The challenge of achieving this should not be underestimated. It impacts business targets, personal incentives and even shareholder perceptions (and is one of the reasons that KPIs need to be adjusted as we describe later in measuring the transformation).

In "pipeline" servitization models, digital technologies are used to transform defined value chains without benefitting from the network effects brought about by the sharing of data within a wider ecosystem. Where benefits from such network effects can be identified in the market, servitization alone represents a sub-optimal approach. In these cases, you should, in addition, seek to leverage platform ecosystems.

17.4 Platforms Ecosystems

A *platform ecosystem* depends on two prerequisites:

- There is value for each participant in the ecosystem from sharing data.
- There exists a (neutral) platform operator.

Platforms may fail to offer effective business models for a number of reasons, including:

- Buyers and sellers cannot find each other easily (especially in the B-to-C market).
- The positive value of sharing data is negatively outweighed by competition in the market or intellectual property considerations.
- Transaction costs of using the platform are too high: if transaction costs are perceived to be too high, the market will not take off unless a platform operator is willing to take the risk of reducing transaction costs, perhaps in exchange for a contractual agreement regarding the usage of data.
- Regulatory constraints (e.g., licenses to operate in certain sectors in certain geographies, taxation, and employment law).
- Lack of the required levels of trust (between the users of the platform and the platform operator). This can be a particular concern if one platform user insists on assuming the role of platform operator, as it can prevent necessary trust from other platform users (who assume that the platform operator will favor their own position).

A potentially attractive scheme for the platform model is to have an independent third-party act as platform operator. They would then take on the risks associated with growing the number of participants and also offer contractual agreements which, for example, would guarantee the data sovereignty for all parties.

To some extent, this is the role played by the Digital Giants in the B-to-C market, although there are perhaps significant question marks over the transparency of their contractual agreements and in the way they are able to respect data sovereignty requirements.

In the B-to-B market, General Electric made a notable move into the world of platforms with the launch of their Predix Industrial IoT environment. For a number of reasons, mostly organizational, commercial and contractual, Predix struggled to deliver against expectations and was eventually spun off into a separate company. This perhaps represents an important lesson in how difficult it is to manage a digital business under the same governance model as traditional business.

If you decide to pursue a strategy of leveraging existing platform ecosystems, you must first assess whether the platform ecosystem will be one-sided or two-sided.

17.5 One-sided Platforms

If your platform of choice is one-sided, your strategy should be one of maximizing the operational efficiencies from using the platform. Such efficiency gains may come in the form of sharing some of your operational data in exchange for access to a larger volume of data from other platform users, which you can then use to derive additional value. An example of this might be an automotive company joining the "HERE" platform (introduced in the chapter on Platforms and Ecosystems) to share data from their connected cars: in return it would gain access to a wealth of contextualized road data without having to collect it through its own cars (Fig. 17.1).

The prerequisites of engaging through such a model will be:

- Adhere to a defined and agreed data architecture model so that your data can be properly interpreted by the ecosystem and, in turn, you are able to use and analyze data contributed by other platform members.
- Check whether your data sovereignty will be appropriately respected within the data usage control policy dictated by the platform operator.
- Check that your internal policies and procedures meet the requirements stipulated by the platform operator for use of data.
- Check how data will be shared between platform users (does it need to be shared in its raw form or can it be anonymized and/or summarized)—how will this align with your business strategy?
- Check what limits will be placed on the usage of shared data (time limits, scope, etc.) What commitment, if any, will there be to destroy data once these limits are reached?

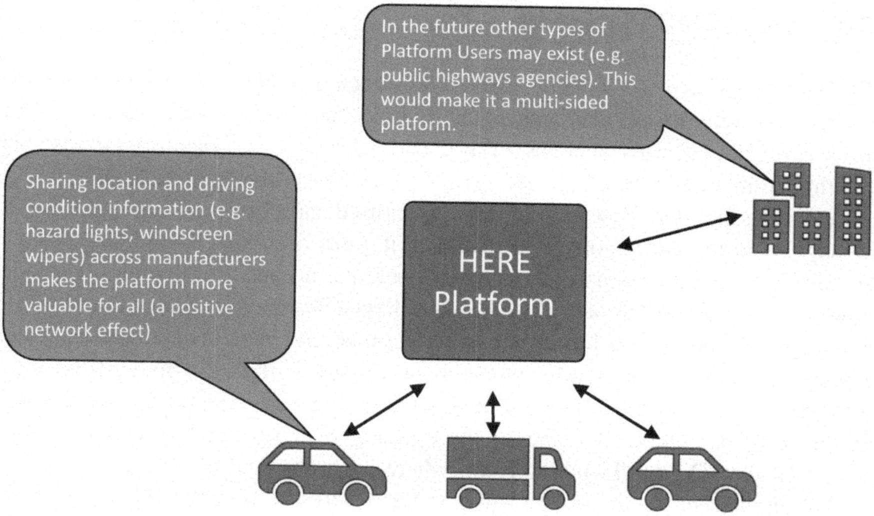

Fig. 17.1 HERE platform, current and future. Authors' own figure

In general, when the access to a large and diverse dataset is critical (e.g., to train Machine Learning algorithms), the one-sided platform approach is a recommended strategy. This is because there is a clear, common, and consistent goal shared by the platform user community.

The success of "HERE" can be explained by the shared vision of automotive companies wanting to offer autonomous vehicles able to operate at autonomy level four (at least). Having access to contextualized road network data for algorithm training that covers a full range of driving conditions is something that would be very difficult for an individual vehicle manufacturer to achieve on its own.

The same logic can be applied to most of the vertical markets that are seeking to exploit artificial intelligence (e.g., health for epidemiology[1] and payment systems for fraud detection), they all need to exploit the value of a given data economy as widely as possible.

Interestingly, pursuing a single-sided platform strategy can be a stepping stone to a multi-sided platform approach. Having established a credible and sustainable platform user base in a single-sided context, consider what other adjacent or even tangential markets might benefit from joining the platform, thereby creating a multi-sided environment. The attractiveness of accessing a ready-made critical mass of users overcomes the "chicken and egg" problem of building ecosystem viability from scratch, when the value for early joiners is very minimal.

[1]The study of the distribution and patterns of diseases.

17.6 Two-sided Platforms

If the platform is *two-sided,* value is derived by each member of the ecosystem from other parties' interactions. The value is both direct (e.g., buyer and seller exchanges through retail platforms such as eBay), and indirect (e.g., data-driven insights resulting from such exchanges, that drive further business opportunities).

Revisiting the Skywise example (Fig. 17.2) used earlier in Part II, when EasyJet participates in the Airbus-operated platform, it gains access to agreed sets of production data for the Airbus planes that it operates. It can, for example, be made aware that a certain batch of Airbus A320s suffers a design issue which could result in operational failures. Such insight can allow preventive repairs on affected planes, leading to avoidance of significant costs (or worse). Airbus, for its part, benefits from participating airlines' in-flight data, which it can use to help improve designs for the next generation of planes. Data exchanged in such a way can be a key enabler of the "Digital Twin" concept, where each physical plane has a comprehensive digital representation of a whole range of physical parameters ranging from design specifications to operational performance and maintenance history. The ability for Airbus to rapidly acquire structured data from EasyJet about operational performance and even customer experience feedback can inspire and significantly reduce design iteration cycle-times and therefore reduce the time to market for new models.

The best way to test the appropriateness of a two-sided platform is to consider the theoretical benefits that vertical integration could bring to the business model of your company. In this context, vertical integration is the incorporation of two successive but disparate operational processes into same enterprise.

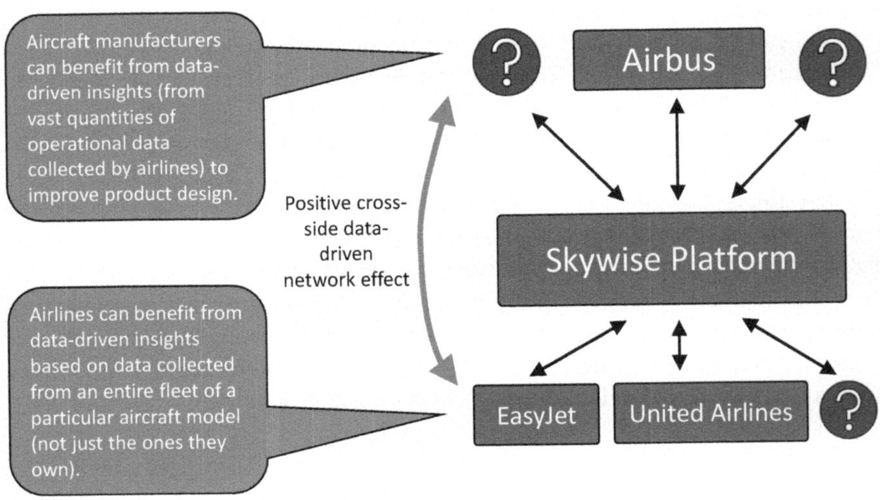

Fig. 17.2 Skywise platform. Authors' own figure

In the case of Skywise, vertical integration simulation would mean analyzing the business benefits for EasyJet and Airbus if Airbus was to operate the planes currently belonging to EasyJet. Assuming that such integration means that there would be no data transaction costs between production and operation, what benefits might Airbus get in terms of product lifecycle management (especially in design and production) and what benefits could EasyJet see in terms of operation and maintenance?

The same exercise can be performed by simulating the vertical integration of airplane design and customer management in the context of building new products and services. As described earlier, the potential benefits would be reduced time to market and improved operational efficiency.

With two-sided platform strategies, the challenge is to realize the theoretical vertical integration benefits (through zero-cost data exchanges) while actually leaving each partner of the ecosystem in control of its own management and strategy.

Having established the theoretical benefit of multi-sided platform engagement, the next step will be to decide and agree how business benefits will be shared between partners of the ecosystem, and which portion should be shared with customers (and how).

It should be understood that the example we have shown is somewhat simplified because it ignores the multi-homing challenge which would normally have to be faced. In our example, Air France would at least have to share data via both an Airbus provided platform and a Boeing provided platform —this is a complex situation in terms of intellectual property management if the two platforms are one and the same (Airbus will tend to be reluctant to provide visibility of its data to Boeing). If the provided platforms are separate, there remains a problem for Air France, in that it does not have a single view of its entire operational fleet.

17.7 Platform Creation or Participation

It must be recognized that a key challenge when determining your strategy for platform ecosystems is to decide whether your company is strong enough to act as the initiator of an ecosystem (perhaps with the potential to act as the platform operator), or whether it should look to participate in one or several existing ecosystem(s)—not forgetting the challenge of multi-homing.

Building a new ecosystem may seem to be the holy grail for a platform business, but this approach needs to be very carefully considered. Getting such a strategy wrong has resulted in the demise of several companies and has put many others on the verge of a major disruption.

The first temptation is to create an ecosystem that specifically revolves around your company, with a parochial view of maximizing your benefits, usually to the detriment of other participants. You take for granted the fact that other target members of the ecosystem will be happy to enter such an asymmetrical relationship. In such situations, the ecosystem is very unlikely to reach a critical mass because other businesses will not perceive sufficient benefit from participating in it.

Another potential mistake is to insist on acting as the platform operator for the ecosystem that your company is creating. In such situations, independence and trust are always difficult to establish, and other members will almost inevitably have doubts over their data sovereignty if the roles of platform operator and user are confused.

17.8 Creating an Ecosystem for One-sided Platforms

The best approach (evidenced through companies like HERE) is to create a joint venture where the main participants in the ecosystem can exercise their influence via a third-party company that acts as the platform operator. Nevertheless, this approach is not without its challenges, particularly in regard to the perceived openness of the ecosystem to potential new partners who are not shareholders of the initial joint venture. However, once the ecosystem reaches its critical mass, and if the contractual terms binding its members appear to be fair to both existing and new partners, such an approach can be a good and workable solution.

This kind of solution is a good fit for one-sided platform but is difficult to implement for two-sided platforms, especially where there is the additional multi-homing challenge to resolve.

17.9 Creating an Ecosystem for Multi-sided Platforms

If to begin with we exclude the challenge of multi-homing and we assume that all potential partners will belong to only one ecosystem, it is clear that one company within a potential ecosystem needs to take the lead. An initiating business can create the kernel of an ecosystem by launching an analysis of multi-sidedness with a few potential key partners that cover the main data complementarities. This would be achieved through the simulation of vertical integration, as described earlier. If the potential business benefits appear attractive enough, the relevant businesses could create a joint venture to provide the platform or agree to let one participant assume this role. The platform operator (joint venture or individual business) may choose to build the platform or outsource its development to an external third party (platform host). The platform operator will still be responsible for establishing and governing the fundamental prerequisites of common data architecture and data sovereignty, as mentioned earlier.

17.10 Dealing with the Multi-homing Challenge

If platform ecosystem members are only interacting with a single platform operator, the challenge of respecting data related Intellectual Property is relatively self-contained. However, as soon as businesses need to engage in more than one potentially competitive ecosystems, the issue of multi-homing comes into play and must be addressed.

To help explain the potential problems that this brings, consider the situation where a contingent (or gig) worker is concurrently working for two competing organizations. The insights that the worker is privy to during his/her engagements may be viewed as a serious conflict of interest and could result in their employment contract being terminated by both organizations—neither party then benefits from the value that the worker might bring. Of course, legally binding non-disclosure agreements could be drawn up to mitigate against IP leakage, but these are still hugely dependent on trust.

Apply this scenario to the world of data, and in particular sensitive data like product design specifications or operational performance records, and it is clear that platform users will be reluctant to share information that may become unintentionally accessible by competitors (or any unapproved party). In this case, it is the responsibility of the platform operator to offer data exchange interfaces (typically APIs) that ensure highly configurable and granular permissioning of data, i.e., data is only shared with agreed parties for the intended use.

Referring back to the Skywise platform example, EasyJet would share operational data that is only permissioned for use by Airbus—Air France would have no access to EasyJet data unless explicitly allowed through some kind of mutually agreed value exchange (in this instance, the platform may well become the mechanism through which value exchanges are monitored and monetized). Air France would only share its data on Skywise as it relates to its Airbus aircraft—Boeing-related data would never be shared on the Airbus platform. Such control demands very precise data taxonomies and permissioning mechanisms and some forward-thinking platform operators are exploring the use of Blockchain technologies to provide immutable audit trails and smart-contract-driven permissions to establish trust within such complex data exchanges.

For a company participating in multiple platforms by design, it is considered important to maintain a degree of independence from the platform operator with respect to the definition and governance of services. That way, the platform operator has to bear full responsibility for ensuring adherence to the data sharing protocols.

The situation is similar to that encouraged by the Open Banking initiative and PSD2, where competitor banks are obliged to exchange specified customer-related financial data when instructed to do so by the respective customer.

18 Planning an Iterative Transformation —Setting the Strategic Transformation Direction

In the chapter on Starting the Transformation, we have explained how to analyze existing data about your organization, conduct surveys, run stakeholder interviews and focus groups, and assess your competitors and your market. In the previous chapter, we have also explained why and how special consideration needs to be given to the foundational transformation themes. Having performed this analysis, you will need to group individual ideas together to form your potential transformation workstreams. This can be quite a complex exercise and will need to be done interactively and collaboratively. A potential workstream will often contain several items which may not be obviously related. For example, a workstream to reduce the call waiting time for customers contacting a help desk may be based on the following feedback and suggestions:

- Complaints from customers.
- A statistical correlation between low customer satisfaction scores and high call waiting times.
- A suggestion by someone to implement chat bots for frequent help desk queries.
- Frustration/attrition among help desk staff.

Remember that, at this stage, the clustering does not have to be 100% accurate, but rather it has to be sufficient to ensure a manageable number of potential workstreams (typically ranging from 10s to low 100s). At this stage, remember that you are only identifying potential workstreams. In the rest of this chapter, we will explain how to choose the right mix of the most promising workstreams for your digital transformation, while in the chapter, on Enduring digital transformation, we will describe how to determine which concrete steps should be planned for the next transformation iteration.

H. Tardieu et al., *Deliberately Digital*, Future of Business and Finance,
https://doi.org/10.1007/978-3-030-37955-1_18

18.1 Workstream Classification

Selection and prioritization of workstreams should primarily be based on balancing the following three criteria:

- *Return on investment*: how large will the benefit be compared to the investment needed?
- *Timescale*: how long will it take to start realizing the benefit?
- *Certainty*: how likely is it that the anticipated return on investment and timescale will be achieved?

We have found that many executives seek to understand these three aspects and take them into account for their decision making. A rule of thumb often applied is that if two out of three of these aspects are desirable, then a workstream should proceed. For example, a modest return on investment is fine, if it can be achieved quickly and is highly likely to be achieved. Or a risky (low degree of certainty) workstream will still make sense if the payback will be fast and large.

Only one of the three measures being positive does not necessarily mean that a workstream should be ruled out, but certainly more careful consideration will need to be given to whether the balance between return on investment, timescale, and certainty is justified.

To enable the selection and prioritization of workstreams on this basis, we recommend the use of several models to classify and present candidate workstreams so that these trade-offs can be more easily visualized, discussed, and understood.

18.2 Classification Based on Level of Certainty

For every workstream, there will be two types of uncertainty. Firstly, there will be uncertainty about the implementation. For example, if you are implementing a change that relies on a very new technology with which you have little prior experience, then there will be a high degree of uncertainty about how to implement it. Secondly, there will be uncertainty about the benefits that will be achieved. For example, even if you are very confident that you can roll-out a new workforce management system, you may have less confidence that it will achieve the desired benefits. It can be useful to plot workstream characteristics on a chart such as the one shown in Fig. 18.1, which also enables a very impactful color coding based on the overall level of certainty.

While this type of chart can be very useful, it is not always easy to quantify the level of certainty associated with a given workstream. To aid this, the Cynefin framework (created by Dave Snowden, and having its roots in complexity science) (Snowden and Boone 2007) can be a useful tool. Cynefin defines four contexts for decision making: obvious, complicated, complex, and chaotic (Fig. 18.2).

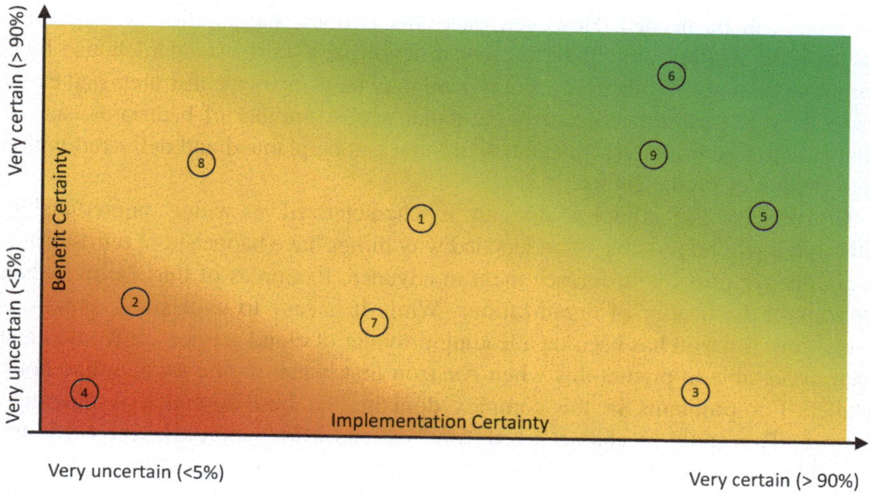

Fig. 18.1 Classifying workstreams based on benefit and implementation certainty. Authors' own figure

Fig. 18.2 Authors' interpretation of the Cynefin framework devised by Dave Snowden. Snowden and Boone (2007)

In the Obvious and Complicated domains, it is possible to predict outcomes (with a reasonably high degree of certainty). Obvious problems are those where, for a given type of problem, there is a standard, well-defined solution (best practice). One example of such a problem might be a password reset: once the problem is categorized as a password reset request, then the steps taken to achieve this result will be the same in every case. An important point to clarify is that obvious does not mean that the solution is necessarily easy or that anyone can do it. It may require a great deal of skill (for example installing a gas boiler). However, the solution will be well defined and understood.

In the complicated domain, it is also possible to predict outcomes, however the actual course of action will tend to vary from problem to problem. This is a domain where good practice can be applied and where some level of analysis, design, and planning will be needed. However, once this is done, the solution will be quite assured. An example might be the construction of a fairly standard house by a building company. While every plot of land may have its own constraints and every house may be customized to meet particular needs (number of bedrooms, size of kitchen, etc.), in principle, it is an activity that can be planned and delivered with a high degree of predictability.

Conversely, the complex domain is characterized as being unpredictable: although it will be possible to understand why things have happened in retrospect, it is not always possible to foresee them in advance. Examples of this abound when we look at the history of organizations. While it is easy to understand retrospectively how Amazon has become a leading provider of cloud services, it would have been impossible to predict this when Amazon first began its life as an online book retailer. For problems in the complex domain, the best approach is emergent practice. This could be characterized as a "test and learn" approach where you try something out, learn from the results, and adjust your future approach accordingly.

Taking this one step further, the chaotic domain is one where the relationship between cause and effect is impossible to understand, even in retrospect. Examples of this are particularly notable in politics where, even with hindsight, it is not always easy to explain or understand (for certain) how particular events have unfolded. In addition, the chaotic domain is characterized by having severe time pressure, where immediate action is required even though outcomes will be uncertain.

The central region in the Cynefin framework is used to represent disorder, which is defined as a state of not knowing which domain a particular problem inhabits. It should be noted that, when a problem is in the disorder domain (and if no effort is made to properly categorize it), people will tend to use their preferred approach (their default modus-operandi) to solving it. For example, people who prefer a test-and-learn lean start-up approach may apply that to problems that would be best solved using a standard solution or by using a more traditional analysis/design/plan approach. Conversely, those who are accustomed to delivering projects with a fixed cost, time, and scope may erroneously use that method to tackle a problem in the complex domain (where accurate planning and forecasting will simply not be possible).

A final point to note about Cynefin is that the domain of a problem will vary depending on the organizational context. What for one organization may be an obvious problem may, for another, be a complicated or complex problem. To help people classify problems using Cynefin and taking this into account, Liz Keogh has developed five questions people can ask themselves about a given problem (Fig. 18.3). In general, if the statements higher up in this model are true (4 and 5), then the problem will be in the complex domain for your organization. Problems for which statements 2 or 3 are true will tend to be obvious or complicated. And problems for which statement 1 is true will tend to be firmly in the obvious domain.

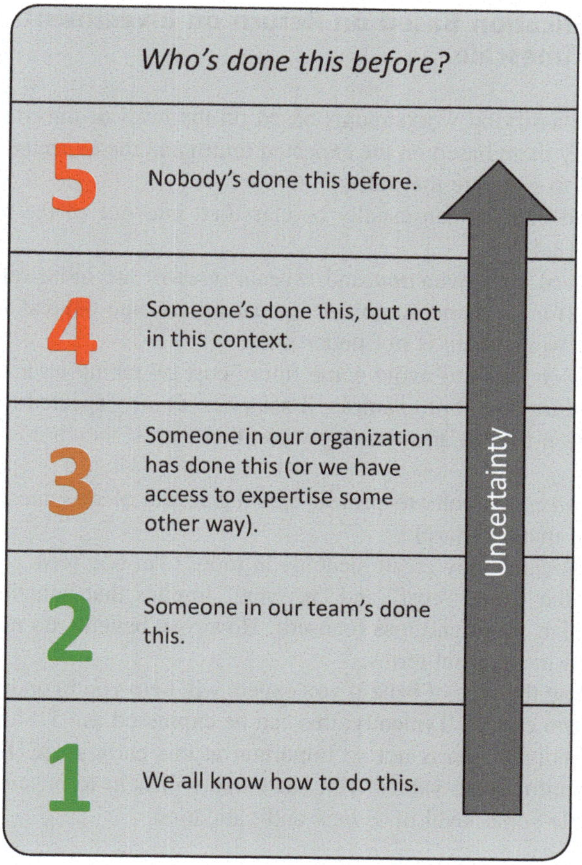

Fig. 18.3 Assessing uncertainty by asking "Who's done this before?"—Based on work by Liz Keough. Keogh n.d.

Used in combination with the information provided in Part I and Part II of this book, you should be able to build up a good picture of the level of certainty associated with a particular workstream. In general, technologies that have been established for longer will have less implementation uncertainty than emerging ones, and switching to a new business model will have greater benefit uncertainty than optimizing existing processes.

Be mindful that identifying workstreams as having a high degree of uncertainty should not lead them to be discounted, rather it should be used to inform the transformation approach in order to reduce risk as much and as early as possible (a topic we will cover in more detail in the chapter Enduring digital transformation).

18.3 Classification Based on Return on Investment and Timescale

In addition to classifying workstreams based on the level of uncertainty, it is also useful to classify them based on the expected return and the expected timescale that will be needed to generate that return.

The expected benefits can usually be classified into one of the four categories shown in Fig. 18.4.

The benefits of *cost reduction* and *revenue growth* are quite self-explanatory: reducing costs (for the same output) or increasing revenue beyond what would be achieved if the workstream is not undertaken.

Cost avoidance seeks to avoid some future cost by taking an action before the cost is expected to arise. For example, if salary costs are expected to rise, then the use of automation may be more strongly justified than if they are expected to stay the same.

Revenue protection looks to protect existing levels of revenue (e.g., by innovating to retain market share).

Some workstreams may create benefits in more than one area.

Our use of the words "cost" and "revenue" implies that benefits are financial (and, in particular, profit and loss focused). However, benefits do not always have to be quantified in financial terms.

Understanding the type of benefit you expect will help you to understand the size of the benefit you expect. Typically, this can be expressed as "T-Shirt sizing" (XS, S, M, L, XL) as precision is not so important at this early stage. However, associating some approximate values with each size will help to ensure some consistency and enable some level of review and validation.

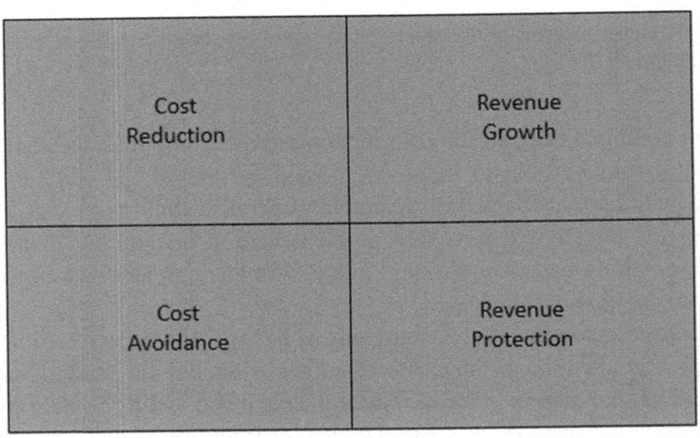

Fig. 18.4 Categories of benefits. Authors' own figure

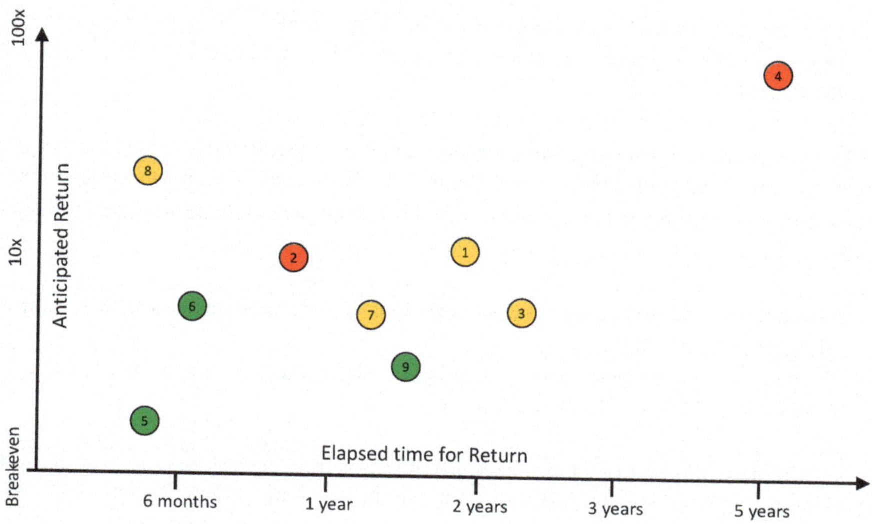

Fig. 18.5 Classifying workstreams based on expected return and timescale. Authors' own figure

In addition to understanding the size of the benefit expected, it will also be necessary to estimate the cost of implementing the change in order to calculate an approximate return. Again, this exercise does not need to be particularly precise at this stage.

Finally, for each workstream, an estimated time to realize the benefit is needed. A very important point is that you estimate the time to achieve the return on investment, rather than the time to implement the change. A change may take one year to implement, but you may not start seeing value from it until another year has elapsed, and the return on investment may not occur until a further two years have passed. In this case, the time estimated to realize the benefit would be four years.

Once the return and the timescale for each workstream has been estimated in high-level terms, they can be plotted on a chart, with each workstream also being color coded based on the level of certainty identified previously, as shown in Fig. 18.5.

There are a few things to note about the approach taken:

- The axes use either logarithmic or Fibonacci-like number sequences.[1] These encourage people to be less precise for longer timescales/bigger benefits.
- The minimum value on the Anticipated Return axis should be break-even. Any workstreams that do not expect to do better than break-even should not be considered (it is worth restating here that benefits are not always financial and break-even in this context equates to benefits that outweigh the costs).

[1] A Fibonacci sequence is one in which each number is the sum of the two preceding numbers.

- It is typical (though not always true) that the items with a higher expected return and/or a longer expected timescale will also have a higher level of uncertainty.

This method of presenting workstreams enables executives to use their judgement to prioritize and select workstreams by balancing return on investment, timescale, and certainty. Their decision-making approach will be unique, but typically will consider:

- The need to include some workstreams that will deliver results quickly with a high level of certainty.
- Whether or not to place some "big bets" where there is uncertainty and/or a long timescale, but a high potential payback.

Note that, while at this stage, executives are setting a direction for the digital transformation, they are not committing to the full benefit, budget, or timescale for each workstream. Rather they are signaling where they see the high-level priorities for the organization at this time, based on the input collected from across the entire organization. Commitment from the Executive Committee is not sought until the first transformation iteration has been planned (as described in the chapter on Enduring Digital Transformation). Furthermore, the choice of workstreams is not carved in stone: the Executive Committee will have regular opportunities to add or remove workstreams as the digital transformation progresses.

Given this context, this level of analysis will often be enough to enable workstreams to be chosen. However, in certain cases (particularly where several workstreams seem evenly matched and it is not clear which ones should be chosen), analyzing workstreams in terms of cost of delay and using the weighted shortest job first approach can be beneficial.

18.4 Cost of Delay

Cost of delay, which was first described by Donald Reinertsen (Reinertsen 1998), is the opportunity cost associated with not doing something. In some cases, the cost of delay is linear (i.e., lost revenue is proportionate to the delay). But, in many real-world scenarios, the cost of delay is nonlinear (Fig. 18.6). For example, cases where there is an early mover advantage have a cost of delay that is an s-curve (i.e., being late to market will have a disproportionally negative impact on revenue). Another example of a nonlinear cost of delay is when there is no benefit to delivering something early, but a significant penalty for delivering late (for example a regulatory fine). It is worth noting that, despite the name, the "cost" may not be merely financial (for example it could be reputational or environmental damage).

18.5 Weighted Shortest Job First (WSJF)

Weighted shortest job first (WSJF) is an approach to portfolio planning that considers both the cost of delay and the length of time it will take to implement a given initiative. To explain, let's work through a simple example, after which we will consider some of the caveats and real-world complexities that it is useful to be aware of.

Let's assume that we have a team of people that will be delivering three initiatives (A, B, and C). In Table 18.1, you can see, for each initiative, how long it will take to complete (if the whole team works on it exclusively) and the value it will deliver per month when it is completed (a linear cost of delay in each case). We have then calculated the weighted cost of delay by dividing the cost of delay by the duration.

One surprisingly common approach to scheduling is to ask the team to multi-task and deliver all three initiatives in the same timeframe. If the team does this, it will take them 24 months to complete all the initiatives, giving a total cost of delay of 4.32 million (the shaded area in Fig. 18.7).

Another approach is to ask the team to focus on one initiative at a time, starting with the one that delivers the highest value first. This is illustrated in Fig. 18.8 and gives a total cost of delay of 3.3 million (instead of 4.32 million when the team were asked to work on all three initiatives in parallel).

However, in this case, total Cost of Delay is minimized even further if the team is again asked to focus on one initiative at a time, but this time starting with the one that has the highest weighted cost of delay. As shown in Fig. 18.9, this reduces the

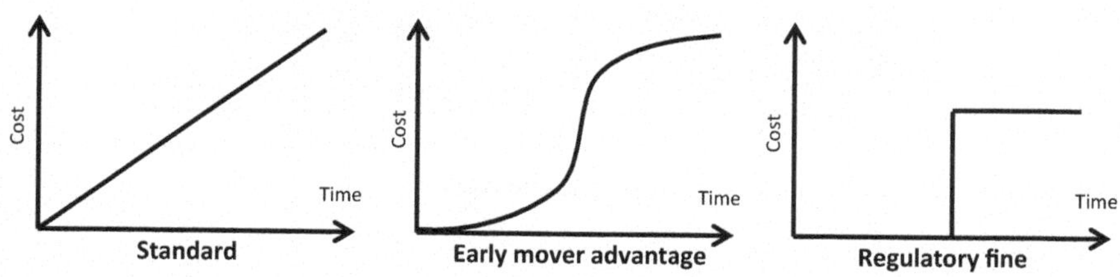

Fig. 18.6 Examples of different cost of delay functions. Adapted with permission from original (Daly et al. 2017)

Table 18.1 Example calculation of weighted cost of delay (table compiled by authors)

Initiative	Time to complete	Value when complete (cost of delay) per month (k)	Weighted cost of delay
A	3	50	16.7
B	9	60	6.7
C	12	70	5.8

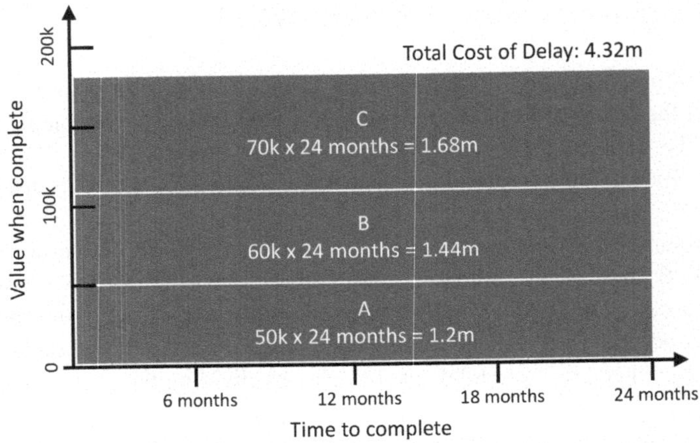

Fig. 18.7 Cost of delay if all tasks are completed in parallel. Authors' own figure

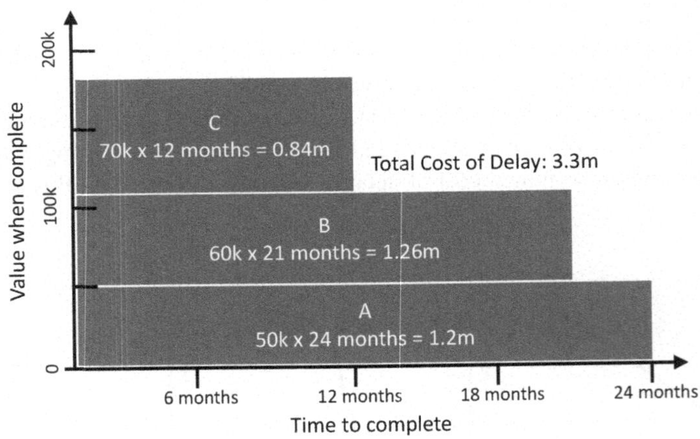

Fig. 18.8 Cost of delay when tasks are completed in order of highest cost of delay first. Authors' own figure

total cost of delay further still to 2.55 million, just 59% of the case where the team were asked to work on all the initiatives in parallel.

The first approach we described (asking the team to work in parallel on all three initiatives) is clearly not the most sensible approach, in this simple example, however this is only because we were able to make the following assumptions:

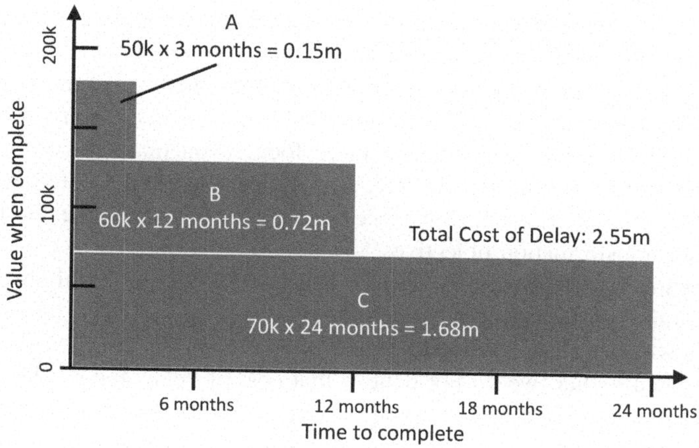

Fig. 18.9 Cost of delay when tasks are completed in order of highest WSJF first. Authors' own figure

- That the same (fixed) team would be working on all three initiatives.
- That if the whole team focused on one initiative at a time then it could be delivered proportionately more quickly (in other words, everyone working on initiative A would deliver it in 3 months instead of 24 months).

Many transformation workstreams will not fulfill these criteria. For example, it is unlikely that the same team assigned to transforming business models will be implementing process automation for customer contacts. Many workstreams will also have an elapsed time that does not relate to the number of people working on it (e.g., where there are key dependencies on third parties). However, we would still recommend that you carry out analysis to determine which workstreams these conditions do apply to and, in those cases, seek to avoid running them in parallel.

If you do avoid multi-tasking, then in our example, you can clearly see that WSJF is an effective way to determine in which order initiatives should be sequenced. However, note that WSJF is reliant not just on the assumptions previously listed, but also the following additional ones:

- That the cost of delay is linear.
- That there are no other dependencies between the initiatives.

If the cost of delay is not linear, then the WSJF approach does not necessarily result in correct prioritization. If some initiatives have a much lower cost of delay initially, then it could make sense to start these later. Conversely, if some have a much higher cost of delay at the outset, then these will usually need to be prioritized.

In other cases, dependencies exist where one initiative simply cannot be started until another one has been completed or is underway. For example, as we have already highlighted in Foundational Transformation Themes, some workstreams relating to Strategy, Business Models, and Platforms and Ecosystems will need to be initiated before other workstreams (more focused on optimization) should be started. The converse can also be true, sometimes you need to start with some "quick wins" that optimize existing processes in order to create time and budget to fund grander transformation objectives.

We hope that this explanation of cost of delay and WSJF has highlighted that the number of transformation workstreams started in parallel should be limited to only those cases where it makes sense to do so.

As we stated earlier, we do not believe that cost of delay and WSJF should be the primary methods used to select and prioritize transformation workstreams, but they can be useful ways to analyze workstreams where the balance of return on investment, timescale, and level of certainty does not yield a clear "winner." In these cases, we have found that cost of delay (and especially considering different cost of delay curves) can greatly assist prioritization. While WSJF is not so commonly applicable to digital transformation workstreams, it can still be a useful "tie breaker" where it is difficult to decide which workstream should be started first. It is also a very useful reminder that the correct sequencing of activities has many nuances and can have a large implication for the return on investment of the overall digital transformation.

References

Daly, et al. (2017). https://atos.net/wp-content/uploads/2018/02/atos-the-digital-business-continuum.pdf. Accessed October 26, 2019.

Keogh (n.d.). https://lizkeogh.com/cynefin-for-everyone/. Accessed October 26, 2019.

Reinertsen, D. (1998). *Managing the design factory: A product developers tool kit*. Simon & Schuster Ltd.

Snowden, D. J., & Boone, M. E. (2007). A leader's framework for decision making. *Harvard Business Review*, November 2007 issue. https://hbr.org/2007/11/a-leaders-framework-for-decision-making. Accessed October 26, 2019.

Measuring the Transformation—KPIs for Understanding Transformation Progress 19

Logic would dictate that in all meaningful transformations, it is important to have a vision of: "What good looks like"; an understanding of the levers of change that will be deployed; and a clear measure of the impact that those levers are having. Without such clarity, transforming businesses risk pursuing somewhat ethereal flights of fancy or suffering status quo stagnation. Before we look at the way that a business might determine a set of balanced KPIs, let's consider some of the factors that make good and bad measures of performance.

19.1 Understanding the "Why?"

The ancient proverb "*Where there is no vision, the people perish*" can certainly be applied to the business environment. If an organization fails to have clarity of purpose, it is hard to motivate employees and excite customers. Conversely, inspiration, loyalty, and engagement can all result from well-constructed mission and vision statements. Some of today's Digital Giants choose to articulate visions that probably extend way beyond the scope of their direct influence (e.g., Tesla —"*accelerating the world's transition to sustainable energy*"; Google—"*To organize the world's information and make it universally accessible and useful.*"; or Uber—"*To bring transportation—for everyone, everywhere*"). While it is not necessary for digitally transforming businesses to set their compass according to a particular global grand challenge, it is important to be able to articulate a mission that is more than one of simply making money and generating shareholder value. In fact, it is very interesting to observe the increasing trend for consumer sentiment to be driven by factors such as environmental sustainability of products and services, ethical supply chains and economic fairness.

Simon Sinek's Golden Circle model (Sinek) emphasizes the importance of understanding "why" an organization exists. Not what it makes or does, or how it goes about achieving its results, but what is its purpose or belief. In this chapter,

H. Tardieu et al., *Deliberately Digital*, Future of Business and Finance,
https://doi.org/10.1007/978-3-030-37955-1_19

although we are not exploring the way that a business should create or articulate its vision, the question "why?" is still key when developing a meaningful set of enterprise transformation metrics. If measures do not ultimately support the realization of your business's "why?" they risk being counterproductive.

19.2 The Problems with Measures

In many enterprises, KPIs have almost become an industry in themselves. The world of digital allows almost every business transaction to be measured, analyzed, visualized and monitored—But what value do these measures really bring? We have encountered many situations where much relied on KPI measures are reported as being "in tolerance" (green across the board), yet business users of the related services are far from satisfied with the level of service they actually receive. There could be many reasons for this, but at a fundamental level we believe it is a symptom of:

- Measures are not "Key." They don't address the heart of what end-users are really looking for. Businesses should ask themselves how many KPIs are appropriate—the clue is in the word "Key." Having many disparate indicators risks taking the focus away from the real "why" behind an enterprise.
- Measures are not really linked to desired outcomes. They are somewhat arbitrary measures of loosely related activity. For instance, "Application Server availability"—having server availability is of course important, but it is only one link in the overall service availability chain. Fixating on the maximizing of such measures will be unlikely to drive overall positive change and may ultimately become counterproductive.
- Measures become more than just "indicators," they become the *raison d'être* for some parts of the organization. Employee recognition and reward then become more connected to the achievement of somewhat parochial KPI's than to desired wider business outcomes.[1] This can be especially the case in organization cultures that are strongly personal bonus-driven.
- When businesses encounter service delivery problems, there is a tendency to create another metric to monitor the perceived cause of the problem—this measure then becomes yet another embedded, operational focus that risks distraction from the real "why?" Somewhat perversely, we have found that poor performance always tends to attract more attention and "management help" than good performance.

[1]This scenario is nicely reflected by Goodhart's Law: https://en.wikipedia.org/wiki/Goodhart%27s_law [accessed 26/10/2019].

It is important to realize that usually "what gets measured gets managed." Measure the wrong things and you will end up managing the wrong things: for example, a measure of employee utilization may well be helpful as a relatively independent measure of efficiency—but in an environment of growing cost pressures there is a tendency to drive utilization ever higher to a point where teams actually become less productive as all slack is removed from the system. Such a scenario can lead to a vicious circle of greater cost pressures, even greater utilization targets and even lower effectiveness which in turn leads to greater cost pressures.

The "gaming" of measures, intentionally or subliminally, is a real risk for those criteria that are more input than outcome-driven: overstating sales opportunity pipelines based on generous win-probabilities may support individual bonus achievements but does not necessarily lead to sales being realized.

19.3 Toward High Impact Measures

Digital transformations often demand a different way of thinking about customers and service delivery models and their associated measures of success—businesses must avoid falling into the trap of simply finding additional measures of performance to layer on top of established traditional measures. They must take the opportunity to completely rethink indicators of digital business success and consider carefully how they will shape organizational objectives and behaviors.

It must also be recognized that removing certain measures could (at least in the short term) unbalance some existing control mechanisms and care should be taken in these instances—however, it is often the case that the impact of certain measures is significantly less than some would like to believe (usually because they were not great measures in the first place). A careful and objective review of measures and reports should be carried out to determine which ones can be dropped without unduly destabilizing business operations. A simple way to assess the appropriateness of a measure is to weigh up the relative value (or impact) of a measure versus the difficulty of deriving it.

The impact value of a measure can be highly subjective and needs to be considered against the backdrop of your overarching mission and vision. Measures of customer sentiment or retention are highly valuable in understanding levels of engagement and intimacy, whereas a measure of sales pipeline against internal targets is a somewhat self-serving comparison.

High impact measures will tend to be lead rather than lag indicators: Proactively dealing with problems (vehicle maintenance, personal health care, infrastructure, etc.) is usually more cost-effective and less disruptive that after a failure event—businesses that can encourage pre-emptive treatments have a clear market differentiator.

None of this dismisses the importance of core “Hygiene factor” measures, such as revenue, free cash flow, and staff turnover, but think about whether these are symptoms of success/failure or real driving forces for your transformation program and whether they will tend to drive the right or wrong behaviors in support of your transformation goals.

Table 19.1 gives examples of the types of measures you may have depending on their impact and ease of collation.

Going back to the fundamental question of “why,” it should be no surprise that truly meaningful digital KPIs will have a strong alignment to anticipated business outcomes. They will be aligned to either the “Scale in Operation” or “Intimacy with Customer” axis of our “Driving forces behind Digital Leadership” graph (see Introduction).

They will tend to have a focus on things like “maximizing customer value” or “growing employee empowerment” (to minimize unintended operational inertia within business processes). These might be considered to be somewhat nebulous concepts and difficult to define, let alone measure, but this should not be seen as an excuse to revert to type and focus on things that are easier to deal with. Some guiding principles might be:

- Can a measure be clearly evidenced and quantified?
- Will a change in the measure lead to a direct impact on the desired business outcome?
- Is there unambiguous organizational responsibility and accountability for the measure?

Table 19.1 Complexity and impact of performance measures (table compiled by authors)

High impact value/difficult	High impact value/easy
Transformation target: The difficulty of generating the measure could indicate that source systems are not well aligned to the desired direction of travel or control. Measures should be analyzed to identify where the mismatch lies. If either the measure or its method of collection can be simplified, they should be	Likely to be *true KPIs*. They are perceived as valuable in terms of providing management control signals. Their relative ease of generation implies that related activities are well aligned to the measures. It may still be however that the wrong processes are being focused on and therefore the wrong measures being derived
Low impact value/difficult	Low impact value/easy
Problem children: This could be an area of ambiguity. It could be the case that these are measures that have always been produced, but no one does anything with them anymore. It could also be that the measure is so hard to accurately determine that no one is prepared to put any faith in the outcome	*Vanity measures*: It is likely that these are produced to justify personal agendas. The measures have no real impact on tactical or strategic business operations (hence low value). Such measures should be candidates for de-prioritizing or dropping. It is worth checking whether anyone actually does anything with measures that are generated. We have observed many occasions of regular, detailed reports being produced that no one ever reads let alone acts upon

By way of example, consider a retail business that is seeking to digitalize its sales and customer engagement model. The desired business outcome of maximizing customer value might be broken down into influencing factors of:

- Convenience of buying experience.
- Efficiency of end-to-end supply chain.
- Continuous improvement and innovation in products and services.

Each of these, in turn, can then be considered in the light of how digital can enable the desired outcome. For example, the convenience measure might be determined by the degree to which controlling systems are integrated. It is unfortunately not uncommon for supposedly digital services to break down when unanticipated events are encountered. How many times do consumers get frustrated because apparently simple actions cannot be completed through fully online channels but instead drop out to non-digital channels? This is seen when failed online deliveries are returned to a post office depot and then have to be collected by hand rather than rescheduled, or when websites display a comprehensive product catalogue, but with no means to execute a purchase. In these cases, a potentially helpful outcome measure might be "The number of customer engagement functions that can be delivered purely online or with the ability to seamlessly switch engagement to an informed and empowered agent". In this online retail context, any customer engagement functions that cannot be seamlessly executed digitally are a potential source of frustration and perceived drop in "convenience of buying experience."

All of the above does not mean that lower-level measures are not useful—having online digital capability is of no use if the supporting server infrastructure is not running correctly. The core business vision needs to be distilled down to behavioral drivers, but lower-level metrics must not be a barrier to maintaining strong customer-centricity and they should certainly not be considered to be "key."

19.4 Input and Output Measures

We would broadly categorize measures as being:

- *Input measures*. These are typically things that it is easier to directly influence (even though they may not necessarily be easy to achieve). For example, percentage of business processes that are digitalized; number of employees reskilled; level of executive sponsorship for transformation initiatives. Input measures tend to relate to the levers of change and by their very nature are more transformation or transition related.
- *Output measures*. These are typically measures which determine whether the desired outcomes of transformation initiatives are being realized. Output measures tend to be more strategy related, being linked to a vision of "what good looks like."

An eye should always be kept on the interplay between input and output measures, remembering the difference between cause and effect. Service desk responsiveness to customer queries could be an effective "output" measure that supports positive customer intimacy; a corresponding "input" measure could be service desk utilization. In this case, if there is too much focus on the "input" measure, responsiveness could take a hit as service agents become overloaded at times of peak call volume.

19.5 Avoiding Some Pitfalls

- It is easy to fall into the trap of "paralysis by analysis" when there is the perception that the more indicators you have, the more control you are in. The risk of digital is that you can measure just about anything you want to.
- One version of the truth. Try to ensure that measures are taken from a single, trusted source of data. It is all too easy to work offline in spreadsheets to produce graphs and tables, where the underlying data is tweaked a bit to support a particular desired message.
- Over-reliance on data. People often assume that just because data is presented in a complex report or spreadsheet it must be right. Don't try to overinterpret data—"lies, damned lies and statistics!" as the saying goes.
- Traditional measures don't always surface the benefits of digital and so they are not always recognized. Just because I book 100% of my time, does not mean that I am 100% productive. Relying on such measures will usually lead to adverse, unintended consequences: It might be easier for people to bide their time and keep booking to an existing job code rather than to look to demonstrate flexibility in finding another job.
- If you focus too much on input measures, you will tend to know the "cost of everything but the value of nothing"; i.e., you have little perspective on whether all your efforts are actually getting you to your target model.
- Avoiding the "rear view mirror." If measures are only available at the end of the month, it may well be too late to take any meaningful actions. Measures should be timely without causing information overload.

19.6 Characteristics of Good Performance Indicators

- Measures should be aligned to achieving your target model and should show a balance between input and output measures.
- Measures should be clear and understandable, ideally presented as interactive visuals.
- They should be easily accessible and "pushed" to those who need to know them.

- There should be responsibility and accountability for each measure; that is, there will be clear ownership of any actions required as a result of failure to reach the required levels.
- Measures should allow you to be positively respond to emerging trends in a timely manner. They should therefore be regular and comparable overtime.
- Measures should ideally include a degree of predictive and prescriptive insights. Consider how you can apply analytics and AI to bring additional operational and strategic value add.
- It should be easy for employees to understand what they have to do in response to particular KPI trends.

19.7 Transitional and Digital Business KPI's

We have seen in the chapter on Starting the Transformation, that it is helpful to have KPI's that are aligned to transformation themes, and to the enablers of that transformation and the foundational characteristics of the target business model.

You will need to work out the most appropriate measure for your specific situation, however here are a few pointers as to the kind of focus on input and output measures that you might consider:

Digital business KPIs (these should be strongly linked to the target model therefore aligned to the objective of driving customer intimacy and operational scale):

- *Customers* (output measure): Net promoter score (includes customer sentiment). Get this right and marketing costs decrease;
- *Operations* (input and output measure): Efficiency, flexibility, and maximized utilization of digital and physical assets (this brings you scale);
- *Partner ecosystems* (Input and output measure): Partner engagement, shared value (a fundamental of the platform model);
- *People* (output measure): Employee engagement (a combination of satisfaction and empowerment);
- *Trust* (input and output measure): Security vulnerabilities, breaches, adherence to CDR[2], and CSR values (both internal and external);
- *Innovation* (input and output measure): Investments, new value propositions (approved business case net worth, and return on investment).

[2]Carbon dioxide removal: the set of activities and technologies that target the large-scale removal of carbon dioxide from the Earth's atmosphere.

Transitional KPIs (linked to driving behaviors that help take you to the target model):

- *Transformation initiatives* (output measure): Progress against specific initiatives (e.g., adoption of digital expenses process);
- *Business models* (output measure): Split of revenues or volumes between old model and new delivery model, e.g., shift to digital channel. This may be a measure that can be "input" influenced by e.g. ceasing to provide non-digital channels;
- *Processes* (input measure): standardized/digitalized/automated/integrated (percentage of core processes);
- *People reskilling and redeployment* (input measure): training and certification, role mobility, individual development plans (equipping workforce of the future);
- *Organization flexibility* (input measure): People and processes able to work seamlessly across the organization (breaking down the silos);
- *Leadership* (input and output measure): Executive sponsorship, visibility, articulated strategy and vision, 360 feedback on trust.

Reference

Sinek, S. The golden circle presentation. Published online at https://simonsinek.com/commit/the-golden-circle. Accessed October 26 2019.

20 Enduring Digital Transformation—Delivering Incremental Value from a Long-Term Vision

In earlier chapters, we have described how to get started with your digital transformation: how to decide at a high level which workstreams will be needed, how to put appropriate governance in place, and how to measure the transformation by introducing and adjusting KPIs. In this chapter, we explain how to implement your digital transformation iteratively and sustainably. But first, let's take a step back and understand why it is essential to use an iterative approach to transformation.

20.1 An Iterative Approach to Transformation

Traditionally, organizational transformations have been managed as a project or program which has the aim of moving the organization from the "current state" to a future "target state". Like any project, there will be a defined scope, budget, and timeline. And the business case for starting the project will be based on an estimation of the value of the benefits expected to be achieved when the "target state" is reached. Transformation projects like these are often planned over a multi-year time horizon.

We can think of planning these transformation projects as similar to planning a physical journey to get from where you are now to where you want to be. This is represented, very simplistically, by Fig. 20.1.

However, in practice, there will be many parts of this journey where you don't quite know the best route to take at the outset. In fact, you will discover knowledge as you progress through the transformation that will change your understanding of what the best next steps should be. Car navigation systems all plan a journey at the start, but in the light of new information (road closures, traffic congestion, etc.) they will reroute to get you to your destination as fast as possible, even if not by the original route (Fig. 20.2).

H. Tardieu et al., *Deliberately Digital*, Future of Business and Finance,
https://doi.org/10.1007/978-3-030-37955-1_20

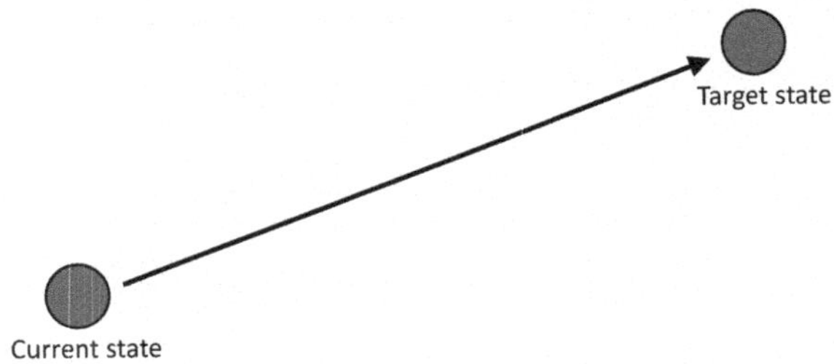

Fig. 20.1 Traditional "current state" to "target state" approach to transformation. Authors' own figure

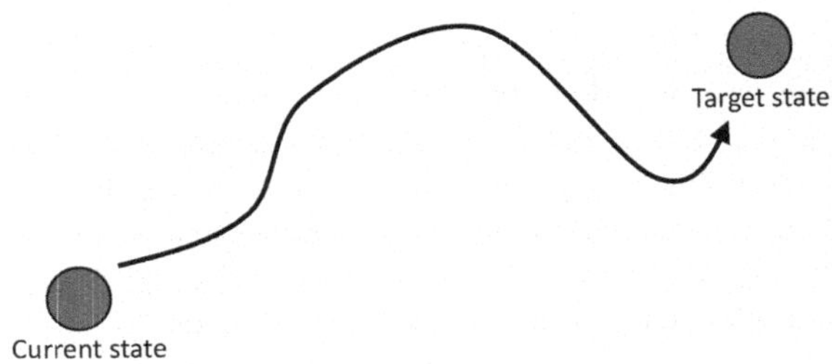

Fig. 20.2 Adjusting course during the transformation. Authors' own figure

But, in one way, this analogy breaks down. Although, for the sake of clarity we have, up until now, talked about the target state as if it is a static quantity, in a digital transformation, you cannot anticipate with any certainty what the target state should be. This is partially because, as we have seen in Part I, trends in technology, business, and society are evolving so rapidly. But it is also because our estimate of the value of the benefits associated with the target state will not be 100% correct. It may be completely wrong or it may be quite close, but it will never be exact. We will get a clearer view of where we want to get to as we proceed through the transformation, and the target state must be adjusted accordingly.

It is probably better to think of a target zone (which will be determined by your overall purpose and strategy) rather than a fixed target state (Fig. 20.3).

In summary: for a digital transformation, you cannot know in advance what the target state should be and, even if you did, you cannot know exactly how you will get there. This is why an iterative approach, where the learning from the previous iterations feeds forwards into future iterations is essential when tackling a digital transformation.

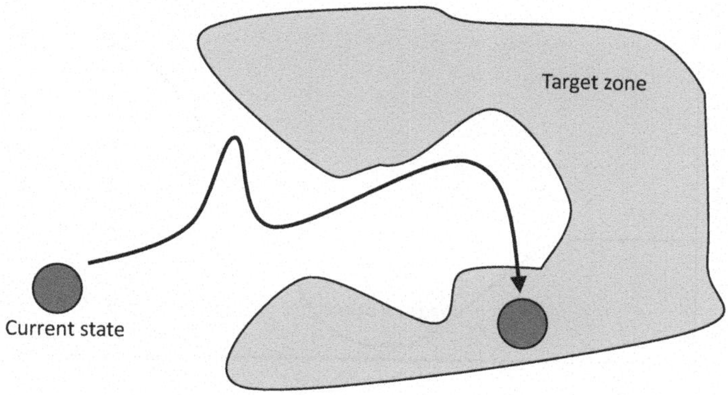

Fig. 20.3 Replacing "target state" with a "target zone". Authors' own figure

20.2 The J-Curve and the Trough of Despair

Also important are the psychological and sociological implications of managing a transformation as a single large plan. A well-understood concept is the J-curve of change (Fig. 20.4).

With most changes, there will be a delay between investing time and money to make the change and realizing a benefit. In fact, during the change, it may feel like things are actually worse than before the change started. Anyone who has renovated their home will know the feeling well: with dust everywhere, no working kitchen, and every day filled with the loud noise of building work in progress, your house feels significantly less comfortable than it did before the work started.

Often this low point in the J-curve is referred to as the "trough of despair." The deeper and longer this trough of despair is, the more likely it is that people will start to question whether the change will be worthwhile. This is another reason why, as we explained in the chapter Starting the Transformation, it is essential that people across the organization are engaged with and have bought into the transformation; that they believe that the effort to get to the target state will be worth it; and that they can sustain this belief, even in the face of difficulties and setbacks.

It is also another reason why a large transformation should be broken down into smaller chunks (iterations), each of which will deliver some smaller benefit, in a shorter period of time, and at a lower cost. When deciding on the timespan for each iteration, you must be realistic both about how quickly you can implement changes and also about how long your organization will be willing to persist before starting to see benefits. Typically, iterations will be between 1 and 3 months in length. We have found it very rare to see transformation activities that can start to deliver benefits in less than 1 month. It can even be a challenge to realize benefits within 3 months. However, if iterations extend beyond 3 months, people can quickly become frustrated by lack of visible results and, what's more, the feedback loops

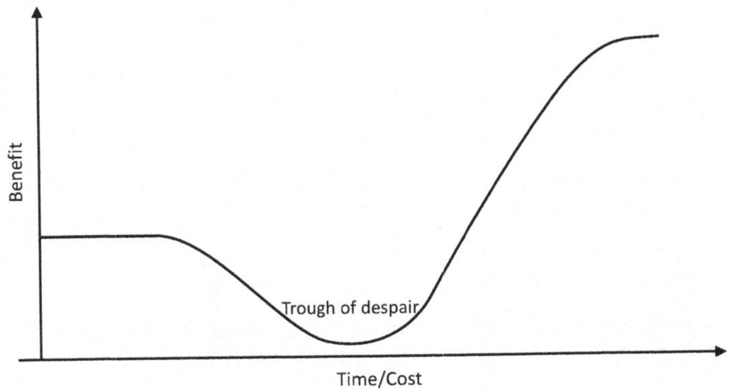

Fig. 20.4 J-curve of change. Adapted from a presentation by Anderson (2017)

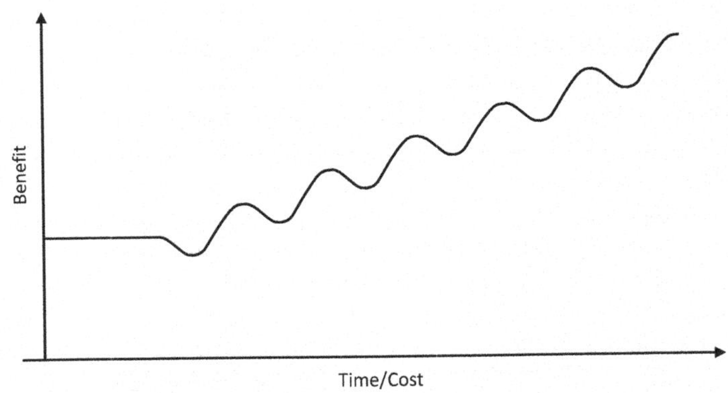

Fig. 20.5 Impact of iterative transformation on the J-curve of change. Adapted from a presentation by Anderson (2017)

(discussed in more detail later) become longer and the opportunities to adjust the direction of the transformation may be perceived to occur too infrequently.

The shape of each separate J-curve in Fig. 20.5 is the same as the large J-curve shown previously (in Fig. 20.4). But, by making each one shorter, the depth and breadth of the troughs of despair are reduced. In fact, the shorter you make each iteration, the more it approximates a straight and upward-trending line. It should also be apparent that, with this approach, the maximum risk exposure is lower, and the payback is faster.[1]

[1]We first saw this concept of evolutionary change explained in terms of the J-curve when it was presented by David J Anderson at the Lean Kanban North America 2017 conference.

An implication of this is that organizations need to become comfortable with and embracing of continuous change. One useful framework for understanding how an organization must operate in order to sustain this kind of continuous adaptation is the Digital Business Continuum (Daly 2018).

20.3 Decomposing Workstreams into Activities

We have already discussed in previous chapters how to identify, prioritize, and select transformation workstreams and group these into transformation themes.

However, for most workstreams, it will not be feasible to implement them within a single iteration and therefore they will need to be sub-divided into transformation activities. It is not necessary to identify upfront every single activity that will be necessary to deliver one workstream; you only need to sub-divide sufficiently to plan the first iteration.

The activities that a workstream can be broken down into will fall into one of five categories (see also Table 20.1):

- *Big bet*: a high-risk, high-payoff activity that can be completed within an iteration
- *Experiment*: an activity that can be completed within an iteration with the main goal of gaining knowledge to inform future iterations
- *Option*: an activity that keeps a future option open that might otherwise become closed[2]
- *Strategic*: an activity that is part of a set of activities needed to deliver a benefit (which is only realized when all activities have been completed)
- *Quick win*: a low-risk activity that will deliver benefits within an iteration.

If you have used Cynefin (described in Planning an Iterative transformation) to categorize your transformation workstreams, this will help you identify the category of activity that might make the most sense for a given workstream, as shown in Fig. 20.6.

What you will notice is that for workstreams that have less certainty, early activities will focus on increasing this level of certainty. A workstream that is in the complex domain may need a set of experiments which, once completed, move it into the complicated domain. Once in the complicated domain, a set of pilot projects could be implemented. Once these are completed (and with the experience gained), the workstream might move into the obvious domain. It therefore also follows that today's bets, options, and experiments, are what generate the strategic projects and quick wins of tomorrow.

[2]For a more in-depth discussion of options, see Commitment: Novel about Managing Project Risk, Olav (Maassen et al. 2013).

Table 20.1 Comparison of categories of transformation activities (table compiled by authors)

	Big bet	Experiment	Option	Strategic	Quick win
Risk	High	Low (provided it is made safe-to-fail)	Low	Medium	Low
Return	High	Indirect value from information/knowledge gained	Indirect value based on the benefit of keeping the option open	Dependent on workstream	Dependent on workstream
Timescale	Can be completed within an iteration	Can be completed within an iteration	Can be completed within an iteration	Task completed within one iteration, but more than one task (in multiple iterations) needed before benefits delivered	Will deliver benefits within one iteration
Example	Launch a new product in a new market to try and gain a first-mover advantage	Pilot a new tool with one development team to see if it improves productivity	Expose product functionality via APIs to enable potential third-party integrations at a later date	Migration of 10 teams to a unified service management platform, which will provide a better end-to-end solution at a lower cost but only once all users have been migrated	Implement automated chatbots to be the first point of contact for online queries

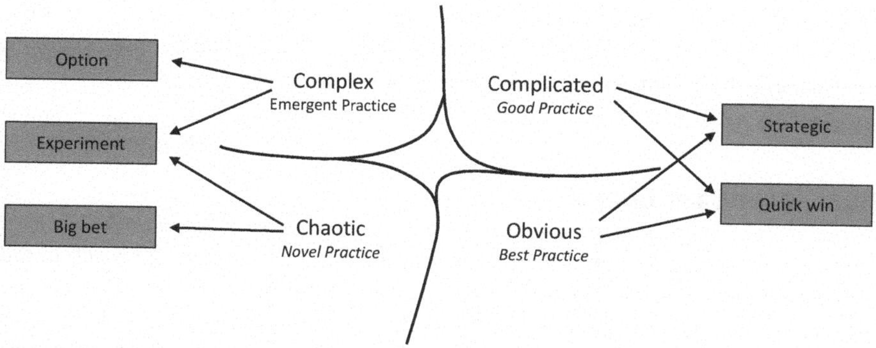

Fig. 20.6 Authors mapping of Cynefin domains to determine the types of activity that will be the most applicable for a transformation workstream. Authors' own figure

20.4 Planning an Iteration

Having selected workstreams, how should you decide which transformation activities should be included in the next iteration?

The first requirement is that any iteration must have a high probability of delivering a net gain. This means that some quick wins must be included. For these, there should already be a good understanding of what needs to change, how to change it, and a high confidence that the change will produce the expected benefits. Do not underestimate their importance: they demonstrate to everyone in the organization that successful change is possible and delivers results.

However, most iterations should also include activities in the other categories. They will not provide benefits within this iteration, but they will enable benefits to be delivered in the future iterations.

To have a high chance of each iteration being successful, you need to ensure that enough benefit will be delivered by the quick wins to justify the total effort included in the iteration. It is also important that stakeholders understand the category of each item in the iteration so that, for example, a bet is not considered to be a failure if it doesn't payoff.

Once an iteration has been planned, the Executive Committee must commit to it. They should agree that it is consistent with the workstreams that they have selected, and they should understand which activities are expected to deliver direct benefits within the iteration versus those that aren't.

In some cases, you will only be able to identify a small number of quick wins, which will severely limit your capacity to pursue workstreams that are less certain. Sadly, this is not an unusual position, especially where organizations have relentlessly pursued quick wins for many years without doing anything to deliver value in the longer term. The low hanging fruit has all been picked, the plants have died, and no seeds have been planted. In these cases, the Executive Committee will have to decide if they wish to insist on a net benefit for each iteration (and have a very slow start to the overall transformation) or agree to some of the first iterations not having a net benefit (but plant the seeds for tomorrow).

20.5 Feedback Loops

As we have explained, one of the reasons for adopting an iterative approach to the transformation is that the experience and learning from previous iterations can be fed forward into the next iteration. In the model, we are recommending (please refer back to Fig. 16.2) this happens at a number of different levels and over different timescales aligned with the transformation governance structure described in Starting the Transformation:

- At the end of each iteration, workstream leads re-evaluate the certainty, benefit, and timescale of their workstream and propose activities for the next iteration based on the results of previous iterations. They may also propose to drop their workstream.
- The digital transformation board selects activities to be included in the next iteration.
- The Executive Committee agrees and commits to the next iteration.
- Every 2–4 iterations, the Executive Committee reassesses the workstreams in progress (and those which were not originally selected) and decides whether to start new ones and/or drop existing ones.
- Every 4–8 iterations, the exercise to understand the current state and identify new workstreams and, potentially, new transformation themes is repeated.

We have found that this approach balances the need to invest in the long term with the need to demonstrate results quickly. It maintains relative stability in terms of long-term vision and goals, while also enabling responsiveness to changing circumstances. It balances planning and control (of what is well understood) with an ability to experiment and take risks (where this is the best approach).

20.6 Evolutionary Versus Revolutionary Change

While we are clear that the only way to successfully start and maintain an enduring digital transformation is to manage it iteratively, individual transformation workstreams (and even transformation activities) may be implemented using either an evolutionary or revolutionary approach. To understand this, it is useful first to define the difference between using an evolutionary or a revolutionary approach to implementing change. It might be tempting to think that the difference relates to what you change and/or the end-result. However, the distinction is, in fact, subtler.

An evolutionary approach to change takes the current state and seeks to identify small changes which could be made. If a change produces a positive result, then the change is kept, if not then it is reversed. Then a new change is tried. Just like in biological natural selection, adaptations occur via small adjustments and survive if they prove beneficial, otherwise they die out. Evolutionary change always builds from the current state (what you do now) in small increments.

A revolutionary approach to change takes the current state and seeks to replace it with something different (which is expected to be better).

By way of an example, let's consider a company that wishes to switch from a functional to a cross-functional organization. An evolutionary approach could be simply to freeze recruitment into the functional teams and enable the business-oriented teams to recruit the needed skills. Another evolutionary approach could be to create one cross-functional team at a time, with people perhaps initially retaining their existing hard reporting lines, then replacing them with dotted reporting lines, and then removing the functional reporting altogether. In contrast, a revolutionary approach would be to design a completely new organization structure and then roll it out in one go.

As another example, let's consider a company that wishes to improve its ability to develop software. An evolutionary approach would be to assess current pain-points and challenges and then adjust in small increments (perhaps adding some test automation in one step, code reviews in another, etc.). A revolutionary approach would be a company-wide roll-out of a new method (like Scrum).

Even changes to business models can be implemented in either way. Transitioning from being a shrink-wrap software vendor to a SaaS provider could be achieved using a revolutionary approach: rewriting your product from scratch as a SaaS offering, and then very rapidly discontinuing the legacy product. Alternatively, a more evolutionary approach is also possible: starting by offering a hosted solution, then multi-tenanted,[3] then full SaaS with the customer still having a shrink-wrap option available during the transition.

This evolutionary approach is very much how Adobe created their Creative Cloud offering. A decade ago Adobe was the leading developer of creative software (with products like Photoshop for photo manipulation, Lightroom for photo library management and Premier Pro for video editing). All of these were desktop applications which could be purchased for a one-off cost and installed by users on their desktop computers (from an installation CDROM supplied in a physical box). In 2011, Adobe launched Creative Cloud as a way for people to download, install and use these applications while paying for them via a subscription model (a fixed monthly charge which included all future version upgrades). The technical change was minimal (consisting mainly of software to manage the downloads and licensing). In 2013, Adobe took a step further and announced that they would no longer be releasing new versions of the standalone software packages, thus starting to push users toward the subscription model. Adobe are now also redeveloping the

[3]Multi-tenancy in software means that a single instance of the software solution serves multiple tenants (group of users who share a common access but with specific privileges).

original applications to be cloud enabled (e.g., they can run as a desktop application, on a tablet, on a mobile phone, or through a Web browser, with cloud storage linking them all together). Additionally, Adobe are also developing and releasing new applications (like their Adobe Spark video creator) via a freemium model: they can be used for free with certain restrictions and limitations, which can be removed by taking out a subscription. Although the change has been implemented in an evolutionary manner over the course of many years, Adobe's business model is now unrecognizable compared with the one from ten years ago.

In general, the trade-off between an evolutionary or revolutionary approach is one of "risk versus speed". Evolutionary approaches tend to be lower risk but slower. Revolutionary models can be faster, but riskier. Of course, judgement is always needed, but typically revolutionary approaches should be chosen when the risk of changing too slowly outweighs the risks associated with moving quickly and disruptively.

20.7 Evolutionary Approaches to Change

The Kanban method as described by Anderson (2010) has done much to popularize the idea of taking a Systems Thinking approach toward organizational change (in fact, the recommended approach for implementing Kanban is known as STATIK, which stands for Systems Thinking Approach To Implementing Kanban).

The principle of Systems Thinking is relatively straightforward: rather than trying to understand how a system works by analyzing its internal workings, you instead consider the system to be a "black box" with inputs and outputs. A Systems Thinking approach to organizational change is based on this principle. First you understand what the main inputs and outputs of the system are and then determine what changes in those you would consider to be desirable. For example, desirable changes in outputs might include higher quality, shorter lead-times, less wastage, or reduced costs. Once you understand the inputs and outputs to the system (and what desirable improvements in those would look like) you create a hypothesis for what might result in a positive change. For example, your hypothesis might be "We believe that less multi-tasking will result in higher quality". Next you would implement this change and measure the impact. If it is positive, then the change is retained. If it is negative, then the change is rolled-back. With this approach, not too much time is spent trying to determine in advance whether the hypothesis is likely to be correct, the emphasis is very much on implementing the change and then measuring the actual results. The important thing is to find ways to make each change both safe-to-fail and easy to roll back if it proves to be detrimental. This is enabled in our transformation model by an emphasis on using options and experiments where necessary to reduce workstream risks.

Building on these concepts, Mike Burrows has developed the Agendashift engagement model (Burrows 2018). It provides a method to explore opportunities for change with stakeholders, prioritize them and implement them in an evolutionary fashion. It is a model that could be applied in any context where a transformation workstream or transformation activity is seeking to deliver changes in an evolutionary way.

20.8 Revolutionary Approaches to Change

The two examples of revolutionary change that we most often witness are mass roll-outs and restructuring.

Mass roll-outs seek to implement a new process, tool, or even business model, across the whole organization in as short a timeframe as possible. As discussed earlier, a mass roll-out approach should usually only be chosen when the additional risks of such an approach (which can be significant) are outweighed by the risks of changing too slowly. Even so, do keep in mind that mass roll-outs in large organizations are rarely achieved in very short timeframes. The often-cited case study of Salesforce implementing agile ways of working demonstrates this: even with complete executive commitment to the change (and dedicated time and budget combined with external support), it still took 3 months to roll-out to 200 engineers followed by another 12 months of on-going refinement before they achieved the benefits they were expecting.

Restructuring an organization is based on the belief that making changes to the way people are grouped together inside (and potentially outside of) the organization and/or changing its make-up (e.g., more/less offshore, more/less engineers compared to managers) will have a positive impact on how the organization operates. Although it is quite possible to restructure in an evolutionary way (as described earlier), it is a change that, in practice, we see often implemented as a revolution.

The most obvious (and common) example is where people's roles and responsibilities and their reporting lines within the company are adjusted. One experienced manager shared with us their insight that "I've been around long enough now to no longer believe that the answer to every problem is to restructure." His observation rings true because often we find that reorganizations do not achieve the expected outcomes. Sometimes this is because the problems it is trying to solve were misdiagnosed as being caused by the existing structure. Other times it is because changing responsibilities and reporting lines "on paper" does not instantly dissolve years of organizational history and, therefore, people actually continue to behave very much as they did before, even many years after the change was made. Sometimes they continue for long enough to be reorganized back into the original structure! Perhaps this is another reason why some people cynically refer to organization restructuring as like "rearranging the deck chairs on the Titanic." Our advice would be to think carefully about your target organization structure (using the advice in the chapter on Organization Structure as a starting point), and, if possible, make the changes in a gradual, evolutionary way. If a revolutionary approach is needed, then at least try to use some experiments to sense check whether you are likely to achieve the intended benefits and to learn what difficulties you may experience along the way.

A less common type of restructure is the creation of a new company. This might be a wholly owned start-up, a carve-out of part of the existing business, or a joint venture together with customers and/or partners (or even competitors). Contrary to the more commonplace change in roles, responsibilities and reporting lines, we have seen this to be quite an effective approach. It works well when the independence of the new organization (which usually equates to greater speed and agility) has significant value. The new organization does not need to be bound by the existing rules and processes and often this enables a much more entrepreneurial spirit among its employees. The new company is accountable for and judged by the results it achieves, not on how it achieves them.

In some cases, it may make sense to re-integrate the new company after a period of time. In these cases, the new company has been created to provide an initial boost to innovation and agility, the benefit of which diminishes as the market matures. In other cases, it may make sense for the new company to retain its independence, or even to be sold.

As we have seen earlier, sometimes the creation of a separate company (often a joint venture) makes particular sense in the context of operating B2B multi-sided platforms, where some level of independence of the platform operator from the platform users can be a crucial factor in signing up enough platform users to achieve a critical mass and make the platform business viable.

References

Anderson, D. J. (2010). *Kanban: Successful evolutionary change for your technology business*. Blue Hole Press.

Anderson, D. J. (2017). *Lean Kanban North America 2017 conference* https://www.youtube.com/watch?v=RsayVfMVjbU. Accessed October 26 2019.

Burrows, M. (2018). *Agendashift: Outcome-oriented change and continuous transformation*. New Generation Publishing.

Daly, et al. (2018). The digital business continuum. Atos https://atos.net/wp-content/uploads/2018/02/atos-the-digital-business-continuum.pdf. Accessed October 26 2019.

Maassen, O., Matts, C., & Geary, C. (2013). *Commitment: Novel about managing project risk*. Hathaway te Brake Publications.

Conclusion to Deliberately Digital: Enduring Transformations

21

At the turn of the decade, we celebrate the thirtieth anniversary of the Web and mark the time when digital-native millenniums become the numerically dominant demographic in our companies. In the introduction of this book, we recalled the long appropriation (a whole generation) for the electrical engine to dramatically change the efficiency of factories in which it was deployed. As we encounter such a generation shift in the world of digital, we anticipate something of a perfect storm in the impact that digital technology will have on business models, processes, products, and services. We expect mindsets to progressively shift from "why digital?" to "why not digital?"

The way in which new technology and ideas will be adopted by industry to drive innovation in real-world solutions and services is the essence of sustainable digital transformation. But will such adoption support a deliberate and enduring change in business models and strategies, or will it be simply treated as an enabler of quick-win efficiency programs? Will innovations strike at the heart of business process and culture or will they merely encourage temporal techno-solutionism?

On the subject of innovation, the French Anthropologist Pascal Picq has posed the following question:

> Are technical inventions becoming innovations which are changing society, or is it their appropriation, their usage by individuals, which has this effect? (HBR 2018)

The Harvard Business Review—France records him as answering:

> It is appropriation; it cannot be anticipated. Some things are emerging without any prior need. They may not be selected because there is no need. But if they are selected, they can change the world as they serve as the basis for an invention to become an innovation. Innovation can change practices and society. Previously, the goal was to fight things like disease and despotism. Today our world is changing aimlessly. Inventions emerge without answering an absolute need in our society. We are in a world where solutions are waiting for problems. We are in a completely Darwinian world.

Looking at the digital leaders in business today, it is evident that "survival of the fittest" is much more than an accidental emergence of winning characteristics: there

H. Tardieu et al., *Deliberately Digital*, Future of Business and Finance,
https://doi.org/10.1007/978-3-030-37955-1_21

is a clear understanding of the power of data, from the perspectives of insight, context, connection, and value. Data is put to work in truly disruptive ways, exploiting the way that new business models can grow at the speed of digital, unencumbered by legacy models, and physical assets. For incumbent enterprises wishing to ride the wave of digital opportunity, there is a need to understand the new data-centric business paradigm and discover how to transform their existing operational and cultural DNA.

Executing a digital transformation brings with it a double uncertainty regarding the pace of new innovations and their acceptability by the staff of the company and its customers. We have in front of us multiple inventions which have been described in Part I, but we also have new economic models for data which have their own characteristics, and which need to be pump primed to take off, and then regulated in order to prevent their monopolization.

At a time when most companies are preparing or executing their digital transformations, we are in a world which has been hugely influenced by both the incredible success of the platform model and the skepticism it has created for citizens all over the world regarding abuse in terms of usage of data.

Companies will have to navigate very unpredictable environments in terms of regulation (where data access and control of data usage are still evolving) to try to combine the necessary privacy and data availability for analytics and machine learning.

In this competitive environment, incumbents and new entrants will have different cards in their hands with hopefully a clear view of the benefits that can come from sharing business data in common ecosystems.

Successful transformations demand a very deliberate and strategic approach which covers an enterprise's values, business model, organization, people skillset, culture, customer engagement, and measures of success. All of these factors will be underpinned with how data is used, shared, and monetized to create differentiated and hence value-added services. With data as an almost limitless resource in a world that is increasingly facing physical sustainability challenges, enterprises cannot ignore the shift in emphasis, even though it may disrupt long-held emotional attachments to established models. We have attempted to highlight the characteristics of digital business that will help surface the required attitudes and approaches for achieving success as a digital leader.

We have an optimistic vision of the future with the clear feeling that such a combination of opportunities has not occurred for several centuries; the future is yet to be played out, but we hope that this book will help you to take full advantage of the opportunities presented by digital.

Reference

HBR. (2018). Le travail d'une vie. *Harvard Business Review*. France 15/03/2018. https://www.hbrfrance.fr/tag/le-travail-dune-vie/. Accessed 26 Oct 2019.

Part IV
Case Studies

Introduction

Abstract In Part IV of this book, we describe a number of market specific case studies spanning energy, healthcare, mobility, financial services and manufacturing. Each case study explains how digital is changing the context in which companies are operating, what new challenges and opportunities this creates and how the concepts presented earlier in this book are (or can be) applied to take advantage of them. We hope that, regardless of which sector your company is focused on, these case studies (and the concrete examples they contain) will provide you with inspiration for your own digital transformation.

In the following pages, we lay out a number of market-specific case studies. We have included them as a source of inspiration for your own business transformation journey. They highlight notable winning approaches, adopted by some of the enterprises that have been able to attain digital leader status, and also offer thoughts on how particular digital technologies have been used to enable new ways of working and trading. They are by no means an exhaustive analysis of all markets, and there are many industrial sectors that are not explicitly covered. However, we have continually found in our digital transformation engagements that taking inspiration from successes in other markets and applying that thinking to your specific circumstances is a powerful way to help articulate a vision, win stakeholder buy-in, and de-risk your own strategy for digital leadership.

As you read the case studies, consider some of the parallels, in terms of business challenges, that you see with your own situation. Try to discern why certain strategies were followed and what made them successful: What can you learn from their approaches? In particular, think about the radical shifts in business models that have been embraced and the creative ways that digital technologies have been deployed to achieve both scale in operation and intimacy with customers.

Case Study 1: The Digital Transformation of Energy and Utilities (Focus on Electrification)

22

The global energy industry is driven by a need to support projected population and economic growth in a manner that minimizes carbon impact. This is leading to powerful dynamics driving a need for transformational change across the entire energy generation, distribution, and consumption value chain. The major trends include: an evolution away from oil, coal, and natural gas, and toward carbon-neutral sources such as renewables, hydrogen, and (in some countries) nuclear; a move toward electrification of the entire energy distribution system; and the evolution of smart grids[1] which are enabling more effective management of supply and demand. Digital technologies are critical to enable the resulting more complex and interdependent energy systems and to ensure our global climate is maintained in a manner conducive to the future well-being and prosperity of the human race. Energy and utility companies, that have historically been very capital asset-driven, are now having to embrace new digital business models and ways of working.

22.1 The Context

The human race has a huge and growing requirement for energy (Fig. 22.1). This trend is driven by population and economic growth, and it will continue despite improved consumption management. The International Energy Authority (IEA) estimates the annual investment required to meet the world's changing energy needs will grow to reach $2000 billion by 2035.

[1]An electrical grid which includes fairly intelligent, often digital components including smart meters, smart appliances or renewable energy sources.

H. Tardieu et al., *Deliberately Digital*, Future of Business and Finance,
https://doi.org/10.1007/978-3-030-37955-1_22

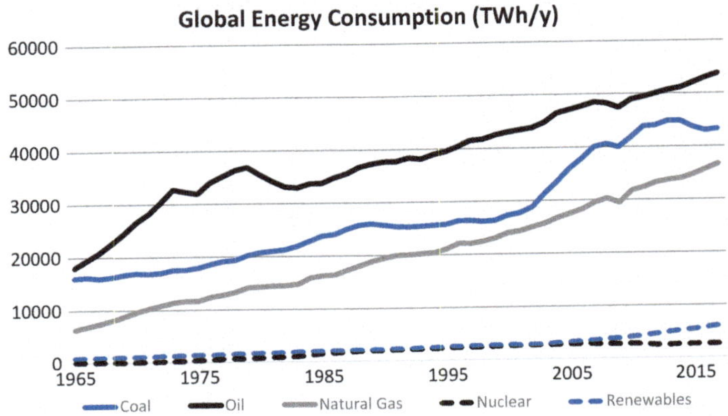

Fig. 22.1 Global energy consumption trends over the last 50 years. *Source data* Ourworldindata (2018)

At the heart of the challenge we face, is the need for a more sustainable energy model. The energy systems of the future are expected to include a combination of characteristics:

Renewables and Nuclear:

An increasing momentum toward renewable energy sources such as solar, wind, and hydro-electricity, and a move away from burning fossil fuels whether from oil, shale gas, or natural gas. In some countries, we will see the growing use of nuclear energy to provide a dependable base-load supply. In others, and notably in Germany and in Japan, there are significant on-going concerns over nuclear safety which, for the time being at least, will lead to decommissioning and termination of nuclear supply.

Electrification:

The move to electricity as a prime energy medium is growing in importance, and it is now being adopted at scale in several new sectors, most notably in electric vehicles, but also in heating and cooling. Two major economies taking a lead on this are China and India.

Smart Grids:

As our energy mix changes toward renewables, there is a need to manage our distribution networks differently. In the past, electricity power grids were relatively straightforward to manage, because the supply from generation facilities could be turned up or down according to demand. Today's power grids are getting more complicated because the renewable generation sources now supplying them are by their nature variable, largely based on weather.

The solution to managing this new complexity is to create a "smart grid" that automatically adjusts to changing supply from alternative energy sources, informed by insights from smart meters on the demand side (customers). This enables energy providers to regulate the use of customer appliances, both to align the demand with available supply and also allowing consumers to benefit from shifting their energy consumption to times when overall demand and prices are at their lowest.

22.2 The Challenge in Electricity

Our global electricity production and distribution system continue to evolve as the share of renewables increases. By 2030, renewables are targeted to represent 32% of electricity production in Europe (2030 climate and energy framework), and this change is making a big impact on how energy is managed.

Historically, our electricity system has been highly centralized. Electricity was produced by large energy plants using coal, gas, or nuclear energy (the producer); transported at high voltage by transmission system operators (TSO); and finally distributed to homes and companies by distribution system operators (DSO). Production was regulated by the TSO on the basis of DSO consumption forecasts which, in turn, were based upon historical data and weather predictions.

Today, two factors have changed:

1. Solar and wind energy are regarded as essential to enable carbon impact reduction. But their production is intermittent and has significant variability according to prevailing weather conditions.
2. Electricity can now be produced anywhere in a given region without any significant scale economies from centralized energy production.

These changes have required the evolution of a more complex provisioning and commercial model, including a complex pricing scheme which guarantees that all the energy produced by solar or wind will be bought, even if there is already adequate supply from other sources.

Figure 22.2 illustrates how the electricity ecosystem is evolving to account for these changes. Key differences compared to the traditional model are:

- The creation of aggregators that act as an intermediary between consumers and the TSO, balancing supply and demand between consumers and producers.
- Smart cities: we are seeing parts of cities and towns beginning to act as an aggregator themselves, especially in newly built areas.
- The emergence of new players bringing increasing digitalization of the end-to-end supply chain.

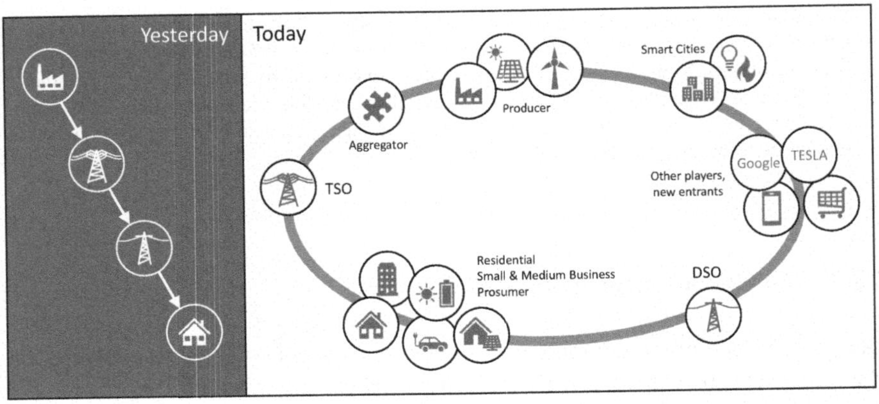

Fig. 22.2 Ecosystem of electricity players yesterday and today. Authors' own figure

Industry structure aside, another key challenge is the load balancing and synchronization of an electricity distribution network that relies on alternating current being transmitted at a defined voltage and frequency. Even small deviations (around 1%) can produce very damaging effects and therefore have to be corrected in a matter of seconds. Historically, network balancing is achieved by monitoring network voltage and frequency and turning on or off generation facilities as required, when deviations are observed.

Today, with the growing contribution of renewable generation in the transmission and distribution network, two new challenges need to be faced:

1. Production cannot be as easily adjusted to demand since it is subject to its own variations determined by the weather. Demand follows its own, often very different pattern: consumers want to use electricity whether or not the wind is blowing.
2. The inertia from conventional rotating machine generation represents a significant ally in maintaining network stability. If the proportion of total network power being generated by such means drops below around 70%, other effects can overcome this inherent inertia and cause major operational issues.

Network operators and power generators have to start looking at alternative approaches to maintaining a stable base load. These can include technologies such as batteries and pumped storage.

More reactive demand management will also play a significant role hence the rise in importance of domestic and industrial smart meter technology.

As most countries plan to evolve their electricity mix toward 100% from renewable sources, there will be an increasing demand for smart digital technologies to help manage transmission and distribution networks at a local, national, and even international level.

22.3 Platforms for Balancing the Electricity Ecosystem

Regulations in many countries, including Europe, oblige Producers, TSOs and DSOs to be separate companies in order to increase competition at every level of the value chain. Today, this constraint is limiting data sharing between the various players of the ecosystem, resulting in none of them having access to all the necessary data to perform efficient power generation balancing when faced with a high proportion of renewable intermittent energy.

One way of overcoming this challenge is to create an industrial data platform to connect the players as depicted in Fig. 22.3.

Such an industrial data platform may face negative feedback from the regulator, but we believe it is one of the foundational enablers of an electricity ecosystem that is able to address the challenge of intermittent renewable electricity generation. The approach is equally applicable in other industries that face problems with access to data that cuts across supply chains and ecosystems.

Nevertheless (and specifically in the context of the E&U industry), two regulatory obstacles may hinder the adoption of such industrial data platforms:

Firstly, regulation authorities which have required the independence of producers, TSOs and DSOs may object on the grounds that such a platform will create an unfair advantage for participants, and thereby distort competition principles.

Secondly, the European General Data Protection Regulation (GDPR), or its equivalent in other geographies, can constrain the use of smart meter data because electricity consumption data is perceived to be private data. In France, where more

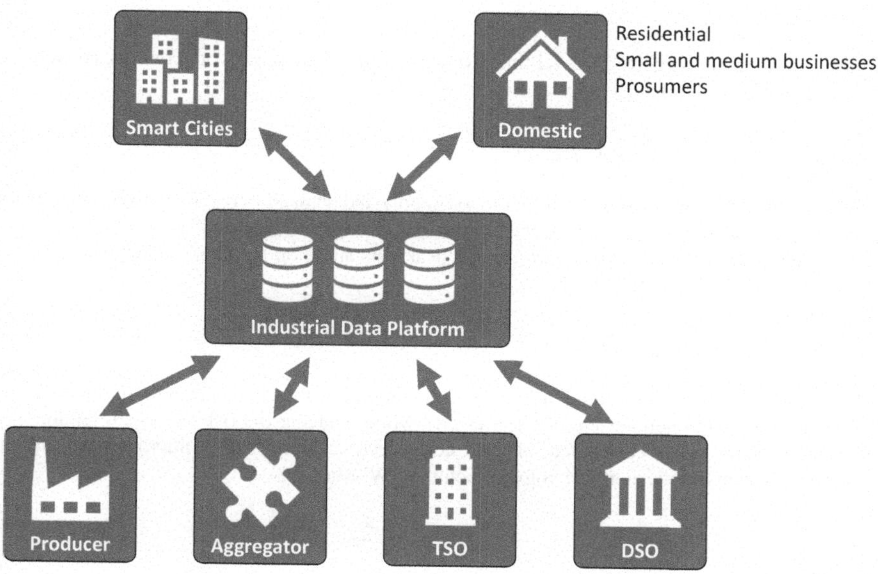

Fig. 22.3 Electricity balancing platform for the future. Authors' own figure

than 20 million smart meters have been installed, only 3% of them are uploading their data, because consumers have not agreed to its use (CRE 2019).

We see ever more clearly that this situation needs to be sorted out by regulatory *sandboxes* which reflect temporary relaxations of regulations in order to better understand use cases and associated business cases. Sandbox participation is carried out on a voluntary basis with the overall process being driven by an independent authority like the "*Commission de Régulation de l'Énergie*" which has the responsibility, in France, for energy-related regulatory matters.

The energy case study is a good illustration of the difficult challenges ahead of us in a changing ecosystem where the technical context is also rapidly evolving.

22.4 How Energy Firms Are Using Digital Technologies to Improve Customer Intimacy and Drive Efficiency and Scale in Operation

As the entire energy value chain changes, its transformation is being accelerated and enabled by digital technologies at every stage. Below are a few noteworthy examples. You may wish to consider how such approaches can be adapted to your particular business circumstance.

22.4.1 Transmission and Distribution

Smart Grid Electricity Distribution:

> Grid optimization is enabled by real-time load balancing, effective network controls, and an end-to-end model linking supply and demand.

National Grid—Load Forecasting:

> Machine learning can now be used to forecast supply and demand in real time and optimize economic load dispatch. For instance, in the UK, Google's DeepMind is working with National Grid to predict supply and demand peaks; its ambition is to help reduce national energy usage by 10%. (FT 2017)

Distribution Automation (DA):

> DA systems use sensors, remote terminals, and computer software to integrate renewable, intermittent energy sources into the power grid while reducing the risk of system failure. These systems have become feasible and cost-effective due to major improvements in wireless telecommunication technology, including Wi-Max.

Managing Supply Shortfalls:

There is potential for artificial intelligence to be used for more effective management of electricity shortfalls by advising consumers as to how they might usefully adjust their non-critical consumption patterns.

Drones for Network Inspection:

It has been predicted that, by 2020, some 50% of all electricity transmission and distribution utilities will be using drones to inspect service lines (Karpowicz 2018). This will enable a reduction of asset and service costs, achieving anticipated savings of up to 30%. (source IDC Energy Insights)

22.4.2 Retail

The opportunity is to provide highly responsive customer services with well-designed "customer journeys" supported by tightly integrated engagement channels and enabled by effective use of customer data.

OVO Energy is currently the leading UK energy retailer by customer satisfaction, winning the 2019 uSwitch Supplier of the Year award for four out of the past five years and achieving a customer satisfaction score of 88%. They also came first in the uSwitch awards for Best Online Experience, Best Rewards, Best Account Management, Best Meter Reading Services, and Best Billing Service. Key to their success is that their founder Stephen Fitzpatrick designed the whole company from scratch around what would be best for the customer. He invested in the best technology so that business was as rigorously cost efficient and customer friendly as possible (ovo.com 2019).

22.4.3 Consumption

The opportunity here is to provide energy consumers with much greater visibility and control of their energy use, with the ability to make more efficient and cost-effective decisions that reduce their costs and carbon impact.

Home Energy Management:

The Nest thermostat uses AI to help homeowners manage their energy consumption more effectively. Data sources include Nest's occupancy sensor, weather conditions, home temperature, homeowners' phone or car location, and consumer behavior in changing the set points. Once Nest has had few days to gather and learn from these data sources it can help homeowners dynamically manage the heating or cooling of their property.

Tracking Renewable Energy Consumption:

Power Ledger's peer-to-peer platform is being deployed in Japan to track renewable energy consumption from an initial 100 solar rooftop customers across three of the country's nine regions. The aim is to scale it up to over 55,000 rooftops within just two years, by the end of 2020. (Business Wire 2019)

Understanding the Costs of Running an Appliance:

Verv (a UK start-up) is using AI to "fingerprint" the consumption pattern of each domestic appliance, using electricity meter data. This will enable householders to learn exactly what it costs to run their dishwasher or fridge and, in turn, will put pressure on manufacturers to develop more energy-efficient products. (World Economic Forum 2018)

Peer-to-Peer Charging for Electric Vehicles (EV):

On the demand side, EV owners still tend to suffer from "range anxiety", given the relative lack of vehicle recharging points available to them and the time taken to charge a vehicle. On the supply side, many EV owners have paid for their own charging points at home, and they are interested in earning money from their investment. New software apps enable these two parties to come together, using Blockchain technology to ensure trusted peer-to-peer transactions.

Zero Energy Buildings:

It is now possible to create buildings in which the amount of energy used by the building and the amount of renewable energy created by the building is equalized on an annual basis. Key enabling technologies include a combination of IoT, AI, solar panels, batteries, and LED light systems.

22.4.4 Generation

Power generation is an asset-intensive business and demands effective asset life-cycle management.

Augmented Reality:

GE renewable energy has run a successful trial of Upskill's Skylight platform for smart glasses. In initial trials, this delivered a 34% productivity improvement for GE's field engineers. Without the assistance of augmented reality, GE's wind turbine assembly workers would typically need to keep stopping what they were doing; check if they were installing parts correctly; reference a manual; or, if needed, call someone more experienced to make sure they were doing their task correctly. When supported by augmented reality none of this was necessary: the glasses could be used to project digital checklists, diagrams, instructions, images and videos directly into the user's line of sight. (BrainXchange 2018)

Immersive Hybrid Reality (iHR) Laboratory:

Fife College, Scotland has created a laboratory which provides highly realistic training environments for scenarios that are difficult or impossible to simulate in real life. For instance, it is not workable to use on-the-job training to teach a student how to inspect an actual offshore wind turbine because it would be over 325 feet above the water in a dangerous environment which is expensive and difficult to reach. However, in the iHR laboratory students can carry out realistic and detailed inspections of a virtual wind turbine, with simulated changeable weather conditions, while still seeing their own hands and holding real tools. (Energy Live News 2017)

Digital Twin:

A Digital Twin is created when physical assets such as a wind turbine are mapped to a digital platform. The digital replica can then be used to analyze the efficiency, condition, and real-time status of the asset throughout its lifetime. Benefits include the ability to detect when an asset is not performing at its best and to carry out preventative maintenance before a failure occurs.

22.4.5 Storage

Efficient battery storage is a critical enabler of our new multi-source renewable energy systems, and it creates the opportunity for a bi-directional energy marketplace.

Virtual Power Plant:

Stem's software-driven storage acts as a virtual power plant (VPP) to respond to diverse load requirements.[2] It offers storage as-a-service to the "behind-the-meter"[3] commercial and industrial segment, as well as to utilities and grid operators. Stem's approach is to bring together reliable energy storage hardware with predictive, cloud-based analytics seamlessly and in real time. Their data analytics software combines weather forecasts and historical and real-time usage data to predict when electricity usage will peak at a given site. The system rapidly and automatically responds to spikes in demand, drawing on stored power to reduce costs for customers without requiring operational changes.

Bi-directional Electric Vehicle Power:

TenneT is a European transmission system operator, primarily serving Germany and the Netherlands. They are currently exploring ways to integrate flexible capacity supplied by electric vehicles into the electricity grid. TenneT are doing this in partnership with energy services provider The Mobility House and automotive manufacturer Nissan (TenneT website 2018). Their vision is that Nissan electric vehicles could help stabilize the network throughout Germany, and the intelligent charging and energy management software developed by The Mobility House could enable automated control of the charging and discharging process.

22.4.6 System-Wide Resilience

As energy firms get more connected, they need to ensure that their operations are fully resilient end-to-end. Cyber-security is paramount for an industry that is part of any country's critical national infrastructure.

[2] https://www.stem.com/. Accessed 26/10/2019.

[3] An electrical or gas device or facility that resides onsite, at the owner's property (at the household's or business' side of the meter), not at the side of the utility; for example, an onsite renewable energy generating facility.

CESER (UK):

CESER is the UK's Office of Cyber-security, Energy Security, and Emergency Response. Their purpose is to advance the research and development of innovative technologies, tools, and techniques which together can reduce risks to the nation's critical energy infrastructure posed by cyber and other emerging threats. At present they are working to ensure that by 2020 resilient energy delivery systems are designed, installed, operated, and maintained so that they are able to survive a cyber-incident while sustaining critical functions.

References

2030 climate & energy framework. European Commission. Published online at https://ec.europa.eu/clima/policies/strategies/2030_en. Accessed October 26, 2019.

BrainXchange. (2018). Embracing digital transformation: real-life use cases in energy & utilities. https://brainxchange.com/embracing-digital-transformation-real-life-use-cases-in-energy-utilities/. Accessed October 26, 2019.

Business Wire. (2019). Power ledger and sharing energy announce scalable partnership to evolve renewable energy in Japan. Marketwatch.com, 22/01/2019. https://www.marketwatch.com/press-release/power-ledger-and-sharing-energy-announce-scalable-partnership-to-evolve-renewable-energy-in-japan-2019-01-22. Accessed October 26, 2019.

CRE. (2019). Report of WG3 of "*Comité de Prospective*" *Commission de Régulation de l'Énergie*: Give sense to consumer data November 2019.

Energy Live News. (2017, June). Virtual reality turbine training materialises in Scotland. https://www.energylivenews.com/2017/06/19/virtual-reality-turbine-training-materialises-in-scotland/. Accessed October 26, 2019.

FT. (2017). DeepMind and National Grid in AI talks to balance energy supply. *Financial Times*, 11/03/2017. https://www.ft.com/content/27c8aea0-06a9-11e7-97d1-5e720a26771b. Accessed October 26, 2019.

Karpowicz, J. (2018). How will drones assist in maintaining power & utilities networks? *Engerati blog*, 20/03/2018. https://www.engerati.com/transmission-and-distribution/blog-entry/maintenance-asset-management/how-will-drones-assist. Accessed October 26, 2019.

Ourworldindata (2018) https://ourworldindata.org/energy-production-and-changing-energy-sources. Accessed October 26, 2019.

Ovo web site. (2019, March). OVO Energy awarded uSwitch Supplier of the Year 2019. https://www.ovo.com/ovo-energy-awarded-uswitch-supplier-of-the-year-2019/. Accessed October 26, 2019.

Tennet website. (2018, March). TenneT, The mobility house and nissan work together on stabilizing the power grid. https://www.tennet.eu. Accessed October 26, 2019.

World Economic Forum. (2018). Here's how AI fits into the future of energy. Article published in association with Raconteur. Olivia Gagan. https://www.weforum.org/agenda/2018/05/how-ai-can-help-meet-global-energy-demand. Accessed October 26, 2019.

Case Study 2: The Digital Transformation of Health Care

23

23.1 The Context

The healthcare sector represents one of the largest and most exciting areas for digital transformation. The World Bank has estimated that global spending on health will increase from US$9.21 trillion in 2014 to $24.24 trillion in 2040 (Global Burden of Disease Health Financing Collaborator Network 2017, with an uncertainty interval from $20.47 trillion to $29.72 trillion). Despite this huge and growing opportunity, health care has been relatively slow to embrace the new opportunities of digital. This is partly for regulatory reasons and partly for reasons of culture.

However, there is a growing awakening across the healthcare sector that change is urgently required. Our global population is increasing, and it is aging. As we age, the likelihood of developing more complex combinations of health conditions increases. When coupled with advances in diagnosis and treatment, the impact on our societies is considerable.

Main areas of concern include: healthcare affordability, patient experience, treatment efficacy, healthcare capacity, and system efficiency.

The affordability of health care is a global challenge with healthcare expenditure forecast to increase at a faster growth rate than our underlying economies over the remainder of the twenty-first century. Already in the EU, health expenditure in the largest 15 national economies is circa 11% of GDP, and in the USA this stands at 16% of GDP (Institute for Fiscal Studies 2017).

Patient experience is being compromised due to a lack of integration of care across primary, secondary, and tertiary care services. This can lead to poor patient experiences, and it contributes to overhospitalization of patients with long-term chronic conditions. As our populations age and the possibilities of health care evolve, there is a significant danger that we become "overhospitalized." We are already seeing signs of this in the UK where hospital admissions in England have recently risen to record levels with 16.2 million admissions during 2015–2016, up from 12.7 million ten years ago (NHS Digital, November 2016). Patients aged 65–69 made up the single largest group of patients with 1.3 million admissions in 2015–2016. If all these

H. Tardieu et al., *Deliberately Digital*, Future of Business and Finance,
https://doi.org/10.1007/978-3-030-37955-1_23

hospital admissions were strictly necessary, increasing hospitalization might perhaps be acceptable, but this does not appear to be the case. Two-thirds of UK hospital beds are occupied by the one-third of the population with a long-term condition. These long-term conditions also require the most care and are therefore the most expensive to manage in a hospital environment. If patients with long-term care needs could be treated at home, this would free up scarce and expensive hospital beds and potentially deliver better patient outcomes, given that there is much evidence to suggest that long-term stays in hospital are not good for you.

Treatment efficacy is not as good as it needs to be, and this is being held back for several reasons. Treatments have tended to be designed and optimized on the basis of mass trials, and they have been prescribed based on population-wide needs. It has been found that pharmaceutical interventions are effective in only 30–60% of patients due to differences in the way that individual patients respond to and metabolize medicines (Graham 2016). Today's treatments have also typically been developed to address stand-alone conditions as opposed to the combinations of conditions from which we increasingly suffer. In addition, medication compliance has been hard to monitor or manage, resulting in many patients not taking their medicine as needed. As a result, they either take longer than necessary to recover or, perhaps, never recover fully, leaving them with lifelong care needs.

Healthcare capacity is hindered because the onus for care has tended to rest on the shoulders of healthcare practitioners and not on the patient. Given there are a finite number of doctors and nurses available, and only so many hospital beds we can afford, it has proved very hard for health services to find or provision the required level of resources necessary to meet demand. Meanwhile, the scarce resources we do have are being put under unnecessary pressure.

Healthcare system efficiency is greatly compromised because it has become highly complex without the required underlying transformation necessary to manage this complexity effectively. The growing management challenge resulting from this is leading to a growing administrative cost burden. And supply chain inefficiencies mean that the cost to serve the healthcare system is far too high, with too many handoffs and too many "middlemen" making a margin.

A rare study in 2010/2011 comparing administration costs in different countries found that administrative costs accounted for 25.3% of total US hospital expenditures and that this percentage was increasing. Next highest were The Netherlands (19.8%) and England (15.5%). Reducing USA per capita spending for hospital administration to Scottish or Canadian levels would have saved more than $150 billion in 2011 (Himmelstein et al. 2014).

23.2 Healthcare Digital Transformation in Practice

Digital transformation is now enabling amazing changes in health care. As a direct consequence of these changes, we will see new healthcare systems emerging that are citizen-centric, with highly effective, personalized treatments; with more integrated forms of care, from doctor's surgery to hospital and community care at home; and with more efficient operating models that cut through the current complexity. Here are two examples of the changes we see:

Patient journey:

> Digital technologies such as mobile apps, medical services platforms, artificial intelligence, and data analytics tools are helping health care to become patient-centric, with citizens personally engaged in their lifelong well-being and actively participating in their own care programs.

Treatment efficacy:

> Digital technologies, such as high-performance computing, are now enabling the mapping of entire human genome profiles at an increasingly affordable cost. These genomic profiles are being used to develop new personalized treatments targeting the specific phenotype[1] of each patient. Other digital technologies, such as Internet-connected sensors, are being used to provide feedback between patient and clinician to ensure medications are taken as prescribed. And we are at the beginning of new forms of drug being created that target multiple conditions for an individual patient; early pilots are underway to discover these formulations using quantum algorithms.

Let's take a closer look at these areas.

23.3 Optimizing the Patient Journey

From a citizen standpoint, there is now much work being done to help people take more control of their "patient journey." This can be supported through enabling patient access to relevant personal healthcare data and insights (e.g., via their mobile devices) and helping them understand what action, if any, they need to take based on the symptoms they are showing. People are already showing a growing interest in engaging with a variety of online healthcare services. A key challenge to overcome is that there is so much health-related information available online that it is proving difficult for people to identify that which is relevant and avoid being misled.

A good way to address this is through formally health-accredited apps. These apps can be connected, with an individual's permission, to their electronic patient record. Extending this approach further, such an application could also signpost other relevant apps as part of an "ecosystem of accredited and approved patient-centric services" to support the individual through the next steps in their patient journey, for instance: setting an appointment with their local GP; providing

[1]The set of observable characteristics of an individual resulting from the interaction of its genotype with the environment.

required permission to healthcare practitioners to access their electronic health record (EHR); uploading any images to share with their practitioner in advance of their appointment; managing their prescription; making any necessary payments and keeping track of their healthcare bills; seeking advice on how best to manage their condition; and getting connected into a trusted social network of other sufferers of their identified condition. Applications like "Doctor Care Anywhere" are opening up access to such a range of services.[2]

From a healthcare practitioner standpoint, there is a parallel opportunity for an app ecosystem to help them better improve their patient interactions and improve productivity. A healthcare practitioner app ecosystem could prove useful in enabling medics to quickly learn about a new hospital or other care facilities they are working in; discover the local services and resources available to them, and how these can be accessed; and connect into local hospital systems.

A personalized patient journey:

> Let's imagine a patient journey for a given individual. In this example, we shall consider someone who has a family history of cardiovascular problems. The patient's journey begins with a visit to the doctor who obtains a DNA profile based on a blood sample. Note: The cost of such profiling has fallen exponentially from £100 million in the year 2000 to less than £100 today (NHGRI 2019). The DNA profile is compared against a sample population of others who have suffered from the condition in question. Three risk indicators are identified leading to the patient being prescribed a personalized program of care based on their clinical, social, and genomic profile. The patient is advised to wear a device, perhaps one embedded in their clothing, to help them monitor their condition over time. Data from this device is fed into a trained algorithm to detect for anomalies. After many years of such monitoring, a worrying change is identified. An echocardiogram is carried out, and a need for a heart valve replacement identified. A new valve is printed using 3D printing based on the echocardiogram images. The doctor seeks guidance from a surgeon who subsequently conducts the operation with assistance from robo-surgery and augmented reality. This may seem somewhat science fiction when articulated in this way, but all the component technologies referred to are already in use today (Atos Digital Vision for Health 2019).

23.4 Enhancing Treatment Efficacy Through Precision Medicine

Science and technology are advancing to enable a more proactive approach to patient care focused on maintaining their wellness for as long as possible, instead of treating a disease once it has occurred.

There are four key elements to precision medicine: predictive, preventive, personalized, and participatory. One medical field in which this is being applied is diabetes, a chronic condition affecting a large and growing number of people in the

[2]https://doctorcareanywhere.com/ [accessed 26/10/2019].

developed world. Imagine a situation in which a doctor can profile a set of patients potentially at risk (predictive); proactively alert them to the risk they face (preventive); propose a program of health care specially targeting each patient's own risk indicators, based on their individual genomic profile (personalized); and subsequently engage them to manage their own risk through relevant behavioral change, including patient tracking of the impact of such changes (participatory) (Precision Medicine: Changing the way we think about healthcare 2018).

Successful execution of each of these steps is dependent on bringing together some critical digital technologies. Data must be brought together from a variety of sources. Machine learning is required to identify underlying patterns and highlight those at risk. The derived patient insights must be converted into actionable alerts, initially for the clinician and then for the patient. These insights must be made available conveniently and securely to all relevant parties.

Focusing on AI: The emerging opportunity for artificial intelligence in health care

> Of all the digital technologies currently being deployed in the transformation of health care, one that really stands out for us is artificial intelligence.
>
> Healthcare operations generate large and increasing volumes of data, both in relation to general management of care facilities and in relation to medical activities. Administrators and practitioners alike are increasingly interested in how they can better exploit this data, whether for operational efficiency or improved patient outcomes.
>
> On the administrative side, a long-standing healthcare challenge has been the continuing growth in administrative personnel required to run our increasingly complex healthcare systems. And on the clinical side, medics are interested in how to augment productivity and performance.

There are a great many areas of opportunity for medical practitioners. Here are just three examples:

- Triage of patients coming into accident and emergency (A&E). A&E can be a highly pressurized part of a hospital. All kinds of patients are coming in for help ranging from, at one end of the scale, someone using A&E effectively as others use their general practitioner (GP) service to, at the other end of the scale, people who may look OK at face value but inside may be bleeding to death from an internal injury and need urgent attention. One possible use of AI is to monitor the vital signs of people coming into A&E to assist nurses with a rapid patient "triage" service.
- Monitoring of a patient's vital signs during a stay in hospital. The current requirement is for nurses to check a patient's vital signs (heart rate, blood pressure, and temperature) every four hours while they are in hospital. This is a time-consuming process, and it requires careful concentration by the nurse to ensure errors are not made. And meanwhile, four hours is still quite a large gap: time enough for problems to occur which may not be picked up, especially if a patient is on a private ward. Digital technologies are now being developed which can both alleviate the pressure on nurses and also provide more continuous patient monitoring and alerts. One very innovative approach to this we

have seen does this using camera technology, whereby heart rate is determined by detecting very small movements as the patient's face pulses in and out with each heartbeat (oxehealth.com).
- Radiology analysis. Radiology is a critical service in health care used, for example, in breast screening for cancer. A challenge today is that there are not enough radiologists to meet demand. AI, and specifically machine learning, can help improve the productivity of radiologists through pattern matching that learns to detect tumors from radiographs. The great benefits of this machine learning approach include: The learning model keeps improving the more examples it is shown (it can learn from some of the best radiologists, so helping all patients get a high quality of care and thereby reducing variability of patient outcomes); the machine learning model never has a bad day and never gets tired, so can significantly enhance the overall performance of a radiologist team.

23.5 The Challenge in Health

The health market can be segmented into two sides:

- The providers (e.g., hospitals, pharma companies, etc.).
- The payers (e.g., social security, insurance, etc.).

Patients are in the middle: seeking to get the best and most appropriate treatment.

The effective interaction between these two sides of the health market is becoming increasingly data dependent: whether this be clinical data, payment data, or personal profile data.

Such medical data is potentially highly personal and sensitive and is increasingly held in digital form as electronic health records (EHRs). Most of the time, these are created in the hospital or clinic where the patient is treated. In some countries, unique "patient medical dossiers" are created by the payer organizations to track all reimbursements for a given patient. While patient medical dossiers are unique, it is often the case that a patient will have as many EHRs as treatment facilities that he or she has visited.

Access to meaningful health data is currently plagued by problems of disaggregation, permission, privacy, and consistency.

It is hard for care providers to obtain a holistic view of patient history, and it is hard for the payers to make a meaningful correlation between the success of treatments and the money they spend on them.

Finally, GDPR seeks to guarantee health data privacy for patients, with patients being able to opt in or out of permissioning access to their EHR. Lack of comprehensive visibility of health data can present very risky situations (e.g., in the case of epidemics). Recently, some European countries like France have decided that by default every newly born child will opt into a "patient medical dossier" (Burnel 2018).

Without a data platform that appropriately facilitates data exchanges between patients, healthcare providers, pharma companies, and payers, current healthcare models will quickly become unsustainable.

23.6 Industry Platforms in the Health Ecosystem

Health information exchange (HIE) platforms are expected to underpin the healthcare industry's interoperability vision.

Gartner defines an HIE "*as a platform and trust alliance that facilitates the exchange of patient-related information among independent healthcare organizations. Participants in an HIE are organizations that, by prearrangement, exchange data through the HIE for the purpose of coordinating and improving care and patient safety*" (Runyon 2019).

They see three major trends:

1. The fundamental value of an HIE is about securely exchanging patient information with legitimate stakeholders (payers, providers, laboratories, trust networks, patients, and other HIEs) to reduce medical errors, better coordinate care, and improve outcomes.
2. Both third-party and HIE vendors rely on industry interoperability standards, protocols, and trust alliances for secure patient data interchange.
3. Managing patient identity and consent at scale will become more important as inter-HIE transaction activity increases to support community-based care globally in the wake of Trusted Exchange Framework and Common Agreement (TEFCA) in the USA. The basic opt-in and opt-out current models will no longer suffice as HIEs go nationwide.

Interoperability for health data has been identified as a key challenge for many years; however, it has difficulties in finding a sustainable economic model because a multi-sided market approach has not been used.

The health market is confronted by the dilemma of an absolute necessity to contain cost and improve efficiency to survive, while at the same time supporting a national community responsible for population well-being including the poorest and most in need.

The necessary use of data for better efficiency is less a business-to-consumer issue but rather a business-to-business issue where a non-regulated exchange of data between provider and payers may well lead to resistance to sharing in order to parochially increase profits.

Addressing these challenges will require:

- Promoting HIEs by offering regulations combining efficient data exchange and privacy protection.

- Defining interoperability rules and generic APIs to facilitate analytics and AI based on data collected by different HIEs.
- Establishing the business value of data exchanges of different data types balanced against the impact of potential privacy breaches.
- Respecting local situations (e.g. developing countries desperately in need of driving efficiency, but at the potential risk of lack of privacy; Europe being permanently challenged by legal considerations linked to GDPR).
- Consideration of the possible benefits of analytics but also having in mind the additional capabilities of AI which can only deliver if machine learning is fed with enough data.

References

Atos Digital Vision for Health. (2019). https://atos.net/en-gb/united-kingdom/digital-vision-programme/digital-vision-health. Accessed October 26, 2019.

Burnel, P. (2018). The introduction of electronic medical records in France: More progress during the second attempt. *Health Policy, 122*(9), 937–940. https://www.sciencedirect.com/science/article/pii/S0168851018303245. Accessed October 26, 2019.

Gameiro, G. R., Sinkunas, V., Liguori, G. R., & Auler-Junior, J. O. C. (2018). Precision medicine: Changing the way we think about healthcare. https://www.ncbi.nlm.nih.gov/pmc/articles/PMC6251254/. Accessed October 26, 2019.

Global Burden of Disease Health Financing Collaborator Network. (2017). Future and potential spending on health 2015–40: Development assistance for health, and government, prepaid private, and out-of-pocket health spending in 184 countries. *The Lancet, 389*(10083), 2005–2030. https://doi.org/10.1016/S0140-6736(17)30873-5. Open Access, Published 19 April 2017. Accessed October 26, 2019.

Graham, E. (2016). Improving outcomes through personalised medicine. NHS England, 07 September 2016. https://www.england.nhs.uk/wp-content/uploads/2016/09/improving-outcomes-personalised-medicine.pdf. Accessed October 26, 2019.

Himmelstein, D. U., et al. (2014). A Comparison Of hospital administrative costs in eight nations: US costs exceed all others by far. *Health Affairs, 33*(9): *Advancing Global Health Policy*. https://www.healthaffairs.org/doi/full/10.1377/hlthaff.2013.1327. Accessed October 26, 2019.

Institute of Fiscal Studies, UK Health Spending. (2017). https://www.ifs.org.uk/uploads/publications/bns/BN201.pdf. Accessed October 26, 2019.

NHGRI. (2019). The cost of sequencing a human genome. National Human Genome Research Institute. https://www.genome.gov/about-genomics/fact-sheets/Sequencing-Human-Genome-cost. Accessed October 26, 2019.

NHS Digital. (2016, November). Hospital admitted patient care activity 2015–16. https://digital.nhs.uk/news-and-events/news-archive/2016-news-archive/hospital-admissions-hit-record-high-as-population-ages. Accessed October 26, 2019.

Runyon, B. (2019). Market guide for health information exchange platforms. Gartner, 09 April 2019. https://www.gartner.com/en/documents/3906722/market-guide-for-health-information-exchange-platforms. Accessed October 26, 2019.

Case Study 3: Autonomous and Electric Vehicles

24

Many commentators, analysts, and vehicle manufacturers claim that the realization of the dream of driverless vehicles is just around the corner. We already have mature, driver-assisted technologies (levels 1 and 2 automation) in use on our public roads, and self-driving vehicles (levels 3 and 4) are being intensively tested with the expectation that they will be available on the market sometime in the 2020s. The potential value of this transformation is significant, with promises of fewer accidents, reduced carbon emissions, lower traffic congestion, and the freeing up of driver time. It is also expected to free up valuable city center land that is currently used for parking. The challenge of reaching fully autonomous driving is not only in the technology but also in the associated regulations, liabilities, and ethics.

24.1 The Context

Given that human beings have become pretty used to driving their own cars, with some really enjoying doing so, you might be forgiven for wondering why autonomous vehicles are currently attracting so much attention.

Autonomous driving is motivated primarily by the following desires:

- Preventing the 1.35 million road deaths (WHO 2018) and many other serious injuries caused by traffic accidents: BCG has estimated that widespread adoption of autonomous vehicles in cities, especially if they are shared (for instance, in the form of robo-taxis), could reduce road deaths by 90%.
- Making our cities and other major conurbations more attractive places to live by reducing the amount of road space and parking space occupied by cars: BCG has estimated that shared autonomous vehicles in cities could reduce the total number of cars on the road in major cities by 60%, enabling more efficient movement of people and freeing up roadside space and car parks from their current role of storing cars (Boston Consulting Group 2016).

H. Tardieu et al., *Deliberately Digital*, Future of Business and Finance,
https://doi.org/10.1007/978-3-030-37955-1_24

- Freeing up the billions of hours spent annually by people driving their cars and, especially, improving our economies by making it easier for everyone to efficiently complete the journeys they need to get to work: Americans as a collective whole drove 2.45 trillion miles in 2014 (Tefft 2018), averaging 293 hours each behind the wheel or almost a month's worth of 10-hour driving days. Over an entire lifetime of driving, this could amount to 37,000 hours. Much of this time could be better spent if freed up by autonomous driving (e.g., to work, study, sleep, shop, communicate with others, or be entertained).

24.1.1 The Five Stages of Autonomous Driving

The path toward autonomous driving has been pursued for some years, and it is often described as a five-step journey as set out in Fig. 24.1. Level 0 is where the driver controls everything, including steering, brakes, throttle, and power. Level 1 gets a little more interesting with most functions still controlled by the driver, but with the option that key functions such as steering or acceleration can be performed automatically. Level 2 enables the car to perform more than one automated function at the same time, supported by additional contextual information. The driver can be disengaged physically from operating certain functions of the vehicle, with their hands off the steering wheel and their feet off the pedals. Importantly though, the driver needs to be ready to re-engage at any time, should the need arise. Level 3 enables drivers to completely shift safety-critical functions to the vehicle, under certain conditions. The driver must still be ready to intervene, but they do not need to have quite so much oversight as before. Level 4 represents the beginning of fully autonomous vehicles, with the vehicle performing all safety-critical driving functions, while monitoring road conditions for a complete trip. The limitation here is

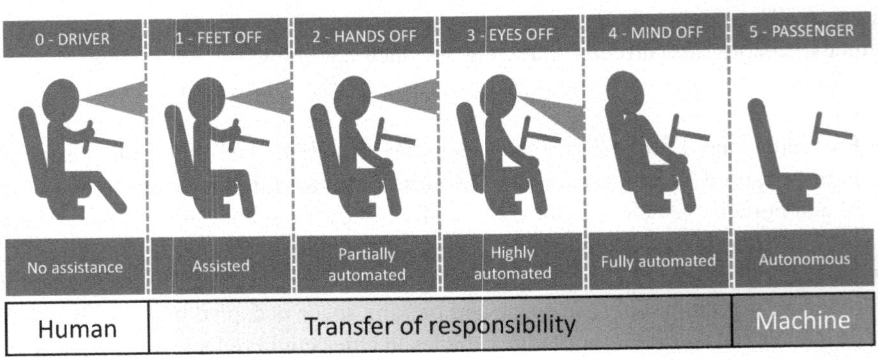

Fig. 24.1 Five stages of autonomous driving. Adapted from "AI in 2018: waiting for driverless cars to become a reality" (Assis 2018)

that the vehicle cannot be relied upon to operate in this way for all road scenarios or weather conditions. Level 5 is achieved when the autonomous vehicle's performance is equal to that of a human driver, except in certain more extreme environments.

At the time of writing, leaders such as Tesla have reached level 3. Getting to level 4 or level 5 is a substantially greater challenge that requires significant transformation in which digital technologies are deployed within vehicles and in the wider external environment in which the vehicles operate (MarketWatch, January 2018).

24.1.2 The Evolution of Autonomous Driving

The real growth in interest for the autonomous car market came from technology-led platform organizations such as Uber and Google (Waymo). They positioned the transportation challenge primarily as one of branded mobility enablement, instead of the (then prevailing) industry norm of branded car design.

As Uber (launched in 2009) and other related mobility platforms (such as Lyft) took off, some of the major car manufacturers started to pay attention. For instance, Daimler invested in mobility provider mytaxi in 2014 and then Hailo in 2016. In February 2019, Daimler and BMW announced a €1 billion joint venture called "Your Now" which incorporates mytaxi and Hailo under a new brand called "Free Now." In parallel to Uber's arrival came another major disruptor in the form of Tesla, who launched their first electric vehicle, the Roadster, in July 2009. They offered a new vision for electric and autonomous driving and quickly grew to a market capitalization greater than Ford. Today, all the world's leading manufacturers are working on autonomous and electric vehicles.

As an integral element supporting both Uber-style mobility services and Tesla-style electric and autonomous vehicles, cars need to be connected to the Internet in order to support critical services such as road traffic analysis and navigation systems. This connectivity is also proving valuable in other areas such as infotainment, roadside assistance, and vehicle diagnostics. As vehicles become ever more autonomous, they will need to connect to the wider road infrastructure in which they operate.

Taken together, these four components of mobility services (shared, electric, autonomous, and connected) now form the basis of the strategy for leading automotive firms. The acronyms may vary (for instance, "ACES" for VW, "CASE" for Daimler), but the meaning is the same.

The value at stake for the automotive industry is very large: The global car market is currently worth in excess of $2 trillion (Kuhnert et al. 2019). Car manufacturers could take comfort from the fact that, at present growth rates, the number of cars on our roads is predicted to grow from 1.01 billion to 2.0 billion in the next 15 years, potentially doubling the size of the market (source: HERE). However, this comfort could prove to be misplaced. There are those who take the view that we will only need 40% of current car volumes on the road to support our growing population's future mobility requirements as we evolve to autonomous shared vehicles. If this is true, then those who stick to traditional automotive business models will find themselves fighting for a share of an ever-decreasing market.

An important point to note is that there is a widely, although far from exclusively, held view that vehicle electrification is a technology evolution that is highly complementary to that of vehicle autonomy. Tesla has adopted an all-electric strategy for its "fully self-driving cars," while Alphabet's Waymo is using plug-in hybrid electric minivans. The debate hinges on the challenges of maximizing vehicle range (to minimize charging downtime), provision of the significant amounts of electric power required for onboard sensors and computing systems, and simplicity of power train production and control. It will be interesting to see how things develop in terms of battery capacities, fast charging times, and even hydrogen fuel cell adoption. Interestingly, flying car start-up Alakai claims its vehicles can fly for up to 4 h covering 400 miles on a single load of hydrogen fuel which can be replenished in 10 minutes.[1] Whatever the eventual outcome, we consider it worthwhile addressing developments in the electric vehicle market in parallel with that of autonomous vehicles.

As we shall describe shortly, having mature autonomous driving technology is necessary, but far from sufficient, for the emerging mobility service ecosystem. There is a need to provide vehicle charging infrastructure, develop an intelligent mobility service infrastructure backbone to reduce the compute and sensing overhead in a given vehicle, and create a "real-time" Digital Twin of the road network-related environment so that autonomous vehicles have an up-to-date view of the changing world around them. This shift toward a mobility service-driven business model will have a significant impact on companies that have been bastions of product manufacturing. If they are unable to transform their strategies, they risk becoming unbranded, white labeled, commoditized suppliers to the leading mobility platform operators. But, on the other, if they can themselves become a mobility services leader, there is the potential for exciting new business models and associated new revenue streams arising from a growing range of innovative mobility services.

Perhaps it is not surprising, given what is at stake, that the scale of investment being made in autonomous vehicles is very large. Our analysis of The Robot Report data on venture capital investments indicates over $7.4 billion of funding was raised for autonomous vehicle development in the first 7 months of 2019 alone. This includes substantial sums raised by just four major players: Aurora ($1.73 billion, Hyundai Motor Group and Baillie Gifford), Uber ($1 billion), Cruise ($1.15 billion, with investments from GM, Honda, SoftBank Vision Fund, and T. Rowe Price), and Argo AI (raised $2.6 billion, with VW as lead investment partner) (The Robot Report 2019).

[1]https://alakai.com/. Accessed 26/10/2019.

24.2 The Challenges

24.2.1 Regulatory and Legal Considerations

As we discussed in Part I, it is the nature of technology to evolve faster than the regulatory and legal framework for a given market. The current state of international law as embodied in the Convention on Road Traffic (UNECE 2018) states that the steering of a car can be carried out by an automated system if the driver can take over at any time. So, for now at least, automotive manufacturers need to retain a steering wheel for their cars.

Another more difficult legal challenge for automotive firms is how to address liability in the event of an accident. At present, when an individual human driver causes a single accident, the liability does not typically fall on the manufacturer, except perhaps in the rare case of an underlying design fault in their vehicle causing the incident. The good news here for manufacturers is that this currently limits the manufacturer's liability in a controllable manner. However, in the future this will be different, with liability moving away from the driver and to those who design, build, and operate the autonomous driving platforms which have replaced them. There are two difficulties for manufacturers to negotiate. Firstly, their algorithms will be investigated to assess their design attributes and how these contributed to the accident. There will be an expectation of transparency and explainability, and this, in itself, may expose AV operators to liability. Secondly, there is the problem of how to manage claims across the multiple accidents that will inevitably occur (in mixed mode manual and autonomous environments), even if overall accident numbers are significantly reduced compared to the current status quo. This could expose AV operators to class action lawsuits, with the potential for large compensation payments.

Studies have been undertaken to determine how safe an autonomous vehicle will have to be compared to a human-driven vehicle before the public will consider AVs to be acceptable (NHTSA 2018). Current research suggests they need to be 100 times safer, but even this contribution to safety and lives saved may not protect the AV operators from the legal exposure they would face within the current legal and regulatory framework.

At present, the leader in AV is Waymo (www.waymo.com), a subsidiary of Alphabet. As of early 2019, we assess their best hypothetical performance is one lethal accident per 80,000 h of driving. Our working assumption here is that one in a hundred of Waymo's current system disengagements could potentially create a lethal accident in open road conditions, if no human driver was available to immediately take over. If we were to take a more pessimistic view (e.g., one lethal accident for every ten disengagements), this would indicate a current performance of one lethal accident every 800 h. On this basis, and with current rates of improvement, we would not expect to see the threshold for public acceptability to be crossed until 2029.

24.2.2 Cost to Provide Versus Customer Willingness to Pay

There is a view that, with technologies available by 2020, the additional cost of an autonomous car capable of level 4 or level 5 driving would be between $75,000 and $100,000 more than a conventional one. And there are those who think this could be a conservative estimate given the number of sensors required.

There are a number of studies now available which have assessed the consumer's willingness to pay for autonomous vehicles. As in most areas of human consumption, this amount varies by context and by related tastes and preferences. According to a study in 2017 by IHS Markit (IHS 2017), on average US consumers are willing to pay $780 for full autonomous driving. Another study showed this to be $3500 for partial automation and $4900 for full automation.

In practice, it appears that some consumers are already proving their willingness to pay, for example through choosing to buy services such as Tesla's Enhanced Autopilot (a $5000 option that allows you to take your hands off the wheel for a short time) or their full autonomous driving system (priced at $8000). However, Tesla has not released data on how many of their customers have bought these services to date. What's more, for many of Tesla's cars these amount to a relatively low percentage of the total cost of the vehicle.

Over time, it is expected that the technologies enabling autonomous driving will greatly reduce in cost. However, the current gap in cost to deliver versus realistic sales price means that the initial buyers of autonomous driving vehicles are likely to be major commercial fleets of robo-taxis whose business case is substantiated through the removal of current driver costs and the ability to extract maximum revenue through high levels of utilization.

24.2.3 Environment

There is a great deal of media focus currently on the nature and makeup of autonomous vehicles themselves. There is less focus on the wider environmental context required to make autonomous driving viable. We expect to see a much more complex and holistic picture begin to emerge as autonomous vehicles start to become more pervasive.

There are two key challenges impacting the current viability of AV design. One is the need to reduce the AV technology cost overhead; the other is the need to reduce AV power consumption.

We've already touched on cost. Key AV cost drivers include intensive onboard processing power and a variety of sensors potentially using a range of expensive technologies including LIDAR. While the cost of these technologies is expected to drop considerably in the coming years (e.g., through technology evolution, economies of scale, and other learning curve effects), the power requirements of these technologies cause another issue: The power overhead of AV's is such that it can reduce the effective range of an electric vehicle by up to 30% (Teraki 2019).

In our view, there will be a need to take much of the compute and sensing requirement outside of the vehicle and to put it into a new mobility-as-a-service platform.

24.2.4 Cyber-Security

AVs create a wholly new and pervasive cyber-challenge which the emerging mobility services industry must address. In essence, AVs are becoming another Internet-connected device, and the sheer scale of AV evolution will doubtless be attractive to the tendency of malicious agents to follow market opportunities available to them. Areas of potential vulnerability include endpoints in the vehicle and the underlying communication infrastructure outside and inside the vehicle. Sources of threat include: state agencies, organized crime, and insiders hacking their own vehicles.

From a communication standpoint, there are a number of potential vulnerabilities: wireless communication networks; Internet access and an internal network inside the car, enabling routing of messaging to devices inside and outside the vehicle; the car's CAN bus to connect its ECUs, sensors, and actuators; connections to additional driver services, such as collision warning systems, speed warnings, and safety alerts; vehicle-to-vehicle communication systems, for instance to enable notification of any road works or accidents ahead; and IoT-related services such as traffic flow data sharing, presence of people, and notification of any other possible hazards (Hartzell and Stubel 2017).

Mobility services providers are responding with layered protection systems which attempt to isolate different types of cyber-hazard. Ultimately, however, no computer system yet devised is invulnerable to attack, and there will inevitably be an "arms race" between mobility services providers and the threat actors they face.

24.3 Industry Platforms for Autonomous Vehicles

Sergio Marchionne, the now sadly deceased CEO of Fiat Chrysler, argued strongly for greater car industry consolidation and cooperation. He felt that there was far too much duplicated investment which did not benefit the consumer and which led to excessive industry investment in R&D to the detriment of shareholders.

Autonomous driving currently represents exactly the kind of challenge Sergio Marchionne had in mind: Substantial, sustained investment is required over a number of years and ultimately, there is insufficient justification for multiple parallel investments.

A key problem for the mobility services industry is how to create trusted, practical, effective, and affordable level 4 autonomous driving which is a significant challenge, even for the most attractive use cases mentioned earlier involving robo-taxi car sharing. In a bid to address some of these challenges, the emergent mobility services industry is developing a new *cooperative intelligence* capability. The idea is for intelligence to be distributed between the car and the infrastructure, thus reducing the computing needs on the car and consequently the electrical consumption. Such a scenario will be facilitated by the advent of 5G, expected in 2020.

One example of this cooperative intelligence is Japan's new Dynamic Map Platform (Public Relations Office of Japan 2018). Dynamic Platform Inc was established as a response to the Japanese Government vision described as "Society 5.0," and it was founded jointly by a number of Japan's leading companies. The ambition shared by its founders was to create the high-definition and up-to-date maps necessary to support autonomous driving. They are now working together with other industry partners to collaborate in efficiently updating the Dynamic Map Platform database. The digital maps they are creating include a large volume of dynamic data such as traffic regulation and roadwork information, accident and congestion data, and pedestrian and signal information. This is combined with more static, high-definition 3D information, including road surface information, lane information, and information on 3D structures. The information provided by Dynamic Map Platform is critical to efficiently improving the cognitive performance of an autonomous driving system through cooperation with a vehicle's onboard sensors. Some of the benefits of this cooperative intelligence include:

- Helping the vehicle to estimate its current position.
- Helping the vehicle to recognize road signs.
- Supporting environment recognition.
- Enabling the vehicle to access data for relevant objects beyond the range of its sensors.

We are seeing similar cooperative ventures being set up elsewhere, including Europe and the USA. In Europe, three major German automotive manufacturers (Audi, BMW, and Daimler) were recently joined by Continental and Pioneer to create a platform (HERE—already described in the chapter on Platforms and Ecosystems) able to share data collected by all connected cars from the three manufacturers. Just as we have described for Japan's Dynamic Map Platform, this shared data will give each stakeholder access to road environment data at all times of day and throughout all seasons regardless of weather, so enabling them to feed their evolving machine intelligence algorithms.

Such a scenario will only take off if all players understand how to function effectively within a mobility services ecosystem in which they learn to operate as one player within a codependent multi-sided market. To illustrate this:

- Automotive manufacturers will only adopt cooperative intelligence if they can be assured of a widely distributed intelligent infrastructure, enabling customers to use AV services on many roads.
- Regional authorities and cities will only equip their infrastructures if they believe that a sufficient number of cars will be able to benefit from it.

As for all ecosystems, this chicken-and-egg problem is the first critical hurdle to be overcome by somehow "priming the pump." It seems likely that specific high-value routes will be enabled first, with take-up potentially further encouraged by only making these routes accessible to shared AVs. Even for this limited scenario, a key dependency is to establish the right regulatory framework and, for something as critical as autonomous vehicles, a certain time lag must be expected: For example, in France it has taken 5 years to create the regulatory environment. While governments cannot always move quickly, when they are suitably motivated significant resources can be applied, as is now the case in France:

- In August 2015, the Energy Transition Law authorized the French government to allow circulation of fully or partially automated vehicles on public roads.
- In March 2018, the regulatory context for AVs was established.
- Finally, the law on new mobilities (LOM),[2] when adopted, will define foreseeing driver's inattention and driver absence, driver attention and inter-distances, traffic law revisions, liabilities in case of accident, and data protection and privacy.

Ultimately, the launch of the AV ecosystem will be enabled through what we might describe as "a regulatory sandbox." This will enable the viability of the use case to be safely tested and proven, and it will allow all players in the ecosystem to identify their opportunities and risks to inform their business cases.

We have seen in this chapter that autonomous vehicles have the potential to deliver significant benefits. But we have also seen that there are many challenges to achieving the dream of level 4 or 5 autonomy. These challenges include being able to provide this autonomy at a cost that consumers are willing to pay, with a level of safety that is acceptable to the public (while also meeting regulatory and legal requirements) and with power requirements that do not inordinately constrain vehicle range. As we have seen, servitization can address the cost challenge (by switching to a mobility-as-a-service model). Platforms and ecosystems will enable data sharing between vehicles and intelligent infrastructure, which then has the potential to improve safety while simultaneously reducing vehicle power consumption and increasing range.

References

Assis. (2018). https://www.marketwatch.com/story/ai-in-2018-waiting-for-driverless-cars-to-become-a-reality-2017-12-27. Accessed October 26, 2019.

Boston Consulting Group. (2016, July). Self-driving vehicles, robo-taxis and the urban mobility revolution. https://www.bcg.com/en-gb/publications/2016/automotive-public-sector-self-driving-vehicles-robo-taxis-urban-mobility-revolution.aspx. Accessed October 26, 2019.

Hartzell, S., & Stubel, C. (2017). Automobile CAN bus network security and vulnerabilities. https://canvas.uw.edu. Accessed October 26, 2019.

[2]https://fr.wikipedia.org/wiki/Projet_de_loi_d%27orientation_des_mobilit%C3%A9s. Accessed 26/10/2019.

IHS. (2017). Survey finds varied autonomy and safety technology preferences for new vehicles, IHS Markit Says. Press Release 03/08/2017. https://technology.ihs.com/594402/survey-finds-varied-autonomy-and-safety-technology-preferences-for-new-vehicles-ihs-markit-says. Accessed October 26, 2019.

Kuhnert, F., et al. (2019). *Automotive trends 2019*. PwC Research. https://www.pwc.com/gx/en/ceo-agenda/ceosurvey/2019/themes/automotive-trends.html. Accessed October 26, 2019.

MarketWatch. (2018, January). Accessed October 26, 2019. AI in 2018: Waiting for driverless cars to become a reality. Original source material: Evercore ISI, SAE International. https://www.marketwatch.com/story/ai-in-2018-waiting-for-driverless-cars-to-become-a-reality-2017-12-27. Accessed October 26, 2019.

NHTSA. (2018). *Automated vehicles for safety*. National Highway Traffic Safety Administration. https://www.nhtsa.gov/technology-innovation/automated-vehicles-safety. Accessed October 26, 2019.

Public Relations Office of Japan. (2018, January). Safer traffic with dynamic map. https://www.gov-online.go.jp/eng/publicity/book/hlj/html/201801/201801_04_en.html. Accessed October 26, 2019.

Tefft, B. C. (2018). American Driving Survey: 2015–2016. (Research Brief). Washington, D.C.: AAA Foundation for Traffic Safety. https://aaafoundation.org/wp-content/uploads/2018/01/19-0226_AAAFTS-2018-ADAS-Research-Brief-Update_v1.pdf. Accessed October 26, 2019.

Teraki. (2019, May). Autonomous cars' big problem. https://medium.com/@teraki/energy-consumption-required-by-edge-computing-reduces-a-autonomous-cars-mileage-with-up-to-30-46b6764ea1b7. Accessed October 26, 2019.

The Robot Report. (2019). https://www.therobotreport.com/category/investments-funding/.

UNECE. (2018). Report of the Global Forum for Road Traffic Safety on its seventy-seventh session. United Nations, Economic and Social Council, Economic Commission for Europe, Inland Transport Committee, Global Forum for Road Traffic Safety, Seventy-seventh session, Geneva, 18–21 September 2018. http://www.unece.org/fileadmin/DAM/trans/doc/2018/wp1/ECE-TRANS-WP1-165e.pdf. Accessed October 26, 2019.

WHO. (2018). *Global status report on road safety 2018*. Geneva: World Health Organization. License: CC BYNC-SA 3.0 IGO. https://www.who.int/violence_injury_prevention/road_safety_status/2018/en/. Accessed October 26, 2019.

25 Case Study 4: The Digital Transformation of Insurance

Insurance firms are now entering a critical phase of disruption and renewal. Their existing primary markets of motor, home, health and life insurance are all being transformed by the emergence of customer aggregators and powerful platform-based ecosystems.

Platform-based ecosystems are showing potential for radical insurance innovation as firms seek access to vast volumes of new data and look to establish new engagement points with customers. At the same time, aggregators threaten to further disassociate insurers from their customers, leaving them as little more than easily interchangeable commodity service providers.

Nevertheless, the opportunities presented by fresh and broader data-driven insights are allowing leading firms to create a plethora of risk reduction and management services to complement the insurance cover they already provide.

25.1 The Context

The insurance industry has been relatively slow to digitally transform, and there are several reasons for this: new entrants have been reluctant or unable to carry insurance risk on their balance sheets; incumbents have been held back by legacy technology; and the incentive to transform has been reduced by the existing books of insurance policies, which offer assured revenue streams, at least in the short to medium term.

The traditional universal insurance model has enabled affordable insurance for all by offsetting the cost of covering higher-risk customers with that of lower-risk customers. In a world of imperfect information, this made sense for both the insurer and the insured because it was not clear to either party the precise risk any one customer represented.

H. Tardieu et al., *Deliberately Digital*, Future of Business and Finance,
https://doi.org/10.1007/978-3-030-37955-1_25

This situation is rapidly changing. As our world becomes ever more connected, it is increasingly possible for insurers to have a much more precise and up-to-date view of the relative risk of any given customer and to price their insurance cover accordingly. Examples from car insurance include policies paid for "as you drive" (with insurance costs directly linked to time spent driving) and policies paid for "how you drive" (with insurance costs directly linked to personal driving behaviors).

Insurer insight into customers is not only helped by the growing availability of data but also by the means to analyze and utilize it using new techniques in artificial intelligence (AI). The capability of AI available to insurers has been increasing rapidly through advances in compute power, new ways to access this through cloud computing, and new platform-based AI tool-sets. Three areas in which insurers are now using AI include analysis of human speech using chatbots; analysis of photographic images using convolutional neural networks; and analysis of unstructured data using machine learning.

Chatbots are proving to be a highly popular way for consumers to interact with businesses and are rapidly evolving into virtual assistants with an increasing range of functionality. One successful early mover in these technologies has been insurer Lemonade.

On December 23, 2016, Lemonade's virtual assistant "AI Jim" broke a world record. A Lemonade customer had his Canada Goose Langford Parka stolen. Without any delay, the customer was able to enter details of the theft into Lemonade's smartphone app, speaking into the camera to describe what had happened. Although the process up to this point had taken only a few minutes and required no paperwork, it was what happened next that broke the world record: in just three seconds, the customer's claim was paid. During this time, some impressive work was going on in the background: Lemonade's AI Jim reviewed the claim; cross-referenced it against the customer's policy; ran 18 anti-fraud algorithms; approved the claim; sent instructions to the bank for payment transfer; and informed the customer that their claim was paid. As you might imagine, the customer was delighted and gave their experience a five-star rating. (Lemonade blog 2017).

There is a danger for insurance incumbents that the value from their traditional business models is beginning to slip away, in part driven by a change in customer behavior as they move from asset ownership toward service consumption. This is impacting insurers in several of their core markets as younger generations rent their homes, use as-a-service platforms to furnish them (Feather), take holiday lets (Airbnb), use mobility services (Uber/Lyft), and engage in the evolving experience economy during their leisure time. All these trends point toward opportunities for new business models based on deeper customer insight and the ability to offer contextual insurance flexibly on-demand. They also point toward a shift in the primary buyer of insurance away from consumers, and toward the businesses that are providing the core services (with insurance bundled in).

Digital transformation is enabling insurers to create customer value in new ways. Firstly, through changing how they interact with consumers (e.g., via digital customer journeys which simplify and improve the insurance experience). Secondly, through the creation of new digitally enabled value propositions, offering significantly greater customer value than has previously been possible.

This is evidenced through services such as the following:

- More personalized and customized insurance (such as the UK's Drive Like A Girl).
- Situational insurance on-demand (e.g., insuring a car driver for one hour at Cuvva).
- The ability for consumers to share risk with others through peer-to-peer insurance that encourages reduced claims in anticipation of rewards (for instance, as provided by Friendsurance).
- A variety of risk mitigation and prevention services (whether for automotive, home, or travel).
- A variety of ancillary services related to risk reduction in a given ecosystem (e.g., InsurTech[1] increasingly integrates digital service provisioning with related services to increase customer engagement and value).

Our chapter on Strategy described the evolution and value of new ecosystems which are helping to transform our global economies in so many markets. The data gathered through these ecosystems is invaluable for insurers, as are the insights created by the major platform operators which underpin them.

The transformational impact on insurers is only now beginning to be felt. Insurers have a natural fit with these ecosystems because they can help to mitigate and manage risk for all participants. They can even support sub-ecosystems with particular groups of consumers or corporations. Examples of such ecosystems include mobility services, health and energy, each of which is explored elsewhere in this book. One tangible example of mobility services is that of Tesla, which now offers lifetime car insurance when customers buy their cars. It is worth noting that this example clearly changes the customer relationship for the insurer toward corporates and away from consumers.

As insurers work to innovate their business models, customer experience and services, they are discovering a need to urgently revisit how they operate. Their challenge is to become more agile and responsive to changing demand, but at a cost that enables them to remain competitive. Leading firms have adopted intelligent process automation as they seek to make core processes faster, cheaper, and more reliable, and they are open to new business partnerships which can help them accelerate and assure this evolution. As part of this evolution, incumbents are waking up to the potential for Blockchain technologies to further transform their performance. An example is B3i, an organization incorporated in 2018 and 100%

[1]Digital start-ups specialized in the Insurance market (FinTech is used for those specialized in banking).

owned by 17 insurance companies. B3i is currently working on a Blockchain solution (due to launch in January 2020) targeting "property catastrophe excess of loss" insurance on Corda's distributed ledger technology (Insurance Journal 2019).

The broader ambition for some insurers is to use Blockchain technology in a way that enables faster on-boarding of new customers through a trusted and notarized know-your-customer (KYC) Blockchain-based application and then to offer smart contracts which self-execute according to defined policy conditions being met.

25.2 Challenges and Opportunities

Learning to collaborate with InsurTech: InsurTechs are now operating in every part of the insurance industry value chain. This might concern insurance industry incumbents but, in fact, McKinsey has found that only around 10% of InsurTechs are seeking to disrupt the insurance business model. On the contrary, nearly two-thirds are actively looking for opportunities to collaborate with incumbents (McKinsey 2019).

The typical differentiating strengths of InsurTechs are as you might expect: they offer agility to respond more quickly to new opportunities, they are effective in realizing value from data, they know how to create compelling digital experiences, and they know how to ensure simplicity. These strengths can complement very well the value offered by established insurance firms who bring to the table other valuable qualities such as well-known brands, large customer bases, access to large data volumes, and access to funding for investment.

Avoid disintermediation by aggregators: Customer aggregators began as relatively simple Web site portals or Internet search services that enabled customers to get comparative quotes based on their specified requirements. They are now evolving into more sophisticated advisor platforms including broker services and, in some cases, robo-advisory services. Aggregation turns out to be an outstanding business model, which McKinsey has estimated to generate EBITDA[2] of between 30 and 40% (McKinsey 2018). Today, up to half the insurance policies sold online in Europe are now sold through aggregators. The field of insurance customer aggregation is itself highly dynamic. We are seeing aggregators that began in one market area, evolve into others. For instance, while Check24 began in the insurance market, others now active in this field did not (such as MoneySuperMarket which began in mortgages).

The aggregator model benefits from powerful positive feedback loops. Insurers are attracted by the opportunity to use aggregators as a channel to win new customers. As more insurers sign-up, more customers are attracted by the growing choice the aggregators can offer. The growing range of options available to aggregators also serves to increase their conversion rates, therefore reducing their customer acquisition costs.

[2]Earnings Before Interest Tax Depreciation and Amortisation.

The danger for insurers is that it is the aggregator who holds the customer relationship and, critically, the customers' data, with insurance companies left in the dark. If incumbent insurers fail to respond to this challenge, they risk losing their ability to access the customer insights they need to create compelling new offerings. And even if they do retain this ability, they need to be mindful that it can suit certain aggregators, such as price comparison websites, to design their platforms in a way that controls the differentiating element their customers can see. In the worst case, insurers may find themselves in the invidious position that their only remaining differentiation comes from the price they offer and the specific appetite they have for risk.

Find a new role in an evolving ecosystem: Given that insurers are currently losing in this battle with aggregators for their sales channel and for their insurance policy customer engagement, they need to either move into aggregation themselves or look elsewhere for new innovation opportunities. The new business ecosystems referred to at the start of this chapter are showing great potential. Already we note that 7 of the largest 10 companies in the world today are ecosystem providers (including Amazon, Apple, Facebook, TenCent, Alibaba, Alphabet, and Microsoft), but this represents only the beginning of the ecosystem evolution, with new ecosystems evolving in key areas relevant to insurers, both in B2C (such as in wealth management, housing, health, and mobility) and in B2B (such as in transport and logistics).

Insurers can extend their offerings into each of these platforms by defining their role in new ways, for example by:

- Helping firms to identify and manage new ecosystem risks, such as those in mobility services arising from autonomous driving.
- Helping ecosystem participants to reduce or even avoid key risks, for instance, through influencing driving behavior.
- Providing additional services to reduce the impact of problems such as car breakdown.

One example of an insurer taking steps to define a new role for themselves is that of Progressive. They have partnered with Zubie, a specialist in vehicle-track-and-trace and engine diagnostics, to help customers determine the impact of their driving behaviors on their insurance premiums.

Revising the approach to risk: Insurers have traditionally depended on actuaries to determine and evaluate risk. In addition to having skills in statistics, actuaries have broader skills and experience in complex areas such as life expectancy, health care, weather, and accidents. Given the significance of their work, it is interesting to note that the actuarial profession is very niche, with perhaps only 70,000 practitioners globally (The Actuary 2017); salaries are high, typically well into six figures in dollars or euros.

InsurTech is now bringing a fresh perspective to the actuarial challenge by addressing it through the deployment of artificial intelligence. These new players are becoming adept in harnessing the growing volumes of new data streams now available (both unstructured and structured). These data sets are derived from sources including telematics,[3] wearables,[4] social media, and news events. The AI-based models they produce are highly dynamic, and they can respond in real time to changing risk factors. Incumbent insurers can build new partnerships with InsurTech to complement their "human" actuarial skills with data-driven algorithmic models.

Examples of today's leading risk evaluation InsurTechs include Israeli start-up Atitdot (a cloud-based predictive analytics platform), FitSense (working with wearables data in Life & Health insurance), and Wunelli (working with car telemetry data in the field of car insurance).

Reducing the cost of fraud: Fraud has always been a factor for insurance companies. In Europe, insurance fraud is largely gang-related so the focus for fraud prevention is largely in third party as opposed to first party fraud (i.e., fraud conducted by a party other than the insured). InsurTech FRISS uses AI for real-time risk detection, and the firm uses this to help insurers prevent fraud before it happens.

In the UK, the Insurance Fraud Bureau has been set up to lead the industry's fight against organized insurance fraud. Two key areas of focus currently include:

- "Ghost broking," which is the sale of fake insurance policies to the general public. Since 2017 the IFB has seen a 67% increase in ghost broking activities in the UK and they currently report 60 on-going cases, each of which might involve hundreds of policies (IFB 2018).
- "Crash for Cash," which is the deliberate attempt to cause accidents for financial gain. This is believed to currently cost UK insurers £336 million per annum (IFB).

Simplifying claims management: Claims management now begins even before a customer faces a material loss, with the evolution of risk reduction and risk avoidance services. Once a customer wishes to make a claim, the process begins with first notification of loss (FNOL), followed by claims processing, loss assessment and remediation, and finally claims settlement.

Traditionally this process involved 5–7 touch points across 5–7 business silos, and the customer experience was designed in fragments by dissociated teams working only on their element of the process. From a customer perspective, this can leave their interactions feeling disjointed and more complex and introduce potential for mis-steps and associated delays.

Leading insurance firms are now taking a customer-centric view on their design of claim management, leading to simpler and more cost-effective engagement models through the entire claims cycle. As they do this, they are introducing digital

[3]A discipline that merges telecommunication engineering and computer science to gather and manage information that enables the tracking and controlling of remote objects.
[4]Electronic devices—usually capable of some data gathering, storage and/or processing capability—which can be worn in clothes or as accessories.

tools for each process element including digital customer engagement from any device, digital claims ecosystem integration, digital claims prevention services, the use of analytics, AI and automation for claims handling, and digital customer feedback. All this is supported by a new digital operating model covering front and back office process digitalization.

Addressing cyber-security: Cyber-security represents both a risk in itself and a new business opportunity for insurers.

Insurers initially lagged behind other financial services providers when it came to cyber-security, mainly because they were not initially targeted as extensively as others (notably banks). However, as other industry players have strengthened their cyber-profiles, attackers have moved on to what they perceive to be weaker targets and insurers have suffered accordingly.

A particular cyber-concern for insurers is to protect the growing number of digital channel touch points they manage and to safeguard the rapidly increasing volume of data they hold. Banks may hold the customers' money, but insurers hold the customers' data.

A recent example of such an attack was on the US-based Fortune 500 company First American Financial Corporation whose Web site was found to have caused a leak of hundreds of millions of documents related to mortgage deals going back to 2003 (Krebson Security 2019).

A new business opportunity, arising out of new cyber-security risks, is to offer cyber-risk insurance cover for businesses. Currently, the market is at an early stage of development. One of the most critical factors yet to be addressed is access for insurers to cyber-breach data. In the UK, the Association of British Insurers has recently asked the Information Commissioner's Office (ICO) to make anonymized cyber-breach data publicly available. As of August 2019, this approval has yet to be provided.

In the absence of effective cyber-risk cover, the cost impact to businesses can prove very significant. For example, in September 2018 British Airways (BA) was notified by the ICO of its intention to issue a fine of £183.39 million for infringements of GDPR (Information Commissioner's Office). One issue was the diversion of BA Web site traffic to a fraudulent site. Personal data of around 500,000 customers was believed to have been compromised in this incident.

There are opportunities in this field for insurers beyond cyber-risk cover alone. As for other elements of their business models, there is potential for them to engage in a wider cyber-risk ecosystem including both digital capability experts and those holding sensitive data.

Ensuring transparent ethical standards: The financial services industry suffered significant reputational damage following the financial crash in 2008, with the consequential loss of consumer trust. Subsequent regulatory changes such as GDPR require insurers to manage customer data transparently and securely, to only keep what they legitimately require, and to ensure customer permission for its use. If insurers are to access the data they need, they have first to re-earn the trust they have collectively lost.

One insurer leading the field in this area is French insurer AXA. AXA now requires all new contracts to respect a standard called RSE (*Responsabilité Sociale des Entreprises*). AXA's insurance products are now examined before launch against fifteen ethical standards, and a minimum score must be achieved before a product is launched. These standards include taking into account disabilities, protecting private data, and integrating prevention measures. For instance, on the environmental measure, points can be attributed if the contract offers "green incentives" such as preferring an environmentally friendly approach to rebuilding after an accident or disaster.

25.3 Industry Platforms for Insurance

Given the dynamic shifts occurring in favor of platform businesses across all key markets for insurance, it is now crucial for insurance companies to develop their own platform strategies.

Insurers can engage in platform-based industry ecosystems in three ways which we will now explore: supporting an existing industry ecosystem, creating an insurance innovation ecosystem, and creating their own industry ecosystem.

25.3.1 Supporting an Existing Industry Ecosystem

This is the easiest route for insurers but perhaps the hardest one when judged in terms of ensuring their long-term profitability.

Here are a couple of current examples:

- Generali insurance and Liberty Mutual are engaged in serving Google Nest's evolving ecosystem in the home.
- Geico is supporting Uber's ecosystem in mobility services.

The reason it is easy for insurers to participate in many of today's leading platform-based ecosystems is that they are seen as an essential component in building and maintaining stakeholder trust.

Insurers enable and assure trust through taking on the risks arising from the consumption of platform-based service offerings. The organization offering the service constitutes one side of the multi-sided market, while the insurer represents another side. Sharing of data is not a challenge because data is created only at the point that the service is provided, and the insurer will only cover the risk if they are able to access the data and hence provide informed cover.

For instance, in the past, Uber has had insurance-related issues. One such example occurred in Hong Kong, where local authorities sent a powerful message by arresting seven Uber drivers for carrying passengers without insurance to cover third-party risks. The drivers were fined, and they lost their driver's licenses for twelve months. Meanwhile, Uber lost market share as other drivers were more reluctant to sign up to the platform.

Geico's innovation for Uber is to offer ridesharing drivers one adaptive policy which they can use whether their ridesharing app is on or off. Geico claims that their policy provides more complete cover than either Uber or Lyft's own policies. For instance, if the driver has their ridesharing app on but is waiting for a rider, Geico's insurance fully covers them, which they claim is not the case with many other policies which would only offer partial cover in this scenario.

A danger for insurers adopting this strategy is that they could easily find themselves commoditized, with low profitability, and the potential to be substituted at any point for another insurer willing to accept even lower returns.

25.3.2 Creating an Insurance Innovation Ecosystem

A more ambitious opportunity for insurers is to build an insurance ecosystem of complementary insurance-related firms. For instance, Munich Re has created an insurance innovation ecosystem through its Digital Partners subsidiary. The Digital Partners ecosystem includes Trov (on-demand insurance providers) and Wrisk (mobile phone channel operator offering motor, home and travel insurance).

An insurance ecosystem is attractive because it enables the orchestrator to access the skills and capabilities of complementary firms (especially InsurTech start-ups) and, through this, accelerate the evolution of their offerings.

25.3.3 Creating Their Own Industry Ecosystem

The most ambitious and challenging opportunity for insurers is to orchestrate their own platform-based ecosystem: bringing together different services from multiple participants into one platform.

For instance, Discovery's Vitality Health has created its own ecosystem focused on well-being. Vitality's key insight is that people tend to "under-consume" wellness, unless helped along the way; if you can offer something that enables them to live better lives, and save money as they do this, they will jump at the opportunity. And this is great for Vitality Health too because it reduces the risks that they take on when insuring customers, therefore improving their profitability.

The Vitality program has evolved into a complete wellness system which enables customers to live healthier lives, helping them decide what to eat and what exercise to take. Vitality customers currently take part in 70,000 gym visits per day, and to date they have bought hundreds of millions of dollars-worth of healthier food using their Vitality card to obtain discounts.

Vitality Health has found that using their platform data has enabled them to reduce health risks by 22% (source: McKinsey).

Vitality Health's platform has proved attractive to other insurance companies, and it has enabled the business to penetrate new markets which the firm would otherwise have found difficult or impossible to enter. For instance, Vitality Health now partners with Generali in Europe, John Hancock in the USA, Pin An in China, and AIA across the Asia Pacific Region.

Vitality has now extended their offer into mobility services, as they take an even broader view on customer well-being. Their mobility service encourages safer driving using a mobile app which provides insights into the "driving DNA" of a given driver. This lets them know who is driving a car and how they are driving it. If you drive better, you get lower insurance premiums. Other ecosystem benefits include cheaper petrol and access to roadside emergency assistance should you need it.

References

Information Commissioner's Office. (2019). Intention to fine British Airways £183.39m under GDPR for data breach. https://ico.org.uk/about-the-ico/news-and-events/news-and-blogs/2019/07/ico-announces-intention-to-fine-british-airways/. Accessed October 26, 2019.

Insurance Journal. (2019, October). Blockchain Initiative, B3i, Deploys Cat Excess of Loss Product for January Renewals. https://www.insurancejournal.com/news/international/2019/10/15/545507.htm. Accessed October 26, 2019.

International Fraud Bureau. (2018, February). IFB supports IFED's warning about ghost broking scams. https://insurancefraudbureau.org/media-centre/news/2018/ifb-supports-ifed-s-warning-about-ghost-broking-scams/. Accessed October 26, 2019.

International Fraud Bureau: Crash for cash. https://insurancefraudbureau.org/insurance-fraud/crash-for-cash/. Accessed October 26, 2019.

Krebson Security. (2019, May). First American Financial Corp. Leaked hundreds of millions of title insurance records. https://krebsonsecurity.com/2019/05/first-american-financial-corp-leaked-hundreds-of-millions-of-title-insurance-records/comment-page-1/. Accessed October 26, 2019.

Lemonade blog. (2017, January). Lemonade sets a new world record. https://www.lemonade.com/blog/lemonade-sets-new-world-record/. Accessed October 26, 2019.

McKinsey. (2018, December). Friends or foes: The rise of European aggregators and their impact on traditional insurers. https://www.mckinsey.com/~/media/McKinsey/Industries/Financial%20Services/Our%20Insights/Friends%20or%20foes%20The%20rise%20of%20European%20aggregators%20and%20their%20impact%20on%20traditional%20insurers/Friends-or-foes-The-rise-of-European-aggregators.ashx. Accessed October 26, 2019.

McKinsey. (2019, May). A new industry model for insurtech. https://www.mckinsey.com/industries/financial-services/our-insights/insurance-blog/a-new-industry-model-for-insurtech. Accessed October 26, 2019.

The Actuary. (2017, December). Strength in numbers. https://www.theactuary.com/opinion/2017/12/strength-in-numbers/. Accessed October 26, 2019.

Case Study 5: Atos—Transforming Customer Experience and Contributing to Business Strategy

26

The authors of this book all belong to the Atos Scientific Community which was originally formed in 2009 to be a catalyst for innovation and thought leadership for the benefit of Atos and its customers. As a diverse, non-hierarchical, self-organizing, and multi-disciplinary group of over 150 employees, the community embodies many of the principles described in this book.

26.1 Creating a Vision and Driving Thought Leadership

The Atos Scientific Community is personally chaired and sponsored by the group CEO but is given a very free reign with respect to the areas of technology and business that they research.

All members carry out their Scientific Community duties in addition to a regular "day job" and typically spend 10–20% of their time on:

- Building a five-year vision for technology and business, particularly for the markets which Atos serves.
- Creating proofs of concept (PoCs) and proofs of value (PoVs) to support research.
- Contributing to the company's R&D program, especially as part of the Alliance with Siemens, which has created MindSphere, machine intelligence platforms and security platforms, as well as many other innovations.
- Sharing its vision and thinking with customers via customer innovation workshops.

The five-year vision which is articulated in the "Journey 20XX" documents (Journey 2022 was delivered in November 2018) is published in a two-yearly cycle:

H. Tardieu et al., *Deliberately Digital*, Future of Business and Finance,
https://doi.org/10.1007/978-3-030-37955-1_26

- During year one, research topics are nominated according to their anticipated key impacts over the next five years ahead. These topics could be generic (technical, ethical, business models, and new ways of working), or sector specific (renewable energy, health, and insurance). Peer voting on topic proposals determines the 15–20 topics which will form the future research landscape. Year one is dedicated to investigating the topics and writing position papers and whitepapers which are only published if they exceed a minimum rating standard in peer reviews.
- At the end of year one, the community's editorial board starts elaborating an overarching vision that considers the cumulative impact of the diverse research topics. Some topics have causal relationships, others are simply happening at the same time. Year two is devoted to aligning the vision with the wider range of topics.

The "Journey" vision document describes future challenges and opportunities that are expected to arise from evolutions and revolutions in business models, technologies, regulation, ethics, etc. This vision is then instantiated by market sector to reflect specific anticipated impacts on various businesses.

The experience gained, after five iterations of this process, is that major innovations are not always detected in the first year when we deepen our understanding on the selected topics but rather when we align vision thinking with each of these topics.

This holistic approach undertaken with a significant community has proven to be efficient for an IT service company like Atos. We believe that it can be replicated in medium and large companies as a way to prepare their own digital strategy.

26.2 Approaches to Innovation in Atos

Atos uses storytelling extensively in its work. For instance:

- Scientific Community. Ideas are developed and shared using images and video as opposed to written documents. This helps to create much stronger engagement among colleagues during the process of developing thought leadership tracks and associated innovation themes.
- Strategic Conversations. Narratives are created for engagement with the largest clients. This narrative is used to frame five strategic conversations which are placed into a collaboration platform accessible by internal delivery units, clients, and partners. These conversations are supported on the platform using multi-media, including podcasts and videos. Atos is currently experimenting with mixed reality to explore how they can engage different stakeholders in these conversations in a more immersive manner.
- StratHacks (one of Atos' Executive innovation "stepping stones"). The StratHack innovation format was developed to help executives cocreate high-value solutions to their biggest strategic challenges. A key part of the methodology is that of

helping executives visualize their challenge and the means to address it using a combination of storyboarding and "rich pictures."
- Visioning and Alignment workshops (one of Atos' Operations innovation "stepping stones"). V&A workshops help clients to accelerate value realization from their strategies by creating common purpose, priority, and plans, and importantly, a common language to discuss them, between business and IT operations. The methodology for these workshops begins by bringing clients' intentions to life using video. These videos help articulate what it is that clients are trying to achieve through their transformation and the implications and value of this from both a business and an IT perspective.
- Deals. Atos works on many very large deals in a typical year, with some deals taking 12–18 months to come to fruition. Storytelling is now a key part of the bid process. Storylines are developed iteratively from the earliest stages in the bid cycle to help bid teams to understand the value they are seeking to create and also to position that value with the client.

Our recommended approach to customer experience transformation is grounded in three key elements which we have seen exemplified in the Atos Agile CX (Customer Experience)[1] Laboratory environment:

- Listening to your customers directly. Even though clients undertake their own on-going customer research, it is invaluable to complement this with your own research into your "customer's customers." There are many ways Atos does this, including a variety of qualitative research and observational techniques such as in-depth interviews, group discussions, accompanied shopping, and mindful visits to the client's outlets (including "mystery shopping," where you act as a customer yourself). Often, it is helpful to use these techniques in combination, because it builds up a rounded picture of the customer experience. For instance, if an end customer has just told you about a problem area they have experienced with your client, we find it really helpful to undertake a store visit to see how this bears out in practice as we "walk in the customer's shoes." Atos also does this for digital experiences. For example, in their CX Laboratories they also sometimes use eyeball tracking as they interview customers as they navigate a client's digital services (such as a mobile app, a customer portal, or a Web site) to help better understand usability.
- A creative space in which to do Design Thinking. The elements we have found to be most useful include a large write-on/wipe-off "white wall" (on which you can also put myriad post-it notes); a large table that people can stand or sit at as they work together; and an airy room with a relaxed feel and enough space for a team to move around in comfortably. These practical matters aside, the most critical

[1]Customer experience is the result of the interaction between a company and a customer. It is generally used in B2C scenarios, although it is sometimes used to describe citizen experience in Government-to-Citizen (G2C) scenarios. CXCX is composed of the customer journey, the brand touch points and the environments (offline and online).

thing is to ensure a diverse mix of skills and experience in the room. This is critical to opening up and exploring new avenues.
- A customer experience development space to refine the customer offering. This is where Atos' process design teams get to work. They typically begin by creating "wire frames" (simply drawn "screenshots" of what the customer may need to see on their device), which are then iterated and refined with customer input. Once this is broadly right, work starts on designing the graphical user interface (GUI), aiming for something that feels simple and intuitive to the customer. Only once everyone is satisfied that they have the right interface, does work start on writing the software code that turns the experience that has been designed into a digital service.

As Atos develops the code to support the new services, they exploit a variety of key tools to accelerate delivery. Together these tools enable faster releases of software to support the new service; automate key tasks (including automation of test cases); minimize IT barriers using templates; and strengthen the necessary collaboration between business operations and IT.

Once this work is complete, Atos' ambition is always to minimize the learning required for a customer to adopt the new service.

26.3 Recognize, Exploit, and Assure Your Most Critical Information Assets

In addition to the above CX Laboratory design environment it is essential now to have a fourth stage in the customer innovation process focused on realizing value from data for new services.

Recognizing this opportunity in their business, Atos have created AI Laboratories in their major geographies, developed in partnership with Google. It is in these AI Laboratories that they now determine the data they need to support new services; to figure out where this data can come from; to source this from wherever it resides on their client's systems; and to develop and train the models to realize value from this data.

27 Case Study 6: The Digital Transformation of Manufacturing

Manufacturing is under the transformative influence of what has become known as the fourth industrial revolution, a phrase coined in 2011 as part of an industrial futures project conducted by the German government, and it is at the beginning of what is now being termed the fifth industrial revolution, or Industry 5.0.

The first industrial revolution occurred in 1784, with the mechanization of production facilities enabled by water and steam power. The second took place in 1870, with industrial mass production enabled by electrification. The third happened in 1969, with the introduction of electronic production automation, enabled by the first programmable logic controller. The fourth industrial revolution builds on the third, with an array of digital technologies that are now beginning to blur the lines between physical and digital systems.

The promises of the fourth industrial revolution are numerous, including improved standards of living; increased safety and security; and improved capacity for people to do work. At the same time, there are concerns. Some are worried about the displacement of humans from the manufacturing workforce; some are worried about the potential for disruption caused by the failure of opaque and complex systems, including as a result of malicious cyber-attacks; and some are concerned about the potential for misuse (or loss) of rapidly growing volumes of increasingly sensitive data.

The emerging fifth industrial revolution, or Industry 5.0 (EESC 2018), is being billed as the result of the development of our ability to combine a human being's creativity and craftsmanship with the speed, productivity, and consistency of robots.

The rate of change is high, and many firms are struggling to keep pace. There appear to be too many options, too many technologies, and too many areas of simultaneous change. In this case study, we will show examples of how leading firms are bucking that trend and are using the new digital tools to succeed.

H. Tardieu et al., *Deliberately Digital*, Future of Business and Finance,
https://doi.org/10.1007/978-3-030-37955-1_27

27.1 The Context

The impacts of Industry 4.0 are beginning to affect every aspect of how a manufacturer thinks, acts, and operates. This starts to become evident when you look at the range of digital technologies that are now available to manufacturers.

At the very core of Industry 4.0 is the new potential for interconnectedness arising from the Internet of Things. A growing array of sensor technologies is enabling manufacturers to collect data throughout the entire value chain. At one end of the chain manufacturers obtain data from their suppliers of raw materials; and at the other they gather product usage insights from their customers; as well as from many stages in between. The sensors that manufacturers use are connected through pervasive networks using a variety of technologies and communications protocols. Data gathered can be marshaled using Big Data techniques and analyzed in real-time using algorithms created with Machine Learning and Deep Learning. Resulting insights can be used throughout the manufacturing lifecycle, for example, to help manufacturers get closer to customers; enable new business and operating models; and power new business ecosystems.

27.1.1 Getting Closer to Customers

As we described earlier in the Customers chapter, customer expectations continue to evolve as they learn about the new possibilities of digital, especially from their experience of engaging with digital leaders. This re-shaping of customer expectations is asking new questions of manufacturers as they seek to win or retain their customer's business. Two areas of focus include:

- Connecting in real time with each-and-every customer and using this connection to gain deeper insights into each customer's unique behaviors.
- Maintaining trust at every step in the value chain, with demonstrable responsibility and accountability.

Deepening Customer Insight:

> Manufacturers now have the opportunity to know their customers as they have never known them before. But creating insights from myriad, new data sources demands thinking beyond the narrow confines of a traditional manufacturing model. New questions to consider include:
>
> - How can manufacturers better understand what makes their individual customers tick, including capturing insights into their changing needs and wants?
> - How can manufacturers better understand each customer's context, including where and how customers are using their products?
> - What can manufacturers do to use this data to better serve each customer, with more tailored products and services capable of adapting to their changing requirements?

Retained Responsibility and Accountability:

Manufacturers are beginning to gain access to data through the entire journey of a product: from creation through to sale and then use. Consumers now expect manufacturers to exploit this data in a way that safeguards consumer interests. New questions to consider here include:

- How can manufacturers ensure the products and services they sell are used correctly and continue to perform effectively "in life"?
- How can manufacturers provide confidence to the customer that the products they make are created in a sustainable manner, one that is socially acceptable and which is fully compliant throughout every step of the manufacturing process with changing norms of acceptability?
- What can manufacturers do to provide transparency on where in the world the product was manufactured, who physically made it, where and how the necessary raw materials were sourced, and how the product will be recycled once the customer has finished with it?

To begin to answer these questions, manufacturers are reconsidering their business and operating models.

27.1.2 New Business Models

The typical manufacturing business model of the past was a transactional model focused on selling products, with some manufacturers extending this successfully into a through-life service and support model.

The advent of digital technologies supports new business models with the potential to create significantly greater customer value and the potential for enhanced business value too.

27.1.3 Mass Customization

Mass customization is about maximizing the customer value of a given product by shaping it in some way to meet personal requirements and doing so at costs close to those of a standard mass-produced item. As such, it is highly demanding for manufacturers, to the extent that some have really struggled to make it work, including occasional high-profile flops such as the attempt by Levi Strauss to produce customized jeans. Given these challenges, some believe that this may be a niche field suited only to certain manufacturers. However, new and emerging digital technologies, including the Industrial Internet of Things (IIoT) and its associated data platforms, could help to relieve some of the existing constraints.

Two examples of mass customization in action can be seen in Dell and BMW:

Michael Dell brought mass customization to the PC world in the 1980s. His approach was to sell directly to customers and manufacture PCs to the customer's specification as they placed their orders. Dell made this work through just-in-time manufacturing, allowing him to keep inventory low. Dell's customers were able to specify their needs to a detailed level, including memory capacity, screen size, drive type (DVD/CD or Blu-Ray), and number of USB ports. They could even customize the look of their PC, by uploading their own graphics for Dell to place on the front of their device.

BMW, like their peers, have taken advantage of digitalization and the app economy to make mass customization even more compelling for both the customer and the producer.

From a customer standpoint, the front-end experience has become hugely compelling via immersive online car configurators. These enable customers to design their unique vehicle without feeling overwhelmed by the available choices. Even after a customer has bought their vehicle, further customization is now possible by selecting from a growing variety of in-vehicle configuration options, including performance settings and displays.

From a manufacturer standpoint, leading producers such as BMW are working to create a more seamless, automated, and intelligent workflow that enables the efficient fulfillment of customized orders. They are achieving this through the deployment of increasingly interconnected ERP, MES, and SCADA systems, and through advanced robotics.

Enterprise resource planning (ERP) software enables the efficient capturing of customer orders; matched requests for components from suppliers, with delivery scheduled "just-in-time"; and the entry of build requirements into production planning. Manufacturing execution system (MES) software is used to manage the execution of the customer's unique build requirements, including production management and machine instructions. Supervisory control and data acquisition (SCADA) systems control the individual production machines through more granular systems, including programmable logic controllers (PLCs), remote telemetry units (RTUs), and Human–Machine interfaces (HMIs).

Each of these critical systems has been deployed by manufacturers for some time. What is different today is how they are being interconnected through the IIoT with the ability to obtain much more detailed real-time data, from sensors and actuators at each stage of the production process, with new data platforms such as Siemens' MindSphere now available to process this information. At the same time, we are seeing the introduction of easily re-programmable robots capable of working alongside human production line workers, so providing much greater flexibility in the manufacturing workflow. Taken together, these new Industry 4.0 capabilities are creating the potential for much greater coordination and agility throughout the production cycle, and they enable new levels of customization to be achieved.

27.1.4 As-a-Service

IoT technologies are helping manufacturers to move beyond mass customization to product-based services sold on the basis of customer outcomes delivered. These services bring significant lifetime value to both the manufacturer and the customer, enabled by sensors and pervasive networks. As they do this, they also encourage and enable Circular Economy benefits in the spirit of the pioneering work of the UK's Dame Ellen McArthur. This occurs because it is in the manufacturer's interest to reduce their cost to serve through minimizing the physical material consumed by their service through efficient designs and component recycling.

Rolls-Royce aeroengines was an early pioneer of this business model. Around 60 years ago, they developed their "power by the hour" concept, created to support the Viper engine on the Havilland/Hawker Siddeley's 125 business jet. This service aligned Rolls-Royce's manufacturing interest with that of the operator because the operator paid only for engine hours used. Over time, Rolls-Royce created additional services to augment their offer, including engine health monitoring and access to additional engines during off-wing service times, so that continuity of aircraft operation could be maintained.

Today, digital technologies are enabling this model to evolve further, and they are making as-a-service models economically viable in a growing range of applications. Critical technologies include: Internet of Things; cheap sensors; industrial data platforms for real-time analytics; and artificial intelligence for process optimization.

Two further examples of as-a-service in action are:

> Philips now offers lighting-as-a-service, as opposed to simply selling light bulbs. Customers can either buy this as a set of managed services (from design and build through to operate and maintain) or they can simply buy the light they use, as opposed to owning any of the underlying equipment. (Philips 2018)

> Alstom, a French train manufacturer, introduced a new predictive maintenance tool in 2014 called Healthhub. This tool monitors the health of trains, train infrastructure, and signaling systems, and then applies data analytics in order to extend train life. Components monitored include wheels, brake pads, and the pantograph carbon strips that conduct current to power trains from overhead cables. Alstom used to manage train maintenance on a mileage basis, now it can do this on a condition basis, achieving 15% savings in cost of materials. (Alstom 2014)

27.1.5 Products as Platforms

Manufacturing companies are learning from software organizations as they explore ways to develop a core product offering that is modular and flexible, allowing third parties to add their own customized variants which the underlying platform can enable to scale efficiently.

For example:

Google's failed Project Ara (Morris 2016) explored the potential of creating a modular product platform for smartphones, with add-ons sourced from a variety of third parties.

These add-on modules included a loudspeaker, an e-ink screen displaying the weather, an array of microphones, a touch-sensitive square, and a camera. This project created great excitement in 2014 and 2015, but ultimately did not take off.

One of the problems was the immaturity of available technology leading to the modular components creating excess weight and bulk; another was their excessive use of battery power. These technology issues aside, a bigger challenge was with the consumer: it turned out that there were simply not enough consumers who wished to meddle with their phone's hardware, with most preferring instead to buy the more convenient pre-integrated offerings of Apple, Samsung, and others.

Tesla is using the product as platform concept to transform the value they bring customers through the lifetime of their ownership. They are achieving this through software updates, and especially through their over-the-air software updates. When Tesla first began doing this in 2012, their updates tended to include relatively minor changes to the user interface and functionality, such as projected range and driver profiles. Over time, Tesla has become increasingly ambitious, enabling customers to change some of the driving-related aspects of their vehicle, including power output management and air suspension settings. In 2015, they introduced their Autopilot, enabling new levels of driver assistance. Autopilot continues to evolve as Tesla pursues its autonomous driving ambition, with features such as automated steering, lane change, and braking.

Tesla's approach has been truly ground-breaking for the industry. Previously automotive manufacturers were concerned about maintaining customer engagement "in-life," because they thought this would upset their dealer-relationships, and they were concerned about making over-the-air software updates for system security reasons.

27.1.6 Decentralized Manufacturing

Manufacturers are showing increasing interest in producing their products physically closer to their customers. Benefits that are sought from this approach include faster responsiveness to changing needs, reduced shipping costs, reduced energy cost and associated environmental impact reduction, and reduced risk from extended supply chains. Key digital technology enablers include CAD/CAM software, augmented reality, robotics, and 3D printing.

For example: micro-factories are now changing the face of fashion (Golub 2018). The traditional fashion model was "produce, sell, deliver." This was found to be high risk and resource intensive. Fashion houses would get their production sourced from a low-cost economy and seek economies of scale through large production runs, often ending up with excess stock at the end of a season. The micro-factory model is "sell, produce, deliver," with the customer paying for the product before it is produced, and the production delivered locally. The micro-factory process begins via an online e-commerce interaction with the customer, supported by augmented reality so they can "try on" their garment. The order goes into a computerized workflow system, artwork is completed, and the final design is agreed with the customer, all in a matter of minutes. The design is then printed out on a continuous roll of fabric, with printed guides for laser cutting.

When cut, the fabric is stitched together using "sewbots" with human workers completing the hemming. Micro-factories such as these produce no excess stock, and they maintain high sales prices through the level of customization offered.

27.1.7 New Operating Models

If manufacturers are to retain their relevance, it is not enough to have a good business model; the operating model behind this needs to evolve as well. Today's increasingly diverse global markets, with increasingly demanding customers, and tough competition from new entrants as well as incumbents, mean the pressure for transformation is high. At the same time, regulatory and compliance standards demand increased transparency from manufacturers on how their products are produced through every step in the process.

At present, there is much more that manufacturers need to do. Research by Accenture Strategy found that only around 25% of manufacturers globally have an operating model that enables them to dynamically shift resources and activities around their manufacturing network in response to market developments or changes in demand (Rasmus and McKinney 2017). They found this to be particularly true of manufacturers that operate their own manufacturing facilities as opposed to relying on contract manufacturers. Those that do use contract manufacturers tend to be more productive, generate more revenue, and are more profitable. Another challenge is that not enough manufacturers are yet fully embracing digital technologies, with only about 30% of manufacturers currently deploying the most promising digital tools. However, there are examples of leading manufacturers who are achieving competitive advantage through being first to introduce a new practice or a new technical approach, and they are increasingly willing to accept the costs and risks this may entail.

Manufacturers are also continuing to explore the many options available to them regarding how they develop, source, scale, and distribute their products. Key partnerships impacting manufacturing operating models now include: third-party innovators and designers, contract manufacturers, logistics providers, and postponement centers.

These partnerships are enabled by a variety of digital technologies, including advanced collaboration and communication tools, which enable the efficient and secure interchange of information between them. This means that a manufacturer's value chain can operate much more like a codependent ecosystem of firms working toward shared goals, thus, enabling the manufacturer to create and deploy an innovative new product at scale faster than ever before, with a much lower capital expenditure requirement, and with much lower risk. Let's now consider some real-world examples of this.

Some manufacturers complement their own in-house innovation and design capability with those from third-party organizations to accelerate the design phase of a project. Design house IDEO is a well-known example, having worked with Apple to develop their first mouse.

Contract manufacturers have been used for some time to help manufacturers accelerate their time to market for a new product, manage their asset risk, reduce their CAPEX requirement, and support manufacturing efficiency. One of the best-known contract manufacturer relationships is between Taiwanese firm Foxconn and Apple. Foxconn manufacturers for other famous personal computer and smart brands as well, such as Dell and Huawei; Apple also uses other contract manufacturers such as Pegatron.

Manufacturers have worked with third-party logistics providers (3PL) since the early 1970s to support distribution, warehousing, cross-docking, inventory management, packaging, and fulfilment. There are also now fourth-party logistics providers who help manufacturers to manage their 3PL, and some now talk about 5PLs who can support a manufacturer's e-commerce operations. Manufacturers are seeking more strategic relationships with their logistics providers, and some see new opportunities to achieve this through deploying new digital technologies such as drones, robots, smart glasses, and 3D printing.

Postponement centers enable a manufacturer to delay the final customization of a product or its packaging until late in the product cycle to enable a closer match to customer needs.

27.2 The Challenges

27.2.1 Strategy Formulation

Manufacturers now need to formulate their strategy in a manner that takes account of their role in a rapidly evolving ecosystem that includes multiple third parties, both upstream in their supply chain, and downstream in their distribution network. Success demands that these parties interoperate in a coordinated, agile, flexible, and responsive manner in order to create and capture customer value. The research by Accenture Strategy found that while more than half of global manufacturers plan to increase their use of third parties, too many of them are focused on short-term benefits instead of longer-term value creation.

The growing complexity of these ecosystems is creating a premium on understanding the critical points of influence. Those who can do this well will have a significant competitive advantage.

27.2.2 Leadership Skills

The industrial leaders of the future will be required to adapt to a world that evolves ever faster. They will need to be capable of thinking clearly as they deal with uncertainty; they will be expected to have a strong practical understanding of the manufacturing capabilities available to them, along with a willingness to tackle and solve problems; and they will need an innovative mindset, with a willingness to take some risks. They will also need strong people skills so that they can motivate an increasingly diverse workforce.

27.2.3 Accessing Required Digital Skills

Operating a digital factory requires new skills and capabilities. Manufacturers are competing for talent and will need to find compelling ways to attract and retain the people they need. Skills that they will need to source include: digital skills, programming skills for robots and other automation, critical thinking skills, creativity and originality, problem solving, and people management.

Four ways that manufacturers are responding include:

1. Accessing the fast-developing gig economy to bring in new skills on demand as they need them.
2. As a variant on the previous statement, accessing seasoned retired experts on demand, including those who may also have worked for many years for competitors.
3. Bringing in talent, especially digital talent, from technology partners, on a time and materials basis.
4. Outsourcing entire aspects of their businesses to third parties, thus providing immediate access to the skills and resources they need.

27.2.4 Process Optimization Through Digital

The UK 2018 Annual Manufacturing Report (AMR) (The Manufacturer 2018) stated that predictive maintenance offers the potential to increase machine life by 20–40%, reduce machine downtime by 30–50%, and deliver 4–10% EBITDA margin improvements. Currently, there remains a substantial gap between awareness, and investment/implementation. The AMR shows one in four respondents currently has no digital plans while 26% have it on the radar but are unsure how to implement it.

This trend is also reflected in the recent PwC Digital Operations Survey (Jukes and Haffey 2018) which demonstrated that only 1% of UK companies were digital champions and that UK manufacturers risk losing competitiveness: growing their digital products and services at a lower rate than global competitors.

27.2.5 Supply Chain Security and Assurance

Supply chain security is an increasing concern. Risks include theft, fraud, counterfeiting, and cyber-attack. For instance, businesses lose an estimated $22.6 billion globally each year due to cargo theft (BSI 2016).

Meanwhile, consumers expect more transparency over the provenance of goods they buy. There is a growing expectation that each item on a production line will have traceable provenance and that products moving through the supply chain are not tampered with. For instance, in the European-wide horse-meat scandal of 2013 (Horse meat—questions and answers), food products advertised as containing beef were found to contain undeclared or improperly declared horse meat; a smaller number of products were also found to contain other undeclared meats such as pork.

A promising route for manufacturers to address supply chain assurance is through deploying a Blockchain solution to help participants validate activity through each step in the supply chain, and do so in a highly transparent, tamper-proof manner.

27.2.6 Managing IT/OT Convergence

Until recently, a manufacturer's operational technology (OT) tended to be operated separately from its information technology (IT). The evolution of the digital factory is leading to these two technology areas coming together. As this occurs there is a need for IT leaders and business leaders to collaborate closely. Today, this can be challenging. They do not speak the same "language" which can make IT leaders reluctant to engage their OT counterparts.

27.3 Looking to the Future: Product and Service Platform-Based Ecosystems

As described earlier in the manufacturing business model section, models based on servitization and product-as-platform are well understood and are becoming more commonplace. Beyond these concepts we are seeing the emergence of new multi-sided platform-based manufacturing ecosystems. The multi-sided nature of these platforms is beginning to open up fresh opportunities for participants to generate new value for customers and for their shareholders. This value is created by enabling data to be pooled and shared in a controlled manner, while also providing access to powerful platform tools and resources. Taken together these capabilities help participants to innovate their offerings more efficiently and at greater pace than they could achieve acting independently.

From our point of view, one of the most currently interesting multi-sided industrial platform is Airbus's Skywise, launched in June 2017. The initial Skywise participants were Airbus themselves and a small selection of airlines. However,

Airbus's ambition was always much bigger than this, and Skywise now aggregates data sources from a burgeoning industry ecosystem that includes Airbus, its suppliers, airports, airlines, aircraft lessors, and third-party developers. Our understanding is that Skywise is currently on track to include 100 companies by the end of 2019; already 6000 aircraft have been entered onto the platform from 80 airlines.

Prior to Skywise, firms were only able to access the narrow slice of data they could create for themselves. With Skywise, they now have access to an aggregated data set collected from the entire Skywise ecosystem. Commercial confidentiality is safeguarded because firms cannot see the data of other individual ecosystem participants. This new capability is already enabling significant additional value, including improved aircraft design, better services, and better support offerings. For instance, as Airbus CDO Marc Fontaine explains: "*Before we were managing aircraft fleet. Now we can manage aircraft for their entire lifecycle*."

Let's now consider some of the ways Skywise data is creating value for its participants.

The Skywise Dispatch service is designed to improve the production process through a "single version of the truth." This enables improved root cause analysis of recurring missing parts and improved supplier visibility of Airbus's manufacturing demand requirements. The lead supplier for this service was Airbus supplier Premium Aerotec, who found that it yielded time savings of 25%.

Airbus's FOMAX™ is an on-board data transmission and data capture module (codeveloped with Rockwell Collins) which provides a greatly expanded data set. For example, prior to FOMAX™, only about 400 parameters could be tracked on the Airbus A320; with FOMAX™, airlines can track roughly 24,000 parameters. This enables much deeper analysis and enhanced decision-making, including predictive and preventive maintenance, resulting in greater operational efficiency and higher asset utilization. The first airlines to sign up were AirAsia, Asiana Airlines, and Etihad Airways.

Airbus's Connected Experience is an IoT enabled in-flight service, launched in partnership with Gategroup, Stelia Aerospace, and Recaro Aircraft Seating, with other suppliers expected to join later. This service provides real-time links between key elements in the cabin including the galley, lavatory, meal trolleys, passenger seats, and overhead luggage compartments. The intention is to enable enhanced passenger services (such as access to Wi-Fi and third-party media), improved cabin operations (such as remote verification of seat-belt fastening), and more efficient aircraft service management.

The success of Skywise is creating some powerful network effects and, as data volumes grow, there are increasing opportunities for the deployment of machine learning and artificial intelligence algorithms which could add even more value. However, not all firms are happy with what Skywise has achieved, or keen to sign up. For instance, jet engine manufacturers such as Safran are keen to protect their existing profitable business of jet engine maintenance, and they see Skywise as a threat. Equally, we would expect Boeing to be determined not to share their manufacturing data, even though Air France may choose to share the operational data from their own Boeing aircraft.

There is also a wider concern that Skywise is controlled by Airbus, itself the most powerful partner of the ecosystem. Some partners see this as creating an unfair competitive advantage for Airbus, and they would prefer to see either an independent company or a joint venture managing it.

References

Alstom. (2014). Alstom launches HealthHub, an innovative tool for predictive maintenance, 23/09/2014. https://www.alstom.com/press-releases-news/2014/9/innotrans2014-alstom-launches-healthhub-an-innovative-tool-for-predictive-maintenance-. Accessed October 26, 2019.

BSI. (2016). *BSI's Global Supply Chain Intelligence report reveals 2015 top supply chain risks*. BSI Group, 23/03/2016. https://www.bsigroup.com/en-GB/about-bsi/media-centre/press-releases/2016/march/BSIs-Global-Supply-Chain-Intelligence-report-reveals-2015-top-supply-chain-risks-/. Accessed October 26, 2019.

EESC. (2018). *Industry 5.0. European Economic and Social Committee*, 22/11/2018. https://www.eesc.europa.eu/en/agenda/our-events/events/industry-50. Accessed October 26, 2019.

Golub, A. (2018). The digital textile revolution: Why textile micro-factories will change the future of fashion. *WhichPLM*, 15/11/2018. http://blog.else-corp.com/2018/11/the-digital-textile-revolution-why-textile-micro-factories-will-change-the-future-of-fashion-whichplm/. Accessed October 26, 2019.

Horse meat-questions and answers. https://ec.europa.eu/food/safety/official_controls/food_fraud/horse_meat/q-ans_en. Accessed October 26, 2019.

Jukes, D., & Haffey, C. (2018). *Industry 4.0 Global Digital Operations 2018 Survey*. PwC. https://www.pwc.co.uk/industries/manufacturing/insights/industry-4-0-global-digital-operations-survey-uk-findings.html. Accessed October 26, 2019.

Morris, D. Z. (2016). Why Google Canceled Project Ara. *Fortune*, 03/09/2016. https://fortune.com/2016/09/03/why-google-canceled-project-ara/. Accessed October 26, 2019.

Philips. (2018). *Introducing Light as a Service (LaaS)*. Philips. https://www.lighting.philips.co.uk/campaigns/art-led-technology. Accessed October 26, 2019.

Rasmus, R., & McKinney, J. (2017). Manufacturing eco systems. *Accenture*. https://www.accenture.com/_acnmedia/accenture/conversion-assets/dotcom/documents/global/pdf/strategy_8/accenture-manufacturing-ecosystems.pdf. Accessed October 26, 2019.

The Manufacturer. (2018). UK Annual Manufacturing Report 2018. https://www.themanufacturer.com/reports-whitepapers/annual-manufacturing-report-2018/. Accessed October 26, 2019.

28 Case Study 7: The Digital Transformation of Banking—An Industry Changing Beyond Recognition

Banks are faced with major challenges as well as with new opportunities, for the agile few. Open Banking, digital engagement models, and cross-industry platforms are each transformational in themselves. Coming together, as they are, at the same time, banks are being forced to address demanding new questions as they strive to maintain growth and customer relevance, while simultaneously driving down their cost base and maintaining compliance with shifting regulations.

Most banks have been experimenting for a few years with piecemeal digital innovations, including mobile app interfaces, omni-channel engagement, localized process automation, and digital marketing. Each of these innovations is increasingly enabled by innovative partnerships with FinTech firms. Despite their undoubted successes, banks are struggling to move at the required pace and, in most cases, are not yet achieving the transformational change that is necessary to remain competitive.

Unfortunately, for banking leaders, just as they as wrestle with these immediate pressures, there are even greater challenges coming their way. The cross-industry convergence we describe in other chapters is leading to the evolution of new ecosystems, and digital leaders in adjacent markets see big opportunities to accelerate the evolution of their own financial offerings.

28.1 The Context

The retail banking industry is being transformed by the rapid evolution of new digital services. These are being developed by established incumbents and new players, encouraged by increasingly demanding consumers.

H. Tardieu et al., *Deliberately Digital*, Future of Business and Finance,
https://doi.org/10.1007/978-3-030-37955-1_28

As a baseline for retail banks, requirements include:

- The need to design compelling customer experiences that can be tailored to the changing requirements of demanding customers and the need to adapt these experiences for customers over time as they pass through different life stages: recognizing different customer appetites for risk and the different trade-offs they prefer to make with their money.
- The need to integrate multiple channels into a seamless omni-channel experience, one in which all channels work together coherently no matter where the customer touches the bank.
- The need to win back customer trust in the continuing aftermath of the financial crisis in 2008. Key considerations here being greater transparency on pricing; the creation of simpler, more intuitive services that work dependably; and the realization of continuing service innovation, with the customer receiving the greatest benefits from this.

Beyond this baseline, banks also need to consider how they wish to compete within an extended ecosystem, both within banking services and into other sectors, as players increasingly integrate into converged industry ecosystems. And in conjunction with the business model selected, they need to determine the operating model they will follow to ensure they can compete.

28.1.1 Customers

Retail banking customers have experienced exciting new ways to interact and engage with their service providers in other sectors, and they are bringing these same expectations to the management of their financial needs. Customers are not just looking for a digital front-end to their banking services; they are looking for truly personalized interactions with their banks, underpinned by customized products and services designed to meet their specific requirements. And all this needs to be accessible 24/7/365.

According to a global retail banking study in 2018 by Capgemini and Efma, banks have closed the gap with other industries (Efma, September 2018). They are now second only to retail and consumer goods for digital customer experience. In the USA, banks are the outright leaders, driven forward by big players such as Bank of America, Wells Fargo, and Citibank.

An excellent example of the new customer experiences that digital can provide comes from Singapore-based DBS: customers can message the bank via WhatsApp or WeChat; their messages are processed by an automated AI-enabled service; and responses are provided by an AI-enabled Chatbot, which can also provide personalized information and support.

The customer appetite for a digitalized customer experience is evident from Accenture's report Banking Beyond North Star Gazing (Accenture). According to their findings, 66% already execute half of their digital banking transactions online and 71% are open to automated support.

In addition, Accenture has found that 31% of all customers, and 41% of Generation Z (those born between 1995 and 2015), would consider banking services from one of the major digital platforms such as Google, Apple, Facebook, or Amazon.

28.1.2 New Digital Competitors

Retail banks are facing competition from different kinds of digital service providers. For example:

Neobanks

> Neobanks such as Atom, Revolut, Monzo, and N26 are growing strongly with valuations that suggest investors expect this growth to continue. According to Quartz, as of beginning August 2019, Monzo was leading the pack with a valuation of $2.45 billion (its current 2 million users imply a valuation ratio of $1,225 per user). These banks are winning through bringing innovative services which are exciting customers who have become frustrated by things never seeming to quite work as they hope with traditional banks, and with too many hidden charges.
>
> Neobanks are managing to win customers even when they do not yet have a banking license so limiting the scope of services they can provide, one such case being Revolut which had attracted 1.8 million customers by July 2018. Revolut started out as a mobile wallet app, helping customers avoid fees when sending and receiving money in foreign currencies. Since then they have evolved their services with innovations that include: sending money to friends through popular social channels like WhatsApp; helping customers to categorize their expenditure; bill splitting; and a Chatbot interface to support service requests.

New digital payment providers:

> The appetite for digital payments is being fueled by the continuing move toward e-commerce and m-commerce and by the shift toward an interconnected world enabled by Internet of Things technologies. This growth has attracted players such as Apple, Alphabet, and Facebook to create their own payments offerings. It has also attracted a huge amount of venture funding in support of entrepreneurs seeking to create new approaches to payments enablement, such as Stripe, Transferwise, and WePay.
>
> The impact of these new-style payment players is substantial. According to a report by IDC (The Business Value of the Stripe Payments Platform, July 2018), organizations using Stripe attribute a revenue increase of 7% to using the platform, with customers also lowering their processing costs of online transactions by 24% over 5 years. The rationale behind these numbers comes from three areas: reduced development cost when working with Stripe; Stripe's API which enables a single payments platform with a single user dashboard, requiring less management and support time; and Stripe's built-in fraud prevention tools and regulatory compliance measures, reducing the need for any additional software and related staff costs.

New digital lending platforms:

> The new digital lending platforms enable faster credit decisions, an improved customer experience, and 40% lower costs (according to McKinsey, The Lending Revolution, August 2018). Their opportunity arose from traditional banks taking far too long to make their lending decisions, usually between three and five weeks for a small business making a loan request, and too long to provide the requested money, on average three months.
>
> One such example is OnDeck. According to their Web site, OnDeck has so far delivered over $12 billion in lending to small businesses globally and currently enjoys a customer rating of 4.9/5.0 on TrustPilot. Securing a loan or a line of credit is straightforward and fast. By following a simple online three-step process, customers can get a business loan as soon as the same day (OnDeck 2019).

28.1.3 Established Players

Bank of America has been a notable digital innovator, voted No 1 in the USA for mobile banking, online banking, and digital sales functionality in 2019 (Bank of America Web site). As of Q2 2019, Bank of America had 37.3 million active digital banking users and 27.8 million active mobile banking users.

Bank of America service innovations including Zelle, a mobile-based person-to-person payments service, and Erica, a mobile-based banking service based on an AI-enabled Chatbot.

Zelle is owned by Early Warning Services, itself jointly owned by Bank of America and several other major US-based banks. The service is proving popular as an easy way to send money between family, friends, and other people known to the user via a simple mobile app. Money can be transferred in minutes with only a few clicks. The service is proving popular for payments such as bill splitting. Its success is evident: as reported in Q2 2019, Bank of America had 8.0 million active Zelle users and 69 million Zelle transactions totaling $18 billion, up 79% year on year.

Erica was launched by Bank of America in 2018, initially to only mild acclaim, with some saying that it was a case of AI for AI's sake. However, Bank of America's customer base seems to disagree. One year on, by end Q2 2019, the service had achieved 7.7 million users and it had logged over 55 million client requests (source: Bank of America Q2 2019 financial release). Importantly for the bank, Erica has achieved broad appeal, with 15% from GenZ, 49% Millennials, 20% GenX, and 16% baby boomers (source: pymnts.com, May 2019).

Barclays scores highly for the quality of service for its UK retail banking business. An independent survey published in August 2019 by Ipsos MORI placed Barclays fourth for overall service quality among the participating banks (newcomer Metro Bank was ranked first), and first for online and mobile banking services (with Metro Bank ranked third) (Barclays Web site).

Barclays have recently updated their online banking to make it "more simplistic," with an intuitive interface and easy to navigate services. Customers can name their accounts as they wish (such as "rainy day fund"); search their transactions using date ranges and keywords; report a debit or credit card lost or stolen; apply for a new account; and access their Barclays rewards. These may appear to be rather basic capabilities, but they have made a big impact because of the emphasis on great user experience.

As a broader statement of their intent to support customers, a key priority for Barclays is to ensure that "no-one is left behind on the digital journey." Among other innovations Barclays created their Digital Eagles program. By 2017, they had trained over 16,000 colleagues to provide free technology advice to over one million customers and non-customers.

28.1.4 Business Models

Retail Banking is becoming a more complex environment than it was when the key to growth was a large and well-placed branch network. Today, there is a growing variety of business models for retailers to navigate. Here are some that have caught our attention; it is by no means an exhaustive list.

The Relationship Model: A personalized approach to banking services provision

> The Relationship Model was where retail banks began, with empowered local branch managers knowing their customer base well, and then acting accordingly using their discretion. However, banks moved away from this model as they evolved to become multi-channel organizations, using centralized decision-making to authorize customer requests.
>
> The emergence of new digital tools gives banks the opportunity to rebuild their customer relationships in a scalable manner through unprecedented insight into customer lifestyles, tastes and preferences, and through high touch, high relevance customer access.
>
> Some progress has been made with billions invested by banks as they have designed effective digital front-end experiences, often inspired and enabled by FinTech. Transforming what lies behind these digital front ends is proving harder. EY's Global Consumer Banking Survey in 2016 showed that incumbent retail banks were under threat, with 40% of customers expressing decreased dependence on their bank as their primary service provider. The issue was not with the basics of banking but over the extent to which banks truly operate in their customer's best interests.
>
> Winning the customer's trust demands some fundamental transformation in how banks operate:
>
> - Senior management needs to set the right culture, with customer-centric values and principles championed through the business.
> - Banks must become transparent over fees and charges.
> - Customer facing people and services need to be empowered and enabled to make customer-centric choices, supported by the data required to do this effectively.
> - Customer experiences must be designed holistically to offer a coherent engagement that is easy for customers to navigate, with ready access to trusted information and advice.
> - Systems must be adapted to enable more personalized services, along with pricing that recognizes relationship value.

For example: Starling Bank won the British Banking awards in 2019 for being the Best British Bank and Best Current Account. Starling Bank has a customer rating of 4.5/5.0 on Trustpilot, and it has created some passionate fans among its customers through getting most of the above requirements right.

The "Walled Garden" Marketplace: A customer banking services platform supported by a defined set of selected third parties

Banks have suffered in the past from trying to manufacture too many things, which has led them to sometime selling uncompetitive products and services that can undermine customer confidence and trust. The "Walled Garden" Marketplace model enables banks to offer a complete set of competitive offerings, with the bank's own products and services complemented by those manufactured by third parties.

The benefits to banks in progressing a "Walled Garden" Marketplace model include:

- They can focus their own product and service creation in areas of core competence, so increasing the likelihood that they develop competitive offerings with a strong customer value proposition.
- They reduce their manufacturing and compliance costs through limiting the extent of their own offerings.
- They obtain additional revenue and profit through charging a fee to other marketplace service providers on the basis of offerings sold.
- They benefit from network effects: the better the service providers they attract, the more customers they win (and vice versa). And the more customer data they gather, the better the service they can provide to their marketplace partners and to their customers alike.

Getting the "Walled Garden" Marketplace Model to work requires the lead bank to become the customer's trusted guide. As with the Relationship Model, this demands effective use of customer data to help model and assess their changing requirements. Marketplace leaders need to source this data not only from sale of their own manufactured offerings, but also from those the customer has bought from other organizations. PSD2 now enables this access, but only if the requesting bank has the customer's permission, so care must be taken to earn this right.

The "Open Banking" Marketplace: A customer banking platform containing an unlimited set of third parties

Under the "Walled Garden" Marketplace Model, banks corral a set of competitive offerings from a limited set of complementary third parties. The "Open Banking" Marketplace Model differs from this in that it opens up a potentially unlimited set of providers to customers.

Open Banking was pioneered in Europe, initially driven by the UK's Competition and Markets Authority and then implemented Europe-wide following the introduction of the Payment Service Directive PSD2. This directive mandated banks to provide third-party access to customer data should their customers demand it. The Open Banking movement has now become a global phenomenon although the approaches taken vary by geography.

The value for customers is:

- Oversight of all their accounts from any provider through one platform (to use the industry jargon: offering "a single pane of glass").

- Access to a range of other financial services online, such as budgeting and comparison tools.
- Easier initiation of payments from their account to other third parties, such as retailers.
- Ability to link their bank account to cards provided by third parties, enabling these third parties to check the availability of funds to cover a planned payment.

The ecosystem of third parties connected to an "Open Banking" Marketplace can extend way beyond financial services into other markets such as retail, travel, and media. The value for third-party businesses engaging with the customer through Open Banking includes the ability to sell products and services using the increasingly popular as-as-service subscription model with reduced banking service cost, along with a simpler, more assured, and secure means of getting paid.

The Manufacturer Model: A "white label" platform, enabling branded offerings to be composed by third-party customer aggregators

There are a growing number of customer-centric organizations, supported by strong brands and deep customer engagement, which have seen the opportunity to market financial products and services to their customer base. However, many of these organizations do not yet have the necessary banking license to manufacture and sell their own financial products and services, and even if they do have such a license, they may not wish to take on the costs of producing and managing their own financial services offerings portfolio. These costs can be burdensome: including both the cost of the manufacturing process itself and the cost of meeting the growing regulatory compliance demands linked to this activity.

The interests of these customer-centric organizations have found a good match with the complementary interests of established financial services players looking to efficiently scale their distribution and customer access. This is the basis of the Manufacturer Model: the producer gets to spread their costs across a much larger volume of business, and the distributor gets increased revenue and enhanced customer stickiness from an enriched offerings portfolio.

From the Manufacturer's point of view there are some limitations to this model. On the one hand, their margins are reduced through sharing customer value creation with the distributor; on the other hand, network effects are reduced because it is the distributor who holds the aggregated customer data, and it is they who benefit from the learning effects derived from this. It can also be uneconomic for the Manufacturer to extend their reach across multiple markets due to the different regulatory compliance environments they would encounter.

28.1.5 Operating Models

Major banks are facing a continuing struggle to drag their businesses forward into the digital age. Much progress is being made but, despite this, challenges remain. For instance, Gartner has estimated that banks on average spend approximately 60% of their IT budgets maintaining legacy IT, leaving just 24% to grow the business and 16% to transform it (Bain).

The key operational challenge for banks is to develop coherent customer and internal journeys that help them to align and coordinate their activities in a way that delivers competitive advantage.

Customer-centricity:

> In the case of a retail bank, customer journey mapping involves walking through the end-to-end engagement cycle: signing up for a new bank account; getting authenticated and authorized to transact; taking receipts and making payments; monitoring and managing financial behaviors; adding new accounts; requesting help; and addressing issues.
>
> As banks seek to create more compelling customer experiences, they are not just trying to make these traditional steps more efficient: they are working to transform them in some way to create more customer value. For instance, signing up and getting the means to transact used to be managed as part of the same process, meaning that customers would have to wait days before opening their account. Digital banking leaders such as Metro Bank have separated these activities so customers can get a new account set up in 10 min, with their debit and credit cards arriving a new days later.
>
> Working in this way requires strong collaboration between departments who have traditionally been quite separate in banks, such as marketing, operations, credit, and IT.

Intelligent Automation:

> Intelligent automation is transforming the speed, quality, efficiency, and scalability of bank processes. At the most basic level, robotic process automation can be trained to replicate the steps of a human operator for linear processes without the need for any underlying process transformation or systems redesign. At a more sophisticated level, the deployment of AI-enabled Chatbots is allowing banks to personalize the service they provide to customers at scale, with learning mechanisms in place to ensure that services become ever more relevant to customers over time.
>
> The impact on banks is significant. For instance, Bank of America CEO Brian Moynihan has cut 100,000 jobs in the bank over a ten-year period through a cost reduction program enabled by technology. More specifically, Bank of America has stated that they have been able to cut 84,000 h per year through the deployment of artificial intelligence and process automation (source: The Financial Brand—is the banking industry prepared for a world without bankers?).

28.1.6 Partnerships

Wherever banks are seeking to compete within the manufacture-to-distribution spectrum, they now need to partner with other third-party organizations to remain competitive, whether on cost to serve, or customer relevance and value.

For instance: JP Morgan has partnered with OnDeck to fund and deliver small business loans in a day and some FinTechs have grown large enough to offer near bank-in-a-box services to smaller banks (source: Bain).

From an operational and risk management standpoint, partnering is creating new challenges for banks, including issues over data ownership, data security, and ultimately, ownership of the end customer relationship.

28.1.7 Platform Enablement

Legacy banking platforms are notoriously inflexible, with changes being time consuming and expensive to make, and placing a powerful brake on innovation. New banking platforms are bringing an entirely fresh architectural approach which enables a much more agile and adaptive innovation capability. This is proving hugely beneficial for new banking providers; it also brings a major headache for incumbents, 70% of whom are now reviewing their core banking platforms (source: McKinsey, May 2019 survey of 37 banking executives).

Some of the leading new-style platform operators include: Thought Machine, FinXact, 10X and Mambu. Here's a brief illustration of the new value these new platforms can bring:

> Thought Machine is one of the UK's leading FinTechs. They have created a complete banking platform, called Vault, which is capable of being configured to the needs of any bank. It is a cloud native, micro-service API platform. This is good news for banking innovators, because banking applications can be "containerized", meaning that exactly the same application can be run in development, test or run environments (good for accelerating the "insight to implementation" cycle); these containers can also be "orchestrated", enabling rapid scale up or scale down of a bank's compute environment as demand changes (good for low-risk experiments for new banking services); and the "micro-services" element enables the development of smaller applications, so speeding up delivery and making applications much more adaptable to new requirements (good for rapid development cycles).

28.2 The Challenges

28.2.1 Strategy Formulation in a Rapidly Evolving Environment

"Who you were yesterday isn't who you will be tomorrow—or the day after that. It's a state of perpetual reinvention, and it takes clear vision, data-driven technologies, and dynamic strategy," Rob Toguri, Partner, Financial Services Advisory, Ernst & Young LLP (EY, June 2018).

The rate of change faced by banks is forcing them to think harder about their strategic options. More demanding customers, changing competitive environments, tougher regulation, disrupted and reconfigured value chains, and relentless waves of potentially transformative technologies, mean that banks can no longer expect the generic industry strategies of the past to be effective. Banks are starting to make bold strategic moves to enable a more differentiated approach by, for example, exiting geographies and sectors where they have previously operated to enable more focus and, in some cases, by reframing how they see themselves as organizations. For instance, the CEO of Citibank has said that he now views their business as a technology company with a banking license.

As banks make their hard choices on *where to play*, they are also having to reconsider *how to win*. One of the key strategic dimensions evident from the earlier section on business models is whether to manufacture, to distribute, or both and, under any of these scenarios, how to maximize shareholder returns through the right ecosystem evolution choices.

28.2.2 Moving to Distributed Leadership

As banks work to become more agile organizations they are being forced to confront the need to change their leadership style into one that supports a less hierarchical approach: one with more distributed leadership responsibility and with more nimble multi-disciplinary teams.

For instance, an early pioneer has been ING's domestic banking unit. Inspired by digital leaders such as Google, Netflix, and especially Spotify, ING adopted an agile team design, with their people organized into squads, chapters, tribes, and guilds.

ING's squads are the smallest grouping, with nine people with a diverse set of skills focused on a very specific mission. For instance, in ING's case, working on a mortgage application and guided by a product owner who owns the problem statement, the backlog of work, and the "to do" priorities list.

ING's chapters are horizontal groups consisting of team members that work in individual squads but organized by a specialist area such as data analytics. The chapter lead responsibilities include personal development, coaching, and performance management.

ING's tribes are collections of squads and can include up to 150 people. The tribe leader within ING has responsibility for an overall area of the business such as mortgage services.

Finally, ING's guilds are communities of members with shared interests, such as Web technology or test automation; they come together to share knowledge, tools, and best practice.

28.2.3 Attracting the Required Digital Talent

Like other industries undergoing digital transformation, banks are finding it tough to recruit the people they need, especially in critical areas such as data analytics, user experience design, and artificial intelligence. Not only is there a global shortage of these skills, banks also have to compete for talent with firms in other more attractive industries, including the BigTech firms and the FinTechs.

Unfortunately for banks, the problem seems to be getting worse, not better. Capgemini found that 62% of leaders in the banking industry think that the digital talent gap has widened in the past couple of years, which is a higher percentage than executives in any of the other industries they covered.

Capgemini's research points to the key organizational attributes that banks need to consider if they are to win the war for digital talent. The top five attributes are:

- Flexible work-life balance.
- Flat hierarchy and accessible management.
- Open and collaborative physical workspace.
- Clear career development path.
- Upskilling and training program.

Digital talents also value firms with an entrepreneurial culture offering engagement with the local community; committed to a digital transformation program; and where their peer group would be digitally talented.

28.3 Platform Ecosystems

"*Over the next decade we will see more changes in the banking industry than in the last 100 years*" (source: KPMG, Future of Digital Banking in 2030).

As we have described in our earlier section on evolving retail bank business models, there are different viable options available for banks, whether as Manufacturer, "Walled Garden" Marketplace leader, "Open Banking" Marketplace Orchestrator, or White Label utility services provider. Whichever of these routes banks choose, they will find themselves increasingly operating as part of an interconnected and growing ecosystem of partners which enables them to create and capture customer value.

The mix of partners they choose will be drawn from a set of players which would be entirely unfamiliar to a banking executive from only a few years ago, including a growing array of FinTechs, Neo Banks, and BigTech firms. They will also include a growing array of organizations from other sectors as banking services become increasingly integrated into all other industry value chains.

Regulatory compliance across these ecosystems will be enabled through AI-based automated tools, with active sharing across international boundaries and distributed ledger technologies becoming the foundation for trusted interactions between multiple parties.

References

Accenture. (2018). *Beyond north Star gazing*. https://www.accenture.com/_acnmedia/pdf-85/accenture-banking-beyond-north-star-gazing.pdf. Accessed October 26, 2019.

Bain. *New bank strategies require new operating models*. https://www.bain.com/contentassets/a97b9014afc84a76ae9fb723d3e94ead/bain_brief_new_bank_strategies_require_new_operating_models.pdf. Accessed October 26, 2019.

The Financial Brand. *Is the banking industry prepared for a world without bankers*? https://thefinancialbrand.com/86253/banking-future-of-work-training-digital-trends/. Accessed October 26, 2019.

Capgemini. (2017, October). *The digital talent gap*. https://www.capgemini.com/wp-content/uploads/2017/10/report_the-digital-talent-gap_final.pdf. Accessed October 26, 2019.

Efma. (2018, September). *World retail banking report 2018*. https://www.efma.com/study/detail/28603. Accessed October 26, 2019.

EY. (2018, June). *How convergence in banking could be an opportunity for growth*. https://consulting.ey.com/convergence-banking-opportunity-growth/. Accessed October 26, 2019.

EY. (2016). *Global consumer banking survey*. https://eyfinancialservicesthoughtgallery.ie/wp-content/uploads/2016/10/ey-the-relevance-challenge-2016.pdf. Accessed October 26, 2019.

IDC. (2018, March). *The business value of the stripe payments platform*. https://stripe.com/files/payments/IDC_Business_Value_of_Stripe_Platform_Full%20Study.pdf

KPMG. (2019, July). *The future of digital banking: Banking in 2030*. https://home.kpmg/au/en/home/insights/2019/07/future-of-digital-banking-in-2030.html. Accessed October 26, 2019.

McKinsey. (2018, August). *The lending revolution: How digital credit is changing banks from the inside*. https://www.mckinsey.com/business-functions/risk/our-insights/the-lending-revolution-how-digital-credit-is-changing-banks-from-the-inside. Accessed October 26, 2019.

OnDeck. (2019). https://www.ondeck.com/home5-lendstart. Accessed October 26, 2019.

Quartz. (2019, August). *Digital banks are racking up users, but will they ever make money*? https://qz.com/1679197/when-will-digital-banks-like-n26-and-revolut-start-making-money/. Accessed october 26, 2019.

Appendix

Statistical Correlation

A full discussion of statistical techniques for establishing correlation between two variables is beyond the scope of this book.[1] However, it is useful to understand some of the basic techniques and terminology involved.

By way of example, let's consider an organization divided into five business units (A to E), where we wish to establish if there is a correlation between their customer satisfaction scores and their margin per employee.

We start with a null hypothesis: that the two quantities are not correlated. We then want to analyze the data to determine if our null hypothesis is true or false. In Excel, you can use the CORREL function to calculate *Pearson's correlation coefficient*, which returns values between −1 and +1. If this number is zero it indicates that there is no correlation between two variables. If it is 1 (or −1) it indicates that the variables are completely correlated. A positive value indicates a positive correlation (i.e. an increase in one variable correlates with an increase in the other), whereas a negative value indicates a negative correlation (i.e. an increase in one variable correlates with a decrease in the other variable). The further that Pearson's correlation coefficient is from zero, the more strongly the two variables are correlated.

In the example shown in Table A.1, we can see that there is quite a strong positive correlation between customer satisfaction scores and margin per employee. However, what we don't yet know is whether this is statistically significant. To establish this, we can look up the critical value in Table A.2 corresponding to a 95% confidence level for a sample size of n equal to 5 (five business units in this example). 95% confidence equates to a level of significance of 0.05 (i.e., alpha = 1 − 0.95).

If the correlation is larger than the critical value, then the result is significant. Since 0.954 is indeed greater than 0.878339, we see that the correlation coefficient is significant. We commonly state that the correlation coefficient is significantly different

[1]For an excellent set of more in-depth resources and information to help you perform statistical analysis using Excel see www.real-statistics.com [accessed 26/10/2019].

H. Tardieu et al., *Deliberately Digital*, Future of Business and Finance,
https://doi.org/10.1007/978-3-030-37955-1

Table A.1 Example figures for customer satisfaction and margin per employee by business unit

	Unit A	Unit B	Unit C	Unit D	Unit E
Customer satisfaction score (%)	33	50	67	20	72
Margin per employee (k€)	15	26	45	16	44
Pearson's correlation coefficient	**0.954**				

Table compiled by authors

Table A.2 Critical values of Pearson's correlation coefficient for various sample sizes (n) and alpha values

n	α					
	0.2	0.1	0.05	0.02	0.01	0.001
3	0.951057	0.987688	0.996917	0.999507	0.999877	0.999999
4	0.800000	0.900000	0.950000	0.980000	0.990000	0.999000
5	0.687049	0.805384	*0.878339*	0.934333	0.958735	0.991139
6	0.608400	0.729299	0.811401	0.882194	0.917200	0.974068

Table kindly provided by Dr. Charles Zaiontz

from zero with 95% confidence. In fact, since 0.954 > 0.93433 (the critical value for alpha equal to 0.2 when n equals 5), we are actually 98% confident of this result.

There are three main issues that you may face when using Pearson's correlation coefficient, particularly with the type of business data that you might wish to analyze when preparing for a digital transformation.

Firstly, Pearson's correlation coefficient is checking for a linear relationship between two quantities: i.e. an increase in one variable correlates with a proportional increase (or decrease) in the other. This is often not expected to be the case. For example, it may be that higher employee engagement scores correlate with higher productivity, but it may not be the case that a percentage increase in employee engagement correlates with an equivalent increase in productivity.

Secondly, Pearson's correlation coefficient does not work well if your data contains outliers (values that do not follow the expected trend in a significant way). If you have outliers in your data, you will need to manually check to see if there is an explanation for these outliers (e.g. errors in data collection or some unusual business event) and potentially remove or correct them to get meaningful results.

Thirdly, Pearson's correlation does not work with ordinal data where items are ranked in some way. One example of this is when people choose from a Likert scale: there is no way to meaningfully say that someone who is "very satisfied" is twice as satisfied as someone who is merely "satisfied."

This is why we have often found it more useful to use a Spearman rank correlation. This works by first ranking your data points (which can be done using the Excel RANK.AVG function) and then calculating Pearson's correlation coefficient from the rankings (instead of from the original values), as shown in Table A.3.

Table A.3 Example figures for customer satisfaction and margin per employee by business unit including ranking

	Unit A	Unit B	Unit C	Unit D	Unit E
Customer satisfaction score (%)	33	50	67	20	72
Margin per employee (k€)	15	26	45	16	44
Customer satisfaction rank	2	3	4	1	5
Margin per employee rank	1	3	5	2	4
Spearman rank correlation	**0.800**				

Table compiled by authors

Table A.4 Spearman's rank critical values for various sample sizes (*n*) and alpha values

n	α			
	0.2	0.1	0.05	0.02
4	1.000	1.000	–	–
5	*0.800*	0.900	1.000	1.000
6	0.657	0.829	0.886	0.943

Source Zaiontz n.d.

Then you can look up this coefficient value in a table of Spearman's rank critical values[2] to determine the level of statistical significance (as shown in Table A.4).

In Table A.4, *n* is once again the number of data points (which is five business units in our example). We see that, using the Spearman's rank correlation, we can have 80% confidence that the two variables are correlated in such a way that a higher customer satisfaction score correlates with a higher margin per employee.

As you can see, with a Spearman's rank correlation, a higher correlation coefficient is needed to infer a correlation with the same level of confidence (as compared to the Pearson correlation coefficient), but it has the advantage of being able to detect correlations that are non-linear or that contain outliers, and it also works with ordinal data.

It should be noted that a confidence of at least 95% is usually considered necessary when undertaking scientific studies. However, in a business context, and particularly where you are using statistical analysis together with other available information (such as surveys, stakeholder interviews, focus groups, and competitor benchmarking), even correlations with a lower level of confidence can still be a useful aid to decision making. A correlation coefficient of just 0.5 could still be a meaningful and useful result in some circumstances.

Our experience has been that you can use these methods to quickly analyze data to search for possible correlations. However, once you have found a potential correlation, it is best to then present the data in graphical format with a line of best

[2]Coefficient tables for both Pearson and Spearman's rank correlation coefficients can be found at www.real-statistics.com [accessed 26/10/2019].

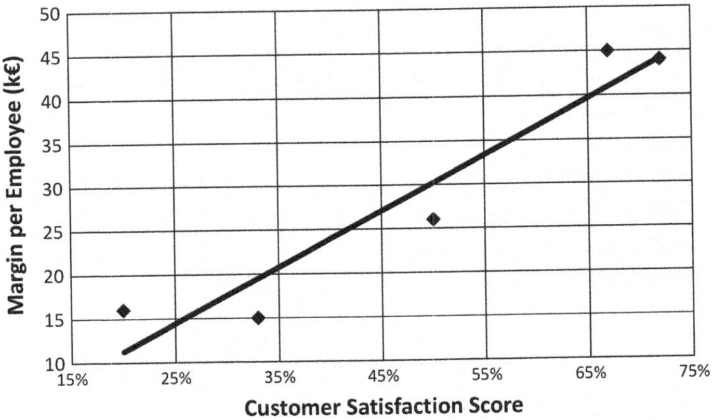

Fig. A.1 Example of presenting a correlation graphically. Authors' own figure

fit (Fig. A.1). Most people find it far easier to interpret and understand correlations by seeing them visually represented!

Finding these types of correlation can often be an interesting starting point for a discussion; however, the results should also be treated with care. Not only can the source data itself be suspect (e.g., a small, unrepresentative sample) but also a statistical correlation does not confirm a causal relationship: Neither the direction of causality nor whether any causality exists can be confirmed. In our example, we cannot know from this analysis whether higher customer satisfaction is leading to higher margin per employee or whether, in fact, achieving a high margin per employee (through other means) is leading to higher customer satisfaction. Or indeed they not be causally related at all, and instead may both be symptoms of the same underlying cause. For example, using chatbots to automate helpdesk queries could result in both higher customer satisfaction (faster more effective service) and higher margin per employee (lower staff costs per customer contact). Finally, there may be no relationship between them at all, and the correlation may be entirely random.

Despite these caveats, when used as a starting point for a conversation, or to support or challenge the outputs from stakeholder interviews and focus groups, this kind of statistical analysis can surface valuable insights.

Reference

Zaiontz. (n.d.). Extracted from http://www.real-statistics.com/statistics-tables/spearmans-rho-table/. Accessed October 26, 2019.

Further Reading

Analysis and Design of Next Generation Software Architecture Art Langer. Ed Springer

AI SUPER-POWERS: China Silicon Valley and the New World Order. Kai-Fu Lee. Ed Houghton Mifflin Harcourt

The four: The hidden DNA of Amazon,Apple, Facebookand Google. Scott Galloway. Ed Transworld Publishers

Machine, Platform, Crowd: Harnessing Our Digital Future. Andrew McAfee & Erik Brynjolfsson. Ed WW Norton Company

The Second Machine Age: Work, Progress and Prosperity in a Time of Brilliant technologies. Erik Brynjolfsson & Andrew Mc Agee. Ed WW NORTON Company

Platform Revolution: How Networked Markets are transforming the economy and how to make them work for you. Geoffrey G Parker, Marshall Van Alstyne, Sangeet Paul Choudary. Ed WW Norton Company

Zero to One: Notes on Start-ups, or How to build the future. Blake Masters & Peter Thiel. Ed Virgin Books

The Net Delusion: The Dark Side of Internet Freedom. Evgeny Morozov. Ed Public Affairs

To Save Everything, Click Here: Technology, Solutionism and the Urge to Fix Problems that Don't Exist. Evgeny Morozov. Ed Penguin Books

Economics for the Common Good Jean Tirole. Ed PUF

The Zero Marginal Cost Society Jeremy Rifkin. Ed St Martin's Press

The Innovator's Dilemma: When New Technologies Cause Great Firms to Fail. Clayton Christensen. Harvard Business Review Press 1997

Competition Policy for the Digital Era. Jacques Cremer, Yves Alexandre de Montjoie, Heike Schweitzer EU Report 2019

H. Tardieu et al., *Deliberately Digital*, Future of Business and Finance,
https://doi.org/10.1007/978-3-030-37955-1

Glossary

Chicken-and-egg (platform problem) All digital platforms face a problem at the start: how to populate their sides (buyers and merchants, landlords and tenants…) to reach critical mass and benefit from network effects. Without one side (i.e., merchants), the other side (i.e., buyers) does not feel compelled to join the platform, and vice versa, hence the "chicken-and-egg" comparison. The "Platforms & Ecosystems" chapter describes certain strategies designed to overcome this problem

Circular Economy a recently proposed economic system that has the objective of optimizing the use of resources by eliminating waste. It looks beyond the current "take-make-waste" linear model, employing the "7R" circular model instead: reduce, repair, remanufacture, refurbish, reuse, redesign, and recycle

Commodification the process by which everything is treated as a commodity and subject to monetization. It is applied specially to sensitive topics: slavery as commodification of people, or indiscriminate data processing as commodification of privacy and freedom. It is often confused with commoditization

Commoditization the process by which a good or service that has economic value and is perceived as distinct or unique, progressively loses its economic value and perceived differentiation. For example, Cloud is the commoditization of computing, since organizations tend to take computers for granted, not wishing to spend large sums on a certain brand of computer, preferring instead to consume computing as a service

Courting a strategy used by digital platform operators to populate their ecosystem s by offering distinct value propositions to different sides of the market. For example, a value proposition to get merchants on board, another to get buyers on board, another to get advertisers on board, etc.

Cynefin (framework) a framework (based on complexity science) designed to improve leadership and decision making, adapting them to today's complex environment. It seeks to encompass the multiplicity of interrelated factors that affect a decision and defines appropriate contexts for decision making

H. Tardieu et al., *Deliberately Digital*, Future of Business and Finance,
https://doi.org/10.1007/978-3-030-37955-1

Digital Business Continuum an approach to running an organization that enables an optimal combination of rapid adaptation and extensive innovation. It is designed for organizations to transform continuously, in a context of disruption, by constantly seizing opportunities and neutralizing threats

Digital Business KPIs a set of key performance indicators designed for digitally transformed businesses, given that traditional KPIs often fail to apply in the new digital context—which often hinders transformation initiatives. See also Transitional KPIs

Digital Sovereignty "The capability of a natural person or corporate entity for exclusive self-determination with regard to its economic data goods," as defined by the International Data Spaces Association

Digital transformation the process in which traditional (non-digital-native) companies embark, aiming to redefine their purpose, business models, portfolio, and ways of working in order to adapt to the new era, marked by digital technologies and new societal values as well as engagement and consumption patterns

Digitalization the process by which digital technologies are used to change a business model, business process, good, or service. It is often confused with digitization, which is a more basic, information-oriented process than digitalization

Digitization the process by which information is converted from an analog representation into a digital representation (paper documents into digital text files, analog sensor signals into digital signals, etc.). It can be extended to eliminating the physical support to an already digital representation (digitizing CDs into signals ready for streaming). Digitization is often confused with digitalization, which is a higher-level process. For example, some companies digitized paper photographs into image files, or music CD into music data streams, in order to digitalize their services: from paper-based to digital photo sharing and albums; from physical CD distribution to music streaming

Ecosystem (digital) "a distributed, adaptive, open socio-technical system with properties of self-organization, scalability and sustainability inspired from natural ecosystems" as defined by Wikipedia

Explainable AI Many artificial intelligence models behave as "black boxes": They provide very good results, but their inner workings do not allow humans to understand how or why the results were arrived at. This hinders their use in certain business situations due to lack of trust. Explainable AI is the set of techniques that aim to make all AI models explainable

Externality a cost or benefit that impacts an individual or organization who did not choose to incur that cost or enjoy that benefit. It can be negative (the water in your town being polluted by an industry in another town) or positive (your fields being better pollinated by bees from near honeymakers)

FinTech innovative technological start-ups that focus on the financial sector, especially in banking (insurance-oriented ones are called InsurTech)

First-mover advantage Traditionally, it is the advantage gained by the first organization to move into a market segment. In digital times, the term has been extended to the advantage gained by the first organization to move into a digital market or digital version of a market segment (e.g., by being the first major digital music provider)

Green button a US, industry-led initiative that enables energy consumers to provide explicit consent for selected third parties to use their related personal data

Holacracy a principle and method of organizational management and governance that eliminates rigid, centralized, hierarchical structures in favor of distributed, horizontal, and self-organizing teams

Industrial data platform a multi-sided digital platform where several industry partners, involved in a given market for delivering products and services, decide to form an ecosystem to jointly exchange and exploit industry data via a contractual relationship

Know Your Customer (KYC) a business activity that aims to verify the identity of customers, often assessing their suitability and risk profiles. It is a basic part of some financial regulations

Mixed data data which is generated by persons (therefore, subject to privacy concerns) and later used for commercial purposes, such as data from smart meters or autonomous vehicles

Monetization the strategy and process by which the value of an asset (in the digital context, usually data) is converted into money. Monetization is only one of the ways in which the value of data can be profited from by an organization: Data can be used as insurance, an option, etc.

Multi-homing a phenomenon of digital platforms that takes place when an organization, which plays a relevant role in several companies' value chains, must participate in those companies' competing digital platforms

Multi-sided market an economic model, mainly described by Rochet and Tirole, in which different groups develop economic activities taking advantage of mutual network benefits

Network effect an economic effect by which the value of a good or service increases as additional users consume it. For example, the more people use the telephone, the more value telephone users obtain (same-side network effect); or the more merchants join a platform, the more value buyers obtain (cross-side network effect)

Pipeline model the pre-digital goods and services model, characterized by a clear, linear flow of inputs and value between the originator, the seller and the buyer. It has been very useful and achieved great levels of efficiency, but it has shown limitations such as its inherent difficulty to leverage network effects and data exchange (aspects in which the platform model excels)

Platform The term platform is often used both in an abstract and concrete sense. In an abstract sense, a platform is the result of the interconnection of stakeholders wanting to establish an ecosystem to leverage network effects. In a concrete sense, a platform is a solution built with digital technologies that allow an ecosystem to interconnect and exchange data in a controlled way for business purposes. Such platforms are distinct from data platforms, typically used for storing and analyzing data

Platform model In opposition to a pipeline model, the platform model is a goods and services model in which an ecosystem of players interconnect, exchange, and analyze data with the objective of discovering insights that will allow new sources of value to emerge. Such value will be monetized by the ecosystem in the form of enhanced or new goods and services, as well as optimized client engagement and time-to-market

Platform operator the party that initiates a platform models, assuming the initial (usually high) costs of platform creation and launching (technology, marketing, etc.) until critical mass is achieved in all sides of the platform

Platform user people or businesses that decide to participate in a digital platform (be it B2C or B2B), owned and operated by third parties, with the aim of making more or better business, and having access to better, cheaper or faster products and services

PSD2 (European Payment Service Directive 2) a European regulation that aims to opening the financial services market. It requires banks to respond to the permissioned requests for exchange of certain basic financial information, to encourage (new) third parties to provide services in competition with traditional banks and financial institutions

Raw data (vs. usable data) data coming from sensors, transactions, logs, and other sources, which may have had a slight degree of processing but has not undergone yet the types of analysis and processing that will extract their inherent business value. In addition, under many regulatory frameworks, raw data is unusable because its owners or originators have not given their consent for the data to be used for business purposes. Only after such permissions are granted, raw data becomes usable data

Refined data Under the metaphor that compares data to oil, refined data is data that has undergone some processing that makes it business-usable to companies (usually other participants in a platform or ecosystem)

RegTech innovative technological start-ups that focus on regulatory and compliance processes

Sandbox (regulatory) A regulatory sandbox offers innovators the possibility to experiment with new products and services that fall outside existing regulation. It allows innovators to experiment freely and without legal or regulatory consequences, while it allows regulators to anticipate market-driven changes. Sandboxes are time-limited, well-defined, and supervised by regulators—who may choose to relax or eliminate specific regulations temporarily for the purpose of the experimentation

Service economy an economy, such as the current global economy, in which services take lion's share in the portfolio of companies and in the total economic activity, either as pure services or as services associated with products (see Servitization)

Servitization the process by which economic assets that have traditionally been commercialized as products are commercialized as services. For example, companies may go from selling cars to selling mobility. Even in cases in which the service cannot replace the product, products have more and more associated services, leading to a service–product continuum

Shadow IT all IT systems, services, and goods being created or consumed in an organization outside the perimeter of control of the IT Department. As technologies are increasingly cheaper and more accessible, as IT Departments have challenges to incorporate them into business (due to skills, personnel or budgetary limitations), and as so-called business departments are increasingly pressured to innovate, many departments have resorted to creating or consuming IT in a rogue manner. This originates many undesired effects, such as lack of budget optimization and control, cybersecurity risks, or compliance risks

Solow paradox Computers enable new activities and the optimization of existing activities. Since their widespread use in business decades ago, this should have led to a significant increase of productivity. However, that has not been the case. As Robert Solow put it, "you can see the computer age everywhere but in the productivity statistics." There are several competing interpretations that aim to explain the paradox

StratHack an innovation session format proposed by Atos (conflating the words Strategy and Hackathon). It consists of highly focused, cocreation workshops targeted at reimagining digital transformation problems through the lens of digital possibilities and persona journeys. It brings together creative inputs from across an organization (from the CxO level down) and often includes trusted partners who can bring fresh thinking and thought-provoking inputs from other companies and industries. They can be very effective at prioritizing transformation initiatives and ensuring maximum stakeholder buy-in

Tokenization (of assets) the virtual, intended, and controlled fragmentation of the value of an asset to democratize and increase the volume of trading. For example, few individuals may trade in skyscrapers, but most individuals could participate in the trade if the skyscraper is tokenized into thousands or millions of digital ownership stakes. Conversely, tokenization would enable an individual to sell 5% of their car or house without the need to sell or mortgage the whole asset. Tokenization is often associated with Blockchain as an effective mechanism to track the tokenization process and subsequent trading and distributed ownership

Transaction cost the cost incurred when trading assets in a market. The widespread use of IT and digital technologies has contributed to significantly decrease transaction costs due to massive access to information, direct contact between parties in a trade, enhanced access to financial means—all of which result in the rapidly decreasing role of agents and intermediaries in trading

Transformation activities In our transformation model, digital transformation—which takes place within a transformation context—is broken down into Transformation Themes, which act as a thematic umbrella for Transformation Workstreams, which are decomposed into specific, detailed transformation activities. The transformation activities are delivered within a single Transformation Iteration even if the whole transformation is iterative in nature

Transformation context In our transformation model, digital transformation—which takes place within a transformation context—is broken down into Transformation Themes, which act as a thematic umbrella for Transformation Workstreams, which are decomposed into specific, detailed transformation activities. The Transformation Context is composed by the external forces and drivers that simultaneously create the need to transform, enable the transformation, and hinder the transformation, according to the relevant key societal, business and technology trends

Transformation Iterations In our transformation model, digital transformation—which takes place within a transformation context—is broken down into Transformation Themes, which act as a thematic umbrella for Transformation Workstreams, which are decomposed into specific, detailed transformation activities. Digital transformation is not a one-time effort but a continuous effort that should be structured in successive iterations that increase manageability, adaptability and learning from doing

Transformation Themes In our transformation model, digital transformation—which takes place within a transformation context—is broken down into Transformation Themes, which act as a thematic umbrella for Transformation Workstreams, which are decomposed into specific, detailed transformation activities. Transformation Themes provide a first decomposition of the overall transformation efforts. We propose eight such themes (strategy, business models, platforms and ecosystems, leadership, customer, organization structure, people and innovation) but organizations may decide to personalize them

Transformation Workstreams In our transformation model, digital transformation—which takes place within a transformation context—is broken down into Transformation Themes, which act as a thematic umbrella for Transformation Workstreams, which are decomposed into specific, detailed transformation activities. Transformation Workstreams are the heart of the transformation. They are defined by the Executive Committee and correspond to the challenges identified by the committee. Transformation Workstreams receive the mandate and budget, which they will cascade down to Transformation Activities. Transformation Workstreams must be wisely prioritized and balanced among Themes

Transitional KPIs a set of key performance indicators that are introduced to track the progress of Transformation Workstreams. They may be adapted over time, but they are unlikely to be required permanently. See also Digital Business KPIs and Transformation Workstreams

Two-sidedness Network effects can introduce positive externalities, such as the telephone network being more and more valuable to a user as more new users join in. Economists have extended the model to two sides, with network effects occurring in the same side (such as the one-sided telephone example) but also as cross-side effects (the more merchants join a digital marketplace, the more valuable it is for a buyer)

Usable data (vs. raw data) Under many regulatory frameworks, raw data (coming straight from sensors, logs, or transactions) is unusable because its owners or originators have not given their consent for the data to be used for business purposes. Only after such permissions are granted, raw data becomes usable data

Index

H. Tardieu et al., *Deliberately Digital*, Future of Business and Finance,
https://doi.org/10.1007/978-3-030-37955-1

The manufacturer's authorised representative in the EU is Springer Nature Customer Service Centre GmbH, Europaplatz 3, 69115 Heidelberg, Germany. If you have any concerns regarding our products, please contact ProductSafety@springernature.com

Printed and bound by CPI Group (UK) Ltd, Croydon, CR0 4YY
22/09/2026
02221059-0012